John Brown in
Memory and Myth

John Brown in Memory and Myth

Michael Daigh

McFarland & Company, Inc., Publishers
Jefferson, North Carolina

LIBRARY OF CONGRESS CATALOGUING-IN-PUBLICATION DATA

Daigh, Michael, 1977–
John Brown in memory and myth / Michael Daigh.
      p.   cm.
Includes bibliographical references and index.

ISBN 978-0-7864-9617-4 (softcover : acid free paper) ♾
ISBN 978-1-4766-1812-8 (ebook)

1. Brown, John, 1800–1859—Influence. 2. Harpers Ferry (W. Va.)—History—John Brown's Raid, 1859. 3. Antislavery movements—United States—History—19th century. 4. Abolitionists—United States—Biography. I. Title.

E451.D35 2015   973.7116092—dc23   [B]   2015000176

BRITISH LIBRARY CATALOGUING DATA ARE AVAILABLE

© 2015 Michael Daigh. All rights reserved

No part of this book may be reproduced or transmitted in any form or by any means, electronic or mechanical, including photocopying or recording, or by any information storage and retrieval system, without permission in writing from the publisher.

On the cover: *Le Pendu (Ecce Lex)* pen-and-ink,
brown washing by Victor Hugo, 1854
(Maisons de Victor Hugo/The Image Works, Inc.)

Printed in the United States of America

McFarland & Company, Inc., Publishers
Box 611, Jefferson, North Carolina 28640
www.mcfarlandpub.com

To Katie, who convinced me to write this book and supported me through the effort. I hope that she and others will enjoy reading it half as much as I have enjoyed writing and thinking about this subject.

To all the marvelous scholars who have already written so many fine books and essays about Brown and about this era of history. Your works inspired and informed me, and I hope I prove myself a worthy voice in the conversation.

And to the people who have conceived the notion that boundaries are conventions that may be transcended, and who have had the courage to do so, despite the cost.

Table of Contents

Preface   1

PART ONE: THE LEHREJAHRE   3
1. How the True World Finally Became a Fable   4
2. Rationality Ex Post Facto   9
3. New Millennium Homes   17
4. The Prejudices of Philosophers and Historians   25
5. Peoples and Nations   34
6. The Stillest Hour   47
7. The Land of Education   55

PART TWO: THE WANDERJAHRE   66
8. All Too Human   67
9. The Stasis   75
10. Beyond Good and Evil   83
11. Skirmishes of an Untimely Man   94
12. The Return Home   106
13. The Child with the Mirror   116
14. Preparatory Men   129
15. The Convalescent Wanderer   137

PART THREE: *DIES IRAE, DIES ILLA*   149
16. The Means to Real Peace   150
17. Upon These Stones   157
18. Like Ashes in the Fall   165
19. The Revelation of John Brown   171

Table of Contents

20. The Metaphysics of the Hangman 180
21. Where Faith Is Needed 190
22. The History of an Error 202
23. The Last Witness 216

Chapter Notes 231
Bibliography 250
Index 255

Preface

During a 2003 discussion about Merrill D. Peterson's *John Brown*, Professor Jonathan Earle of the University of Kansas made an interesting comment about the prospect of writing a biography of Brown: "I think John Brown, for many people, is hard to *view as a normal person or as a human* [italics mine]. If I were going to write a biography, one of the last people I'd want to write a biography about is John Brown. He's really interesting, but we've had 150 years of people in my business trying to 'get inside his head,' and I don't think we've done a very good job at all."[1]

That's quite a statement about the limits of historical understanding, considering that Brown once influenced luminaries like Ralph Waldo Emerson and elicited trans-Atlantic attention. Armies once sung or cursed his name as they marched to kill and die. At one point, *apparently*, a great many people were, if not inside his head, at least in harmony with his story. Furthermore, other "representative men" in historical narrative have loomed at least as large, or more so, without so many shadows attending their stories.

Following after Emerson's view of historical consciousness, the problem isn't the inscrutable cipher of John Brown; it is us. Identity is not individual, understanding is not discrete. But the narratives and metaphors that comprise our society, that underpin our nation, may provide inadequate context for understanding John Brown. In fact, there's something almost threatening about Brown's tale. Many historians might not really be writing about John Brown at all. There may be deeper truths being either supported or challenged, a story that historians attempt to reconcile with Brown's actions.

This story about John Brown—who he was, the choices he had to make, and the mythic figure he became—tracks, in counterpoint, the narrative arc of history in the Age of Revolution, and thus serves as the vehicle for an examination of broader social metaphors and beliefs. At the foundation of the story are the writings of Ralph Waldo Emerson, not merely as a consistently perceptive source of observation and context, but also as a primary philosophical basis for my approach to the historical narrative. Though it may seem circular, in a way this book is my attempt to address the subject somewhat like Emerson might have, had he not been such an integral part of it: History as narrative art, even an interactive truth, one often designed to linguistically, epistemologically frame ethical decisions. Story masquerading as science filling in for religion in order to create fate that was, in reality, an illusion.

This book, while academic, is meant to be read like history's companion art form—the novel. The narrative builds sequentially, not in interchangeable pieces like a text. I have utilized my own historical imagination, drawn from contextual knowledge of sources, evaluations of plausibility, and even memories of my own Kansas upbringing to bring the narrative together. In fact, in many ways, this book is a personal intellectual journey that began when I was a youth, staring up at John Steuart Curry's *Tragic Prelude*, wondering about all the forgetting that went into the tepid histories I had been taught about the titanic figure I saw in that painting.

History, as an act of communal narrative, might be more about forgetting than about remembering, as Benedict Anderson postulated in *Imagined Communities*. As he tells it, Ernest Renan, writing in 1882—a little over a century after the Declaration of Independence, the inauguration of the Age of Revolution and of nations, and after most of those nations had committed deicide, fratricide, parricide, or genocide[2] of one form or another in an effort to comprehend what they were—penned a lecture entitled "Qu'est-ce *qu'une nation?*" in which he illustrated the non-linear process of the creation of historical identity in a nation in the Age of Revolution—in this case, the French people or, "l'essence d'une nation est que tous les individus aient beaucoup de choses en commun et aussi que tous aient oublié bien des choses.... Tout citoyen français doit avoir oublié la Saint-Barthelemy, les massacres du Midi au XIIIe siècle."[3] (The essence of a nation is that all individuals have many things in common, and that all have forgotten much. Every citizen is obliged to have already forgotten the French Saint-Barthelemy, the massacres in the Midi in the thirteenth century.)

History is not the record of the self-consciousness of nations, it is an art form that invents nations in the imaginations of multitudes will never know each other, but will somehow carry in their mind an abstraction of community. Renan alludes to this and assumes a memory in the minds of his French readers of the anti–Huguenot pogrom of 1572, and the brutal papal extermination of the Albigensians. But, those same readers were "obliged to have already forgotten" the events which he said that they remembered, and in fact would only have known—since they took place centuries prior—due to the very system of state education that demanded forgetting. It is a selective forgetting though, in which victims and assassins from wildly varied cultures blur unnamed into a metaphorical conflict between fellow Frenchmen. The system of state history constantly "reminds" readers of a conflict that they are obliged to forget out of civic duty, in order to inscribe it as a collective and almost fraternal narrative.[4] Even the raw and cataclysmic memories of slavery, injustice, and civil war were eventually subjected to this legerdemain. An understanding of all the tragic absurdities surrounding the life and death of one man obliges one, on the other hand, to remember. Forgetting is what makes this story, more than many, so very incomprehensible.

When we look carefully at our stories—our histories—we might find that the differences between fact and miracle are highly subjective.

Part One:
The Lehrejahre

What could have been done more to my vineyard, that I have not done in it? Wherefore, when I looked that it should bring forth grapes, brought it forth wild grapes?

For the vineyard of the Lord of hosts is the house of Israel, and the men of Judah his pleasant plant: and he looked for judgment, but behold oppression; for righteousness, but behold a cry.

—Isaiah 5:4, 7

John Brown from an early daguerreotype, 1840s. Regarded by the family as the best picture of him (Library of Congress.)

1

How the True World Finally Became a Fable

> *... what does history yet record of the metaphysical annals of man? What light does it shed on those mysteries which we hide under the names Death and Immortality? Yet every history should be written in a wisdom which divined the range of our affinities and looked at facts as symbols. I am ashamed to see what a shallow village tale our so-called History is.*
> —Ralph Waldo Emerson, *History*

The story of John Brown begins in Torrington, Connecticut, on May 9, 1800, with a single sentence written by Owen Brown in the twilight of Owen's life in 1849: "John was born, one hundred years after his great-grandfather. Nothing else very uncommon."[1] It is one of few memories of John Brown written before 1856 when the story—and John—would become so much more, and would transform past and future with a disfiguring, tragic gravity.

In 1793, twenty-one-year-old Owen Brown—the rootless son of an impoverished widow—had married a minister's daughter named Ruth Mills, who was among what he referred to as "the better class of people."[2] But love was stronger than class divisions and they dreamed of raising a family together. Those dreams seemed to be cursed in the beginning. In his brief memoir Owen omitted the joy and trepidation that he and his wife must have felt at John's birth. Their first two children had died as infants, and as time advanced Ruth's hopes of childbearing grew dimmer. After the death of the second, the couple decided to adopt a boy named Levi Blakeslee. By the time John was born, Owen was 29 years old, making his way in a world swept up in revolutions and religious movements by working as tanner of middling success.

Owen Brown had not had an easy life. In 1776 his father—Captain John Brown—had left to fight with a Revolutionary militia, only to die of dysentery. His mother was left with eleven children to support in the new society, and "for want of help," as Owen recalled, "we lost our crops and then our cattle, and so became poor."[3] The children were scattered to relatives, including Owen, who spent 1777 with his grandfather. He lived on the move, searching out opportunities during the winter months, returning home in the summer to help with the farm. In time Owen and his brothers built moderately prosperous lives, but the shadow of early hardships kept Owen on the move to make sure that he provided for his family—that he never "failed," the term for business insolvency.

Their unwritten worries for their newest baby eventually faded as John grew to be

1. How the True World Finally Became a Fable   5

The house in Torrington, Connecticut, where John Brown was born (Library of Congress).

a rudely healthy boy, wiry of build and sober of demeanor, fond of rough play, with a belligerent, mischievous, sometimes resentful streak that would earn him approbation and admiration as a youth and beyond.

On October 16, 1804, Owen visited the new town of Hudson, Ohio, returning to Torrington to excitedly inform Ruth that they were the proud owners of a small parcel of land where they could build a new home for their family. Torrington was the family's third home, but this migration was more than the whim of an orphan of the Revolution who had grown a bit accustomed to a nomadic, rootless lifestyle.

Americans (a tenuous identity, uncertain in the minds of most) were flowing westward at a prodigious rate, free of the Crown's restrictions. With the new tools of cartography available to them, Congress saw nearly endless possibilities for expansion.

Connecticut's "Western Reserve" became a popular destination, luring men like David Hudson, who built the town that bears his name. After Hudson purchased the land, he recruited people he felt would help him to engineer an ideal community. Owen was not as prosperous nor as educated as most of Hudson's recruits, but he possessed important skills that fit Hudson's scheme, skills which he would pass on to his son John.

Most important to Hudson for the maintenance of community harmony, Owen shared his narrative identity; he was a Congregationalist and a Federalist. The opportunity was impossible for Owen to refuse. He would have a home, and perhaps the kind of respect that would free him from poverty and make him worthy of his beloved Ruth. "I came with the determination," he wrote, "to build up and be a help in the seport of religion and civil order."[4] So the oxen leaned into their burdens, the harness creaked and the wheels slowly rumbled along in the seven week journey to their new home, miles rolling slowly by as the family moved ponderously west.

For five-year-old John, it was a world of towering mountains, and rivers running beyond the imagination. Mighty oxen turned the world under their hooves as clever wild turkeys dashed in and out of sight. He had a child's wondrous pride in being able to help his father drive their little caravan to their new home. They met alien brown men who spoke in strange tongues and who frightened John at first, but his father taught him—contrary to the opinions of nearly all whites—that these men were neither monsters nor vermin.[5] John kept their company, but they were also becoming scarcer with every passing year, fading into the mists of history, which Owen declared was "rather against" his wishes.[6]

In the Western Reserve a young Indian boy gave John, as a token of their friendship, a small yellow marble. He had never seen such a thing, a remarkable bauble of light and color. One day to his horror he lost it, and he wept and searched the world for it. He also cherished a little squirrel, sadly bob-tailed from being injured when John captured it. He did his best to atone for the injury, "to screen himself from blame; or from punishment," over the accident, caring for the squirrel as a tame pet. But in time the squirrel, too, was lost, and for nearly two years John mourned for it and searched the forest. An inability to endure loss was a fault John would always struggle with.

He wept for those losses, but there were graver ones. A young ewe had been given into his care by his father. Healthy until adolescence, it suddenly sickened and died without explanation. It was a troubling financial loss, but the ewe's death brought with it a long melancholy with questions about the caprice of the world and the nature of love and attachment. John had always been "quite skeptical" about religious dogma, but his doubts about his future were deeper still, so he became "to some extent a convert to Christianity" and yet a "firm believer" in the Bible.

Around this time John's mother sickened and died. In December of 1808, Owen Brown inscribed her headstone with this farewell:

> She was a dutiful child,
> A Sprightly youth, a Loving wife,
> A tender parent, a Kind neighbor
> and an Exemplary christian.[7]

Such a loss for a child of that age is profound, for as he becomes an adult he will re-experience the grief in real and immediate ways as the memory meets with growing understanding. So it was for John, who was deprived of a connection to women, and had he not overcome his diffidence to some degree later in life, it may "have proved his ruin."

Less than a year later, Owen married Sally Root, who found herself opposed by three cleverly willful boys who were stubbornly determined to make their new stepmother feel unwelcome. John and his younger brother Salmon once rigged a ladder to give way when she was halfway up, dropping her to the ground with bruises to both body and pride. John later regretted his mischief, and reflected that Sally was a "sensible, intelligent, and on many accounts a very estimable woman."[8]

John's world changed in 1812. There was a war, and a highly successful campaign by the British had driven General William Hull's army near the Browns' western homestead. Even underachieving armies require food, so an enterprising Owen arranged to sell beef to the soldiers. John was given the daunting task of driving the cattle "more than a Hundred Miles" to the army's camp. Children on the frontier contributed to the homestead and assisted their parents in many ways, but this journey was made in solitude. He drew "notice and distinction from the people among whom he fell from the fact that this boy of twelve had conducted his drove of cattle a hundred miles alone."[9]

His mind was alight with the fictions of history, of war and glory. For two years his interest in reading history had provided the basis of a rough education, kept him from poor company and trouble, and gave him representative men to follow. But among the regimented assassins he saw and heard only cheating, deception and treason. Death and disease befouled the country, and the overall effect "went so far as to disgust him with military affairs" to the end of his days.

Weary and dispirited, he found respite on the return journey at the home of a United States marshal who was effusive over John's industry and courage. In the marshal's house a hardworking, intelligent slave, a boy about John's age, did "numerous little acts of kindness." The boy was wretched and clothed in rags, and slept in the bitter cold while John ate at the marshal's table and was praised for every trifle. But the boy, "more than his equal," was beaten before John's eyes with an iron shovel.[10] And if John Brown went mad, then his madness sounded like iron on flesh. He wondered at the plight of a motherless slave child and whether this spectacle meant that God was dead.[11] After that terrible day he declared "Eternal war with Slavery."

Brown grew to be a tall man of around five feet ten inches, with an untamed shock of thick, dark brown hair. Those who met him often remembered him as more than six feet, and one of the most common physical descriptions of him is "tall." He had intense, bombardier blue eyes, which in repose were often dim and half-lidded, but could blaze with anger. A thin, grim mouth, hawk-like nose, high cheekbones and hollow cheeks gave his face a stern aspect. He was slender but muscular, fond of tan-colored wool coats and white shirts when he wished to dress for society, and he always wore boots. He was also very tidy, particular about his home and his dress, and his manners and the manners of his friends and family. When he walked it was typically with his hands clasped behind his back, and his eyes downwards as if in thought.[12]

Brown was a startlingly intense man, earnest and quietly emphatic, yet he could surprise with a keen sense of humor. He delighted in the colorful, garrulous, and bombastic speech of his black friends. He loved the nuances of spoken English, and seemed to savor his own direct and carefully chosen phrases. When he laughed, his eyes shone with tears while his severe mouth broke into a smile, and his whole body would shake and rock with mirth, though not a sound came from him.[13]

His intensity went hand in hand with his imperious ego, a fusion that eventually metamorphosed into a vision of himself as an instrument of fate. For a time he built a life of modest success, earning a measure of respect from the serious and intelligent among those he esteemed. But this respect, as he told it, fed a dark part of him, a vanity and conceit that drove his younger brother to angrily refer to him as "A King against whom there is no rising up." Brown had a haughty disdain for rivals, and as for his friends he usually tried to sway them to his will even in the smallest things. For example, he would coerce coffee drinkers into drinking tea, simply because he wanted and enjoyed tea.[14]

As his story grew, he collected nicknames as some people do clothing, sobriquets like "border chieftain," "Old Covenanter," and most commonly and simply, "the Old Man."[15] Defining his writings and speeches was his abiding religious faith, and he tried to be true to his God as best he knew how.

This is the story of John Brown, a myth that defines a tormented space within American culture, perhaps the only myth that modern Western history has produced.[16] This is also a story about John Brown's story as both a summary and a counterpoint to American history up to his death and beyond. The story of John Brown also questions the nature of historical belief, since that tale was largely written by Brown in his 55th year after much blood and pain. Did a lone twelve-year-old boy journey for 100 miles, and did that journey define the man he would become? But the age of John Brown was one where myths and ghosts had been discarded. People no longer relied on irrational stories to guide their actions, no longer fed those stories on blood, no longer committed crimes for ghosts. It was a rational age, one in which the myths of the West had been replaced by a far more rational representation of life and will—History—which supplemented or replaced Christianity as narrative justification for inflicting all manner of horrors. Like any good ancient story, history has spitefully narrated people that challenged its own mythic assumptions, and the hierarchies and subjugations it sanctifies.

Knowledge is a mirror, yet people may only see life, however dimly, by looking back in the imagination. "This human mind wrote history, and this must read it. The Sphinx must solve her own riddle. If the whole of history is in one man, it is all to be explained from individual experience. There is a relation between the hours of our life and the centuries of time." The specious present, like a Gothic cathedral, stands as a collapsing of successive occurrences, process and structure, story and fable, crafted by us, and yet not by us.

During Brown's life the structure itself was rebuilt into the words and ideas of a rational world, where understanding is supposed at the outset to be attainable, provided the story complies with comprehensible laws and broadly understood human motivations. Words and ideas like "ideology," "liberal," "conservative," "capitalism," "socialism," "communism," "industry," "working-class," "middle-class," "proletariat," "aristocracy," "statistics," "sociology," "psychology," "journalism," "utilitarianism," and "nationalism" took on their current meanings or were invented then.[17] To paraphrase Max Weber, the success of nationalist and capitalist ideologies was the narrative identity they offered to the new, post–Westphalian civilizations, and the identity compelled people to perform and therefore renew the reality their words crafted.

John Brown's story is the story of that age. It is part of the tangled root system of our presentation of reality today. Proof may be a social construct, so the difficulty of John Brown's story is that it chillingly suggests that most of the ideas which form the narrative presentation of the world died a little on the gallows with him December 2, 1859. His death had a lot to do with history in a rational age.

2

Rationality Ex Post Facto

The Fathers made the fatal blunder in agreeing to this false basis of representation, & to this criminal complicity of restoring fugitive slaves: and the splendor of the bribe, namely the magnificent prosperity of America from 1787, is their excuse before God & men, for the crime. They ought never to have passed the Ordinance. They ought to have refused it at the risk of making no Union ... the bribe, if they foresaw the prosperity we have seen, was one to dazzle common men. And I do not wonder that most men now excuse & applaud it. But crime brings punishment, always so much crime, so much ruin.
—Ralph Waldo Emerson, *Journals*

Ralph Waldo Emerson was a philosopher born within three years of John Brown. His intellectual career mirrored the transition of American culture during the Age of Revolution from a roughly religious colonial foundation to its secular-scientific nineteenth-century form. He despaired of an ability to write anything as profoundly rational as an "Essay of Hume," despite his "immoderate fondness for writing," and so as a young man decided his imagination was best suited for the Unitarian ministry and the study of theology, "which is from everlasting to everlasting 'debatable Ground.' For, the highest species of reasoning upon divine subjects is rather the fruit of a sort of moral imagination, than of the 'Reasoning Machines' such as Locke & Clarke & David Hume."[1] Emerson was as responsible for this story as anyone.

As Emerson's transparent eye looked on the age, his professional life tracked the re-writing of civilization from the ministry to secular intellectualism, but in response to that narrative he developed a questioning and critical anti-rationalism. It vexed Emerson that a supposedly rational age nurtured the deepest irrationality. It defied all reason and understanding, and led him to write in his essay "Self-Reliance": "As men's prayers are a disease of the will, so are their creeds a disease of the intellect." His anti-rationalism may have been one of the most rational notions of his day.

He is an elusive narrator, full of cheerfully proclaimed contradictions. It would have vexed him to know that his writings would later give semi-literate anti-intellectuals ideas, as well as the scholarly imprimatur such people ironically crave. Emerson's greatest concern was the dialectic within the mind between received wisdom and living power and the resulting social reality, otherwise stated as the nature of understanding and wisdom in the transitory space between being and becoming. He was an unapologetic post–Christian amoralist; whatever morality was contained within his writings was human, but only dubiously humane, which led Herman Melville to write: "His gross and astonishing errors and illusions spring from a self-conceit so intensely intellectual and calm that at first one hesitates to call it by its right name. Another species of Mr. Emerson's errors, or rather blindness, proceeds from a defect in the region of the heart."

This fault was prominent in the American simplicity of Emerson's earliest works, despite their occasional fits of black pique. They were infused with the optimism of a benevolent deity, an inherently good humanity, and the providential free-will derived from his Unitarian education. Unitarianism was perhaps an under-sophisticated faith, one that was ill-equipped to comprehend the darkly and divinely sarcastic God of Job with the same demonic eloquence shown by John Calvin, patriarch of Melville's and Brown's Reformed faith. Unfortunately, Emerson's Unitarianism would not sustain him long through the moral outrages of his age.

The heavy orthodoxy of Calvinism would have been a burden for Emerson, who chafed under even the spare and mostly unenforced *doxa* of his progressive denomination. His search for the answers that his church failed to provide led him instead to the study of Hinduism, Confucianism, Buddhism, Zoroastrianism and Islam, and he liberally seeded his journals with the most prominent thinkers in those traditions. Among his doctrines, Compensation was merely a secularization of early theological mandates mixed with certain karmic ideas, while the conceptual Oversoul was an aspect of the eighteenth-century project of harmoniously translating the Heavenly City to the historicist state. His search for ways to understand life revealed a steadily shrinking and interconnected world in which it was ever more apparent that any particular faith was merely one possibility among many.

His was the most capable, most far seeing philosophical mind of his generation, perhaps the only American at that point to have thought about the conduct of life at the level of the greatest European thinkers.[2] He was both a keen observer and harsh critic of the broader epistemological program taking place around him, and he seldom wasted an opportunity to turn his hammer upon the age in order to sound its ideas when struck with something other than a desperate desire to believe.

He left behind a singularly cohesive narrative thread during the age, both in his public writings and in his journals. The journals served as a reflecting pool that he could gaze into in his later life, since "Man is an animal"—unique in all

Young Ralph Waldo Emerson (Library of Congress).

of creation—"that looks before & after." He hoped that he would someday look back and be able to know that he had been able through "the awfulness of virtue to press & prevail over the false judgments, the rebel passions & corrupt habits of men." These flaws in humanity were the products of narrative identity and historical thought, as "We blame the past, we magnify & gild the future and are not wiser for the multitude of days. Spin on, Ye of the adamantine spindle, spin on, my fragile thread."[3]

Historians were kind to Emerson—who stood alone in an era that desperately needed philosophers—far kinder than he was to them. At the root of Emerson's philosophical questioning was a horrified disgust with the banality of man. Man's unwillingness to confront, comprehend and transvaluate his epistemological fantasies led Emerson to a place of aloof isolation from the ethical concerns of his day. Despite man's wondrous accomplishments, he sneered at the endless parade of idiocy and the justification of ethical horrors derived from the insights of science and history.

Emerson thought a great deal about history. History was the great project of the age, the program of building of a new collective identity. It was historians, and not philosophers like Emerson, who wrote the age. The foundational moment of American history is the Revolution. Not the confused events that actually happened, but the thread of historical agency that gained its name and identity in the writings of historians, most prominent among them George Bancroft.

The Revolution became incarnate in Bancroft's multi-volume *History of the United States* (1834–1878). His premise was straightforward: if the United States is the freest and greatest and most democratic of all nations, and if the narrative of human history is one that moves inexorably towards democracy, then isn't the history of the United States the grandest tableau for the study of history? He built an origin myth on a mountain of research, where "with one impulse, the colonies sprang to arms; with one spirit, they pledged themselves to each other 'to be ready for the extreme event.' With one heart, the continent cried: 'Liberty or Death.'"[4] In Bancroft's mind if the colonists had not been so unified in purpose, they should have been. In fairness, his commitment to the "truth" was genuine, and he believed his studies were rational.[5] But the story he told happened, in a way, in 1812.

For those who put stock in the "great dates" of history, 1812 stands as one of the most formative. The American state entered the Napoleonic wars, its first conflict as a sovereign entity. The first academic chairs of history were established less than two decades after history was declared at an end with the proclamation of Year One of *la Révolution*—the first in 1810 in Berlin, the second in 1812 in Sorbonne. The year was also the beginning of the end of Napoleon's *Grande Armée,* and his *imperium.*

The emperor was raised to power while liquidating the American Revolution's ideological cousin. He understood history's power to philosophically define social reality, and so exploited to the fullest the opportunity provided in a country where *la Révolution* had swept aside all historic barriers. As first consul he had written a pamphlet entitled "Parallels between Caesar, Cromwell, Monck, and Bonaparte" and had it circulated as a test of his imperial ambitions; it was poorly received. Those parallels gained popularity after the army decided to dispense with the civilian government altogether. Similarly, he legitimized his *Imperium,* so fresh and new, by rapidly aging it with the thaumaturgy of history and ancient symbols, "that is, what has always existed," as he later said at St. Helena.[6]

The result of the emperor's mastery of accepted realism was the death of millions and a France that was geographically smaller than he found it. In the process of ruining his young nation, he burdened France with staggering debt, which compelled him to sell an expansive swath of American land stretching from the Mississippi delta into the northwest, doubling the size of what Thomas Jefferson called "the Empire of Liberty."[7] The emperor reassured himself and justified the sale by stating that not only would it affirm "forever the power of the United States," but also that it would give "England a maritime rival who sooner or later will humble her pride."[8]

The emperor's great problem was England's naval blockade of Saint-Domingue, which had long prevented reinforcements from reaching Vicomte de Rochambeau, who was attempting to re-establish slavery in order to provide sugar to fund the emperor's war chest. Rochambeau had taken over the expedition to Saint-Domingue, ordered by then–First Consul Napoleon Bonaparte after Napoleon's brother-in-law, Charles Leclerc, died during the colonial rebellion.

Saint-Domingue had been in open rebellion under the leadership of Toussaint L'Ouverture ever since the fall of the Bastille inspired the slaves of the sugar fields to rise up and break their chains. Thousands of Europe's soldiers perished suppressing the rebellion in the New World. But once *la Révolution* was liquidated at home and power consolidated on the Continent, Napoleon turned his attention to the colonies. Leclerc, his glory-hungry officers and 30,000 French soldiers were dispatched to Saint-Domingue to eliminate the last vestige of resistance and to regain the pride that had been wounded by defeat at the hands of slaves.

After he arrived, Leclerc promised freedom and equality under the Napoleonic Code to Toussaint's men in exchange for integrating with the French army, but his true mission was subjugation. By this treachery, Toussaint was seized and spirited away to a French prison in 1802, where he died in April 1803, in a cold cell in the Jura Mountains. His jailers delighted in humiliating and abusing this figure who had risen up to challenge the emperor. Leclerc deemed him so dangerous that he advised his master, "you cannot keep Toussaint at too great a distance from the sea and put him in a position that is too safe. This man has raised the country to such a pitch of fanaticism that his presence would send it up again in flames."[9]

Under Leclerc's rule, Saint-Domingue was peaceful for a time. But once Leclerc's true mission became known the island burned again, and smoke and fire hung in the air over Cap-Français. French soldiers who didn't die jaundiced and vomiting black blood in the tropical fields as victims of Toussaint's greatest ally—yellow fever—were slain by the infuriated former slaves. Leclerc himself perished of the fever. His successor, Rochambeau, was spared the fever but spent nine years in a British prison after he was snared by the blockade around Saint Domingue.

By then Napoleon was master of Europe, but however haunted he was by defeat and the loss of the jewel of the French colonies to rebellious slaves, there was little he could do. His empire faced an existential threat in a reorganized and English-led opposition, and his treasury was being hungrily devoured by his standing armies. So he finalized the sale of the Louisiana Territory for a pittance. While he hoped to banish the ignoble past and use the funds to secure greater glory, the emperor also said of the sale as he walked away that it thankfully meant no more "damn coffee, damn sugar, damn colonies!"[10]

Jefferson moved in time to suffocate and destroy Haiti, the Western hemisphere's second republic. The resort to violence by blacks was taken as confirmation that they were unfit for freedom, notwithstanding the violent birth of the American state. Also, the triumph of "Jefferson and Liberty" in the 1800 election had depended on the Three-fifths Compromise which allowed Southern slaveholders disproportionate political power.[11] Jefferson owed them his victory, and comfort after another event in 1800, when the slave-blacksmith Gabriel Prosser attempted to raise his hammer in insurrection in Richmond, Virginia. The literate slave Gabriel had read of Toussaint, and saw in that recent history all that he was and might become.[12]

The United States was the only nation born out of the revolutions of the age in which the successor government strengthened the institution of slavery. Emancipation had followed in every other just as it had in France, where former black slaves breathed free only briefly before they were once again manacled by Napoleon, idol of the martial pseudo-nobility of the West. During the Constitutional Convention of 1787, James Madison had observed that "the institution of slavery and its implications formed the line of discrimination" during the deliberations. Madison, a slave owner, pronounced to the convention that the "distinction of color" defined "the most oppressive dominion ever exercised by man over man." He nonetheless assured the Virginia delegation that should they ratify the Constitution it would provide "better security than any that now exists" to the institution of slavery.[13]

The words "slave" and "slavery" did not appear anywhere in the Constitution; euphemisms like "other persons" and "bound to Service" were employed. As Luther Martin noted with a sneer, the true words might have been "odious to the ears of Americans" and thus were actively excluded to preserve the illusion of *We the People*. He also wryly observed those same disingenuous writers were "willing to admit into their system those things which the expression signified."[14]

The Constitution was only possible because of the inclusion of the fugitive slave clause of Article 4, which made everyone an active legal accomplice in the "peculiar institution," and the three-fifths clause, which gave political power to Southern whites based on how many black slaves they owned. This arrangement led to Southern slaveholders winning the presidency in twelve of the sixteen elections up to the momentous year of 1848, and from that year until the pivotal election of 1860 every president publicly supported slavery even if they weren't slave owners. The political structures of the Constitution cannot be separated from the fact that by 1860, the economic value of slaves exceeded the sum of all monetary investments in railroads, banks and industry combined.[15]

The South's share of total U.S. capital, in terms of slaves, was 30 percent. Of the 7,500 individuals in the United States with assets greater than $111,000, 4,500 of them lived in the South and owned slaves.[16] Though poorly industrialized, Southern states were the heart of the nation's wealth. The fugitive slave clause and all the future laws which metastasized from it deepened the Southern addiction to slavery. As Alexis de Tocqueville would observe, when faced with the prospect of living in equality with former slaves, most northerners had chosen the "great advantage" of "exporting" their bondsmen to the South, and rather than freeing the slave in the North, merely changed "his master to a Southerner instead."[17]

"We the People" as an imagined entity was first defined in a document that "We the People" never called for, and never voted for in popular referendum.[18] "We the People" also lacked any context or conceptual form, so relied upon appositional others which were better understood for definition. With three types of people neither explicitly or implicitly identified in the Constitution—Indians, slaves and citizens—it would have been largely meaningless. "We the People" was defined by the fear that unified southern slave owners terrified of conflict with northern merchants haunted by Shaysite uprisings.

Reflecting after the American Civil War, Emerson wrote: "It is commonly said of the War of 1812, that it made the nation honorably known: it enlarged our politics, extinguished narrow sectional parties."[19] And there were few things that Emerson held to be as contemptible as common opinion. By the year 1812, fear was pulling the new republic apart just as easily as it had held it together, and Americans had little faith in their government.[20] During the emperor's reign, American political elites constantly looked overseas for the reference points by which to theorize about their own political destiny as a nation. Parties in the United States had coalesced largely around their orientation to the two principal European powers. Jefferson's Republicans identified—however much at arm's length by the time of the emperor—with the idealized French revolutionaries while warily eyeing British power. Federalists, for their part, viewed the specter of French Radicalism in America with great fear, and clung ever more tenaciously to the language of English liberty.[21] Each regarded the other as the puppet of European masters.

Federalists heaped scorn on President James Madison after he suspended trade with Britain in 1811. They believed this was the result of French pressure to indirectly join the Continental system.[22] England retaliated with orders in council that established a blockade to circumscribe American trade with Europe. When the blockade resulted in the loss of vessels and impressment of sailors, it also effectively created a national pride to wound, arousing American bellicosity over the insult to their sovereignty and the impingement on trade revenue.

The emperor was less than forthright concerning the role the French had played in the destruction of American merchantmen, but the overall anxiety resulted in a declaration of war against Great Britain on June 19, 1812. Unable to reach Britain, the Americans decided to strike at Canada—and if their own territory was expanded in the end, so much the better. This aggression brought a small British detachment to America with a mission to do enough damage to distract the Americans from invading Canada while discrediting the Madison administration, thus putting an end to the fiasco.[23]

In August of 1814 the British force advanced on Washington in what is one of the most storied episodes of the war. The city was largely vacant by the time they arrived; the citizens had abandoned it out of fear of both the British and a potential slave insurrection. Hundreds of escaped slaves fought alongside British Royal Marines with great effect despite their limited training.[24] All along their march, escaped slaves performed admirably as spies, guides and messengers, which not only smoothed the road for the British, but also reduced the size of American forces confronting them, since many had to be diverted to armed watch of the slaves.

On the 24th of August, 4,500 British routed the 7,000 Americans defending

Bladensburg, Maryland, in an event derisively referred to as the Bladensburg Races. Among those fleeing were the president and his cabinet, scattered to the countryside in the chaos, unable to communicate. From there the British made their way to the White House. After a toast to "Jemmy's health," they communicated Whitehall's displeasure with American actions in Canada by putting to torch the War, Navy, Treasury and State Departments, as well as the presidential residence.[25]

Vice Admiral Sir Alexander Cochrane then directed his men towards Baltimore. But after failing to capture the city, they withdrew, safeguarding 2,400 slaves who had seized the opportunity for freedom offered by the presence of British soldiers. The freed slaves were, with very few exceptions, settled free in other lands—primarily Nova Scotia—a point of contention between the American government and Whitehall for a number of years. The defense of Baltimore was observed and recorded in verse in Francis Scott Key's "Star Spangled Banner," though his composition would remain in cultural obscurity until the early twentieth century.

The British mission was a success, and talk of secession and disunion was rampant in the United States. To preserve American unity, President Madison desperately required a satisfactory end to the war, so by October of 1814 he instructed his London delegation to accept peace *on any terms* and without any guarantee of the trade rights for which they had presumably declared war in the first place.

The Treaty of Ghent was signed Christmas Eve of 1814. It didn't reach Washington until February of 1815, but it was still welcome news to Madison, who had spent over two years overseeing the debacle. Taking British success into account, the treaty was quite generous, but the British were eager to put the irritating distraction behind them and return to pressing struggles in Europe. Curiously, when the treaty arrived, the city was already celebrating. And the revelers had no knowledge of the treaty's passage in Parliament.

This curiosity was the founding of American history and the narrative identity of the nation. The celebration was for a lopsided victory won by the defenders of New Orleans, a victory that forever linked Andrew Jackson's legend to that of the nation.[26]

The Treaty of Ghent had been signed prior to the Battle of New Orleans. Due to the delays of time and distance on communication, the outcomes of both of these events were unknown in Washington, D.C., when January 12 of 1815 was declared a day of national prayer, fasting, and humility. News of the Battle of New Orleans traveled slowly overland through a cruel winter and arrived to a dispirited Capitol and to a president in desperate need of hopeful tidings on February 6. But this news had not been delayed as much as the Treaty of Ghent was by a vicious season of Atlantic storms. The treaty arrived in Washington on February 12, a week into a celebration begun on the 6th.

For the immediate observer the initial impression was that Andrew Jackson had won the war. And not even Jackson's foes questioned that. But the battle was meaningless, since it took place a week after the Treaty of Ghent was signed. Nonetheless, in the celebratory moment the president's residence was hastily whitewashed to conceal the scorched memory of the farcical Bladensburg Races. The White House stood as brilliant metaphor of the nation's hasty reinterpretation of the war, a reinterpretation made possible by an isolated and curiously meaningless event. "Seldom has a nation so successfully practiced self-induced amnesia."[27]

Historical fame has eluded Madison, who once proved himself the Constitutional Convention's most noteworthy thinker when he improved the Articles of Confederation right out of existence. However, Andrew Jackson, who contributed to American society in ways that were perhaps less constructive, was transformed from a mere human into an historical definition, as in terms like "Jacksonian America" and "Jacksonian Democracy." But the climate of opinion, "I am sorry to say, will bear a great deal of nonsense. There is scarce any absurdity so gross whether in religion, politics, science, or manners, which it will not bear.... It will bear Andrew Jackson for President.... There's more of the fool in the world than the wise."[28] The Battle of New Orleans eventually propelled him to the presidency and ensured that he would eclipse Madison. After Jackson's election, John Brown never voted again.[29]

This twist of cause and reconstruction is George Bancroft's story. Bancroft was of the elite New England class from which the Federalists drew their support, yet he was distinctively different due to his prominent place within the Massachusetts Democratic Party. His history represented the climate of opinion of the post–1814 America of "Jacksonian Democracy," though he didn't really know "any more than he tells," nor thought deeper than politics over any "reason why these barren facts should be preserved in modern ink."[30] After the war, the Revolutionary past and the nation that emerged absorbed a certain chauvinist character from this fictive feedback loop.[31] During the rise of Jacksonian America, the Federalists disappeared in the shadow of their opposition to the war, leaving only Bancroft to blend their political acumen—long concerned with the value of hierarchy in balancing the nature of material progress—with his own unique ability to articulate his country's exceptionalist sentiments.[32] Emerson felt there was a kind of "mockery in printing ... these withered marrowless facts, like the dead body of an officer ... dressed out in his regimentals, powdered & pomatumed, & sitting up in the bier, going to his own funeral."[33] Jacksonian America became the American Revolution because of a curious wrinkle in time surrounding a battle of dubious meaning.

3

New Millennium Homes

So what is truth? A mobile army of metaphors, metonyms, and anthropomorphisms—in short, a sum of human relations which have been enhanced, transposed, and embellished poetically and rhetorically, and which after long use seem firm, canonical, and obligatory to a people: truths are illusions about which one has forgotten that this is what they are; metaphors which are worn out and without sensuous power; coins which have lost their pictures and now matter only as metal, no longer as coins.
 —Friedrich Nietzsche, *Untimely Meditations*

As a man of ideas, Brown formally joined the Congregationalist church in 1816 to pursue a career in the ministry. He studied classic languages and rhetoric, as well as grammar and mathematics at Moses Hallock's school in Plainfield, Massachusetts. Brown's father was respected and land-rich, but hardly wealthy, so John attempted to work his way through school in the grueling tannery trade. He was a proud craftsman, a hard worker and a very intense young man. Once, Moses Hallock boasted that he was strong enough to pull apart one of Brown's hides with his bare hands. He strained and struggled and failed, and Herman Hallock always remembered Brown's expression of "very marked yet kind immovableness ... on seeing father's defeat."[1]

Brown later transferred to the Morris Academy near the "abolition and anti-slavery center" of Litchfield, Connecticut.[2] His studies were cut short, however, when an eye infection kept him from his books and his work. The poor, more than any, are the victims of caprice in matters such as this, and he was forced to recover in his father's home.

Studies abandoned, John started a tannery in Hudson with his older brother, Levi Blakeslee. These were bright days for the brothers, and it was a good time and place to be a tanner; the wild primeval forests were a riot of creatures, and the methodical extermination waged by white settlers would bring a fortune of hides their way. The brothers spent long days in the difficult, malodorous work of tanning. The two would laboriously scrape the hides of fat and flesh, and soak them in a caustic brine to remove the fur. After that, the hides would be rinsed in the nearby stream, and then steeped for days in a solution with ground tree-bark to impart color. Brown was modestly prosperous, and he purchased his bread from a neighbor named Mary Lusk, a woman who had been made a widow during the 1812 war.

But you cannot hide from your demons forever, not even on a brightly productive little homestead. One evening a fugitive slave happened upon them while they worked. He was frantic, wide-eyed with terror, weak from hunger, and bore the scars of years.

He begged the smelly and blood-covered Browns to shelter him, if only for a night. Levi and John looked at each other, and after a short exchange John hastily led the young man to the barn while Levi dropped his work to run to town for food. The sun was setting.

There was a faint rumble in the distance, and soon John and his charge realized it was the sound of hooves. Knowing the pursuers would likely go for the barn first, John had the fugitive climb out the back window to hide in some bushes outside. But this night, at least, the rider was merely a neighbor returning from town, and after he passed, John ran out to find his fugitive.

John swore he remembered hearing the man's heartbeat before finding him trembling behind a fallen tree. It was a bitter reminder that out there, beyond his little home, were evils that could reduce a strong, capable man to trembling and incoherent terror. John Brown clenched his jaw and swore, once again, to fight slavery for the remainder of his days.[3]

He and Levi remained happily busy, so busy that it was getting difficult for Brown to keep his floors as carefully sanded and swept as he liked. Though a bit of a rough bachelor, he was fastidious, and decided he needed to hire Mary Lusk as his housekeeper. So she and her nineteen-year-old daughter Dianthe moved into John's home, and before long John was smitten with the "remarkably plain" but amiable and gentle girl who kept her mother company through the day and lit the home with song. John had been shy and diffident around women since the death of his mother, but he worked up the courage to propose to Dianthe, and the two married on June 21, 1820.

Neither dark memories nor an uncertain future mattered when John Brown, Jr., was born a year later, on July 25, in Hudson. Jason was born soon after on January 19, 1823, and the third son, Owen, arrived on November 4, 1824. With a new family to care for and a country of possibilities before him, John decided in 1826 to make a journey like the one his father once made to Hudson, and the family went to Randolph, Pennsylvania.

In Randolph, John cultivated a twenty-five acre plot and built a log home, a tannery, and a barn. Within the barn was a carefully concealed room built to harbor fugitive slaves as they escaped to English soil in Canada, where they could breathe free under the protection of the Crown. James Foreman, an employee of Brown's, said that Brown considered it "as much his duty" to shelter those runaways as to bring to justice, say, a horse thief.[4] It was a duty he owed as much to personal convictions as to the community. His hidden cellar was in a valley traced by the densest network of escape paths in the Underground Railroad. If his cellar was a social duty anywhere, it was there.

During this time Brown also joined a Masonic fraternity, but he left in protest after the mysterious disappearance of William Morgan, who had authored a book about the Freemasons and proposed to expose their secrets. Brown became thereafter a vociferous supporter of a loosely organized anti-mason movement, which drew support from religious opponents of secret societies, various free speech advocates and the political opponents of Andrew Jackson, who happened to be a Mason. The public frenzy over Morgan's unsolved disappearance and the secretive society was inflammatory. After Brown spoke in Meadville, Pennsylvania, his hotel was surrounded by angry Mason supporters. He was frightened enough to purchase a gun, and he practiced until he was a decently accurate shot. He would not use those skills for thirty more years.[5]

He started a school, and employed fifteen people at his tannery. It was imperfectly managed according to modern business practices; he would turn away customers rather than sell them hides with the "least particle of moisture" or any imperfections.[6] Though he could have assigned a commodity value to the hides based on their condition, in his pride he simply refused to sell. His financial life was seldom precisely calculated, and neither were his employment decisions. He once hired a local man on the verge of becoming homeless, but only on the condition that the man would accept clothing and food as payment in advance. Local officials and merchants regarded him as "evil and unprincipled" due to his aggressive activity organizing resistance to evictions in Erie and Crawford counties.[7]

President Andrew Jackson (Library of Congress).

John and Dianthe's family continued to grow, while he kept busy as the clerk for the church and postmaster for the post office, both of which he established. Frederick was born on January 9, 1827, and two years later they welcomed their first daughter, Ruth, on February 18, 1829. Living happily with the rewards of his work, his new life was the stuff of the dreams and ideals of a kind of mythological "American story." In his community, to be considered half as "enterprising and honest ... and as useful" as John Brown was a high compliment.[8]

But by 1830, no one had coined any phrases as nonsensical as "the American Dream." A related and equally mythical concept—"liberty"—was remarked upon by the French historian Michel Chevalier that in America it was not merely a mystical but also a "practical idea," meaning "a liberty of action and motion which the American uses to expand over the vast territory that Providence has given him and to subdue it to his uses."[9] It was part of the narrative that led John Brown to purchase one of the inexpensive and large plots in northwest Pennsylvania, in order to pursue the lifestyle "of the [Biblical] patriarchs."[10]

The ideal of the yeoman-farmer was a common dream that involved a political autonomy gained not just from God but from a household centered production model. To be a property-owning farmer—a patriarch—meant moral autonomy and theoretical insulation from the vicissitudes of the market revolution often reduced in narrative to the personal differences between an eccentric Virginian and an equally eccentric West Indian.

The fate of Brown's Randolph fortunes were part of a transformation of private life that was redefining words like "freedom" and "power." The yeoman-farmer was the archetype of Jefferson's frontier, and when Thomas Jefferson opened the West he opened both a mythic future-past and an inescapable and tangible fact of life. Jefferson—a man with colossal debts who had wealthy friends and penitent historians to save him from ignominy—believed that by extending the frontier he had also extended far into the future the day when an overpopulated and class-divided America could no longer support freedom.[11] Territory was integral to sovereign franchise.

To complicate things, capitalism was re-defining the concept of what even constituted "property," which led James Madison in 1829 to warn that a property-less majority was being created that would imperil the union. Madison had once advanced property qualifications as a means of curbing public excesses, but eventually determined that such ideas were no longer compatible with the age, as they violated the principle of rule by consent. During the time the Browns lived in Randolph, challenges to property qualifications for public participation was well underway, but would not be complete until 1860. The final assault on freedom as defined by property would come when the western states entered the Union with laws allowing all adult white males the vote, or when territories like Kansas allowed the same under Federal law.

The home-centered yeoman remained a vital myth for a long time, and those producers enjoyed considerable choice regarding the extent of their market participation. However, part of the contradictory impact of the spreading market economy was that it not only redefined the value of productive property, but also enmeshed those yeoman-patriarchs in market relationships whether they desired it or not. The expansion of capitalism served to weaken individual control over one's future, paralleling the inception of the word "individualism" in the 1830s, yet it also paradoxically brought about a loss of control by individuals over their private lives. "Jacksonian" America long held to the idea, dating to John Locke, that labor was the source of wealth and that the worker—unless he was a slave—was entitled to the fruits. The ideal yeoman-farmer was upheld as a critique of capitalism and the commoditization of labor.[12]

The eventual collapse of John Brown's private financial life had less to do with work than it did with capital, a problem that arose in his first business venture. Due to a specific kind of bark that grew there, Randolph was an attractive place for a tannery. But it was short on local livestock and hides and sparsely populated, presenting fundamental difficulties that a good bark-dye could not offset. In an effort to establish a successful trade, Brown came to an arrangement with a cattle-rancher named Seth B. Thompson. Brown sold Thompson's cattle to the locals for beef, and also processed the hides to send back to Thompson, who would sell them in the more populous Trumbull County region near the Ohio-Pennsylvania border.

It was successful for a time, and in 1831 Brown was able to award a plot to his assistant, James Foreman, in recognition of "faithful service," while purchasing 200 more acres for himself.[13] But the economy was changing; people who bought the beef were slow to pay, and Brown was struggling to comprehend credit and finance. His ventures survived for a time on loans from Thompson and by selling piecemeal his expansive land. By 1832, the community pillar could no longer afford even the down-payment on an oxen team, and he was having as much trouble paying his creditors as his debtors had paying him.[14] Brown could not fully articulate in his letters the conditions that his story, on a small scale, represented in the world at large.

A period of runaway inflation began in 1812 in American markets due to involvement in the emperor's wars. To curb similar future calamities, the Second Bank of the United States was chartered in 1816 to manage the nation's wealth and that wealth grew from cotton and textiles. It was the raw material of the industrial revolution and its sale underwrote investments in every new enterprise as well as the urbanization and factories of the British Midlands and the American Northeast. It was the flood that broke the traditional limits of "yeoman-farmer" society and rushed onward to fuel a growth never before seen in history. But technological innovations alone did not crowd out older modes of production. The end dissipative structure of the West depended on the productive capacity of its environment, the fuel, as it were. Without the cotton fields of the American South, Britain would have been unable to grow beyond the "cul-de-sac" of labor, land, food, fuel and other raw materials which had held back China, among others.[15]

Inflation, collapse, crises—this period saw the first of these phenomena, at least in a form recognizable to modern finance. That is because prior to approximately 1750 there was virtually no economic growth in all of human history. (And prior to 1812 there was no history as understood academically.) America's own history coincides with a period that suddenly deviated from the norm. America itself may be little more than a cultural system formed around the ideas underlying that growth, growth of a magnitude that might be an aberration, never to happen again—less a culture than an abstraction of power.

Economic growth, put simply, is the remittance of expectations of monetary interest, the exponential expansion of the monetization of the act of moving matter about in relation to other matter. To that end, physical technologies certainly helped, as did a continent of low-hanging economic fruit, but the abstraction underneath the growth was money and finance.

Money, whether paper or metal, is an abstraction. It is an illusion, a metaphor, a representation of time, change, and causality that enables the idea of work to be carried forward or backward into time. It is a device, a thought machine that cultures outsourced a variety of ethical decisions to, and then forgot that there ever were ethical questions while accepting money as fundamentally true. Money from the future (loans) does not make bread nor bridges, yet people believe that it does. As a data form, a quantification of a dissipative social structure, it carries within its movements cultural values and narratives that go far beyond numbers.

Emerson wrote, "Among the marks of the age of cities must be reckoned conspicuously the universal adoption of cash-payment. Once it was one of many methods."[16] But after monetization, there was no alternative for social coexistence outside of monetary exchange. Money, in the end, is the delicate thread that determines who is master, and who is slave, since "growth" is also a function of predictive expectations. The system needed to grow to live, and since money itself does not form bread, or clothes, the metaphor eventually had to be culturally grounded in the very real and physical world. Metaphor became flesh in black slaves, the dark nexus of cultural transubstantiation.

One of the fundamental doubts Emerson had about abolitionism was the relationship of the movement to the system; did abolitionists actually understand and believe what they asked for, and truly desire it as an end? Speeches were one thing, but "whilst we sit here talking & smiling, some person is out there in field & shop & kitchen doing what we need, without talk or smiles.... The world asks, do the abolitionists eat sugar? Do they wear cotton? Do they smoke tobacco? Are they their own servants? Have they managed to put that dubious institution of servile labour on an agreeable & thoroughly intelligible & transparent foundation?"[17]

When the slaveholder cracked his whip, the foundation of a complex and dynamic world economy cried out and set the enmeshed gears into motion. They were remarkably efficient, producing 80 percent of the textile industry's raw materials. Output had increased by a factor of twenty from the ratification of the Constitution through 1859. Steady, efficient growth upheld an intricate financial system that traded and speculated on the outcomes, and the portability and profitability of this most important commodity was imminent to the web of capital interest that stretched from New Orleans to New York to London.[18]

In 1824, speculators purchased cotton—largely on piles of credit—based on predictions of a relatively small crop yield. The cotton was bought at dear prices and "turning out" some of the factory workers in anticipation, then quite contrary to expectations, the crop was exceedingly large. The news crept like a shadow from the Mississippi Delta to New York and beyond, cotton prices plummeted, and merchant firms could not repay their loans. Rationally, as expected, they demanded remittance from their debtors, and the results, iterated tens of thousands of times across the West, paralyzed the markets in the year that Brown established his tannery.

Nathan Biddle's Second Bank of the United States limited widespread economic disaster when it checked, to a degree, both speculation and available credit by making and calling in its own loans, and by forcing state banks to redeem credit in a number of forms of convertible currency. The relative stability offered by the bank also gave the merchants the breathing room to develop workable solutions for hedging against the producers' efficient productivity. In order to avoid another situation where they would be left holding bad debt, the merchants collectively insisted on shipping cotton on consignment, which meant that the planters bore all the risk until a textile company made the purchase.

As the economy's largest lender, the bank limited the excesses of frustrated individuals but also propelled growth by lending directly to individual entrepreneurs, particularly enslavers who were always ready to buy more people to harvest the wealth of the cotton field. In 1832 the slave-trader Isaac Franklin noted that both the Bank of the United States and the "Planters Bank" were infusing the slave trade with capital to spur growth.[19] Franklin, a veteran of the 1812 war whose wealth came from a 640 acre North Carolina bequest to his father for service in the Revolutionary War, was one of the most prominent and wealthy slave traders operating in the financial heart of the slave trade between Natchez and New Orleans. In the years to follow, fully one-third of the U.S. Bank's capital was bound up in those slave markets. Cotton buyers consumed the remaining balance in the form of commercial credit, which kept prices steady, and the money made its way in loans to planters who were awaiting their actual payday for their product.

This structure operated in a kind of feedback loop, encouraging the purchase of more slaves to grow more cotton in anticipation of paying those loans, and Franklin became wildly wealthy exporting slaves from Virginia into the expanding West. His

Tennessee estate, named "Fairvue," was far more impressive than his famous neighbor's more humble manor, called "The Hermitage."[20] The entire edifice was borne on the bleeding shoulders of people cruelly exploited, toiling in the fields where the margins were to be found. Without the ability to draw cotton from slaves, or the ability to sell the bodies to people who wanted to draw cotton from them, the entire system collapsed.[21]

The cruel cultural acceptance of the productive exploitation of slaves assured markets about the future, making intricately exponential interest possible. Their bodies, on the other hand, were the final hedges against insolvency. As the idea went, no matter what else happened they would either draw enough cotton so that the debtor-planter could pay his debts, or the debts could be discharged by their sale. As a form of "value" that fluctuated far less than the cotton they harvested, they became the standard unit of mortgage guarantee for loans.

Slave-traders created alternatives to Biddle's bank, like the Consolidated Association of the Planters of Louisiana (C.A.P.L.), the institution that Isaac Franklin referred to as the "Planters Bank."[22] Its purpose was to "securitize" slaves, further hedging investors' losses, a scheme that worked so long as the broader financial system remained sound.

Under the C.A.P.L., planter-borrowers would mortgage land and slaves to the bank for credit in half the value of those assets. In order to legitimize its investments, the C.A.P.L. secured $5 million in bank bonds, half from the state of Louisiana, and half from Baring Brothers of England. Thus the slaveholders' largest collective investment was converted into multiple income streams, all of which ended in a pool of credit available for lending at rates highly favorable when compared with expected production. A clever slave-trader could engage multiple lenders on the same collateral or use short-term borrowing to buy more slaves to borrow against as well.

By the time the entire system had run its course and the slaves were fully monetized, a wide population was participating in slavery's expansion. An investor purchasing bonds from Baring Brothers would find each one priced at $1,000, roughly the price of one slave.[23] This piece of paper, made of the shivering shards of thousands of lives, was much preferred by investors over purchasing one complete life, where escape, malaria, or rebellion made treating a human beings as transparently fungible very difficult.

Shaped and incrementalized, securitized and rationalized, black slaves were translated into any number of metaphors, just like a table, which is a metaphor that exists only in the minds of people, and stands for the time and change of the hands that crafted it. But commodity-humans, being more than objects, might have quite different ideas from their masters concerning what they represented in an abstract world, and those individuals could, unlike a table, do more than stand: they could rebuke, and even kill. One of the most noteworthy uprisings happened in 1831, the same year that President Andrew Jackson began his historic and brutal fight with Nathan Biddle's Bank of the United States.

As the fight progressed, Franklin's optimism about the state of credit in December of 1832 yielded to "distress" about the market, but he would "endeavor to bear up," knowing that should he and his associates "loose everything," they could find ways to "robb far more."[24]

By 1832 half of the bank's balance sheet was deeply bound to Mississippi and Louisiana, and from there spread in the ways described into the lands that Jackson had directly or indirectly cleared of Indians, and yet the bank was not loved by those Southern debtors, or even by Jackson. It is important, however, not to read Civil War sectional divisions onto Jackson's economic politics. His statement that the bank had made "the rich richer and the potent more powerful" was certainly so, and was spoken from his genuine desire to be a protector to the weak and helpless, at least those of a certain color.

Jackson's ascendancy to iconic political and historiographic status marked John Brown's withdrawal from the process, though the two were highly similar. But Brown's singular hatred of slavery and fury over the injustices done to black folk drove him to spurn Jacksonian America. Otherwise, Jackson, like Brown, was a man of considerable force of character, imperfectly educated, prone to strong prejudices, and equally prone to forming personal enmities. He was also a leader of significant abilities with generally good instincts and a desire to faithfully discharge his duties. He was always kind and gentle with women and children.[25]

The turmoil within the banking system was not the only calamity to beset Brown, as his Randolph fortunes declined. He was ill during much of 1831 and 1832 with the ague, an antiquated term for a terrible set of malaria or typhoid-like symptoms. The agonizing teeth-grinding fevers and shivering fits kept him from work, and his business ailed with him as much as with its decaying web of connections. Then his son Frederick, only four years old, died on March 31, 1831.

4.

The Prejudices of Philosophers and Historians

The desire for "freedom of the will" in the superlative metaphysical sense, which still holds sway, unfortunately, in the minds of the half-educated; the desire to bear the entire and ultimate responsibility for one's actions oneself, and to absolve God, the world, ancestors, chance, and society involves nothing less than to be precisely this causa sui and, with more than Munchhausen's audacity, to pull oneself up into existence by the hair, out of the swamps of nothingness. Suppose someone were thus to see through the boorish simplicity of this celebrated concept of "free will" and put it out of his head altogether, I beg of him to carry his "enlightenment" a step further, and also put out of his head the contrary of this monstrous conception of "free will": I mean "unfree will," which amounts to a misuse of cause and effect.
—Friedrich Nietzsche, Beyond Good and Evil

In 1831 a fiery young reformer named William Lloyd Garrison published the first installment of *The Liberator*, which became the epistolary of, and defined, "abolitionism." His introductory issue was inflammatory. "I will be as harsh as truth," he wrote, "and as uncompromising as justice. On this subject, I do not wish to think, or to speak, or write, with moderation." After all, would one moderately save one's wife from a rapist, or a baby from a fire? Garrison thought not, and declared, "I am in earnest—I will not equivocate—I will not excuse—I will not retreat a single inch—AND I WILL BE HEARD. The apathy of the people is enough to make every statue leap from its pedestal, and to hasten the resurrection of the dead."[1]

Born in 1805, Garrison grew up in a family broken by economic vicissitudes, and began writing and publishing when he went to work at age 13 for the *Newburyport Herald*. By 1830, he had turned his pen and words on slavery. He was "a man of great ability in conversation, of a certain longsightedness in debate which is a great excellence, a tenacity of his proposition which no accidents or ramblings in the conversation can divert, a calmness & method in unfolding the details of his argument, and an eloquence of illustration, which contents the ear & the mind." And yet the delivery of his message suffered "by his continual wearisome trick of quoting texts of scripture & his judaical Christianity & then by the continual eye to numbers, to societies. Himself is not enough for him."[2]

Garrison briefly joined the American Colonization Society, but broke with them, to write the *Liberator*, and a year later founded the New England Anti-Slavery Society, and immediately after, the larger American Anti-Slavery Society. These societies were partly a reaction to the colonization groups, which he felt advocated a fundamentally un–Christian solution to the nation's original sin. A significant portion of the colonizationists were dedicated to the cause of colonizing *free blacks* in order to protect slavery, not to end it. Fundamentally, Garrison thought, "the Question between the Colonization & the Abolition men was 'whether you should remove them (the negroes) from the prejudice or the prejudice from them.'"[3]

Most, if not all, abolitionists were racists, and only by the most painful of mental contortions can one dispute this fact. Emerson wryly observed that "the abolitionist (theoretical) wishes to abolish slavery, but because he wishes to abolish the black man."[4] Even intellectuals as subtle as Emerson were not innocent, and his early journals have some shocking bigotry and racism. He once claimed with no shame that race determined "different degrees of intellect" and that it was natural that "some should lead, and some should serve."[5] There was nobility in the abolitionists' impulse to emancipate the slaves, but after emancipation most abolitionists were colonizationists, and would have sent the millions of black men and women anywhere but the United States. Emerson's early crude writings were barely distinguishable from the orthodoxy of opinion held by opponents of slavery like Abraham Lincoln and, prior to him, Henry Clay, who was among the founders of the American Colonization Society in 1817, one of the first organized groups dedicated to the end of slavery. The lasting legacy of this group is the troubled nation of Liberia.

So "abolitionist" is a vague label, a term that is as much the generalization of historians and demagogues as anything else. It doesn't apply to everyone who opposed slavery. The millions of black slaves and freemen in America did not require a social group, creed, or political organization to hate slavery and desire its abolition. It is a bit awkward to define Frederick Douglass as an "abolitionist" given what that term can mean. To be an abolitionist—the individual practitioner of a particular "ism"—implied at a basic level an acceptance of the validity of the social contract and the engagement of the subject as an intellectual issue, a philosophical matter extrinsic, perhaps, to one's own life.

Nonetheless, Garrison's abolitionist words were defining, and *The Liberator* electrified public opinion on New Year's Day of 1831. But they were just words. Most were obliged to have already forgotten the events of January of 1811 outside of New Orleans. It was 1831, and people were trying out the taste of the new word "nationalism" on their tongues, symbolized by a spectacular

William Lloyd Garrison (Library of Congress).

4. The Prejudices of Philosophers and Historians   27

victory in that same city, and by a gleaming white house in the capital. Who wished to remember the fear when the spirit of Toussaint reached the port city, or the crows reveling on the emancipated heads of black men, impaled on pikes, empty and sightless sockets beckoning other rebels to the grave?

Certainly not comfortable New Englanders, who greeted Garrison's *Liberator* with nervous praise. Virginians—warily eyeing the rising abolitionist sentiment north of them—were decidedly less pleased. In fact, they stunk with fear, despite their boasting of the "enlightened" condition of slavery in their state, and the supposedly happy and submissive slaves that such beneficence created. In their fear they made of their state an armed garrison of some hundred thousand men whose sole purpose was to be ever watchful for insurrection.[6]

New Orleans was far away, and 1811 on the other side of an amnesiac divide. But Virginia was so close to that white house, and in August of 1831 a fatherless slave named Nat, called the Prophet by fellow slaves, beheld a vision of a black hand covering the sun and knew it was the time to rise up and slay his enemies with their own weapons.[7] All slaves must of necessity be fatherless, born as ghosts with no surety in their world save for the master's caprice, and so he was also called Turner, after Benjamin Turner who owned him first, who passed him to Samuel Turner, though Nat's first and only ownership was not recognized by white Americans. When Samuel died, Nat and his wife had been sold to separate masters.

The ghosts of violence beset the master's house, slaying sixty people as the rebellious slaves went from house to house with steel and club. The slain were chosen for death by their white skin, and only extreme poverty could by sympathy stay the killing hand, those poor whites being hardly better off than the slaves bringing death to their masters.[8] Eventually the militia arrived, numbering twice as strong and armed with guns, and the insurrection ended in fire and blood.

The peace that followed echoed with screams and was awash in blood. Heads gazed dumbly over the plantations, food for the crows, as 200 black slaves perished for white fear. Nat, called Turner, was eventually captured, and his punishment was worthy of his biblical aspirations, the kind traditionally reserved for prophets and for those who oppose kings. He was skinned, beheaded, and his body cut in four. Virginia made it law that no black man should henceforth learn to read.[9]

Accusing eyes looked to Garrison, for they remembered the uncompromising immediacy in his calls for abolition. However, Nat never read a single northern abolitionist publication, let alone Garrison's, which was new and was circulated only sporadically in the South. When Nat gave his command to kill, it was not the voice of northern abolitionism, but the command of Ezekiel to spare none. Southerners, however, needed a reason, an extrinsic cause that would not demand of them the courage to contemplate their society and way of life. Better to simply blame Garrison. The eight months between the first *Liberator* and Nat's crusade was a convenient enough sequence, and after 1831 northern abolitionism and slave insurrection were unified in the slave owner's mind. Poor Garrison was just as afraid of insurrection and of black people as those southerners were.

Nat's insurrection served to change, or perhaps clarify, a variety of philosophical positions on slavery. Garrison did not slouch in defending himself from southern accusers, reminding his audience that where he differed from those southerners was primarily in his view of moral causation. In this he was, as in most things, honest. He abhorred insurrection and violence as much as they, but where southerners believed that black people must be kept enslaved to prevent such horrors, Garrison believed that only liberation would accomplish peace. This is to say that all parties believed that black people were the source of violence and the disruption of civilization; southerners held that it was endemic to their character, those ungrateful beasts that were as untamable as a lion, while Garrison adopted the position that slavery and the injustices perpetrated by whites had made beasts of black men.

Garrison had written as early as January of 1831 that he did not "preach rebellion ... but submission and peace."[10] Submission to the success and vindication of the Leviathan state, the machinery of nations, that it might function properly once black people were emancipated, but not fully, for they would need to be educated as in a great cultural experiment. He didn't really know if black people could be a part of the nation, and four months before Nat's rebellion the *Liberator* printed essays like "Another Dream" which narrated a race war, the spilling over of the vengeance of slaves, where a fictional narrator was forced to witness "three savage Negroes" cutting down his wife and child while he improbably survived to witness in prose.[11]

Garrison genuinely cared about black people and their plight, but those who fight animal cruelty love the animals no less. His theories regarding abolition were just theories. The redemption and perfection of the state was the end goal. The Virginia uprising gave him recent historical fodder to emphasize his point, and the issue of March 10, 1832, featured a hypothetical recollection, in poetry, of the violence as viewed by a white citizen.[12]

Slavery was once viewed almost as a necessary evil in the South, an unfortunate but necessary fact of harmonious life. The violence of Nat's revolt challenged many assumptions, and southerners realigned their philosophies on slavery to the health of society. The Virginia legislature was briefly locked in furious debates, news of which spread through the slave population, who began to dare to hope for emancipation. It was a vain hope. People may have debated the pleasing fictions which horizontally justified the evil, but monetary value of each slave and the potential cost of colonization were indisputable. And under no circumstances were southerners going to manumit black slaves into white lands; surely even the abolitionists saw the horror of that?

So, faced with a perceived convergence of the enemy within and the enemy without, southerners expanded their militia system and founded schools like the Virginia Military Institute. Additionally, the legislature passed laws like the aforementioned literacy proscriptions, to try to ensure the slaves would never revolt again. The "enlightened" South then earnestly undertook the self-mutilating process of becoming a military society, dedicated at all costs to preserving a slave-based civilization that was no longer seen as unfortunately and historically necessary, but rather as "the greatest of all the great blessings."[13] Logics and horrors multiply when confronted by truth, and Emerson caustically remarked, "I do not wonder at feeble men being strong advocates for slavery. They have no feeling of worthiness which assures them of their own safety. In a new state of things they are by no means sure it would go well with them. They cannot work or facilitate work or cheer or decorate labour. No, they live by certain privileges which the actual order of the community yields them. Take those and you take all. I do not wonder that such would fain raise a mob for fear is very cruel."[14]

Southern feelings of isolation on the issue were not unfounded. The forgetting of slavery as fundamental to the founding and the national narrative was already taking place as historians attempted to make reality fit the bald fictions that Luther Martin had once derided in the U.S. Constitution. Bancroft dedicated more pages of his *History* to slavery than most of his peers, but only to move it to the narrative periphery of the New England heart of the Revolution, ensuring that there was "not enough [of slavery] to affect the character of the people." It was, in his estimation, "essentially a southern institution." He then exonerated the Puritans he revered of their own historic complicity in slavery while attempting to give the South some redemption by ultimately placing the entire evil at the doorstep of the Crown.[15]

By 1859 southerners would fully internalize the notion that New England Puritans were historically dedicated to the veritably Jacobite notion of society-ending abolition, and its companion evils of feminism, secularism, liberalism, and the like. Puritans were not, in the main, anti-slavery rebels, though John Brown's Calvinist speech and rhetoric would reinforce such a narrative and accelerate the divergence of historical identity between North and South, as historians like Bancroft tried to grant the northeast historical absolution since he could not grant abolition. Like Brown, many abolitionists, were descendants of Puritan traditions, though altered a hundred ways through deism, Congregationalism, Enlightenment philosophy, and even Transcendentalism. But John Brown was a curious sort of abolitionist, both of that movement and yet not.

Abolitionism was an intellectual position, arrived at through careful consideration and with the state as its end. It was a thing of facts, a classification, like "a church is a classification," but merely a new one, "as Benthamism, as Abolitionism, as Calvinism … & the neophytes take the same delight in subordinating everything to their new terminology.… But in all the unbalanced minds (& whose is not so?) the classification is idolized, passes for the end, not a specifically exhaustible means."[16] John Brown hated slavery, but his end was the value of the individual; should the state accede to that end, so much the better, but hardly necessary.

Though Brown enjoyed Garrison's "judaical Christianity" in the *Liberator*, his preoccupation was his family. Despite his incomplete training as a preacher, he raised that family in a manner consistent with the most doctrinaire New England Puritan tradition. As John, Jr., remembered, his father kept a ledger of his petty transgressions, and had him pay it off in "strokes from a nicely-prepared blue beech switch, laid on masterly." But one day the balance had run too high, and John Brown could not bear to exact payment for every petty sin, so he stripped off his own shirt, dropped to his knees, and had his son administer the remainder to him, commanding him to strike harder "until he received the balance of the account" and "drops of blood showed on his back where the tip end of the tingling beech cut through."

A confused young John, Jr., later recognized it as a lesson in the doctrine of atonement, but at the time he had not read "the ponderous volumes of Jonathan Edwards sermons which father owned."[17] Brown loved his son—he loved his entire family—and his severity was his way of seeking to do right by them the best he could in a changing world. Corporal punishment was common then, but Brown came to this disciplinary solution after long exasperation, and out of a confirmed policy not to threaten his children. And though he was severe, he ignored the popular advice of a New York Methodist leader who "every other week" took a horsewhip to his wife "in order to keep her in subjugation, and because she scolded so much."[18]

Because he remembered his own impish youth he was attentive to the spiritual development of his boys, and every morning and night he solemnly prayed "in the old-fashioned, Presbyterian way," standing and leaning forward on the back of his chair while the entire family participated in the reading of Bible selections. Devout, but not a scold, religious, but abhorring excessive cant, he was "simply an inspired paternal ruler" caring for his family as he knew how, and his demeanor evoked conformity simply by example.[19] In conversation he quoted the Old Testament "from one end to the other," and was domineering during religious discussions.[20]

He used his financial success as well as he could to become an honest man and to serve his God. The Sabbath in the Brown home was dogmatically austere, a time for the most serious reflection and moral education, devoid of play or any kind of frivolity. On those days he would gather his family and all his employees together for religious observation. Sometimes there would be a preacher in Randolph, but often Brown served in that role, delivering sermons in the Congregationalist church he founded. "Providence," he intoned, "unfolds to our darkened minds, Three cardinal traits in the character of the true God, vis Justice, mercy, and love of propriety."[21]

The New England frontier where John Brown came of age had been the scene of two "Great Awakenings"—waves of religious revivalism that swept the region. Owen Brown converted during the second of these movements, which he recalled as an event so profound that the like had not been seen "since the days of Edwards and Whitfield."[22] Owen took his new faith seriously, and raised John accordingly. It may have helped that Owen had a painful stammer—the worst a neighbor had ever heard—but spoke clearly when he prayed or read the word of God.[23]

The Edwards that Owen referred to was Jonathan Edwards, a Calvinist theologian who lived from 1703 to 1758, and wrote a number of definitive sermons and sophisticated essays on Calvinist pre-destination and the will. His volumes filled Brown's bookshelf, works about judgment in a secular world, works about destiny in a narrative reality based on the idea of free will. When Brown became part of the narrative, his later violent actions were often emplotted as a mind out of its time, driven by an incomprehensible theology to enact revolutionary social theories. The man who didn't believe in free will thence had none, and moved though life like a well-intentioned and anachronistic biblical prophet to commit the violence demanded by an uncompromising faith.

This faith was illustrated by one of the most famous sermons in American history, "Sinners in the Hands of an Angry God," by Jonathan Edwards. But Edwards was a prolific writer, and those "ponderous volumes" on Brown's bookshelf were more than iterated copies of that one sermon. It took volumes to record the myriad sophisticated works by the only theologian during the first Great Awakening to represent the delicate balance between intellect and passion instead of becoming a part of the antinomian and anti-intellectual character of revivalism. Edwards' famous sermon, invoked so frequently, is a slight aberration in a broadly intellectual body of work.[24]

4. The Prejudices of Philosophers and Historians

An understanding of Edwards, and Brown, is not best found in "Sinners," but rather in an essay titled "A careful and strict Enquiry into the *modern* prevailing notions of that Freedom of the Will which is supposed to be essential to Moral Agency, Vice and Virtue, Reward and Punishment, Praise and Blame." Specifically, Edwards was considering the Arminian notion of freedom of the will, in which said freedom is supposedly necessary in order to be capable of virtue or vice, and thus be subject to praise or blame.

One must first understand what Edwards means by will, and how moral action is perceived as a sequence of events linked by the necessity of cause and consequence. He develops his argument in a framework seemingly borrowed from John Locke's chapter on "Power" in the *Essay Concerning Human Understanding*. Edwards commences his definition stating, "The faculty of the will is that faculty of power or principle of mind by which it is capable of choosing: an act of will is the same as an act of choosing or choice." Edwards defines "choice" broadly: "So that whatever names we call the act of will by—choosing, refusing, approving, disapproving, directing, liking, disliking, embracing, rejecting, determining, directing, commanding, forbidding, inclining, or being averse, being pleased or displeased with—all may be reduced to this of choosing. For the soul to act voluntarily is evermore to act electively."[25] Such acts of will, or "volition," are the effects of antecedent causes, and are the cause of voluntary actions, or "vulgar causality," in which man acts freely.

Edwards maintained that while men may choose their voluntary actions, they never choose contrary to their desire, nor desire contrary to their will. The notion of "liberty," he elaborated, is in "common speech" nothing more than "power, opportunity, or advantage that anyone has, to do as he pleases."[26] But this has absolutely nothing to do with acts of volition. Men may choose their actions, but have no ability to choose their will. The truth or falsity of this was, according to Edwards, irrelevant. Man cannot create his mental states *ex nihilo*, and to propose such a thing is to propose an infinite regress, a senseless absurdity.

Locke, whose ideas were central to the founders' thinking, maintained that the very phrase "free will" was nonsensical, and likewise maintained that the truth of determinism was largely irrelevant. It is only man's ability to postpone a decision long enough to reflect on the consequences of a choice that even allows man to call a behavior "voluntary."[27]

A crafty theologian first and last, and a philosopher in between, Edwards was concerned—after demonstrating the logical absurdity of free will—with asserting that the grace of God was the extrinsic factor which began and completed the causal chain and made it intellectually and morally feasible, the "natural law" which governed the will. Men were helpless before the will of the God of Job, but Edwards did not write that they were strung like puppets on a terrible and irrational belief. They arrived at a position of helplessness through reason, with a theological conclusion: Men who cannot cause their own will can certainly not sway the mind of God, thence helplessness and dependence on mercy and Providence. God, as John Brown knew and phrased more simply, was no "respecter of human affairs."[28]

George Bancroft, representative author of the "climate of opinion" of the age in which John Brown lived, read Jonathan Edwards's *Freedom of the Will* as a Harvard undergraduate and enthusiastically embraced it as an "immortal treatise" and a brilliant reformulation of Calvinist theology.[29] He wrote, "He that would know the workings of the New England Mind in the middle of the eighteenth century, and the throbbings of its heart, must give his days and nights to the study of Jonathan Edwards."[30] Edwards's concepts, in many ways, defined the meaning of "freedom" for Bancroft, for whom the imagined community of the United States took the place of—or united with—Edwards's God as the narrative cause of freedom and determinant of the will.

Edwards's *Freedom of the Will* is highly consistent with modern notions of philosophical physics and psychology.[31] Stripping it of narrative weight and of theological intent translates it into working historical theory as well. To simplify, the will follows the last *perception* of good, and man perceives good in a consistent fashion, often with little regard to actual events. Following Locke, the language of faculty psychology regarding these matters is merely a convention, a way to communicate a unitary self under different aspects, and like John Brown said in his sermon, redemption is historical, since human knowledge can only discern God through divine action in the world through time.

Edwards's argument was tailored to absolutely crush the Arminian position preached by George Whitefield and later by John Wesley, which asserted above all else that grace and dignity required fundamentally unimpaired and self-directed freedom of the will. One of the itinerant preachers of Wesley's "method" came to Randolph in 1832 and visited with Brown in a neighbor's home. The preacher spoke so rapidly and flippantly that Brown—a slow spoken man—never had an opportunity to discuss the issue. John Wesley, an Oxford trained cleric, may have set creditable intellectual standards for Methodism, but his American followers were seldom interested in sustaining them. They were vigorous circuit riders, adept at working the emotions of the under-educated; accordingly their achievements in terms of numbers "saved" were truly extraordinary. In fairness, John Wesley appears to be the only Christian thinker of his time to argue against slavery. By the time the unnamed Methodist visited Randolph, the sect was well on its way to becoming the largest Protestant denomination in the United States.[32]

Brown was irate about the encounter, and arranged for a public debate to settle the discussion. It would be conducted in questions and answers—an impediment to the fast-talking conversion methods of the Wesleyans—and over the course of twenty-four questions as James Foreman recalled, the "clergyman confused him Self So much, that he gave up the debate and although a Clergyman has amounted to little or nothing Since."[33] Brown's faith, subtly intellectual and broadly representative, was in decline though. By the year of his death faith in America would be defined by people more like the confused preacher and by the philosophical simpletons that were the preacher's religious heirs.

Since Brown left no treatises on the subject, the full extent of his comprehension of the subtleties of Edwards's theology must remain, as with many matters of his mind, pure speculation. The fact that he was also imperfectly educated has further shaded estimates of his intellectual depth, though this in truth meant little in a time before the Wisconsin system. But if it amuses later Americans to beam fondly on a president who was self-educated in a log cabin, so be it.

Among those who met him, or spoke with him, or knew him even indirectly, whether they were friend or enemy, the only person who ever said anything disparaging about John Brown's intellect was John Brown. His was a thinking theology as taught by

Edwards, and which he in turn taught to his Randolph parishioners when he admonished them that they were in fact sinners in the hands of an angry logic: "Our reason will tell us in a moment that these are just the requirements we might expect from the true God, were we now for the firt [sic] time (in our lives,) called into his awful presence to learn our duty. Nothing but an incomprehensible stupidity on our part, can keep us from breaking out at once in strains of the most exalted praise; when we reflect that God is ever reasonable. His language to erring man, is; 'come & let us reason together.'"[34]

Brown's sermon discussed the character of man and the shaping of will and thence choice, a rational and intelligent God's desire that His rational and intelligent creatures join Him as well in justice, mercy, love, and humility. Even in the depths of poverty, Brown would always have his books, and he was a well informed and thoroughly read man. Before poverty there was a room dedicated to the library, and the little school, and long discussions in front of the crackling fire in the depths of winter, and though he led the debates, he had little regard for people who did not hold reasoned opinions of their own.[35] He would be the last, perhaps, to say a word on his own intellect. After all, "What can so properly become poor, dependent, sinning, & self condemned mortals, like us; as humility? How can any one on that very account question but that the character of the true God is so far at least set before us?"[36]

The Browns had another son whom they named Frederick, and they struggled along as the Randolph community slowly, almost imperceptibly at first, withered away. The debts mounted in the creeping, insidious manner that only optimism can feed, and by the end of 1831 Brown was hopelessly in debt to Seth Thompson and to a variety of banks. Just as slow, just as chilling, Dianthe began to ail. It began with confusion, a mental deterioration, the pieces falling apart subtly and gracefully like fluttering autumn leaves. Then her heart fluttered just the same, and fevers came and went like brushfires, deepening her brittle malaise.

Despite their trials and poor health, on August 7, 1832, Dianthe delivered another son. This one, unlike the others, was born not flush with life but with twilight chill, and the little baby perished hours after birth. Three days later, Dianthe followed her newborn baby and "went to her rest." It was all so sudden, really. She had been so beautiful and healthy, and had sickened and died barely two-thirds of the way through what might have been considered a normal life for people who did everything right.

John Brown had done right. He had kept his faith, and worked hard, and cared for his community and his family. When Dianthe perished he was so ill and tired that he barely had the strength to bury her.[37] His neighbors clothed Dianthe in her wedding gown, cradled her dead baby in her arms, and the two were lowered into the earth to rest forever in that tender, cold embrace.[38] What did it all mean? Lost in a senseless world, family and faith shattered, Brown eventually recovered enough to write to Seth Thompson about the sad state of the business in Randolph. He explained the travails that had caused him to be so inattentive to their arrangement, and also expressed a mild surprise at the griefless emptiness inside, that he could "think or write about her or about disposing of my little children with as little emotion as of the most common subject."[39]

5

Peoples and Nations

The spirit of the American freeman is already suspected to be timid, imitative, tame. Public and private avarice make the air we breathe thick and fat. See already the tragic consequence. The mind of this country, taught to aim at low objects, eats upon itself. There is no work for any but the decorous and the complaisant. Young men of the fairest promise, who begin life upon our shores, inflated by the mountain winds, shined upon by all the stars of God, find the earth below not in unison with these,—but are hindered from action by the disgust which the principles on which business is managed inspire, and turn drudges, or die of disgust,—some of them suicides.
—Ralph Waldo Emerson, *The American Scholar*

Brown was a broken man, so despondent and "unfit for everything" that he moved in with James Foreman to get some help caring for his children.[1] They were a handful. John, Jr., was eleven, as rebellious and as prone to daydreaming as his father. Jason was an extraordinarily kind and gentle child of nine, who was growing resentful of his strict religious upbringing after being thrashed once for claiming—and believing—that a dream he had was in fact real.[2] Ruth was three, babbling toddler chaos and curiosity, and ambling about behind was Frederick, a sweet two-year-old, too young for anyone to have detected that there was something amiss with him. The unruly brood and their morose father were overwhelming for the recently married Foreman family, and as soon as Brown was even close to able he was gently persuaded to return to his own home.

Life moved on, and the work was no easier, so he hired another housekeeper, this time the daughter of a local blacksmith who had found his way into cruel penury through some poorly chosen business arrangements. Before too long the housekeeper's younger sister was employed to spin yarn at Brown's house. And as Brown watched sixteen-year-old Mary Ann Day turning thread on her wheel, and as he spoke with the steady, reassuring girl, fate led him to love again.

Normally in his presence "everything seemed fixed as fate," but he was painfully shy with her, and she hardly better, so he proposed marriage silently in a letter clutched in his trembling hand. Mary couldn't even bring herself to open something that could so badly unsettle that grim figure.[3] The next morning she found the courage to open it, and not knowing what else to do she left to go draw water from the stream so she could have some time to figure out her suddenly spinning world. John followed, desperate to hear her answer, and the two returned from a long quiet walk together with a bucket of water, newly engaged. They married in 1833. Their first child was a winsome daughter named Sarah, born on May 11, 1834.

Brown first read Garrison's *Liberator* in his father's home sometime between 1833 and 1834, and subsequently took out a subscription of his own.[4] Around this time Owen Brown resigned from his position as a trustee of the Western Reserve College and took a similar post at Oberlin College, a co-educational, co-racial school that was becoming a busy switching station on the Underground Railroad. Owen's resignation was part of a broader fight with the colonizationists on the Western Reserve faculty, a quarrel that split the whole community and resulted in the mild censure of two anti-colonizationist teachers.[5]

These were years when John Brown felt great changes afoot amid the creeping failure of his tannery and the spreading poverty in Randolph. He read about the excruciating tensions in the South following Nat's rebellion, and about recent riots in Philadelphia and New York City, and was convinced that God was preparing to bring down the "house of bondage." He exhorted the citizens of Randolph to be prepared to throw their doors open to the fugitive slaves who would surely soon arrive.[6]

Elijah P. Lovejoy (originally published in *Appletons' Cyclopædia of American Biography*, 1900, v. 4, p. 34. Public domain image. Retrieved from Wikimedia Commons).

During the twilight of his time in Randolph, after poverty had already closed in about them, Brown would hold his children at night and sing his favorite hymn: "Blow ye the trumpet, blow." One evening he explained slavery to little Ruth, and then asked how she felt about having the family adopt some black children, though it would mean she would need to share their already meager possessions. Little Ruth was so moved that she attempted to invite the next black person she met to come live with them.[7] Near that same time, on November 21, 1834, Brown wrote to his brother Frederick about a plan to do something to help his "poor fellow-men who are in bondage."[8]

The first part of his plan was to adopt a black child as his own, and to provide him a good education while also creating an integrated and interracial family. Brown hoped that Christian goodwill would persuade a slaveholder to give him a child, but if not, his family was willing to "submit to considerable privation in order to buy one."[9] Given the economics of slavery, Brown must have been very optimistic about his finances, or he believed so strongly in the rightness of his idea that he was willing to mortgage his family's future on a crippling expense which would never grant a financial return.

Second, he intended to establish a multi-racial school, and Brown had written to his brother in an attempt to recruit him as a teacher. His idea was inspired by recent events, including scandalous troubles in 1833 concerning a school for black girls in

Canterbury, Connecticut. Prudence Crandall had decided to operate the school with Garrison's encouragement, and there had been a predictable white backlash. She and her students were subject to a constant stream of vile invective, and a stream of literal filth on the school's doorstep. The townspeople finally resorted to an old vagrancy law which could have subjected the girls to whippings "on the naked body."[10] The state eventually resolved any legal confusions by simply outlawing all such schools entirely.

Brown believed that the end result of education must of necessity be abolition, and therefore a school must unite the disparate voices of abolition, whether they believed in immediate emancipation or not. The South obviously knew it, which is why they passed the "heaven-daring laws against teaching blacks" which had followed Nat's rebellion.[11] Brown didn't know how the emancipation of the slaves would actually come about, but he knew it must end with the "breaking of their yoke" and that education would "operate on slavery like firing powder confined in rock." The differences between Garrison's "benevolent supervision" and Brown's education plan are slight on the page, but Garrison was more philosophical than specific, and he never intended to adopt a child personally.

These plans would need to wait. Business in the region was contracting. Credit, lavishly expanded and expended during the years of Randolph's growth, was contracting as Jackson and Biddle confronted each other. The loss of half of the bank's deposits compelled it to call in its loans, and Biddle chose to contract monetary policy even further. By 1834 Brown could no longer operate his tannery, and cash was so scarce in that region of Pennsylvania that he couldn't even sell his belongings, nor could any of his debtors remit to him their obligations.

Brown summed up the situation succinctly enough when he wrote, "It is a time of General Jackson darkness here about money."[12] For some time he had been putting off an offer from Zemas Kent of Franklin Mills to return to Ohio and jointly operate a tannery, but now he reconsidered. In April of 1835 Brown finally decided his family's best chances lay in abandoning Randolph for Ohio, but in order to do so he had to write to Kent to plead for a loan to finance the move. A desperately needed $25 arrived just as Brown was on the verge of selling his few remaining possessions as scrap. In May he resigned as postmaster, settled the best he could his "honorary debts," and left with his family for Ohio.[13] The town of Randolph was eventually renamed New Richmond.

Ohio was in turmoil when Brown arrived. Abolitionists from Oberlin College and the Congregationalist Church had been agitating to convert all of Ohio to the cause of immediate emancipation and to rid the valley of colonizationists. The entire Western Reserve had suffered a schism, and by mid–1835 the local churches, schools, and newspapers had largely resolved to align with the abolitionists. As a result, the Presbyterian General Assembly was no longer able to hold its nationally dispersed churches together, and abandoned the Plan of Union between North and South congregations. In a fit of administrative pique the assembly expelled all the abolition churches within the Western Reserve for the crime of harboring too many "ill-mannered fanatics."[14]

Even so, racist crowds in the Western Reserve still held numerous and vigorous protests against the presence of free blacks, and a variety of onerous "black laws" remained in force, relegating Negros to a socially humiliating and subservient status. It wasn't the law that made society exclude black people from certain parts of town and from select schools, and for a white to hire or befriend blacks was to court ostracism and scorn. So soon after arriving, John Brown had hired a free black family, and was sheltering runaway Kentucky slaves.[15] Unlike in Randolph, such an act in Franklin Mills was punishable by laws that were, more often than not, happily enforced. Then in 1836 Congress passed the Pinckney Resolutions, which barred the presentation of, or even the discussion of, abolitionist legislation.

John and his eldest son, John, Jr., then fourteen years old, built a new tannery in the pleasant Ohio summer on Zemas Kent's land. Kent was going to lease the tannery to the Browns, but he changed his mind and instead rented the tannery to his son Marvin. In time the town would bear the Kent family name. Kent paid Brown a disappointing sum and left him without the job he had followed to Ohio.

Fortunately for Brown, promising new projects were sprouting like mushrooms in the region, awash as it was in a steady rain of newfound funding from "wildcat banks," each more than willing than the next to help out an ambitious young man. Ironically, Jackson began his fight with Biddle out of a dislike of "all banks," but diminishing and eventually voiding the power of the Bank of the United States had an unintended consequence: the total number of banks doubled between 1832 and 1837.[16] The doubling had started, in part, when the New York banks and the commissioners of the Erie Canal intervened to make funds available to continue a grand project.[17]

It was a "work more stupendous, more magnificent, and more beneficial than has hitherto been achieved by the human race."[18] It's barely poetic embellishment. The canal exceeded by a factor of fourteen the longest ever made in America. It would eventually link the entire northeast and transform myriad local economies into one integrated whole. It brought the Industrial Revolution to the northeastern U.S. by opening the pathway for coal, both use and transport. Before 1825 there was virtually no coal mined in America; the primary fuel for railroad steam and for households was wood. Iron smelting was accomplished by using charcoal. But the canals changed that, and in three short years coal engines would shatter traditional barriers of time, and hot blast anthracite coal furnaces would make steel around the clock.[19]

The canal's tributaries spread from the central artery throughout the body politic, and carried goods south to maintain the slaves, and cotton in return to northern ports. In time this network, and the railroad to follow, would allow merchants to dictate all manner of commodity pricing. One of those capillaries was under construction in Portage County, and property prices were booming. John Brown worked for a time as a canal laborer, and after saving some money he did the most rational thing he could: he and Seth Thompson, his old Randolph cattle partner, joined up again to purchase property near the canal project. Water rights on that land were about to be highly lucrative. Thompson was eager to get involved, and gave Brown $1,134 while promising $13,000 more as soon as he could borrow it.[20]

Ohio's prosperity was dispelling the shadows. And on October 7, 1835, Mary gave birth to Watson, her first son and the first Brown child born in their new Ohio home. Then a year later on October 2 another son was born, this one named Salmon in honor of Brown's brother, a New Orleans attorney who died in 1833.[21] It was also nearing the time when Brown intended to sell his land plots, and hopefully begin work on a new and enduring homestead for his large family.

But just as Brown was preparing to sell, money was becoming scarce again, and it became harder every week to keep up with the mortgage as sales prospects evaporated. Despair was averted for a time when word came that President Jackson had signed a law to distribute treasury funds among the states beginning in January of 1837. Ohio would receive $2,676,000 of this largesse, which "added substantially to the hope of things," enough hope that Brown was able to persuade his father's partner, Heman Oviatt, to loan him more money for a family farm near Hudson, closer to friends and family. He named his property the Westlands.[22] To guarantee the financing and to prepare for the anticipated Ohio windfall, Brown and twenty-one other businessmen formed the Franklin Land Company and on even more credit purchased more land and the water rights connected with the ongoing canal construction.

But then the canal company abruptly changed its plans and opted to draw its water from the nearby Cuyahoga River instead of from the Franklin Land Company's tributaries, and Brown's water rights were made suddenly and sickeningly worthless. Furthermore, widespread anxiety followed Jackson's Specie Circular, and Seth Thompson urgently pleaded with Brown to sell their lands immediately and get out of the business before it was too late. Despite these developments, Brown was certain that better fortunes were on the way, and wrote Thompson, "If we have been crazy in getting in, do try & let exercise a sound mind about the manner of getting out ... let us presume on a merciful Providence (if presumption it be) a little longer. Let us try and trust all with a wise and gracious God, & all will be well some way or other."[23] This, alas, was not to be.

"The land stinks with suicide," wrote Emerson in his journal in 1837.[24] That philosopher was at a loss, perhaps for the first time ever, for words to adequately convey his thoughts on events. So he merely gave bitter and wry thanks of a sort for having left the ministry for a life of letters, and wrote that he was "glad it is not my duty to preach these few Sundays."[25] No, much of the preaching was reserved for vile men in a burgeoning "spiritual self-help" industry that promised material gain in exchange for faith in an odd fusion of animism and a magical Jesus. It was the beginning of a reformulation of classic models of religious help, whereby faith begat character, which in turn led to an almost karmic prosperity. The emerging themes bypassed tedious intermediary steps of human morality and simply promised the genius to manipulate the world in exchange for faith in genie Jesus. These preachers wrote these notions with an accusing finger pointed at the secular philosophies that had supplanted religion, but their ideas did more to harm the interaction between the worlds of physics and faith than anything else, secularizing the mind with a kind of primitive faith in magic.[26]

It was in fact apostate intellectuals like Emerson who vouchsafed the ecclesiastic heritage of the West, both through wiser writings and through scorn for these new preachers of capitalism. "The world has failed," he wrote. "The pretended teachers who have scoffed at the Idealist, have failed utterly. The very adulation they offer to the name of Christ, the epithets with which they encumber his name, the ragged half screaming bass with which they deepen the sentences of sermons on purity, martyrdom, & spiritual life, do preach their hollowness & recoil upon them. They lash themselves with their satire."[27] In 1841 the magazine *Arcturus* declared that "ours is the age of suicide and mysterious disappearance."[28]

It would later be called the Panic of 1837. Half of the country's 850 banks locked their doors, and almost all were in the South, the locus of the collapse. Prior to the panic, huge quantities of capital had funneled into the South via a bank network that had spread like scrambling and thorny bougainvillea in the hollow trellis Biddle's Bank left behind. Cotton prices, which at the beginning of the land boom in Ohio had been eighteen cents per pound, slumped to ten cents as manufacturers found they could not absorb the glut created by the quarter of a million black slaves who broke their hands all while being mortgaged and securitized and resold in financial markets far from those ghost fields. And so the crash began in Britain first, about the time that Jackson issued his Specie Circular, and by March of 1837 the top ten cotton-buying firms were no more.[29] Suddenly, all of the creditors realized that they were also debtors, and their exceptionally rational scramble for solvency, iterated millions of times, created the tragically irrational outcome of systemic "failure."

"Failure" as an idea is part of a defining dialectic, opposite of which teeters the poorly articulated idea of the "American Dream," a concept that gained its meaning in the effort to understand what Emerson was struggling with. "Failure" began as a term used to describe the sudden—unexpected—insolvency of a business. By 1860 the word had become fully personalized, an adjective of individual achievement or lack thereof, a term of narrative confession which went hand in hand with the imagining of capitalism as a rational and scientific idea.[30]

If Emerson—no academic slouch—was having trouble understanding what was going on, and John Brown was powerless to predict or comprehend it, all involved should perhaps be excused given that "capitalism" as a conceptual term had not yet been invented.[31] The intellectual acceptance or rejection of theoretical business "cycles" and their pejorative effects on the working class were immaterial as well, since in 1837 there was no working theory of an "impersonal" business cycle, which meant that even had he been inclined to study business, Brown would not have had a body of theory which would have guided him any better than his faith suffused language.[32]

Brown's faith in Providence rather than in economic rationalism is in some ways the most rational part of the story. At the time, the speculative economic world and the men of finance all utilized a language of divinity to understand their market transactions, and uniformly believed that the economy fully remained within the sphere of divine control. An effort was underway to "naturalize" the language of capitalism, to transform it into something conceptually as beyond liking or disliking as the weather, and by the latter part of the century this feat of linguistic legerdemain was nearly complete, but it was not so when Emerson contemplated the horror in his journal.[33] He didn't even describe it as the "Panic" of 1837 because that label came about after 1857 to describe the irrational behavior of failures; what was a rationally self-interested scramble for liquidity was re-framed as judgment for a lack of faith.

So the victims of the "panic" struggled with the terrible questions of whether they themselves were personally responsible for the calamity, or perhaps rather God, or even nature. It was a commonly held belief as well, one shared by Brown, that a viable tool in God's arsenal of punishments was pecuniary distress.[34] John Brown's approach to business and the fate he shared with so many millions was bewilderingly normal. The bonds between hope and recklessness are as strong as the certainty of the fictions that forge them, and there is little to suggest that Brown was more reckless than others.[35] Americans flatter themselves that their financial success is any more than chance, but the differences between modern theories and nineteenth century ideas of divine Providence are hard to discern in "rational" writings about benevolent markets guided by invisible hands.[36]

Surveying the misery and suffering around him, Emerson the comfortable, conservative New England intellectual began to change. The early expression of this change was in his journals, where he wrote of the "lessons of the crisis" and laid bare the inhumanity and banality of American society, and the confusion over why such misery and destitution should be. The answer eludes when the question does not challenge the climate of opinion, what Emerson called the "atmosphere of ideas." "What answer is it now to say, 'It has always been so?' I acknowledge that, as far back as I can see the widening procession of humanity, the marchers are lame and blind and deaf, but to the soul that whole past is but one finite series in its infinite scope. Deteriorating ever and now desperate. Let me begin anew. Let me teach the finite to know its master. Let me ascend above my fate and work down upon my world."[37]

The financial crisis eventually resolved, but Brown never recovered the "reputation he had achieved of possessing at least good common-sense in respect to business matters" after the washing away of his castles.[38] And since he never recovered the reputation, he never recovered his fortunes, as fortunes were predicated in that time, as they are today, on the capacity for confidence men to sell optimistic fictions to society.[39]

From 1837 until 1844 he tried many ways to make a living, trudging under the weight of lawsuits which hung like chains about his neck. As the crisis deepened, the Western Reserve Bank moved to repossess the Westlands, and to hold them off Brown referred them to the promissory note held by Heman Oviatt. He continued to hope, against all odds, that his Franklin Mills lots would become valuable enough to pay for the Westlands. He hoped because many of the schemes to resuscitate the economy were centered on the canals, but by 1839 those measures would economically finish off the remaining optimistic survivors.

Ill fared the land in 1837, fortunes crumbled, a creeping malaise infiltrated economic life, and the conflict between abolitionists and slave-owners had grown increasingly tense since 1831, while religious revival movements swept the country. "How can such a question as the Slave Trade be agitated for forty years by the most enlightened nations of the world without throwing great light on ethics into the general mind?" wrote Emerson. "The fury with which the slaveholder & the slavetrader defend every inch of their plunder, of their bloody deck, & howling Auction, only serves as a Trump of Doom to alarum the ear of Mankind, to wake the sleepers, & drag all neutrals to take sides & listen to the argument & to the Verdict which Justice shall finally pronounce."[40]

The revival was in town in Franklin Mills, and as John, Jr., recalled in his wry and laconic manner, "Lukewarm Christians were heated up to a melting point, and there was a bright prospect of a good shower of grace." Free and fugitive black folk alike were attending some of the revival meetings, but they were always seated alone, usually by the door of the barn, in a place where it was difficult to see or hear the singers and ministers. John Brown couldn't tolerate it, and resolved one day to rectify this situation, and at the next meeting he rose and took a black family by the hand to his pew, and informed the congregation that they were making an unjust discrimination and should know that God was not a "respecter of persons."[41] Brown sat with his family in the seats by the door.

John, Jr., noted sardonically that the ministers, whose hearts were home not to God but to "another tenant," paid a visit to admonish his father for his scandalous act. But they left, if not humbled, then at least with "new views of Christian duty" after their conversation with Brown, and to underscore the point Brown made certain that for the remainder of the revival his family occupied the forlorn seats previously reserved for the black people of Franklin Mills. A year later in Hudson the Browns received a letter from the Franklin Mills church informing them that they were no longer members, due to an obscure church bylaw which suspended the membership of any parishioner out of communication for a year. Deep down, Brown knew why he received the letter, and as a deeply religious man, the hypocrisy of the church would forever be troubling. As for his sons, their distaste for the racism in the pews caused them to turn from the church and embrace an almost Emersonian agnosticism.[42]

In November of 1837 the abolitionist community was shaken when a man named Elijah Lovejoy was killed by a pro-slavery mob. In 1828 Lovejoy had moved to bustling St. Louis—the "gateway" to Jefferson's frontier, a thriving slave state river port surrounded on all sides by free territories—to become the editor of the anti–Jacksonian *St. Louis Observer* and the headmaster of a co-educational school. By 1832, inspired by the paired social movements of abolitionism and Christian revivalism and by the Christian perfectionist writings of reformers like Garrison, he decided to become a preacher. After attaining his ordination as a Presbyterian minister, he returned to St. Louis to establish a church and resume his editorial job.[43]

On three occasions pro-slavery crowds had destroyed Lovejoy's printing presses after he criticized either the institution or the sheer mendacity of judges and officials who supported slavery. He eventually abandoned St. Louis for nearby Alton, Illinois, a free state town settled mostly by southerners in the fugitive slave-catching trade.

On November 2, 1837, he found himself on the defensive again, publicly addressing the community's desire to bring him up on undefined charges related to his anti-slavery writings in the *Alton Observer*. As he pointed out, no crime had been committed save for the fact that the people didn't like his words. "If I have committed any crime, you can easily convict me. You have public sentiment in your favor. You have [your] juries, and you have your attorney [looking at the attorney-general], and I have no doubt you can convict me. But if I have been guilty of no violation of law, why am I hunted up and down continually like a partridge upon the mountains? Why am I threatened with the tar-barrel? Why am I waylaid every day, and from night to night, and my life in jeopardy every hour?"[44]

Accusing eyes leveled on the citizens of Alton, he charged them with protecting his right to free speech. He acknowledged that though they were easily capable of committing any form of violence on him, if he was not safe in Alton he would be safe nowhere. If civil society had any meaning, the municipal authorities and the community must vouchsafe his rights, and if they would not then he would look to God and make Alton his grave.

Five nights later, the mob he trusted with his safety converged on the warehouse where he had hidden his presses. They fired shots, and Lovejoy returned fire, killing a man. The crowd then sent a boy up a ladder to put torch to the building, but Lovejoy snuck outside and toppled it. Moments later when the comic scene repeated itself, Lovejoy's attempt to tip the ladder was cut short by five shotgun blasts. His press was broken up and thrown into the river. The event shook the entire North, and Emerson, who was growing, however painfully. "You think that because you have spoken nothing when others spoke and have given no opinion upon the times, upon Wilhelm Meister, upon Abolition, upon Harvard College, that your verdict is still expected with curiosity as a reserved wisdom. Far otherwise; it is known that you have no opinion: You are measured by your silence and found wanting."[45]

Throughout the North abolitionists mourned Lovejoy's murder, and reflected on his bravery. Though aggrieved, Garrison took it as confirmation of his philosophy of nonresistance and moral suasion. A martyr Lovejoy might have been, but Garrison thought him a flawed one since he had fought and killed. The entire episode convinced Garrison and his followers that violence was the product of the institution of slavery, and to oppose it by violence was to indulge in the same evil.[46]

Emerson differed, and wrote that Lovejoy had "died when it was better not to live. There are always men enough ready to die for the silliest punctilio, to die like dogs, who fall down under each other's teeth, but I sternly rejoice that one was bound to die for humanity and the rights of free speech and opinion."[47] Ministers in the Western Reserve held commemorative meetings, and exhorted crowds to attend by proclaiming that "the crisis has now come" and that the question was no longer whether slaves could be made free, but rather if all were slaves together under "Southern mob law." Brown sat and listened to one of these meetings and then rose, and in his quiet and emphatic way raised his right hand and consecrated himself before those present to the destruction of slavery.[48] "Rightminded men" had "been called to decide for Abolition."[49]

Into this uncertain world John and Mary welcomed another son, Charles, on November 3, 1837. John, Jr., was a teenager, preparing himself for school and working alongside his father. Jason and Owen were strong boys of 14 and 13, respectively; Owen had shocking red hair and a withered and mostly useless crippled right arm from a childhood accident. Ruth was a studious young lady of 8, but 7-year-old Frederick was showing some disturbing signs. He was slower to develop, mentally, than his siblings had been; one might even say feeble. And he was occasionally afflicted with headaches that would leave him helplessly writhing in agony.

Brown attempted to keep his ventures solvent by herding cattle again. Seth Thompson, Heman Oviatt, and his father gave him their herds to drive east for sale at one of the Erie Canal's bustling ports. Once Brown arrived in West Hartford, Connecticut, he signed a partnership with the firm Wadsworth and Wells to sell them 200 head of cattle every year. Contract secured and first delivery accomplished, Brown left for New York City, which had emerged as the North's financial center after the collapse of Biddle's bank. He was seeking a loan for his property, but failed to secure one, and wrote to his family on December 5, 1838: "I have not yet succeded in my business, but think the prospect such that I do not by any means despair of final success. As to that, may Gods holy will be done."[50] He moved on to Boston, arriving the day after Christmas, where he petitioned three wealthy businessmen for funds. Whatever arrangements were made during that conference gave him the confidence to return home immediately and purchase a flock of sheep on the way.

Spring of 1839 brought another son, Oliver, born on March 9, as well as an endless procession of lawsuits, so another trip east was quickly planned along with a second cattle drive. The herd was sold to Wadsworth and Wells, after which he made for Boston to check on his loan arrangement. Confidence turned to despair, and Brown wrote a distressed letter to his wife on June 12 stating: "I am now somewhat in fear that I shall fail of getting the money I expected on the loan. Should that be the will of Providence, I know of no other way but we must consider ourselves very poor; for our debts must be paid, if paid at a sacrifice."[51]

Sometime during Brown's downward spiral in 1839, a black preacher named Fayette visited his family, and Brown arose and pledged himself and his family to make active war on slavery, and implored God's guidance in this enterprise.[52] The tale is perhaps apocryphal; it is not in the public records, but only facts ever are. The story powerfully symbolized Brown's genuine concern for black people, and his earnest desire to help in some minor way to bring the evil of slavery to an end. It might also, as a matter of history, be more about 1859 than 1839.

Somehow, Americans are to believe that Thomas Jefferson wanted, deep down inside, to free his slaves; he just couldn't because of a lack of free will. He is also forgiven for the many descendants of Sally Hemings, which says everything about the psychology of the historian and nothing about the subject, and changes not a bit the fact that Brown, like Jefferson, acted always according to his will. And it might be rude to recall that Jefferson died five years prior to an event that put to torch the orthodox "faith" of Virginians about the benevolence of slavery and their happy black bondsmen.

Oaths notwithstanding, Brown had no time for war; he was desperate to save his home. The Western Reserve Bank had every intention of seizing his land at the soonest opportunity, and with it his dreams for a family home. Such is the fall of man; with the death of all his aspirations, and nightmares about his hungry children shadowing over his mind, Brown found himself with access to $5,500 in business funds from Wadsworth and Wells. So he stole the money, and sent it to Ohio to secure the Westlands deed from the Western Reserve Bank. Wadsworth and Wells threatened to have him arrested, and to placate them he promised them the Boston money that he despaired of ever receiving.

While attempting to devise a way out of the mess, Brown met a man named George Kellogg of the New England Wool Company. Kellogg spoke with Brown for a time, and became convinced that this incredibly knowledgeable and plain-spoken shepherd was the business partner he had been looking for. Kellogg was so impressed that on June 15 he gave Brown $2,800 towards future wool purchases. Brown, in turn, used that money straightaway to pay Wadsworth and Wells.[53]

Kellogg wanted answers about this dishonesty, about the character of the man who would do such a thing. In his response to Kellogg's demand for an explanation, Brown saved Kellogg and future inquisitors the trouble of condemning him since he had already done so himself. "I have found it hard to take up my pen to record, & to publish, my own shame, & abuse of the confidence of those whom I esteem, & who have treated me as a friend, & as a brother." He explained with utter candor the threat of jail, and what exactly transpired with the money, and the debt that kept him always in its cold shadow.

He promised, however, to make good on Kellogg's trust soon, signing the letter "Unworthily yours."[54] Kellogg, for his part, understood the difficulties of life after 1837 quite well, and was satisfied enough with the answer to not sue.

The shape of Brown's unraveling life was a rickety cabin on his Westlands property. As his desperation grew, Brown took out another mortgage on the land without informing Heman Oviatt, the co-title holder. The autumn found Brown, John, Jr., and Owen in the cabin waiting with shotguns for a creditor named Amos Chamberlain. When Chamberlain attempted to take possession of the property, the Browns menaced him with guns and refused to leave the dilapidated dwelling. Chamberlain finally summoned the sheriff, who took Brown and his sons to the Akron jail for the night. Brown promised Amos Chamberlain a "tedious distressing, wasteing, and long protracted war" to recover his land, but nothing ever came of this dire threat.[55]

With nowhere else to go, Brown turned to his father for advice. By this time Owen Brown was a longtime trustee of Oberlin College, an institution that functioned as both lyceum and as a depot on Ohio's robust Underground Railroad network. The school took pride in the fact that it never lost a single fugitive to slave hunters. Very recently, industrialist-errant and abolitionist reformer Gerrit Smith of New York had given the college a thousand acres of land, not necessarily for academic purposes, and Owen pointed out that the college needed to have this bequest properly surveyed. John Brown therefore made a proposal to Oberlin, whereby he would survey the land for a salary, settle on it with his family to generate productive income for the institution, and also be available as "competent agents should they be kneeded."[56]

Surveying was elaborate work, involving a working knowledge of coordinate geometry and trigonometry, and skill with technical instruments such as a surveyor's compass, rulers and plotters, chains and poles for measuring, and a Jacob's staff. Surveyors acquired their training in a variety of ways, from self-education, to apprenticeships, to night schools. The demand for surveyors in the Northwest Ordinance and later in the Louisiana Purchase prompted many East Coast navigation schools to offer courses in land surveying.[57] Brown was largely self-educated in this field, owned his own tools, and his work never received a complaint of error. Despite the opportunities, he took on very few projects and never made a career of it. But surveyors often travelled for long periods, sometimes by necessity in austere conditions, and Brown had fixed in his mind a dream of living a pastoral life with his family. What we intend, and what we achieve, are often very different.

In July of 1840 he completed the Oberlin survey, and gave his final report to the board, after which they conveyed the deed to "Bro. John Brown, of Hudson." Yet, Brown hesitated to claim it. Heman Oviatt had forgiven him enough for the Westlands debacle to propose a joint sheep-herding and tanning business in Richfield, not unlike that which Brown and John, Jr., had worked to build in Kent. Brown delayed his decision on the Oberlin lands while he considered the tempting proposal, but after the birth of Peter on December 7, 1840, Brown returned to the Oberlin board in January of 1841 to accept the thousand acres for his family and their future. Unfortunately by that time, as money continued to contract in the ongoing and cascading economic collapse, Oberlin had changed its collective decision as well.[58]

The $29 that Oberlin gave Brown in place of the homestead land did nothing for his debts. Creditors hunted him, and everywhere he turned he dragged a paper trail that marked him for moral blame and legal reprisal. The poor know best how a single setback can become a tangled web of misfortune, preventing them from earning money while punishing them for the same. Brown was in court for 21 different suits over the course of his ill-starred financial life, most concerning the period of 1836–1837.[59]

Finally, in 1842, the former community pillar was leveraged into bankruptcy and shorn of his worldly possessions. He was allowed to keep six "old and poor" feather beds, which by an exercise in arithmetic indicates that his twelve children—Austin was born on September 14 that year—may have occupied but five of those. He also retained a variety of foodstuffs, kitchen utensils, a couple of spinning wheels, two mares, two hogs, and nineteen chickens, as well as nineteen sheep "pledged to Heman Oviatt." Additionally, he kept his surveying and tanning tools, 36 academic books, and 11 bibles.[60]

Brown described bankruptcy as a state of freedom in which he would finally be able to demonstrate his sincerity towards Kellogg. As a bankrupt man he was actually free of any legal compulsion to make any payments again to Kellogg, but legalistic evasion was not Brown's way, nor his conception of freedom. Because he had "imprudently pledged" the money for his own benefit, he felt determined by "moral obligation" alone to repay this misdeed "from time to time, as Divine Providence shall enable."[61]

Freedom. Americans then had as little idea what that word actually meant as they do now. The reality of slavery shaped and gave clarity to the definition. "Debt slavery" was a term invented by proponents of the liberalization of bankruptcy laws, which they felt barred a person from future success. Emerson took up a variation of this idea in his contemplations on the meaning of failure in *Self Reliance*. As the market revolution spread, Americans felt that any form of control over their material fates was slowly slipping from their grasp as plutocrats gathered society's financial instruments to themselves under the guise and rhetoric of freedom. These people offered the term "wage slavery" to describe their lack of, to phrase it one way, free will.

What might be called the radical Jacksonian labor movement adopted this idea as well. Social philosopher Orestes A. Brownson published *The Laboring Classes* in 1840— essentially an extensive review of Thomas Carlyle's *Chartism*—which he recalled as being greeted with "one universal scream of horror" from the influential segments of society. Brownson described wages as "a cunning device of the devil for the benefit of tender consciences who would retain all the advantages of the slave system without the expense, trouble, and odium of being slaveholders."[62]

"All is well—all is well," Brown wrote to John, Jr., though he lamented both that his "worldly business has borne heavily," and that he had corresponded so poorly with his son and prayed so irregularly. John, Jr., was practically a grown man now, attending school at the Grand River Institute in Austinburg, Ohio. Though Brown's own life was in disarray, he was very eager to hear of his son's studies, his plans for the future, and any of his difficulties. Above all, Brown regretted that he could not support his son financially, but he hoped, despite all their troubles, to see John, Jr., in the fall, and above all that his son would behave himself "wisely."[63]

It was a special kind of freedom, in the drafty, cramped hovel that the Brown family lived in for that Ohio winter. Little Charles, almost six, may have shown first. It started with a fever, but then came the agony and crippling gut pain as he defecated blood and was unable to eat. His screams were joined by Peter and Sarah—Mary's firstborn—and then by baby Austin, her newest child. John Brown stayed up all hours, holding tightly to his poor children in an ecstasy of grief and tears, as one at a time they slipped through his fingers. Charles perished on September 11, Peter on the 22nd and lovely Sarah the very next day, and finally little Austin on the 27th. When everything has been taken from a man, he is no longer in anyone's power; he's truly free. Brown likely knew that their impoverished living conditions had as much to do with their deaths as anything else. What to do in a world where everything he touched, he broke? God only knew, but John Brown "never fully recovered," and the only thing he felt inside was a "steady, strong, desire; to die."[64]

6

The Stillest Hour

Machinery has been applied to all work, and carried to such perfection, that little is left for the men but to mind the engines and feed the furnaces. But the machines require punctual service, and, as they never tire, they prove too much for their tenders. Mines, forges, mills, breweries, railroads, steampump, steamplough, drill of regiments, drill of police, rule of court, and shop-rule, have operated to give a mechanical regularity to all the habit and action of men. A terrible machine has possessed itself of the ground, the air, the men and women, and hardly even thought is free.
—Ralph Waldo Emerson, *Manners*

But he could not die. On December 23, 1843, the darkest Christmas season of John Brown's life was brightened when Annie's tiny newborn wails pierced the gloom, fiercely alive, stridently demanding love and care. Perhaps he could cling to hope for Mary and his tiny new daughter.

It had been a decade since the loss of Dianthe. John, Jr., was a twenty-two year old man who had largely turned from his father's faith out of a reaction to his upbringing, and Jason and Owen seemed to be doing the same. Time and tragedy had worked their own transformations on John Brown, and though still earnestly faithful, he was not the same father anymore. Or maybe he was, and John, Jr.'s, memory of the towering Abrahamic patriarch was more about him than his father.

Brown's children all remembered the dour, stern puritan. Ruth, born eight years after John, Jr., recalled being struck "quite often" for telling lies, but also a father who believed in instilling moral lessons, not wanton abuse. And he was a skilled nurse, a tireless caregiver who stayed awake beyond the point of collapse bringing the entire family through an outbreak of scarlet fever. And most of all, he loved to hold his children and sing his favorite hymn to them.

Ruth's earliest memory was of her father carrying her easily through the whispering and light-dappled woods to a neighbor's house. At the end of the gathering, a minister baptized the children with a dab of water, but for Ruth the memory with weight of significance was her father, holding her and using his brown silk handkerchief with a lovely scatter of yellow diamond shapes on it to tenderly dry her head. It enchanted little Ruth that he had used such a pretty and valuable thing to clean her. That was the father she loved most, the one who would talk to her seriously and give loving advice and encouragement when they were alone.[1]

But those boys. The daughter of an Ohio employer remembered that Brown could be a "terrible tyrant," but it was the only way "to rule all those swarming children, all

The earliest known image of John Brown, from around 1846, taken by Augustus Washington. The flag is purported to be a banner for the Subterranean Pass Way (public domain image. Retrieved from Wikimedia Commons).

of whom were rebellious, [and] demanded a firm hand." Salmon, now 7, was taking a leading role in marshaling his siblings in mischief, jokes, and the theft of fruit. Mary was so exasperated with him that she dragged him to the woodshed, birch switch in hand, but the impish boy eluded her until he succeeded in wresting the switch from her, resulting in a comical brawl. Brown relied on corporal punishment, but never seemed fond of the necessity of striking his children, and eventually just grew weary of it. Salmon was once fleeing him after stealing fruit, but could not outdistance his father's long stride. Brown beat him severely, but then just sadly looked at him and said, "you are a very bad boy." He never struck Salmon again.[2]

As the years went by, Brown grew particularly close to Annie, who had recalled him to life in his darkest hour. She was his confidante for all of his most secret plans, the ones that had they fallen on the wrong ears could have doomed him. Annie remembered a very strict father, but also a tender man who, after a busy day and even in the middle of the most serious conversations would allow his precocious daughter to climb up onto his lap, and empty all of his pockets of their contents so that she could examine what she found. And even in the middle of the night he would hike out to the well to draw water for her if she was thirsty, insisting that "water that stood in the house was not good to drink." He would know.[3]

When Brown wrote to John, Jr., in January of 1844, he did not mention his four dead children anymore, but wished only to inform his son that they were all in good health, and that a new sister had been born. The sheep were healthy and well, and the tannery was modestly successful. Prospects looked ever brighter thanks to the generous intervention of Simon Perkins of Akron, Ohio. Perkins had taken pity on Brown's misfortunes and also had recognized his keen eye for wool. Though "perfectly advised" of Brown's poverty, he bestowed an opportunity on "the poor bankrupt and his family, three of whom were but recently in Akron jail, in a manner quite unexpected."[4]

It would be Brown's final business venture. Perkins offered to merge Brown's small flock with Perkins's much larger one, and Brown would supervise the combined operations. Brown believed the partnership would prove to be "the most comfortable and the most favourable arrangement of my worldly concerns that I ever had."[5] He worked happily; restlessness abated for a time while he kept his family fed without lawsuits to contend with. On this pastoral Akron homestead he and Mary welcomed another daughter—Amelia—on January 22, 1845. Sarah was born on September 11, three years after her namesake perished of dysentery during the winter of 1843, but as business prospered, Brown had little opportunity to spend time with his new daughter.

After a year, Perkins firmly believed in Brown's forthright honesty, and so turned a benevolently blind eye to the fact that Brown was "not a good shepherd," a bit too fond of sheep-dogs, "because it was then the fashion … but they did more harm than good."[6] Perkins made Brown his trusted agent, and sent him travelling to purchase sheep or to sell wool. Perkins often wrote to Brown during his travels merely to converse, and to keep him apprised of the welfare of his family. In October of 1846, Brown received a letter with sickening news. There had been an accident at home in the kitchen: baby Amelia had been painfully scalded to death, and Brown was not there to save her. "I seem to be struck almost dumb," he wrote. "One more dear little feeble child I am to meet no more till the dead small & great shall stand before God." The tragedy had been Ruth's fault somehow, but Brown implored Mary to not "cast an unreasonable blame on my dear Ruth on account of the dreadful trial we are called to suffer."[7]

He agonized from a distance, and begged Mary to understand that he could not come home right away. Torn between despair and optimism about their prospects and unable to comfort his wife, he urged her to "try to maintain a cheerful self-command" while passing through the storm, and to let their motto be "action; as we have but one life to live."[8]

While travelling Brown grew frustrated with what he perceived as a system of merchant collusion to control prices, and thereby the perpetual indebtedness of the wool producers. As an alternative, in 1846 Perkins and Brown devised a business plan for a new wool depot cooperative. Brown hoped that by consolidating the wool-growers and grading the wool himself to sell on commission, they would be able to command fair prices that merchants wouldn't give.⁹ When Brown called a gathering of wool-men to discuss the arrangement, they came from eight different states to hear the proposal. Unfortunately the conference was hosted by a merchant—not a grower—and the merchants did not have to work overly hard to sidetrack the meeting. Brown was his usual argumentative self, and instead of pushing the agenda, he engaged in heated and friendly debates concerning the merits of different lines of wool.¹⁰

He tried again in February of 1847 in Steubenville, Ohio, and this time there would be no self-defeating "Saxony or Merino disputes to settle." Brown lectured at the event on the proper care, brushing, and deburring of wool, and also wrote a useful pamphlet on how to treat infestations of "Bots," or "Grubs" in their flocks. What concerned him most, however, was the poor reputation of American growers, caused by "slovenly, dishonest habits." As a result, European and other foreign markets were effectively closed to them, leaving American producers "entirely at the mercy of our large manufacturing companies—bodies without souls."¹¹

The convention voted overwhelmingly to form a wool cooperative, and by late 1847, Perkins and Brown were so well regarded that their business was designated the official eastern depot for the region's wool, earning a valuable endorsement from the publication *Prairie Farmer*. But the business struggled, and unsold wool piled up in the warehouse. The anxiety among growers was such that a wool trader named Aaron Erickson visited Brown to see if he was merely an "unscrupulous sharper" running a scam.

He decided that Brown was an honest, forthright man who unfortunately also had an "almost childlike ignorance" of the business of wool.¹² Erickson advised him that his price structure of very cheap low-grade wool and expensive high grade would eventually prove ruinous. Brown demurred; he believed that selling the lower quality product at those prices would serve to lower prices across the entire market for goods which required poorer grades of wool, thereby helping the poor. Conversely, he believed the quality of his fine wools would be recognized and purchased dear by the people who could afford such things. Erickson could not convince Brown that this was not the way the world worked.¹³

However it worked, travel was wearing on Brown, and laboring around the clock at home and as a regional nomad had done little to provide meaningful value to his life. And he missed his family. On one lonely spring day he wrote to his wife that he wanted nothing more than

> to spend a portion of it conversing with the partner of my own choice, & the sharer of my poverty, trials, discredit, & sore afflictions; as well as what of comfort, & seeming prosperity has fallen to my lot; for quite a number of years. I would you should realise that notwithstanding I am absent in boddy I am verry much of the time present in spirit. I do not forget the firm attachment of her who has remained my fast, & faithful affectionate friend.... I really feel ... that you are *really* my better half.
>
> There is a peculiar music in the world which a half years absence in a distant country would enable you to understand.... I feel considerable regret by turns that I have lived so many years, & have done so verry little to increase the amount of human happiness.
>
> In imagination I often see you in your room with Little Chick [Sarah] & that strange

Anna. You must say to her that Father means to come home before long, & kiss some-boddy. I will close for this time by saying what is my growing resolution to endeavor to promote my own happiness by doing what I can to render those around me more so.[14]

To that end, with some time at home at his "own command except the care of the flock," he aided fugitive slaves on the Akron and Hudson lines of the Underground Railroad, which was more dense and more dangerous than ever.[15] It is unclear whether he was an actual "conductor"; Brown's life of abolition work was distinguished by not being a part of abolitionism. But to aid fugitives, one needed to be prepared to fight, and perhaps die, in the attempt to bring them to freedom away from the United States. Brown had long held as true that everyone merely gets a lifetime, and that even "the longest life was short, that it could be shortened but by a few years" and that "death for a good cause was glorious."[16]

In November of 1847, the eloquent escaped slave and darling of the New England abolitionists—Frederick Douglass—sought to meet with the increasingly well known man, whom, when people spoke of him, dropped their voices "to a whisper." After a spare meal in Brown's humble Akron home the two discussed slavery and its possible end. Brown's blue eyes flashed as he grimly denounced slavery as a form of war upon a people who had every right to resist the violence. Brown had a plan, and he spread a map across his kitchen table. "These mountains" he said, pointing a trembling finger, "are the basis of my plan.... God has given the strength of the hills to freedom; they were placed here for emancipation of the Negro race; they are full of natural forts, where one man for defense will be the equal to a hundred for attack."

His plan, which he called the "Subterranean Pass Way," was two-fold and sophisticated: First, destroy the value of slave property by rendering that property insecure. Second, set up a de-facto sovereign state of freed slaves and abolitionists. He would start with twenty-five or so armed guerrillas and set up a mountain stronghold, not far from the slave fields, and make periodic armed forays to free more.[17]

Though Brown was "not averse to the shedding of blood," his plan was not for insurrection.[18] That would have defeated the purpose. Brown's plan at the time was more like an expansion of the Underground Railroad, and slave property was still far too secure despite the railroad's activities. Estimates of the numbers of slaves who ultimately escaped varies wildly, but no estimate is high enough to have significantly impacted the security of a pool of property numbering almost three and one-half million bodies.[19] At the highest estimate, slave-wealth suffered a 3 percent loss over a 40-year span. Only the desperately brave dared to run. Brown's plan would have provided armed surety for the journey, the pride of fighting for their fate, and a destination that was not half a continent away. With such guarantees, maybe the floodgates would have opened.

He thought about starting up a school with his old friend George Delamater, and in a hazily outlined plan that never came about, attempted to unite his new wool business with abolitionism.[20] Free and fugitive black people in Springfield became some of his closest—even only—friends, and he learned from them about the conditions of slavery in the South and about Northern racist stereotypes, like the belief that black people were feeble minded "sambos." That word had only brief English popularity; never clearly among the most vile epithets, but always with negative racial connotations, it appeared in *Vanity Fair* as well as in Harriet Beecher Stowe's influential and controversial *Uncle*

Tom's Cabin. As for Brown, in 1848 he re-appropriated the word in an article titled "Sambo's Mistakes." It was written for the *Ram's Horn*, a free black publication out of New York.[21]

It might be awkward, or even racist, for a white man to write an allegorical confessional with the voice of a fictional black man bearing a derogatory name. However, John Brown is one of the few, if not the only, man in nineteenth-century America who appeared to be almost devoid of racism. Furthermore, Sambo's follies were many of Brown's own. "Sambo" had an unlikely feud with Masons like Brown did in his days at Randolph. And he apparently let petty dogmatic differences with another slave over faith create disunity between them while jeopardizing the fight for emancipation.

Brown was beginning to admit his own inflexibility had alienated possible allies. For years he hadn't spoken with his brother-in-law, Milton Lusk, after a dispute over the keeping of the Sabbath. Later when Milton was feuding with a church over its racism, Brown reconciled with him in a way, acknowledging that Milton had perhaps been "nearer right" in opposing the church than he had previously thought.[22]

And "Sambo's" greatest mistakes were his efforts to mimic the most ridiculous and grotesque white behaviors. Depending on one's interpretative inclinations, Brown's essay was all at once a self-excoriating confessional, an indictment of white—and particularly Southern—American culture, and an exposition of common humanity.

Thankfully for "Sambo," his story ends in redemption. He was enlightened by people like Garrison and Abby Kelley, and realized that the stakes were as high as they "proved to be of late in France in the abolition of Slavery in their colonies." "Sambo" was a man of "*peculiar* quick sightedness" in recognizing his true mistake. Brown was coy about that, but hinted at what it might be by invoking the ghost of Toussaint, and contrasting the example with northerners who "think themselves highly honored" for their prostrate obeisance to the South, and the opportunity to lick up Southern spit.[23]

"Sambo's Mistakes" was cautiously daring, if awkward, social commentary. His sentiments, guised in metaphorical skin, were the only time a white man during the age urged slaves to violently overthrow their tormentors. As Frederick Douglass said, Brown was the only white man he ever met—and he met nearly all those who defined abolitionism—whose sympathies were as if "his own soul had been pierced with the iron of slavery."[24] By 1848, Douglass found that his own speech was becoming "more and more tinged by the color of this man's strong impressions." His audiences were treated to a far more scandalous Douglass, one who openly welcomed the prospect of slave insurrection, and who professed a belief that only blood would end slavery.

It was a disservice to himself and to "Sambo" for Brown to credit so much of his education to Garrison. Garrison came by his abolitionism at the age of twenty-three, during his association with the Quaker-publisher-reformer Benjamin Lundy. Emerson discovered a buried intellectual sympathy for black people after the odious Fugitive Slave Act, a sympathy made possible by the deep philosophical questioning provoked by the 1837 "Panic" and the death of his son. Douglass had profoundly moved Emerson as well, and he wrote in 1844,

> So now it seems to me that the arrival of such men as Toussaint ... or of Douglass ... outweighs all the English & American humanity. The Anti-slavery of the whole world is but dust in the balance, a poor squeamishness and nervousness; the might & right is

6. The Stillest Hour

here. Here is the Anti-Slave. Here is Man; & if you have man, black or white is an insignificance. Why at night all men are black. The intellect, that is miraculous, who has it has the talisman, his skin & bones are transparent, he is a statue of the living God, him I must love & serve & perpetually seek & desire & dream on.[25]

But John Brown's abolitionism was childhood miracles and horrors, by the events he narrated in a lone autobiographical letter written late in life concerning his awakening to the world in 1812. His children recalled that he had often told that story to them, in one way or another, as they grew. Truth might be entirely questionable when it comes to miracles, but all the elements of a working philosophy were in that story. Looking backwards from his encounter with destiny to that tale may not reveal pure abolitionist constancy, but unchanging philosophical consistency is for theories, not necessarily a living thing or a working apprehension of reality. Brown's own fight against slavery grew in complex, unplanned, and perhaps mysterious ways.[26]

The fight was yet to come. Brown was searching for a new home, and in April of 1848 his search brought him to the door of Gerrit Smith's Peterboro, New York, mansion in order to make a proposal. Brown offered to move his family to Smith's prototype North Elba community and teach his new neighbors how to hew a living from field and forest and build a working community. It would be a secure family home with a higher purpose.[27]

Smith, for his part, liked Brown and was struck by his genuine concern for the plight of black people, and therefore sold him 244 acres for only $1 per acre. An impulsive, even erratic reformer, Smith was also a savvy, practical abolitionist. Reformers like Garrison might talk about "benevolent supervision" and education, but no white family in 1848 America was going to live in an all-black community. Brown was Smith's chance to move beyond ideas. But first Brown needed to liquidate the wool business of Perkins and Brown, and do so in a way that would pay their debts.

May 20 of 1848 brought another daughter, Ellen, along with dreams of settling with refugees and beginning anew in North Elba. Settling the wool business was proving to be problematic though. Erickson had been unfortunately right in his assessment of the wool depot's prospects. The partnership stumbled in the regional, if not global, market. The very canal that Brown dug enabled the merchants to bypass his attempt to deprive them of their profits, and his own sloppy bookkeeping and curious pricing compounded the problem. Equally perplexing was the fact that wool output as a whole was on the rise, while the number of woolen establishments was on a steady decline.[28] When Erickson came back for another visit, he found Brown "greatly depressed" and preparing to take his wool to London. Brown felt he could sell it dear based upon some recent comparative price quotes.

Perkins and all the growers had agreed to the idea, but Erickson was appalled. In the wake of recent tariff reform and volcanic political upheavals in Europe, prices were atrocious, and Erickson had found London to be an inhospitable market. But a desperate Brown would not be dissuaded, and he tersely told Erickson that he would succeed where Erickson had failed.

Erickson couldn't have known the reason for Brown's somber mood and smoldering black determination. When Brown started planning for London, infant Ellen had caught a cold. It didn't seem serious. But the cold got worse, and before long she was coughing blood. She died in her father's arms as he walked an endless vigil with her through the night in the small bedroom, rocking her and singing her through her final hours. This child too slipped from his grasp, and when she did he stoically placed her in the cradle and closed her eyes; it was only when she was buried that he fell sobbing to his knees. Now he clung to a hope that was sharp and brittle, desperate for some success after so many debacles.[29]

7

The Land of Education

A house is an escarpment, a door is a refusal, a façade is a wall. This wall sees, hears, and does not want. It could open up and save you. No. This wall is a judge. It looks upon you and condemns you. How somber these closed houses are! They seem dead, they are living.... And the house takes on the look of a tomb. The insurgent in front of that door is breathing his last; he sees the grapeshot and drawn sabers coming; if he calls out, he knows that they hear him, but that they will not come; there are walls that might protect him, there are men who might save him; and those walls have ears of flesh, and those men have bowels of stone.
—Victor Hugo, *Les Misérables*

The Age of Revolution began with *La Révolution* in France in 1789 and with the establishment of the first factory system in England. Old ideas and class legitimacies were swept away, and from them emerged new ideas and ways of ordering the world and the mind. Those twin revolutions happened just as much in the live interplay of human will and intentions as they did in thousands of pages of print, conceptualized into an idea as people attempted to historically understand their present and future. As they endured on the page, echoes of old movements and sound, the past became the product of the ideas that emerged from it. The age drew to a volcanic close in 1848, the year of the Seneca Falls Convention and the Declaration of Sentiments, of the collapse of the firm Perkins and Brown, and the publication of the Communist Manifesto by Karl Marx. It was a year of convergences, the crystallization of ideas and patterns and the shape of things to come and the shape of things past. In 1844, the nature of time and cause had changed forever when a wire between Washington, D.C., and Baltimore instantaneously and silently proclaimed, WHAT HATH GOD WROUGHT! Morse's telegraph was baptized in his faith in divine, historical, manifest destiny, intended to connect the land.

The American Revolution, as a concept, was merely an invocation to things past, an effort to procure post-hoc public acceptance of its inevitability by linking it with a broad English tradition beginning with the Glorious Revolution, which constituted the first use of the term in the political lexicon. When comparing the two, Alexis de Tocqueville observed that the American Revolution "made sweeping changes in the political constitution of the country, and even overthrew the monarchy, but it hardly affected the secondary laws or the customs and habits of the nation.... The apex was shattered, but the substructure stood firm." He went on to describe the American "Revolution" as merely a "change in government."[1] Tocqueville understood revolution

Mary Brown, with daughters Annie and Sarah (Library of Congress).

quite well, having spent much of his life intellectually grappling with the French Revolution.

The American Revolution, rather than being a beginning, was a confused denouement, a post–Seven Years' War mess vexed by problems between London and its colonies that neither could have foreseen and which all failed to adequately address. The Seven Years' War was a global conflict that began improbably in the colonial hinterlands with a colonial governor's attempt to remove a small French construction crew. The result was the massacre of fifteen Frenchmen by a Mingo chieftain attempting to compel British policy.

No one could have known that one desperate British officer's inability to adequately cope with events would lead to a war that would destroy France's American empire, or that the improbable English victory would lead to an insurrection commanded by that same officer that would fracture London's empire.[2] "But now that I think of that even with a changed mind and see what a compliment to England is all this self glorification," Emerson wrote, "and betrays a servile mind in us who think so overgreat an action, makes the courage & the wit of the admirers suspected, who ought to look at such things as things of course."[3]

But for George Bancroft, the Revolution was the beginning, and an extension of a broad "Jacksonian" vision, written in the future imagined in Jefferson's vast western frontier. It was crafted alongside Bancroft's own political career that began in the dark year of 1837. He rose to prominence in the James K. Polk administration as the secretary of the navy and, for a brief period, also the secretary of war, and was instrumental in agitating a war with Mexico fought in the disputed lands at the Texas-Mexico border. Additionally, he ordered the occupation of California by the United States.

Bancroft's narrative was heir to the three great historians of the long nineteenth century, who cast themselves as heirs to a "scientific" legacy stretching from Thucydides to Gibbon, a tradition that purported to distinguish myth from truth. He studied under one of them—Leopold von Ranke, Berlin's chair of history—who made the defining statement that "to history has been assigned the office of judging the past, of instructing the present for the benefit of future ages. To such high offices this work does not aspire: It wants only to show what *actually* happened."[4]

Ranke's narrative was written to demonstrate the historical reality of the revolution from above within Prussia in opposition to the French Revolution. Eschewing broad philosophical ideas about time, space, and cause, Ranke developed an idea based on scientific positivism that he could discern truth without relying too heavily on the human imagination. What "actually happened" was in the archives he indefatigably plumbed, and which he believed would become a story when properly assembled. But lacking a working theory of psychology, he unintentionally philosophized broadly by granting a position of truth to state records over all other sources.

Moreover, his positivism was a belief that through the precious quotes he turned in his mind like shiny stones from a river, reality might be known. Those stones had been shaped, preserved, and brought to their location by the river, and yet what did they say about it? For Ranke, historical truth resided in the connected memory of the state, of society and culture, notwithstanding that those truths were imagined reflections. It was a pleasing seduction, that stories preserved in the appropriate form could be taken as something that causes effects—a subject—and therefore lead to understanding.

Ranke never considered that those stories, like amber, held fundamental errors of reason. He merely wished to elevate his academic discipline to the status of mechanics all while refuting Hume's nihilism. So he replaced Hegel's notion of political states as "moral energies" and "thoughts of God" with a historicist theodicy to the state that condemned contrary views as heretical. Thus history finally replaced philosophy, theology's age-old companion, and assumed its place next to science long after science had done away with God.

Alternatively, Jules Michelet, second great historian of the Age, attempted to make Revolution whole by elevating an essentially Romantic view of the world to the status of science.[5] Nations were an incarnate drama of historical disclosure, as he said: "Let it be my part in the future to have not attained, but marked, the aim of history, to have called it by a name that nobody had given it.... I have named it *resurrection,* and this name will remain."[6] His "discovery" was the national spirit invoked by Robespierre, an idea that grew from the Enlightenment's certainties while at the same time disdaining its inherent skepticism.[7]

By this device he described history not as the uniqueness of individuals, but rather as the singularity of an emergent metaphor formed of *the people's* collective uniqueness. The significance of any person only mattered within the unity that society was struggling to achieve. Fundamentally, *La Révolution* became historical "first cause," since "we" are one, and one is the beginning. Revolution was the light that shone through the darkness of time to bring justice, however late, as "the tardy reaction ... against the government of favor and the religion of grace."[8]

Through the medium of history, Michelet allowed *the nation* to speak for the dead, liberating those forgotten dead from the past's *oubliette,* and helping to "solve for them their own riddle, which made no sense to them" as well as to "explain to them the meaning of their words, their own actions which they did not understand."[9] Bancroft owed many of his plot flows to Michelet too, since a nation that claims such authority for the dead has no philosophical limits on its future. Emerson, a better reader of philosophy, noted that the "sublime creed of the Indian Buddhists was not," perhaps, "meant for a Frenchman to analyze & crack his joke & make grimace upon."

In an enlightened age, a scientific concept of history began with actions that really took place performed by people that really existed, and worked in a one-dimensional diachronic concept of time in which events followed each other in coherent sequence. Within that framework, human actions mirror intentions, and come together in a coherent story. Historical narratives also imply within the story a belief in the philosophically indefensible idea of "free will," though metaphorically narrating "free will" often depends entirely on the assumption that the subject's thoughts ride obediently on the rails of a shared reality. History's tautological endeavor during Brown's lifetime was crafting the very framework by which its subjects were narrated.

Historical destiny, manifest or not, is based on the notion that the past cannot be other than what it was, and by extension the future will not be other than what it will be, which must be logically consistent with the past. This idea, based in scientific "natural law," was fully internalized by Bancroft when he narrated a Revolution that "grew naturally and necessarily out of the series of past events by the formative principle of a living belief." According to him, the revolutionaries "fulfilled their duty not from the accidental impulse of the moment; their action was the slowly ripened fruit of Providence and of time. The light that led them on, was combined of rays from the whole history of the race."[10]

Prior to the eighteenth century humanity's universe was a conceptual one in which the unfolding design of the cosmos proceeded *a priori* from the Creator. But the predictive triumph of observable phenomena made it unnecessary to be haunted by such ghosts. The keepers of the social order drew solace from the belief that their heretics were helpless against a narrative as ruthlessly certain as gravity. "Natural law" in the age of revolution became the historical "first cause" that the Western mind needed to validate the future of social reality. It was an idea as ecumenical as God, grand enough for Hobbes and Locke to both invoke while debating the ethics of despotism.[11] Thomas Malthus may have "discovered" through maps and demographics that somebody born poor would always remain poor, but the wealthy were most enthusiastic to discover the natural law that generosity simply made them poorer.[12]

The future-past of Bancroft's sense of imperial destiny became fixed as *manifest destiny* in 1845 on the pages of John L. O'Sullivan's *Democratic Review,* an intellectual forum for "Jacksonian Democracy."[13] As a concept, it served as pleasant euphemism for a more honest, yet morally compromising, European term: *empire.* It also served as a psychological narcotic for a shaken and troubled nation. Given that the prosperity of the nation depended on appropriating the land of one non-white group, enslaving and exploiting the labor of another, and in 1846 making war on a non-white state (Mexico), "manifest destiny" quickly took on the implied guise of race. The belief system overrode (Whig) objections to the annexation of vast swaths of territory, and categorized the inequities done to the Indians not as matters of historical relativism and growing pains on the path to unity, but rather as the unfortunately unavoidable dictums of science.[14]

"Race," according to the *Democratic Review* on the eve of the Mexican War, was the "key" to the "history of nations."[15] In other words, historians and political leaders were deliberately casting effects as causes, transforming avarice and greed into "natural law." Even Emerson once delivered an unfortunate lecture titled "Genius of the Anglo-Saxon Race" in which he aided in the narrative fusion of racial superiority and nationalism.

The United States ended its war with Mexico in 1848 with its largest territorial gain ever, save for the Louisiana Purchase.[16] This coincided with the (other) French Revolution, an event greeted with considerable joy in certain quarters of America as people imagined the stars of their freedom finally bringing light to despotic Europe. But that revolution was crushed by authoritarian regimes along with all the myriad revolutions that mimicked it across Europe. Slave-owners, bankers, and politicians had not been so enthusiastic for European revolutions, but their suppression and U.S. territorial expansion contributed to a booming cotton economy, quelling a great deal of irritating domestic political agitation that had been endangering both the economy and the sense of national unity which had probably existed at least since 1830 when the word "nationalism" first came into popular use along with the new histories.[17]

The failure of those revolutions also validated nascent American exceptionalism; Europeans clearly lacked the capacity to emulate the United States.[18] And who wouldn't want to emulate America? As Emerson observed:

> The name of Washington City in the newspapers is every day a blacker shade. All the news from that quarter being of a sadder type, more malignant. It seems to be settled that no act of honor or benevolence or justice is to be expected from the American Government, but only this, that they will be as wicked as they dare.... Things have another order in these men's eyes. Heavy is hollow & good is evil. A western man in Congress the other day spoke of the opponents of the Texan & Mexican plunder as "Every light character in the house," & our good friend in State street speaks of "the solid portion of the community" meaning, of course, the sharpers. I feel, meantime, that those who succeed in life, in civilized society, are beasts of prey.[19]

"History repeats itself" Karl Marx wrote, "the first time as a tragedy, the second time as a farce."[20] The people who were being devoured by the systems of predation born of the twin revolutions that had established the modern order drew their inspiration from the system of their oppression. Nationalism was a loose idea, understood as some organizing principle based on a mix of common languages, a shared history, and the bounds of geography. The year 1848 had been in the histories, and the words erupted across Europe as the people attempted seize national identity by acting out how they believed it had happened to begin with.

The people, mostly the poor proletariat, rushed to the barricades and rose up as one to fight for upsetting ideas such as socialism, undefined beyond a vague idea about worker ownership, and democracy, broadly understood as the government by the consent of national male suffrage. In France homes burned, the Second Republic was declared, and King Louis Phillipe fled to England. But as events unfolded, the poor at the barricades found that they were alone; the city slept, and the armies of the bourgeoisie destroyed wood and stone and flesh with bullets and grape-shot and steel. The insurrectionists died alone, they died poor. Who was to blame?

France elevated Louis-Napoleon to the presidency. Louis-Napoleon was a man whose only claim to such high office was his name and some history books. He returned the people to their place, filled the prisons with debtors, and ushered in an era of banking prosperity. Eventually the pretenses were dispensed with, and the Second Empire was declared following a *coup d'état* on December 2, 1851. From the aftermath of 1848, Bismarck and his generals forcibly forged the artificiality known as Germany. The American powerful smiled, never looking down to see that the histories which validated their ravenous ambitions contained within it the same seeds of Europe's 1848. Those seeds were merely waiting for a good storm.

John Brown travelled to post-revolutionary Europe along with the tons of cotton that fed England's factories, picked by slaves who were subjugated by foolish little martinets mimicking Europe's military class. Brown would suffer his measure too, alongside all the poor enmeshed in trans–Atlantic markets. The problem was that the borders of nations restrained only the poor, and the system was arranged for him to fail. In London the very same merchants who were edging Brown in America bought his wool at prices that were insulting and ruinous, and shipped it right back to Boston while retaining as additional profit the money that would formerly have been taken by wool import tariffs. Brown was bankrupt again, perhaps worse off than ever.

It was not for ignorance of his trade that he failed; he knew his wool. An English merchant once attempted to fool the newly arrived Yankee rube, and handed him some poodle clippings. He asked Brown how to best utilize that "wool." Brown rolled it between his fingers, and said drily, "Gentlemen, if you have any machinery that will work up dog's hair, I would advise you to put this into it."[21]

Brown suffered financial ruin in England, but it was also the England that had sheltered Frederick Douglass, and that England must have influenced Brown somehow. Douglass had once found after leaving the blue skies of "freedom" and democracy to arrive under soft gray Irish fogs and the land of the Crown that he was ... free. "The chattel becomes a man. I gaze around in vain for one who will question my equal humanity, claim me as his slave, or offer me an insult.... I dine at the same table and no one is offended. No delicate nose grows deformed in my presence. I meet nothing to remind me of my complexion. I find myself regarded and treated at every turn with the kindness and deference paid to white people. When I go to church, I am met by no upturned nose and scornful lip to tell me, 'We don't allow niggers in here!'"[22]

Brown also visited the Continent, notably France and Germany. He was interested in the different farming practices there. What struck him socially about Europe was the horror of the standing army, the "greatest curse to a country," which drained off all value and lives.[23] After his brief tour he went back to Springfield and resumed his shepherd duties for Perkins. Then the lawsuits mounted from bewildered and hurt farmers, and with them the promise of financial ruination, yet again.

He had sorted as much as 300 tons of wool and put endless hours into Perkins' warehouse, only to fail. Another local businessman named E.C. Leonard later wrote that "Uncle John was no trader: he waited until his wools were graded, and then fixed a price; if this suited the manufacturers they took the fleeces; if not, they bought elsewhere, and Uncle John had to submit finally to a much less price than he could have got. Yet he was a scrupulously honest and upright man—hard and inflexible, but everybody had just what belonged to him. Brown was in a position to make a fortune, and a regular-bred merchant would have done so.... But, as I said, it was a failure."[24]

In 1849 the Brown family finally made the move to North Elba, New York. The experimental, utopian side of the community did not survive, but to Brown it remained the home of his dreams, and settled his family there, at least the family that had not moved on with their own lives. John, Jr., was gone, married to a woman he met during his studies, Wealthy Hotchkiss. Jason too had married, and had started a family with a woman named Ellen Sherbody; their son Austin was born the next year. Ruth was married to a man named Henry Thompson, but they elected to live on the North Elba property.

Owen and Frederick were still with him. Frederick was always by his side; he had been his father's special charge ever since it became apparent that there was something wrong with him. He was slow, and was troubled by terrible headaches and by attacks of black melancholy. And so Brown kept him close, to help him through the world. Frederick loved his father dearly, and was fiercely loyal.

As was Owen, who was minding the homestead one day while his father and Frederick were away. One quiet, sunny afternoon Owen was startled and bemused to see three men stumbling towards his family's simple cabin. He greeted them cordially, since his father had long counseled: "Forget not to entertain strangers, for thereby some have entertained angels unawares," and took them inside where Ruth tended to their abrasions and bites.[25]

One of them was Richard Henry Dana, Jr., an abolitionist who as a child attended Emerson's private school, and later attained some literary fame for his book *Two Years Before the Mast*, about poor merchant sailors. He was also a founding member of the Free Soil Party. That day, Dana had been hopelessly lost in the Adirondacks. He and his friends had navigated to the most prominent landmark they could find, and found their way to near Lake Placid, and the towering mountain with the striking cliff-face known as "Whiteface" or "Cloudsplitter." There, in a clearing, was a small frame house.

Later that evening, John Brown arrived home with Frederick and two black neighbors. Dana thought him as a "grave, serious man" possessing a "natural dignity of manner." The well-educated Dana also found Brown to be pleasant conversation, and "well informed on most subjects, especially in the natural sciences." Though deeply poor by this time, Brown's simple homestead still contained his books.

Among Emerson's complaints about the Abolition movement was what he felt was a lack of philosophical constancy, noting that for all their words, there were essentially still "Two tables in every house! Abolitionists at one & *servants* at the other!"[26] No surprise that Dana was mildly scandalized when Brown sat his black friends at the table as equals and introduced them with all the courteous honorifics of white society: "Mr. Dana, Mr. Jefferson," and so forth.[27] But this was what Brown intended for his little community, no matter what the abolitionists thought.

Emerson both cared and yet did not care specifically about the immediate physical plight of the black man, since to him that was merely a symptom of a philosophical void. "The absence of moral feeling in the whiteman is the very calamity I deplore. The captivity of a thousand negroes is nothing to me."[28] Whatever the state of Dana's own moral compass, Brown saw to it that he was fed and rested and healthy, then gave him directions on his way.

Brown's lawsuits dragged on interminably in the coming months, and he was compelled to reside on Perkins's farm again.[29] Mary's health was suffering too, but while she was receiving treatment they could hardly afford she had the opportunity to see Lucy Stone, abolitionist, suffragette, and inspiration for the women who led the Seneca Falls convention. Public speaking by women was strongly discouraged, but Mary attended her lecture tour, and wrote, I went to hear "for the first time that I ever heard a Woman speak. liked her very well."[30]

Circumstances held Brown in Springfield, but they also led him to form the society he had intended for North Elba. Shortly after passage of the Fugitive Slave Law in 1850, a runaway in New York had been captured, and the fear that the event caused among Brown's friends turned blackly in his gut. The abolitionist press decried the law in 1848 metaphors, casting themselves as Hungarian freedom-fighters overrun by cruel Austrian oppressors from the South.

On January 15, 1851, Brown gathered all of his black friends in Springfield and read to them his "Words of Advice," written to a proposed "League of Gileadites." It was a call to the barricades, for violent resistance to slave-catchers, for their death if necessary. And should a man die trying to defend himself, it could only help others: "The trial for life of one bold and somewhat successful man, for defending his rights in good earnest, would arouse more sympathy throughout the nation than the suffering of all the slaves."[31] Forty-four black men and women signed the charter. Thankfully they never had to rely on Brown's advice.

On May 17, 1852, John and Mary lost a 17-day-old infant. And John was perhaps getting a little weary of life, and longed to spend his final years with his family in North Elba, where all that he saw reminded him of "omnipotence." Returning to Ohio to work and answer court summons, he wrote to Henry Thompson asking him to build a home in North Elba, though he feared at his age that he would not live to see it done.[32] And even if he did, he didn't know that he would be able to live with himself, crying "peace when there is *no* peace" like all the others in a land desperately clinging to a national myth after having put their lives back together since 1837.[33] It had been many years since Brown had formally joined a church, but he was pleased to see that churches in North Elba had renounced "man-stealing." If they were indeed God's own, he looked forward to perhaps uniting with one.[34]

Brown later reflected that his financial troubles

> grew out of one root,—doing business on credit.... Where loans are amply secured, the borrower, not the lender, takes the risks, and all the contingencies incident to business; while the accumulations of interest and the coming of pay-day are as sure as death.... I started out in life with the idea that nothing could be done without capital, and that a poor man *must* use his credit and borrow; and this pernicious notion has been the rock on which I, as well as so many other, have split. The practical effect of

this false doctrine has been to keep me like a toad under a harrow most of my business life.[35]

That summation was as good as any. Emerson noted that trade and commerce had done much to overthrow tyrannies, and might eventually overthrow slavery, but that markets, like all human imaginings, had any number of moral possibilities. "Every reform," he wrote, "is only a mask under cover of which a more terrible reform, which dares not name itself, advances…. Antislavery dare not yet say that every man must … at least, receive no interest for money. Yet that is at last the upshot."[36]

Southern slave-owners also shared Brown's downfall. Every year, the system that their cruel institution fed in turn fed on them. It was the endless chasing of efficient returns in the long nine-month cycle of seed, food, slaves, and harvest which helped bring about the 1837 crash. In that year the planters collectively owed $33 million to New Orleans, and their depressed crop prices earned a mere $10 million.[37] The shortfall devastated the economy, prices never recovered, and planters sought revenues the only two ways they could while doing early calculations on the financial worth of the Union.

Their first option was to utilize pain to achieve a frenzy of labor from those black slaves, drawing ever more cotton from the lash and from blood. This, of course, was a solution doomed to fail; it is impossible to produce out of a problem of overwhelming supply.

But there was another way. At the most basic level, the system stood not on cotton, but on the broken families and broken bodies of mortgaged and hypothecated people. The expansion of that most secure form of capital into new lands had once brought about prosperity for white Americans—why not again? New lands in Jefferson's vast Western frontier and beyond beckoned, lands like Mexico, or even Kansas.

Brown and Perkins dissolved their partnership amicably. But unable to afford the move to North Elba, Brown worked in Akron for a time. He was troubled by recent developments like the Fugitive Slave Law, and his conflicted correspondence to Frederick Douglass conveyed his sense that the slaveholding powerful had co-opted the republic, that the barricades had fallen and no one stirred to help.[38]

If he was looking for proof of a slave-power takeover, perhaps the best evidence was the 1854 "trial" of Anthony Burns, a fugitive discovered and arrested in Boston by slave-catchers. Despite the defense attorney's best efforts, the Fugitive Slave Act made the outcome of the farcical trial a certainty. Boston was outraged that the slave-power, under the imprimatur of the Pierce Administration, could reach into the center of abolitionism and drag black men back into the South's abyssal depths.

John Brown heard the news while fighting his lawsuits in Vernon, New York. He quickly forgot his problems, and nervously paced the courthouse like a caged beast, eyes blazing. A friend talked him out of an impulsive and potentially suicidal rescue attempt.[39] Others tried, like an Emerson acolyte named Thomas Wentworth Higginson, along with some friends and a battering ram. Higginson was wounded and bore a prominent scar for the rest of his days, but the rescue failed.

Some two thousand United States soldiers escorted Burns to a waiting ship on June 2, 1854, through streets hung with black cloth and inverted U.S. flags. The federal government paid nearly $40,000 to return him to his wealthy masters. Once stolen away "Back in to a Land of death," Burns wrote a sadly debasing letter to his attorney, offering himself for sale at a bargain as a means of securing his freedom. His lawyer, Richard Henry Dana, Jr., had once spent an evening at a post-racial table in an Adirondack cabin.[40]

After the fiasco, Garrison publicly burned copies of the court's decision, the Fugitive Slave Act, and the Constitution. Emerson wrote, "I submit that all government is bankrupt, all law turned upside down; that the government itself is treason."[41] Congress had passed the Kansas-Nebraska Act just a few months prior, and after the Burns trial, emigrant aid societies started aggressively recruiting "free men" who hated slavery, and who were searching for purpose in the desperate remains of the economy. According to the societies, opportunity would be found on the "broad and beautiful plains where they go to raise their free homes."[42] Theoretically it was a happy convergence of noble and needful purpose for all parties.

Amos Lawrence, a prominent Boston businessman, belonged to one of the 15 families known as the "Boston Associates" who controlled 20 percent of the city's cotton spindles, 30 percent of the state's railroad mileage, and 40 percent of the state's insurance and banking.[43] He said of the Burns trial: "We went to bed one night old-fashioned, conservative, compromise Union Whigs & waked up stark mad Abolitionists."[44] After the ghastly drama in Boston, the Massachusetts Emigrant Aid Society became Lawrence's *cause célèbre*; he donated so generously that settlers named a Kansas town in his honor. It was "a piece of New England set down in the prairie," complete with attractive brick buildings and the fortress-like Free State hotel. Speculators as well as anti-slavery crusaders flocked to the $5 million colonization effort, and southerners rushed to counter the threat to their "peculiar institution," all coming together in northeast Kansas to decide the fate of slavery on the frontier.[45]

If the Kansas-Nebraska Act troubled Brown immediately, he did not indicate it in his surviving letters of 1854, which speak of farm and family, and his constant desire to move home to North Elba, the last home he would ever know, if only for a moment. Ellen Brown was born on September 25.

Of course, "nobody in Washington" could "explain this Nebraska business to the people,—nobody of weight.... But what effrontery it required to fly in the face of what was supposed settled law & how it shows that we have no guards whatever, that there is no proposition whatever, that is too audacious to be offered us by the southerner."[46] The act led John Brown's sons Owen, with his crippled arm, simple-minded Frederick, and Salmon to leave North Elba in October of 1854 for Kansas to confront the most combustible issue of the day. They settled eight miles outside of Osawatomie, some thirty miles southeast of Lawrence. The land was free, and the cost would be so high.

Brown strongly considered moving with his family to the Kansas Territory. His was a spirit that would bear much, and perhaps demanded to bear much in order to find meaning. And he had borne much, and suffered for it; his follies had mocked his wisdom and leveled his pride. He had waded the fetid waters of illness and death, and the equally malignant waters of truth, and had come through determined to offer his aid to the ghosts that the powerful feared most, and his friendship to those who were most despised.

He was beginning to believe that carrying his burden like a faithful camel into the western plains would be "more likely to benefit the colored people on the whole than to return with them to N. Elba." He was torn between that frontier and the mythical Adirondacks, which he wanted to believe held the promise of freedom for the slaves, and whose beauty enchanted his tired soul. Seeking guidance, Brown wrote to Ruth about his turmoil, and wondered if she and her husband Henry would ask the Negroes of North Elba what his course of action should be. After all, since he had "volunteered in their services" their voices should inform his decision.[47]

Based on their counsel, and on the advice of other friends like Frederick Douglass and Gerrit Smith, John Brown determined to remain in the East. So when John, Jr., and Jason followed their brothers in May of 1855 with their families, Brown wrote enigmatically to John, Jr.: "If you or any of my family are disposed to go to Kansas or Nebraska with a view to help defeat Satan and his legions in that direction, I have not a word to say; but I feel committed to operate in another part of the field. If I were not so committed, I would be on my way this fall."[48]

It was a dark passage to Kansas, particularly for Jason and Ellen. There was a cholera outbreak on the riverboat they were travelling on, and their four-year-old son contracted the disease. He died in Missouri, skin ashen-blue, in agony from hunger and dehydration, while his parents watched helplessly. In Waverly, they asked the boat captain merely for the time to bury their child on shore.

Their tears mingled with rain as they lowered his little body into the ground near the river, their grim task lit only by the violence of "furious thunderstorms." Upon returning to the boat, they discovered that the captain had seized the opportunity to be rid of those ill-starred abolitionists, and had abandoned them, forcing the bereaved parents to journey by foot and wagon through the heart of pro-slavery Missouri lands. But eventually they made it to Kansas.

John, Jr., Wealthy, Jason and Ellen arrived in May. Thunderstorms roiled upwards towards the heavens and lumbered serenely along the southern horizon. Then nervously twitching winds troubled the balmy day, cold breezes carried the ponderous smells of ozone and flood, and the sky eventually darkened as those clouds relaxed with a rumbling sigh, losing their grip on the fury within that it might assail the men below. It was a time that Salmon reminisced as being like "Noah's flood," and he felt the whole territory might be washed away in the deluge.[49]

Amid the peals of thunder, news of violent threats from bordering Missouri began to creep around the eastern Kansas prairie. On the 20th of May, John, Jr., sat down with his pen and wrote to his father of all that he heard and felt.

Part Two:
The Wanderjahre

So I returned, and considered all the oppressions that are done under the sun: and behold the tears of such as were oppressed, and they had no comforter; and on the side of their oppressors there was power; but they had no comforter.

—Ecclesiastes 4:1

John Brown, Kansas warrior, 1856 (public domain image. Retrieved from Wikimedia Commons).

8

All Too Human

When the gods in the Norse heaven were unable to bind the Fenris Wolf with steel or with weight of mountains,—the one he snapped and the other he spurned with his heel,—they put round his foot a limp band softer than silk or cobweb, and this held him; the more he spurned it the stiffer it drew. So soft and so staunch is the ring of Fate. Neither brandy, nor nectar, nor sulphuric ether, nor hell-fire, nor ichor, nor poetry, nor genius, can get rid of this limp band.
—Ralph Waldo Emerson, *Fate*

The story of John Brown's journey to the Kansas frontier took place in the geography of the land and of the mind. The narrative dilates in that frontier, the story of a life delicately suspended in the absurd philosophies of men, their historicist faith, their economic devastation, their sin of slavery—the very things that drove them to stab westward like wretched children scattering before a flood.

On the pages of history the light of civilization spread across those vast expanses. These years on the Kansas frontier are where the historical narratives of John Brown begin. In his fifty-fifth year, his son called to him, a lifetime directed his resolute will, and he went to Kansas to save his children—all of them—and to save his own soul. This was not freedom, but it would make of him history, which is to say it was the beginning of the end of a conceptually grotesque and disfiguring transformation.

By early 1855, letters from his sons about the Kansas territory were making John Brown restless. North Elba was a functioning yet struggling little mountain town, but Gerrit Smith's social experiment was not going anywhere. There were scarce economic and fewer ethical rewards in the Adirondacks, so Brown started to think about a move, and hoped that out West he would find work surveying, or homesteading. His family began preparing for the longest move of their lives, to those apparently prosperous plains.

On the 20th of May, John, Jr., wrote to his father, not of verdant fields, fresh water, and abundant land, but of a conflagration to come, and terrible enemies arrayed against the Browns. "Hundreds of thousands ... armed to the teeth with Revolvers, Bowie Knives, Rifles, and Cannon" were gathering to "fasten slavery on this glorious land." John, Jr., was bristling and bellicose: "The Antislavery portion of the inhabitants should immediately, thoroughly arm and organize themselves in military companies."[1]

Brown had been terribly stern with John, Jr., for most of his life, and continued to remonstrate with him about his agnosticism. But John Brown loved his oldest child, who was much like him in his mannerisms. Despite his own years of hardships, Brown's worried lectures always came enclosed with money whenever he could afford it. Now, in his son's letters, he beheld a future in which a pro-slavery army washed over Kansas, killing his boys and destroying the free-state cause. What did North Elba, or the rest of his work matter compared to this, when in Kansas, reality was blurring at the edges, and men were going to die for beliefs about it? John Brown's sons called to him, and he "fully resolved to proceed at once to Kansas; & join his Children."[2] Abandoning all plans to bring his family, he gathered weapons and directed his terrible gaze towards Kansas.

Eventually the day comes when you know that all that remains is to choose the kind of man you're going to be. Maybe the choice was then, or maybe his path was set when he was twelve years old. Maybe he had no choice but to go under, to a place where man's worst instincts were coming out, where the war against slavery was beginning. It's difficult to tell with any certainty just how much blood was actually spilled in Bleeding Kansas. By 1855 both the territorial and the national press were competing to best narrate the atrocities being committed in Kansas as the struggle over slavery took on ever greater urgency.[3]

The American frontier was certainly a violent place. Unchecked by the interconnected systems of the state, and often peopled by the unreflective and unintelligent, men were anything but angels, providing proof in anecdote for James Madison's aphorism concerning the need for government. But how many died on the Kansas prairie for abstract ideas about freedom and the morals of men, and how many died simply because people are brutes? What kind of truth brought John Brown to Kansas?

There were 157 violent deaths recorded during the territorial years of 1854 through statehood. Of those, 56 may be with confidence attributed to political strife regarding slavery. The remainder—a sad compendium of brawls, land disputes, robberies, and lynchings—merely cry out for justice, or at least for the law.[4] By way of perspective, there were 1,200 violent deaths in San Francisco alone in the three years preceding this period, and 583 in California in 1855.[5] Yet the deaths in Kansas loom larger in narrative, even if they were lighter on the statistical scales of pain. They gained narrative weight after the past was sifted and meaning imposed on it from the carnage to follow. Even at the time, the story had its locus in the center of so many historical ideas, the meanings of which seemed more illusory by the day.

The story, or at least the final accounting of those dead in the Kansas Territory, has long been the victim of willful distortion and incomplete records. The territorial press for both sides was motivated by the same tedious impulses as both the shrillest of journalists and military historians. They needed to gain sympathy, or else convince themselves and any who might read, that the outcome of the tale was inexorable, and that to continue resisting was not realistic.

In the end, the Free-State side emerged victorious and thoroughly overwhelmed their seemingly dominant pro-slavery adversaries. The records of the pro-slavery vanquished were either spirited away to the South to be subjected eventually to further violent loss, or were destroyed as rubbish by the triumphant Free-State Party.

But exactly two people had died violently as a result of the philosophical struggle over slavery when John, Jr., penned his fateful letter to his father, in which he attempted to convey the truth as well as he or anyone knew how. The first was the most ironic: a nameless black man shot by an equally nameless Shawnee Indian while attempting to flee his bonds in March of 1855. The second was a pro-slavery man killed by a Free-Stater in Leavenworth during a heated quarrel at a meeting of the squatters' association.[6]

Was John, Jr., deceptive or ignorant about the nature of the stasis in Kansas? Speaking minor truths and minor falsehoods is a simple thing, but conveying real truth is far more tenuous. There is both secret knowledge and spoken knowledge, dependent upon each other as darkness and light. In this case the relative falsity of Bleeding Kansas may have been the truest secret knowledge, reverberating where the false light of civilization purported to shine, the shadow from the flickering flame of a burning pile of ideas.

The quickening kinesis that was tugging at John Brown and had already swept his sons out to Kansas had compelled the abolitionists to call for a "Convention for Radical Political Abolitionists" to be held that June in Syracuse, New York. The summons went out in April, during John, Jr.'s travels west. Those who drafted the summons, among whom were notables such as Gerrit Smith and Frederick

John Brown, Jr. (Library of Congress).

Douglass, had decided that it was time to reassess their near-helpless political situation, and to gather "for the purpose of enlightening each other's minds, and cheering each other's hearts, and strengthening each other's hands."[7] Though he was not a habitual joiner of groups or movements, John Brown had decided by June to attend. He brought with him a collection of letters from his sons in the Kansas Territory, and a purpose in his heart.

From the 26th through the 28th of June the convention discussed the most acrimonious events and legal developments of the day, to include the Fugitive Slave Law and the inflammatory Anthony Burns "trial" that took place in Boston. Prior to the convention, Boston's Twelfth Baptist Church had purchased Burns' freedom, a fact which did not make the outrage any less raw or immediate.

The recent Kansas-Nebraska Act was exceptionally troubling, as was the reinvigorated struggle to extend slavery into the frontier. That act, and the possible loss of free Kansas, was regarded as the latest example as the failure of "non-extension," a national policy ostensibly intended to result in slavery's eventual extinction. As the attendees noted, no territory had ever been reclaimed from "the enemy" under non-extension. In fact, the most recent Free State to be admitted to the Union under the current non-extension policies had been California, and only at a terrible price.

The Bear Republic had organized itself as a Free State over the opposition of a coterie of southern Californians and a minority of pro-slavery landholders. To the slaveholders this was unacceptable, and therefore their representatives in Congress were not in the mood to entertain California's petition to join the United States. Americans were, however, willing to compromise on this most terrible of subjects. The recent expansion of the national reach of slavery into the tautological spoils of historical "manifest destiny," and a healthy cotton economy, had helped to stabilize the debt structure for the time being. Therefore, for the sake of narrative continuity, California was only permitted by the balance of pro-slavery delegates in the Federal Government to retain its status as a Free State in return for the "Compromise of 1850."

Fundamentally, the "compromise" was an act of extraction by the slave-holding oligarchy: a hostage negotiation at gunpoint. They would *allow* California to abide by its own referendum so long as the Missouri Compromise and the politics of non-extension were made void in newly conquered lands. Those new territories would instead decide the issue of slavery by, ironically, referendum. This was known as "popular sovereignty," the euphemistic proviso which defined the Kansas-Nebraska Act; God help those Kansans if they voted like California. But, perhaps the slave-power had plans for that.

The next part of the extraction involved the demand that the U.S. government assume all of the debts of the state of Texas—one of the newest and largest slave-states—in a phenomenal federal bailout. And the final concession extracted was a greatly strengthened Fugitive Slave Act, institutionalized legal terror that provided for the impressments of ordinary citizens anywhere in the country into slave-hunting bands, effectively drafting them into the South's military-garrison state. Furthermore, the excessively loose terms for identifying a runaway slave—via skin color and the sworn statement of nearly any white person—resulted in a number of free-born blacks being enslaved with no recourse for defense.[8]

The "conquest of free territory by the slaveholders" had become too easy.[9] "Compromise" had laughably lost any connection with English as commonly understood. In practice, the definition of the word appeared to have been distorted into a term that meant yielding to the absurdly strident demands of a slaveholding oligarchy while they shrieked threats of war and secession, all in the interest of maintaining the illusion of manifest destiny.

The solution, the convention proposed, was the active extermination of slavery by the federal government, which the attendees asserted was within the scope of the government's powers. It was a correct interpretation of the powers of the federal government under the constitution, and the starkly clear moral imperative seemed to make the case for outright abolition a fairly self-evident one.

But the attendees felt that the argument would be more persuasive if it appealed to the Western mania for "first causes" and invoked the historicist epistemology of the state in the support of abolitionism. This effort involved dedicating a rather large percentage of printed space in the proceedings to a curious examination of the conditions of founding and the Constitution itself, in order to demonstrate in the historical sense why slavery was an aberration, and equal rights applied to all.

The notion that liberty could extend to blacks dated from the inception of the

American polity, when white citizens were horrified to find that certain "high notions of liberty" had spread through the slave population as a result of the revolutionary struggle. In Charles Town, a week after whites had protested the Stamp Act by proclaiming "Liberty and stamp'd paper," blacks had marched crying out the less ambiguous "Liberty."[10] The convention was therefore either mythologizing the history of the American body politic in order to persuade the mass of the faithful to support abolition, or they were blind to the unique protections that the founders and their constitution granted to the slave-holding class.

Their historical-legal outline was subtly different from Bancroft's delicate treatment. They too characterized slavery as an atavistic holdover from an original English sin, but were slightly more precise in identifying the private interests which were pivotal in expanding the English mercantile empire. In this story, a shared heritage of civil social theory and transatlantic history was also a shared model for abolition, since the Crown had accomplished it.

"Slaves," as Cowper noted, "can not breathe in England; if their lungs Receive our air, that moment they are free; They touch our country, and their shackles fall."[11] The powers the Constitution granted were as broad as Parliament's, if not more so; Americans had in fact lost many freedoms once enjoyed on English soil. Unfortunately, much of the federal government's power had been agreed upon only if it supported slaveholders, contrary to the claims of the abolitionists assembled in Syracuse.

That being said, as the abolitionists saw it there were practical arguments supporting the application of this power for novel and moral purposes. Slaveholders, they noted, were a "petty oligarchy" comprising certainly no more than around 300,000 individuals—just 1 percent of the population—and their threats of dissolution and war seemed a proportionally foolish boast.[12] Would an entire region downtrodden under the system actually unite behind this oligarchy and protect the economic model which supported so few? Hardly so, thought the abolitionists, and the shrill ultimatums from the slaveholders were a compelling reason to force the issue and have done with it.

Abolitionist narratives about founding liberty omitted the opinion of Thomas Jefferson on the subject, an opinion that would have clarified the intellectual roots of the current compromises. "Slavery," Jefferson said, is "a necessary evil, which cannot be practicably eradicated." He feared that the institution would lead inevitably to violent insurrection, but to free the slaves would amount to virtually the same when underlying enmities led to an extirpative war.

Jefferson's political solution was the same one that would forestall the feared Malthusian end-state of society: "diffusion," or "the uninhibited expansion of slavery, without congressional restriction, across … all future territories." His logic was curious; this would make slaves "happier" by distributing them among a greater number of slaveowners, all while simultaneously promoting emancipation by somehow democratizing slave ownership by including more people in the system. It was a bizarre idea that enabling more people to be consumers of slavery would somehow lead them to favor emancipation. How this form of emancipation wouldn't result in a race war while another would is something that Jefferson blithely glossed over, but he felt that somehow the "peculiar institution" would be improved by expanding the shareholder base.[13]

But Jefferson was clear; under no circumstances should Congress restrict slavery.

It would be unconstitutional to regulate "the condition of the different descriptions of men composing a state"; a dubious argument since the slaves were being regulated as property, not as people. He believed restricting slavery would cause a legal and sectional crisis, and bring about the dissolution of the Union. Such were the inevitable fruits of the Missouri Compromise, which he feared would one day "burst on us like a tornado."[14] But the die had been cast, and Kansas beckoned to the fight's partisans.

In a short paragraph about a fairly uneventful evening, the convention's minutes recorded an innocuous administrative item. It read: "A collection was taken up, amounting to $41.30."[15] Though not an inconsequential sum, it was relatively minor compared to the $4,600 the convention collected for the abolition cause.[16] However, such a small thing could have great meaning to someone who had long labored merely to reap dividends of suffering and disappointment. On the morning of the third day, that man spoke.

Before he did, Gerrit Smith set the scene by reading the letters from John Brown's sons, so that the assembled might hear the truth as seen by people actually living in the lands and ideas that had been the subject of the gathering. "These letters," the minutes attested, "gave sad information of the annoyances, and perils, too, that surround the emigrant to Kansas."[17] Then, after a pause for the business committee to announce a report, John Brown took the stage.

His words were not recorded, but they were singularly identified in the minutes as having "deeply stirred the hearts of the audience," an accomplishment in a crowd of lecturers that included Frederick Douglass and Lewis Tappan, and in which essays from numerous famous individuals had been read.[18] This praise was not the kind perfunctorily granted to prominent persons; historical perspective connects Brown with abolition, but at the time Brown was an outsider, known only by Gerrit Smith, and maybe from an obscure article written eight years prior by Douglass in *The North Star*.

According to Brown's daughter Ruth, "Nat Turner and Cinques stood first in his esteem."[19] Their stories had inspired his thoughts on abolition, particularly in later years, and may have guided his words that day. The broad outline of the message he delivered may be faintly discerned in of Lewis Tappan's reply. Once the initial praise and support had passed, Tappan firmly "disclaimed all sympathy with the war spirit as an auxiliary to the cause of abolition."[20] With that dismissal, the convention proceeded with the remainder of the business of the day.

Lewis Tappan's brother Arthur was a co-founder of Garrison's American Anti-Slavery Society. The brothers were both members, and had also been highly influential in establishing Oberlin College. But Tappan was most famous for his involvement with the 1841 court case regarding the *Amistad* captives and their leader, Joseph Cinque.

Cinque attained popular fame in July 1839 when he led a revolt to seize control of the slave-schooner *La Amistad*. He killed the captain, then ordered the navigator to return all the captives home. But the helmsman was able to pilot the ship by night off the shore of Long Island due to Cinque's unfortunate lack of stellar navigation skills. The trickery was revealed when the USS *Washington* intercepted the *Amistad*.

Virginia had long prior successfully lobbied for a ban on slave importation, thereby protecting a monopoly on the greatest source of wealth in the nation. Therefore slave cargo in the United States was a violation of U.S. law. But it remained to be decided if the captives were the legal salvage of the *Washington*'s officers (which they claimed by naval law), or the property of their intended Cuban buyers (and thereafter slaves in the United States, as the Cuban market was a back door to importation prohibition), or even the property of Spain.

An inspired Tappan had daily chronicled the trial for *The Emancipator,* a New England publication akin to Garrison's *Liberator.* Additionally, he arranged for the captives to be tutored in English by Yale University students. Those captives who survived prison would later use those language skills to secure the funds for the return voyage home.

Brown had once employed the *Amistad* drama in his League of Gileadites charter to encourage his friends to unite together for belligerent mutual protection.

> Nothing so charms the American people as personal bravery. Witness the case of Cinques, of everlasting memory, on board the "Amistad." The trial for the life of one bold and to some extent successful man, for defending his rights in good earnest, would arouse more sympathy throughout the nation than the accumulated wrongs and sufferings of more than three millions of our submissive colored population.... *No jury can be found in the Northern States that would convict a man for defending his rights to the last extremity. This is well understood by Southern Congressmen, who insisted that the right of trial by jury should not be granted to the fugitive.*[21]

It was bold when he wrote it, still bold at the convention. Black people knew the consequences of resistance; they had seen the irrational fury and rage of white Americans when confronted by black slaves. The cruelly medieval methods of slaughter acted as psychological balm for those whites by reassuring them of their untrammeled power while transplanting their terror back to their slaves. Brown knew just as well as his friends did how the stories of Nat and Toussaint ended; the *Amistad* story was his effort to persuade his audience that resistance—even armed—in the cause of personal justice could inspire support from whites, like Tappan, sympathetic to their cause. Perhaps the unity and sympathy that the *Amistad* case engendered in white abolitionist circles persuaded him that it was even true. He failed to understand that Cinque's bravery was acceptable because it was exhibited against Spaniards—a Catholic, alien, monarchical colonial power—as opposed to Americans.[22]

It was the line of division between Brown and Garrison, or on that day, Tappan. It was the evolving line of division within the abolitionist community. Frederick Douglass had recently suffered terrible abuse in *The Liberator,* partly due to Garrison's jealousy over his protégé's fame, and partly because Garrison abhorred the dark and violent language Douglass had been employing of late. Yet Douglass's fame grew with his audacity; decades of moral suasion and compromise had achieved nothing but the 1850 Compromise and 1 million more slaves. Something needed to change.

Nat's shadow, or even Toussaint's, must have darkened Brown's words, given Tappan's opposition in the face of general approval for the speech. However, despite the imperfect reception, the response was all that Brown needed to set him on a path the attendees should have foreseen. As they wrote in the proceedings, "If the passage of the Nebraska Bill was the crucifixion of liberty, it was the needful condition of its restored and more glorious life. If Kansas proves its sepulchre, it shall prove, likewise, the scene of its triumphant resurrection."[23]

The moments that change a life and move history often seem so insignificant at the time. There stood a destitute old man, likely dressed in plain and worn clothing, in contrast with the fine suits worn by many of the prominent attendees. He was nearing the twilight of a life marked by so much failure and disappointment and sadness, but he knew that he had at least one last duty, and that was to go to his sons. He spoke, and read the letters from his sons about the stasis in Kansas. By the time he had concluded, he found himself surrounded by people regarding him with admiration and respect, while he held tightly to $41.30.[24]

Afterwards, there was still business to finalize, and talks to be made, and social niceties to be attended to. But those ceremonies ultimately meant little, despite their formality and dignity. Perhaps later some of those present even forgot, for a while, about the shabby old man and his ominous words that day. But for John Brown, the path to Kansas was clear. He had called for war, fortune favored him at last, and in his final years God apparently intended that he, too, should be brave. Brave for the slave children beaten and bloody, brave for his own children like grown John, Jr., or for baby Ellen, whom he would never really know.

9

The Stasis

The received value of names imposed for signification of things was changed into arbitrary. For inconsiderate boldness was counted true-hearted manliness; provident deliberation, a handsome fear; modesty, the cloak of cowardice; to be wise in everything, to be lazy in everything. A furious suddenness was reputed a point of valor. To readvise for the better security was held for a fair pretext of tergiversation. He that was fierce was always trusty, and he that contraried such a one was suspected....
Thus was wickedness on foot in every kind.
—Thucydides, *History of the Peloponnesian War*[1]

A will needs the proper means to attain its ends, so Brown converted most of his cash into broadswords and guns and left his wife and children behind. Coincidentally, on June 29, the day after the Convention for Radical Political Abolitionists ended, John, Jr., wrote another letter to his father in order to report that a convention had been held in Lawrence during which Free-State men had discussed the possibility of organizing and arming themselves in order to oppose the slave power.

The situation in Kansas was bleak. Back on March 30, pro-slavery forces had overwhelmingly won control of the new Kansas territorial legislature, after an election in which voter enthusiasm ensured that 6,000 voters managed to cast ballots. The legislature convened on July 2, and within a week the remaining Free-State members had been unseated, and the government was moved to nearby Shawnee Mission, closer to its Missouri base of support. In the meantime, roughly 1,200 more Free-Staters were migrating to Kansas.[2]

They were not without violent means. Some "friendly associations" like Pastor Henry Ward Beecher in New England had provided some highly coveted Sharps rifles, and John, Jr., hoped that his father might also persuade "one or more capitalists to furnish means to purchase a number of these [rifles]," along with revolvers. He emphasized that "The storm every day thickens ... its near approach is hourly more clearly seen by all ... the great drama will open here, when will be presented the great struggle in arms, of Freedom and Despotism in America. Give us the arms, and we are ready for the contest."[3]

Like many frontier Americans, John, Jr.'s education was predicated on biblical study, particularly when it came to language education. In an era before systemized schooling this was often the only universal option readily available far from the metropole. Thus he learned English in the translated verses of the ancient Hebrews, whose delight in nature was written in their scripture in language both "utilitarian and poetic."[4] He understood Kansas in a linguistically deterministic way. The Hebrews had an agrarian preoccupation with the usefulness and order of nature, with the exception of the royal bower in Song of Songs, biblical gardens, for all their beauty, existed only for utility.

But primacy was given to the weather, particularly the storm, over the land. In the Psalms, the theophany was the wind, and trembling mountains, thick darkness, lightning, and thunder.[5] It was the terrible and sublime nature description of Leviathan that the voice from the whirlwind used to silence Job, confronting him with fearful and unanswerable questions in order to awaken in him an awareness of the limitations of humanity and human knowledge.[6] When John, Jr., wasn't summoning the whirlwind in his letters, his pastoral descriptions noted that the beauty of the land was ideal for ploughing and homesteads. Prairie grass of exceptional quality and abundant quantity waved "in the wind most beautifully," but as always, there was the "tremendous thunder and lightning."[7]

This Kansas of metaphor was the perfect stage. It was one thing in the relatively civilized East, within the increasingly complex and civilizing interdependencies of the state, to philosophically apprehend the nature of slavery and the struggle over a realistic representation of social reality. It was quite another to do so in the westward kinesis that had been written into lands where words could lose their meaning and the social contract was nonexistent, where man stood alone with the precious few intellectual and technological artifacts of his past against a world he was unprepared to meet. It was a land where Leviathan was nowhere to be found, and men could be monsters, unchecked. How Brown oriented himself to this great struggle might have been different had he remained east of the Appalachians, instead of racing west in a war that was already real.

Once John, Jr., was finished with poetically narrating the impending American Armageddon, he added a postscript about finding work, pointing out that all the "jobs of surveying ... have all been under contract for some time, and that the work is moving very slowly. Whether you will, in consequence of this, be able to get immediate business or not, I cannot say." John, Jr., had brought his father's surveying equipment with him, and was optimistic about prospects, for the frontier was vast, and there was still "a great amount of surveying to be done," enough to make of it "a good business here for many years."[8]

John Brown was indifferent to his son's words about work on the frontier. In a sense, all the surveying had been done; the reassuringly rectilinear future stretching across the continent had already been drawn. So he left behind twenty year old Watson to look after Mary and his daughters, and packed up his surveying equipment along with guns, revolvers, heavy artillery broadswords, and extra powder and caps, and left for Kansas.[9]

It was a long journey. He and his teenaged son Oliver, along with Ruth's husband Henry Thompson, had to walk most of the distance. Their wagon, heavy with steel and fire, was pulled by a single long-suffering and ill horse. And while he was on the move, so were events in the Kansas territory.

Within days of Brown's departure, the Kansas legislature had passed a law titled "An Act to Punish Offences Against Slave Property." It was an importation of various de rigueur Southern social codes written to protect slavery following Nat's Virginia insurrection. Brown would be arriving in a territory where speaking against slavery carried a sentence of two years' imprisonment. Printing and circulating such material would mean five years in prison. Sheltering runaways or hosting the Underground Railroad would earn the same. Actually leading fugitives to safety meant a ten-year term or death. Writing or speaking about insurrection meant death, as did the ultimate crime of raising an insurrection.[10]

The Territorial Governor, Andrew Reeder, a rotund Pennsylvania Democrat, was honestly trying to maintain peace and order. To that end, he vetoed all laws passed by the legislature. Though he didn't dare expose their blatant fraud, he argued technicalities, like the illegality of a session because it violated his requirement to seat the government in Pawnee. In response, the territorial chief justice dismissed Reeder's opinions, while the assembly easily secured a majority to override his veto. Reeder faced pro-slavery death threats, and

Owen Brown (Library of Congress).

the legislature petitioned President Franklin Pierce for Reeder's removal. Unknown to the harried Reeder, a far more compliant man named Wilson Shannon had been appointed by the president on August 10, though he wouldn't take office until September.[11] Shannon would prove himself an inept politician, quickly becoming the antagonist of the Free State population while stumbling blindly from crisis to crisis.

On August 14, Free State partisans called a meeting in Lawrence to discuss opposition to the "bogus" legislature and their hated new laws. Among those in attendance were Governor Reeder, special correspondent to the *Baltimore Sun* Martin F. Conway, and Dr. Charles Robinson, a former California politician sent to Kansas as an agent of the New England Emigrant Aid Society. John Brown, Jr., met most of the principals in the Free State movement at the second Lawrence meeting, later that month, as a member of the "Committee on Business." When Governor Reeder was officially fired by the president on August 16, a mid–October meeting in Topeka was planned in order to draft a constitution and a petition to admit Kansas to the Union as a Free State. The organizing Free State opposition also proposed a legal measure to prohibit free black people from settling in Kansas.

Nonetheless, John, Jr., was enthusiastic. On September 14, in Pottawatomie, he confronted a pro-slavery settler with the law-violating declaration that "no man had a right to hold a slave in Kansas." To clarify his purpose, he boldly announced that he was quite intentionally breaking the law, that he would continue to do so, and that should any agents of the slave power attempt to arrest him, he "would surely kill them, so help me God."[12]

To be fair, Pottawatomie was close enough to Free-State redoubts to be a relatively safe place for defiance. The local population was not united on the issue, and were mostly "of the poorer class." Still, the consequences were potentially real and so was his bravery. His wife, Wealthy, blithely wrote to Mary Brown that, "We shall probably get shot for disobeying their beautiful laws, but you might as well die here in a good cause as freeze to death there" in North Elba.[13]

Wealthy hadn't been in Kansas long, and the family's letters back east had read like the promotional literature, full of the lovely Kansas spring and summer. "I *certainly* never saw any region to compare in beauty and in richness of soil," she wrote.[14] But October was around the corner, and the morning's chill edge whispered of the months to come.

All the while, John, Oliver, and Henry were trudging west. In Brunswick, Missouri, they came at last to the Missouri River. Though Missouri was surrounded by free states—and contested Kansas to the west—the river served as a conduit to the South. The town was home to an auction block and a large livestock-type holding pen. Cholera was rampant.

One day, a Missourian approached Brown's overloaded little wagon and convoy, and asked, "Whar you going?"

"To Osawatomie," Brown answered.

The wagon, and Brown's New England accent, aroused suspicions. "Where you from?" the Missourian asked.

"New York."

"You'll never live to get thar," the man concluded.

John leveled his gaze on the man, and in his chilly and placidly earnest manner replied, "We are prepared not to die alone."[15]

Despite threats, they arrived unmolested, travelling through the hills on the California Road, which eventually traced through Pottawatomie towards North Middle Creek and his family's claims. Sunday morning, October 7, John walked into Brown's Station alone with his thoughts; Oliver and Henry went ahead of him the night before. From the road he could see the countryside for miles, and on colder mornings fog traced the ravine-scored prairie, flowing like ghostly rivers around green hillocks like eroded islands. Copses bunched in low areas, and the territory was "better timbered" than Brown had expected, but on the whole he was not as impressed as his children were.[16]

Autumn was already cold and bitter. Keening winds cut to the bone. John's children were living in makeshift shelters, "shivering over their little fires all exposed to the dreadfully cutting Winds Morning and Evening."[17] The crops that John, Jr., and Wealthy had written about lay un-gathered in the fields, and their livestock and horses roamed loose on the prairie. Continuous storms and regional disease epidemics had incapacitated most of the Browns, leeching their morale. Many other settlers had abandoned frontier life altogether to move back to where food and medicine were more plentiful, and where nature's caprice was not so harsh. Fortunately, their enemies shared their woes, and were mercifully quiet.

As always, Brown was a vigorous engine of human industry, and he set to work at once tending to his children, while Oliver and Henry unloaded the weapons, blankets, and surveying equipment. John also bore an unexpected burden for Jason and Ellen; in Waverly he had retrieved the body of their son Austin. Since the boy's death, Ellen had been melancholy and distant, and she and Jason were talking about returning east. Having the body of their lost son resting on their land cheered them some; Ellen tentatively mentioned staying, and Jason returned to dreams of owning an orchard.[18]

After settling immediate concerns for the day, Brown sat down with John, Jr., to learn about the area, and about events that had transpired during the two-month journey. John, Jr.'s account of the pro-slavery laws served as validation for Brown's journey, and despite the clouds hanging over Free State settlers, it was exciting. Brown was in Kansas, and intended that none of his children were going to be shot by the slave power. He also learned that he was just in time for the October 9 vote for Free State delegates.

That Tuesday, Brown went to Pottawatomie with his sons who could still walk, armed with a menacing assortment of knives and revolvers. A quiet, deadly sentinel, he watched for trouble as his sons voted. He left after an uneventful and bitterly cold day without casting his own ballot. It wouldn't have been right; his purpose was to prevent harassment and ballot-stuffing. He was not a Kansas resident and had no intention of making the state a permanent home.[19] Legal rectitude aside, his abstention from electoral politics had been absolute since Jackson's presidency.

Four days later he found the time to write to Mary about the journey and the pitiable state in which he found their children. He was also optimistic; he had expected violence in Pottawatomie, and yet the voting went peacefully and, by all reckoning, favored the Free State cause. Kansas seemed to be "brightening every day," at least in his one week there.[20]

Mary, for her part, was less than pleased with being left mostly alone to struggle in a cold Adirondack home. John was able to send a little money from cattle sales in Connecticut, and swore he would try to do more, but ultimately could offer only words, and pleaded with her to trust in God. "I humbly trust we may be kept & spared," he wrote, "to meet again on Earth; *but if not* let us all endeavor earnestly to secure admission to that Eternal Home where will be no more bitter seperations; 'where the wicked shall cease from troubling; & the weary be at rest.'"[21]

More earthly concerns occupied him soon enough. On October 25, a punishing cold snap brought sleet and jagged winds, and more illness. For a time Brown was the only healthy man on their homestead, facing the elements alone while he harvested the crops, rounded up the livestock, and cut wood for proper homes. By November 2 he had built sturdier lodging, with a functional chimney that delighted Ellen, who found that she could finally warm herself and cook a meal without smoke burning her eyes. Next was a cabin for John, Jr., and once finished with his remarkable feat of work, "a tolerable cheerfulness" appeared to prevail in Brown's Station.[22] Brown deserved a brief respite, and later in the month traveled to Osawatomie to visit his brother-in-law, the preacher Samuel Adair.

The fruits of a seditious October had been a draft Free State constitution, the unofficial election of Andrew Reeder as Free State representative, and a retaliatory pro-slavery meeting in Leavenworth to organize a "Law and Order" political party. During Brown's visit, a messenger from Lawrence rode by the Adair farm, spreading the alarming news that a pro-slavery Virginian named Frank Coleman had murdered a free-state Ohioan named Charles Dow. Dow's death, however tragic, was not part of the "Bleeding Kansas" struggle over slavery, but rather over a property line quarrel; apparently Coleman was cutting timber on Dow's land.

Dow's friend Jacob Branson called for a protest in Lawrence and was promptly arrested by Sheriff Samuel Jones, a Missouri postmaster, for disturbing the peace. The citizens of Lawrence, armed with New England supplied Sharps rifles, subsequently intercepted the sheriff and relieved him of his prisoner. Outraged, Jones called on the governor and on nearby Missouri for help, informing them that an armed mob was in "open rebellion against the laws of the Territory." The pro-slavery militia was mobilized, and the "ruffians" who had made Atchison their home moved on Lawrence.[23]

Such a small thing to begin a siege, but that is the problem with focusing on battles and the mundane increments that define them. The most proximal cause of the siege was the rumbling under the narrative. The citizens of Lawrence, ordinary settlers, were already protecting their city with the most advanced and deadly handheld weapon available: the Sharps rifle. It was invented seven years prior by Christian Sharps, a former employee of the federal armory at Harpers Ferry, Virginia. It was at least three times more expensive than the previous top-of-the-line firearm. The war was already happening; acknowledging that is merely a matter of narrative and cultural preference about beliefs concerning violent historical change.

As the siege began, Brown learned from another runner that more than two thousand ruffians and militia were massed on the Wakarusa River with intent to burn Lawrence. At Brown's Station he hastily packed rifles, revolvers, knives, swords, and bullets into his wagon. It took him until the evening of December 6 to finally be done running bullets, but he was going not for a fight, but for war, to fight off a Southern onslaught he feared Lawrence was unprepared for. He and sons John, Jr., Owen, Salmon, and Frederick travelled through the night to reach Lawrence.

Their way was blocked, but the Missourians parted for them, either because they didn't really want to start killing anyone—at least not yet—or because the Browns, bristling with weaponry, presented a menacing target.[24]

Brown wheeled his payload of death directly to the fortress-like Free State Hotel, where Charles Robinson and James Lane were directing the defense amid a chaos of earthworks construction, endless soldier drilling, and a general feeling of menace. Brown and his sons entered this scene each fearsomely armed with a "short heavy broadsword ... a goodly number of fire arms, and navy revolvers, and poles ... standing endwise around the wagon ... with fixed bayonets pointing upwards."[25] The menacing Brown was a recognized figure after the December polls, and out of gratitude for his ongoing bellicosity and armament, Robinson appointed Brown a captain in the "First Brigade of Kansas Volunteers" and gave him command of a small group of men known as the "Liberty Guards," which included Brown's sons.[26] But Robinson made certain that Brown knew that peace negotiations with the governor were underway.

Brown, however, was not in peace talks. Nor did he serve Charles Robinson, or the officers of the Volunteers. He urged defenders to defend the earthworks with pitchforks during an attack, and striding about with his ancient-looking broadsword he attempted to rally volunteers for a surprise, middle of the night attempt to break the siege by killing the enemy in their sleep.[27] However, Robinson kept Brown in check, and the increasingly disorderly conduct of the ruffians was enhancing Robinson's bargaining position, since Governor Shannon grew daily more fearful that the "pack of hyenas" he had summoned might do something awful.[28]

On Sunday, December 8, Robinson and Lane publicly announced at the Free State Hotel that a peace treaty had been signed. Brown stepped forward from the wary and murmuring crowd and demanded to know the terms. It was unacceptable if the settlement was a capitulation to the "bogus" government. The crowd, however, had little desire to let Brown appoint himself spokesman; some knew well that he was ready for war, and after assurances from Robinson's representatives that nothing had been yielded to the "bogus" legislature, the citizens of Lawrence dispersed with relief.[29]

By December 12, the few remaining bands of Missourians were dispersed under the terms of the peace. The siege that came to be called the "Wakarusa War" was officially over, after claiming exactly zero casualties, and Brown reflected with grim amusement that it was characterized by "a good deal of trickery on the one side and of cowardice, folly, & drunkenness on the other." Robinson had apparently plied the governor with so much drink that the governor had happily signed another document authorizing Robinson to use force against any subsequent pro-slavery attacks. Lawrence's defenders were proud, as was Brown, who felt that Missourian cowardice had left the "Free Statemen organized & armed; & in full possession of the Territory."[30]

Three days later, the Free State Topeka Constitution was ratified, along with the supplemental "Negro Exclusion Clause." Brown was disturbingly silent about it in his letters to Mary, particularly given past reactions to such injustices. He wrote triumphant accounts of the Wakarusa victory to her, Frederick Douglass, the Akron *Summit Beacon,* the Western Reserve *Chronicle,* and some of his northern backers. In the quest for support, no need to dwell on the manifold shortcomings of the "well behaved, cool, determined men" who had exhibited "the high character of the Revolutionary Fathers."[31] No need to dwell on the fact that Negro exclusion clauses had always existed in the hagiographic shadows of such men. The world as it was understood was built on exclusion.

In the colonies, prior to the Revolution, free blacks had the right to vote. Even in the South, though not the entire South. South Carolina was the first to exclude blacks, along with Jews, in 1716. Then they lost the right to vote in Virginia—the economic heart of the slave trade—in 1723. Georgia, a state which knew only property restrictions until 1761, confined the franchise exclusively to white men in that year. But prior to the Revolution, only those states that eventually became the core of the secession movement barred blacks from civic participation.[32]

After American inception, Maryland disenfranchised black voters in 1783, Delaware followed in 1792, and New Jersey in 1807. New Jersey restored black franchise in 1820, but took it again in 1847. Louisiana took the vote from blacks in 1812, and Connecticut did so in 1814. Mississippi followed in 1817, Alabama in 1819, and Missouri in 1821. New York had previously disenfranchised black voters but allowed them to vote in 1821, provided they satisfied a property qualification that didn't apply to whites. Arkansas joined the list in 1836, and the "reform" convention of Pennsylvania disenfranchised blacks in 1838.[33]

The Western territories of the Louisiana Purchase generally had no color basis for the delineation of political rights. The lines of disenfranchisement were typically drawn along with the lines of states when they were admitted into the Union. Ohio disenfranchised blacks in 1803, Indiana in 1816, Illinois in 1818, Michigan in 1837, Iowa in 1846, Wisconsin in 1848, and Minnesota in 1858.[34]

Black disenfranchisement spread at a rate roughly commensurate with the Industrial Revolution. Those black slaves, cheap labor easily distributed and regulated, harvested the fiber that clothed the heretofore ragged masses of His despised poor. And as economic Revolution expanded, the black slave became indispensible, in effect the cause of dreams of power, and of a whole cultural system and social philosophy in the South in which it was ever easier to prove that black people were born to slavery and could never be free. Disenfranchisement was horridly pragmatic; if blacks could vote, even in the Northern states, what would be the fate of the Union?

Despite Brown's reticence to write about the franchise, and the exclusion clause, the frenetic activity of his pen exceeded in volume anything he had ever recorded in such a short span. His three days in Lawrence under siege both changed him and resonated with his working narrative of social reality, already at odds with a great many of his fellow Americans. His writings about the Wakarusa War were an effort to reconcile two variant narratives. One can be seen in his wry disdain for the almost farcical political solution, but that was Charles Robinson's vision of a struggle that was a relatively logical political and legal problem, with solutions that could be crafted in systems from above. Brown saw it differently, and came to Lawrence with visions of war, and the sights and sounds and smells of a city under siege by thousands of enemies permeated his vision.

The truth about the Wakarusa War would not be determined until time had worked upon those truths, and reflection determined whether the dreams formed there could breathe in the atmosphere to follow. All men dream, but it is a dangerous few who may walk among those phantoms and see them with open eyes, and thereby make them possible, willing them into the light of day.

Prior to leaving for Kansas, Brown had visited his eighty-four year old father. Despite Owen Brown's deteriorating health, he saw as clearly as ever, and his son's journey troubled him. So he wrote to his daughter Florella—Samuel Adair's wife—about his forebodings. "He thinks to start for Kansas next week he has something of a warlike spiret I think as much as necessary for defence I will hope nothing more, I hope God will take you all under his care I wish we might all chearfully resign ourselves and all we have for time and eternity to him." Owen concluded this thought with an oddly prophetic fear. "I have thought for some time that Kansas would be the seat of war but did not think of it falling so heavy as I fear it will on my Family."[35] After the Wakarusa War, Adair may have reflected more seriously on that letter.

A few days after writing it, Owen Brown had bid his son farewell. It was their last meeting in this life.

10

Beyond Good and Evil

Whoever fights monsters should see to it that in the process he does not become a monster. And when you look long into an abyss, the abyss also looks back into you.
—Friedrich Nietzsche, *Beyond Good and Evil*

It was quiet for a time after the Wakarusa War. Creeks frozen solid groaned under thick snow and temperatures plummeted to 29 below zero. The Browns peered out from homes almost buried in drifts at a land transformed. Roads and ravines vanished, gray trees cracked under the weight of ice. Brown wrote to Mary about the numb land and the pain of illness, but mostly he wished to tell her, "I do not forget you, even when I have nothing worth writing." And so the family endured the bruising cold, but had to sell Brown's old faithful horse and creaky wagon in order to afford bare rations of cornmeal cakes and bleached-corn coffee. While buying supplies in Westport, Missouri, a restless Brown prowled about and loudly announced his presence as a Free-State man from Kansas, but was ignored by people more concerned with the jagged winds than with a crank looking for a quarrel.[1]

Brown was so very homesick, and desperate to connect across the vast distances with his wife and children. He implored his family to write with every letter, and on February 1 he wrote Mary that as cheerful as it made him to deliver mail to the others, he was mostly grateful whenever "a letter from *you*" arrived. But silence dominated the territory for six weeks as snow dunes crawled like sand in the Kansas wind, and rivers slithered under a foot of ice, and all the mail was cut off.[2]

Wealthy wrote that it was amazing they even lived through that desolation, since "our men have so much *war* and *elections* to attend to that it seems as though we were a great while getting into a house."[3] Despite the paralyzing winter, there was another election, and the Brown men were there, menacingly armed and prowling for trouble. Either out of fear or apathy or simply because of the terrible ice and cold it was another peaceful vote, in which John, Jr., won a seat in the legislature, while Charles Robinson was elected to the governor's office.

February brought movement with the thaw, and belated news of President Franklin Pierce's January 24 Congressional address on the Kansas troubles. According to Pierce, the villains in Kansas were the northeastern emigrant aid societies, and those agencies were delivering a flood of new free state settlers along with the delayed mail. They would be needed, since the president had also declared the Topeka Constitution to be "revolutionary," and warned free-state Kansans that any further organized resistance would be treated as insurrection. Given the climate, John, Jr.'s words for migrants included a goodly amount of advice on navigation and sustenance and equally practical counsel to "come thoroughly armed with the most efficient weapons they can obtain, and bring plenty of ammunition."[4] Missourians, for their part, watched the wagons rolling in and, knowing what it meant for the October elections, called to the Deep South for aid.[5]

Brown missed North Elba and his family so badly that he "seldom" allowed his "thoughts to dwell on it," but unfortunately he could not go home yet.[6] Pottawatomie's polls may have been quiet, but at Leavenworth fights had erupted; one pro-slavery man lay dead, and each side had suffered two wounded. The pro-slavery press shrieked its outrage, urging readers to "leave not an Abolitionist in the Territory to relate their treacherous and contaminating deeds. Strike your piercing rifle balls and your glittering steel to their black and poisonous hearts."[7] The exhortation was largely superfluous; that day near Leavenworth the local Free-State leader was captured and hacked upon with knives and a hatchet. He was then tossed—still alive—on his porch to die in front of his frantically sobbing wife. The pro-slavery press crowed about the murder, and rumors about a Missouri new offensive in the spring were whispered everywhere.[8]

Executive condemnation and "*new;* & shocking outrages at Leavenworth" had driven free-state men to seek sanctuary in Lawrence, which "is again threatened with an attack." Brown was needed in Kansas. He believed Lawrence would be safe until the land fully thawed, but after that the attack would come, and when it did they would "buckle on our Armor."[9]

The free-state legislature continued to defy the president, and John, Jr., attended to his elected post. He cast the only dissenting vote against a measure introduced by Charles Robinson which attempted assuage Pierce by declaring that no measures passed in Topeka would be actually considered law until Kansas was admitted to the Union as a state. In the meantime, pro-slavery territorial officers

John Brown, by Southworth and Hawes, 1856 (public domain image. Retrieved from Wikimedia Commons).

with the aegis of national authority on their side began circulating copies of the pro-slavery legislation passed the previous year.

In April, rumors blew through the Pottawatomie Creek region about preparations "in the U S Court for numerous arrests of Free State men." Pro-slavery settlers were giddy over the possibility of generally enforced proscriptions, while free-state men anxiously organized an armed self-defense company called the Pottawatomie Rifles. John, Jr., was elected captain, but the ranks did not include his father. Brown was averse as ever to joining movements, and likely too proud to take orders from his son. Nonetheless, he was eager to fight. "I have no desire," he wrote Mary, "to have the Slave Power cease its acts of aggression. Their foot shall slide in due time."[10] He was paraphrasing Deuteronomy 32:35, a prominent verse in Jonathan Edwards's famous "Sinners" sermon.

On April 16, a week prior to opening the court's spring term, free-state leaders met in Osawatomie to debate options if the pro-slavery laws were actually enforced. Most of them were in danger of arrest, and a trial with grim prospects. Martin White, a free-state man of conflicted loyalties who was ostensibly opposed to slavery but equally opposed to the presence of blacks in Kansas, suggested that the best option was peaceful submission to the laws. The meeting erupted in anger over this preposterous and cowardly idea to simply give up and trust in the clemency of the pro-slavery party! Others sided with White, deciding that it was best to protect their own and their land, and abide by the dictates of the Shawnee Mission legislature.

A silence started at the back of the meeting, and spread like a slow wave forward. It walked on the steady thud of the Old Man's boots, and stilled the melee as he faced them to speak. His voice was gravelly, pinched and irritated, his message clear; he was an abolitionist, and would kill any agent of either territorial or national government who attempted to force his compliance. With that, White and the conservative faction of the meeting stormed out, and those who remained passed resolutions putting the pro-slavery legislature on notice.[11]

And so the residents of Pottawatomie waited on edge as Judge Sterling G. Cato opened court at Dutch Henry's Crossing on April 21. The establishment was named "Dutch" for the owners, Henry Sherman and his brother William, who had immigrated from Oldenburg, Germany, in 1844 prior to the Kansas territorial organization. And it sat at a crossing on the California Road, where the brothers had prospered running their supply store and tavern. They staunchly supported slavery, and according to the Shawnee Mission laws, a belief in slavery was the qualifying prerequisite for William Sherman to sit on a jury.

It may seem odd that Europeans with no class interest in slavery should defend it, but had the Shermans remained in Germany, they would have opposed the 1848 movements. Europe, after Napoleon's fall, had entered into a period of relative peace, which was paradoxically incubating military nationalism, a grim denial of the hope of the Romantics couched in their scientific metaphors. The new military class of Europe merged the idea of martial honor with *nations* set apart by breed, a pseudo-scientific boundary derived from the histories of revolution and imposed on the possible scope of national unity. This device became a solvent to the sharp class lines emerging with capitalism and recruited eager supporters to the national cause, admitting them to a form of narrative pseudo-nobility. In the Shermans' Germany, "revolution" was crafted from above by the military staff, and the social reforms of the German state were solely devoted to the ends of military victory. The 1853 book *Inequality of Races* by Comte de Gobineau, a tract which feudalized the Victorian mania for racial typologies, was highly influential and broadly representative.[12]

Gobineau had once written to his mentor, the magisterial Tocqueville—the third great historian of the age—in the hope that the latter would provide valuable advice on the absurd *Races* tract. Tocqueville, whose historical schooling was of a pre-revolutionary nature, observed the world through an older mindset that recognized race as more a social construct than a "natural" certainty. He answered Gobineau that he remained "opposed in extreme to your doctrines" and advised that their correspondence ought to turn to other subjects lest it end entirely.[13]

In the American South, Tocqueville had witnessed appalling behavior by a white girl of six towards two adult black women, despite the girl's obvious "weakness and her age." The episode was illustrative of the "immense gap" artificially created between people by nothing more than simple "prejudice and the laws."[14] He decided to trace the little girl's grossly disproportionate social power to what he was certain were repugnant social norms.

Tocqueville found that in the South "the whole white race formed an aristocratic body having at its head a certain number of privileged persons whose wealth was permanent and leisure hereditary. These leaders of the American nobility perpetuated the traditional prejudices of the white race in the body they represented, making idleness honorable." Yet the "poor men" were the key to this system, bound by identity and a desire to ape the wealthy planters.[15] Those five million poor whites outnumbered the slaves—barely. In the Southern martial state, poor whites served as the constabulary, giving them authority and imagined prestige by association with the masters. And, of course, poor Southern whites did not see themselves as laborers, but aspired above all to own a slave, and become part of the Southern culture of leisure. These poor whites, the armed garrison of the South, held the slave system together by brutally transferring their hatred of the system onto the black slaves.

After 1848 the United States was suffering a veritable epidemic of "filibustering societies" formed by an itinerant Mexican War officer class steeped in national myth and the euphoria of violent expansion, and a desire to mimic Europe's martial nobility. They filled their ranks with glory-seeking poor Southern whites. These groups launched private crusades to topple governments and absorb more people by bullet and the sword into the historic unity and into subjugation. The problem was so widespread that President Millard Fillmore's 1851 address to Congress dealt primarily with their disastrous expeditions to Cuba and the Yucatan Peninsula, and not with the deepening North-South divide.[16]

It was connected though. On November 26, 1855, while Brown had been at Adair's residence prior to the Wakarusa War, a summons was published in the *Eufala Spirit of the South* calling for "reliable men capable of bearing arms" to travel to Kansas. The author, Major Jefferson Buford (then a self-made colonel; nothing appeals so to the military mind like rank), was an Alabama lawyer, slaveholder, and veteran of the 1836 Creek War, which began when Alabama squatters and land speculators were defrauding the natives. The conflict ended when the Army forcibly removed the Creek to Indian Territory.

Buford was highly successful canvassing Alabama for recruits. He promised them a forty acre homestead—thus making them voting residents, among other material dreams—and one year of financial support.[17] A month prior to his February 1856 departure he gave a speech in Montgomery outlining his plans to secure Kansas, and thereby the South, to an enthusiastic crowd. A visitor named William T. Merrifield found it rather alarming, and he rushed home to Massachusetts to inform Eli Thayer of the Emigrant Aid Society. To oppose Alabama, the two arranged to send 165 men armed with Sharps rifles to Lawrence.[18]

James P. Doyle was not a member of a "filibustering society," but promises of mythic identity and race-based superiority had brought him to Kansas with his wife, Mahala, and their four children. He was a poor Tennessee white man who had found it impossible to find work back home, but hoped that in Kansas he could eventually live the dream of Southern white men, to be a master and be financially "independent." That concept was summarized once by an Alabama planter who boasted, "On my own place, I have now slave carpenters, slave blacksmiths, and slave wheelwrights, and thus I am independent of free mechanics."[19]

Doyle and his two oldest sons, William and Drury, had joined the pro-slavery "Law and Order" party.[20] They were, in essence, reverting to cultural form. They too were selected for Cato's court, along with the acting district attorney, another Tennessee migrant named Allen Wilkinson. Wilkinson was John, Jr.'s opposing counterpart on the pro-slavery legislature thanks to 150 Missourian votes.

The Pottawatomie Rifles, along with Salmon Brown, Samuel Adair, and John Brown himself, went to Dutch Henry's for the court's opening. Judge Cato was in mid-sentence pronouncing a charge when John, Jr., walked in and stood in the center of the entryway, facing the judge. But Cato addressed the murmuring and fidgeting jury and perfunctorily stated, "The laws passed at the Shawnee Mission were to be enforced and recognized as the statutes of Kansas." John, Jr., relayed this message to the Rifles, and then reentered the court to deliver a written message. Did Judge Cato mean to enforce the laws? Cato was by this point visibly agitated, and he flung the note across the table, testily stating, "The court cannot permit itself to be disturbed by outside issues." John, Jr., went outside and announced loudly enough for all inside to hear that the Rifles would meet at the parade ground. They departed after Brown and an escort walked inside and delivered the April 16 Free State resolutions.[21]

No one was indicted that day for violating any of the "black laws." The court instead heard only mundane charges, from property crimes to petty violence, though only against free-state settlers. It is beyond believability that slave-state settlers were blameless saints, but the composition of the court is well established. Still, with the Rifles ever present, the minor indictments were not pursued either. The court moved to the next county on April 28, and charged a free-state man named James Townsley for assault with intent to kill.[22] In the meantime people in Pottawatomie were making threats and acting with general hostility. Despite constant threats by the Doyles or the Shermans to burn out their free-state neighbors, John, Jr., seemed to believe that they were mostly talk. The Old Man, however, came to despise and even fear these men.

In fact, early in the spring Brown had surveyed his enemies, along with John, Jr. Masquerading as territorial surveyors, the two had dropped a tripod outside of a Buford camp in the Pottawatomie Creek region, and sighted a line directly through. Brown walked with the chain, calmly through the middle, while his son marked the distances. Thinking the Browns to be a pair of government surveyors (and therefore pro-slavery), the men had been casually open about their intent to "clean out" the territory. The Shermans, the Doyles, and Wilkinson were all identified as their territorial guides.[23]

On the 23rd of April a few people in Lawrence heard a gunshot. Sheriff Jones was injured, but staggered to cover before a lone would-be assassin could kill him in retaliation for arresting six free-state citizens. The noise machine of the pro-slavery press decried the "murder" of Jones in piercing volume for nearly two weeks while demanding abolitionist blood, with tragic effects. Chickens and geese must have been scarce, because for want of feathers two free-state men were tarred and cottoned before the month was out. One of them, the Rev. Pardee Butler, had committed the crime of telling the *Squatter Sovereign* newspaper that he would vote as a Free-Soiler. He was informed that should he return to Atchison, he would be hung.[24] And like the previous fall, Atchison called on Missouri for armed help, and Missouri looked to the Deep South for reinforcements.

The South was answering. The day Sheriff Jones was shot, Buford's army, over 400 strong (he exceeded his symbolic recruiting goal), reached St. Louis where his expedition was hailed as the best friends of Kansas in the entire South. From there they boarded the steamer *Keystone* which conveyed them up the Missouri river to Westport. After equipping themselves for settlement, on May 2 Buford's men scattered to plots across the river in Kansas to settle and wait.

His arrival frightened the free-state men and emboldened Missouri's pro-slavery leaders. "The crisis has arrived," the Lafayette (Missouri) Kansas Emigrant Society wrote in May. "The time has come for action-bold, determined action; words will no longer do any good." They went on to add, "The noble Buford is already endeared to our hearts; we love him; we will fight for him, and die for him and his companions."[25] By May 7, Buford was seeking a central location from where he could maintain communications with his colony spread across the prairie.

The sentiments of men quickened with the summer, and the fight came sooner than perhaps anyone would have imagined. At the beginning of May, a Lecompton judge decided to end the free-state movement and indicted all the members of the Topeka legislature for treason. Then, a federal marshal published false claims that mobs of disorderly Lawrence citizens had violently resisted. He called upon all "law-abiding citizens of the Territory" to gather in Lecompton for a raid on Lawrence. They came from all over, those Missourians, in numbers that were less a posse and more an army, drawn like moths by compulsions that they likely hardly understood themselves. After Buford gathered his army, Governor Shannon, still stinging from his embarrassment the previous autumn, armed and deputized the horde as a territorial militia.

On the morning of the 21st if early risers in Lawrence looked at Hogback Ridge, a high limestone hill, they saw the army's first wave.[26] Buford's men arrived next in mid-morning, bearing military-style banners that read, "The Supremacy of the White Race" and "Alabama for Kansas—North of 36° 30'," as well as "Bibles—not Rifles" in reference to the Sharps rifles—Beecher's bibles—carried by the free-state men.[27]

10. Beyond Good and Evil

That evening in Pottawatomie a cloud of dust up the road resolved into a messenger at full gallop, his horse frothy with sweat. "A proslavery army has concentrated outside of Lawrence," he said breathlessly, "and they have cannon! Send help at once!"[28] By nightfall John, Jr., had sounded the alarm and rallied the Pottawatomie Rifles to nearby Mt. Vernon, where they spent the night preparing for departure. The entire Brown clan was healthy this time, including Jason, a man of monastic tranquility who dreamed of planting orchards and who had never struck anyone in anger in his life. Such was Kansas.

The next morning they might have regretted delaying for the night. Once they were underway, another messenger intercepted them near the Marais des Cygnes creek to inform them that Lawrence's leaders had chosen not to fight and had turned the town over to its enemies, who were pillaging it at that very moment, burning the presses—always the dangerous presses—and also the Free State Hotel which had once served as the resistance headquarters. The Rifles sent another runner to nearby Osawatomie to get more volunteers.

So they waited in the confusion for reinforcements. While they did so, yet another messenger found them and told them that it was over; federal soldiers had taken over the wreckage of the town and the invaders were leaving. The company was in disarray over what to do next, but Brown insisted that they proceed. However, their path was blocked near the Wakarusa River. Pro-slavery forces may have left Lawrence, but they hadn't gone far, hovering in their armed encampment in Lecompton.[29]

The Rifles decided that discretion was the better part of valor, and there was no point in riding outnumbered through a gauntlet into burned Lawrence. They would wait for more reinforcements, maybe not go at all. Brown was furious, but made camp with them. If he went on to Lawrence, his sons might follow him, but without the rest of the Rifles his survival odds were slim. However, he had time to reflect on events after making camp, and as he did so he became "frenzied." That Lawrence was burning was enough to kindle his deep anger, but his rage went beyond that.[30]

He was supposed to have been there as a brave witness, to even die for the cause. Had he been, the cowardice of the free-state leaders would surely not have defined the day. Everyone was waiting, and he hadn't been there. Out of doubt he had seen his dreams and nightmares walk from darkness into the day, and he hadn't been there. An awful, helpless rage consumed him, an agony of regret and volcanic fury, desperately wanting to do something, anything, but separated by the stream of time from any opportunity—the frenzy of a man who had seen everything that was, everything that is, and everything that should be somehow torn away. Whatever his thoughts, Brown was never one to spend too long in helplessness.

Eventually he calmed enough to think. Lawrence was burning, pro-slavery forces prowled the Kansas prairie, the Rifles were in disarray, but the story wasn't finished yet; it had a way it was supposed to go, and he had surveyed his enemies. They were agents of the bogus legislature, representatives of the false Shawnee Mission law. They had threatened his family. They had been there all along, and were known by the slave-power. They had hosted and served on the Cato court. Now, if Lawrence had fallen, almost nothing stood between Brown's family and his enemies among Pottawatomie's pro-slavery settlers. The Old Man's mind now fixed on them with white-hot purpose.

It was time to do something to cause a "restraining fear," though they may burn for it in heaven. Brown called his men around him to describe his new plan, saying, "I mean to steal a march on the slave hounds." Buford's men were camped near Pottawatomie and the time for good intentions was past. This would involve "some killing."[31] The Old Man was coming for his enemies, for their sons. His hair was on fire and his heart was burning.

The next morning Brown's party readied for departure, and while he packed their belongings, his sons had their swords sharpened to a razor's edge. Modeled after the Roman gladius, the blades were forged in 1833 for an Army pretending to historical continuity and glory. Despite their significant heft and fearsome appearance, the "Ames Artillery Side-Arm Sword, Model 1833" was never intended as a true combat weapon.[32] Instead, artillerymen used them to hew down grass and brush in order to better position their guns for battle. But better tools wouldn't have been as symbolic. Form follows function, and these swords had, from their forging, always been more historical than practical.

On his way to Kansas, Brown passed through Akron, Ohio, collecting money and weaponry, where "General" Lucius Bierce gave him six of these blades.[33] Bierce had once been the "Grand Eagle" of the Akron lodge in a defunct secret filibustering society known as the "Hunters," who had lodges strung along the Canadian border. The Hunters were organized to abet an insurrection against the Crown known as the Upper Canada Rebellion, or the Mackenzie "Patriot" War. The rebellion was short lived, but violent resistance lingered through 1838, largely due to the Hunters' influence. On December 4, 1838, Bierce led an invasion of Windsor, but his subsequent crushing defeat precipitated the collapse of the Hunters' organization. Many of Bierce's men never returned from Van Diemen's Land. Brown's swords, surplus from Bierce's foolish venture, had been modified from their original utilitarian design with a golden eagle on the hilt. Those decorated weapons had one more curious role to play.

The Old Man crossed the North Middle Creek around sundown on Friday, May 23, lounging in the back of James Townsley's wagon. His broad-brimmed and battered hat cast his face in shadows, a revolver was tucked into his belt, and a gold-eagle sword was at his side. His companions were Henry Thompson, Owen, Salmon, Oliver, Frederick, a Pottawatomie neighbor named Theodore Weiner, and Townsley, who had the unfortunate distinction of being the only man in camp with a wagon and a team to draw it, and who—like many—could not resist Brown's imperatives. John, Jr., who had vehemently disagreed with this plan, did not ride with them. He had instead gone with the remaining Rifles to attempt a rescue of Charles Robinson, rumored to be a captive in Lawrence. As they approached Pottawatomie, the group paused in a grass-choked ravine near Weiner's store, about 1 mile from the Doyle residence, and waited for dark.[34]

A May night in Kansas smells of vibrant spring and viridian beginnings on moist breezes whispering the memory of tattered storms which exploded far away, remnants drifting silently by and periodically blotting the stars and moon so that light could not see the black desires of men below. Every chill was followed by a cloying blanket of summer's promised warmth, as hot as blood.

They hastened across the California Road, hearts pounding as they sheltered in the tree line by Mosquito Creek, which they waded to a point near the residence of James Doyle. They felt a plucked string's tension in the silence, their ears clanging with the chirping of insects and the clank of their weapons, the sucking of their wet boots on the dirt, and their nervous breath. Brown led them to a house and knocked on the door of their first intended victim.

Hearts racing frantically at the precipice they stood upon, the group scattered like autumn leaves after they heard the metallic scrape of a rifle barrel on masonry from inside. Either by cautious habit or by premonition breathed in the social climate of those violent days, the man inside avoided a violent end. This might have benefited Brown and his men as well. It took some time to regroup and calm down, but after that, the mood had changed. Though the first visitation had ended farcically, a moment had been crossed, and a possible future born of it. What had been inconceivable was suddenly possible. They moved on to James Doyle's cabin. This time, their reaction to an alarming interruption was different. Two bulldogs charged from the cabin, but Frederick and Townsley coolly cut one down while the other fled, howling, into the night. The Old Man calmly knocked on the door.

When a voice inside answered, Brown asked for directions to Wilkinson's home. James Doyle barely cracked the door when Brown abruptly grabbed it and burst through, toppling Doyle over. Once inside, the Old Man faced Doyle and his wife, Mahala, who was clinging to a terrified little girl while screaming at her husband, their three sons, and most of all, Brown. The Old Man ordered Doyle and his sons outside, but decided to spare the youngest, fourteen year old John, after a tearful Mahala begged for the boy's life. He was only a child.

The memories of all involved have been conflicted, distorted by guilt and trauma and the bloody rush of more primal feelings. The bodies told stories, now as they did then, when they were a message of fear. Doyle's had a bullet in the head from the Old Man's revolver. He and William were lying together in the road, arms, torsos, and heads savagely hacked. Drury was found cut down in the grass by a ravine; he had attempted to flee.

Next, the Old Man repeated the scene at Wilkinson's place, knocking on the door and asking the way to Dutch Henry's Crossing. When Wilkinson attempted to relay the information without opening the door, Brown's party pressed further. "Come out and show us," they sneeringly insisted. Wilkinson stalled, but they finally ordered him to open the door or else they would break it down. Once it was opened, Brown rushed through and seized Wilkinson, his gun, and his powder. His wife, bedridden with measles, begged the tall, terrible visitor in his broad hat to spare her husband. "You have neighbors?" Brown curtly asked her. She answered that she did, but they were not at home. "It matters not," he replied, distantly sad as he walked Wilkinson into the Kansas night. Wilkinson's body was found in the brush roughly 150 yards away, head and side slashed, throat slit.

From there they moved to the home of James Harris, one of Dutch Henry's employees and a juror on the Cato court. Harris had visitors: a traveler named Jerome Glanville, and another man named John Wightman who had purchased a cow from the Shermans. William Sherman was present, but brother Henry was missing. The Browns interrogated the guests one at a time regarding their involvement with the burning of Lawrence, or any other violent support to the pro-slavery cause. Glanville and Wightman were released shortly. Harris was also released after informing the Browns that Henry Sherman was out attempting to locate lost cattle. But William Sherman was taken to Pottawatomie Creek, and was found there the following morning with his head split open and his left hand cut off, blood trickling into the stream, tiny cells carried in capillaries to join the mighty river and eventually, invisibly diffuse, past the hot New Orleans delta into the beating heart of the sea.

Dutch Henry would have been their sixth victim, but daybreak was coming, and they needed to ride fast for home, so they washed the blood from their blades in the Pottawatomie and rode away. As the horizon off their right side was pierced with the first clean rays of dawn, a shaken Owen whispered quietly to Townsley, "There shall be no more work such as that."[35] The Old Man rode in silence, his shadow at morning striding behind him, and beyond it the screams and wails of widows and mothers. And the flowers for their funerals bloomed from the dead land, no longer warm under a blanket of snow, but stirred by rain into the dawn.

The story that the bodies told was confused. At the most basic level, they were killed by men using fairly crude and heavy weapons, and such a death does not leave a beautiful corpse when all is done, particularly when the killers are woefully inexperienced. Their condition also suggested that the slain were attempting to ward off the blows at the end, which means that their hands and arms had not been bound as in a formal execution, and those heavy blades in clumsy hands fell upon the victims' arms—repeatedly—before striking vital parts. They may also have been cut like so much prairie grass after the killing blow; it was clearly not a business-like dismemberment, but quick, furious butchery. The elder Doyle had a bullet in the head from the Old Man's gun, which according to Salmon—one of the only eyewitnesses—was inexplicably put there nearly 30 minutes after his death. Mahala Doyle claimed in her affidavit later to have heard two shots.[36]

There is perhaps no act more terrible, and certainly none more final, than taking a person's life. But history is too often merely a chronicle of men ending the lives of others, and to historians has fallen the curious task of making those deaths mean something. It would be pleasing to be able to say that John Brown has suffered unique condemnation because he killed people, but people have demonstrated that they are willing to accept and even celebrate killing for the most absurd reasons imaginable.

The significance of these killings, in an historical sense, beyond the immediate atrocity and the lasting condemnation, puzzles. Just prior to the Age of Revolution, the conceptual ordering of time and cause in historical narrative had been fundamentally altered to exhibit a characteristic of linear mechanics known as "returns to scale." The historians and philosophers of the West have been pursuing "natural law" and its underlying principle—causality—ever since. But, natural laws are merely statistical truths. Natural laws, cause and effect, turn out to be only statistically valid and merely relatively true, and small quantities tend to not behave in accordance with them.

It was only five men, weighed against the six on the free-state side that had been killed so far, and certainly Brown's killings weren't the only grisly deaths.[37] When simply weighing statistics, it's unclear why these deaths should have changed anything. This is not to mitigate the deaths by equivocation; that would be as dubious as choosing them for singular condemnation. This is an ethical problem, but one that goes far beyond the fundamental evil of killing. The quest for statistical truth in human narrative had been no less than the quest to craft surety, which by extension tilts the mind towards the future. But if statistical truth can be fundamentally altered by single acts such as John Brown's at Pottawatomie, then social order loses its integrity for a people whose minds depend upon mimicry and a social construct of reality. One man cannot transvaluate morals and have it mean anything, can he?

The Old Man was damned no matter what he did at that point though. The smoke rising from Lawrence and the inevitable march of slavery and predation that it signaled also signified the end of his dreams. He could be damned to live with inaction, or damned by the actions he took, and a man can only act according to his will; there is no choice in this. The only solution was as clear as day to John Brown; he must stand and fight. The grass on the prairie was cut and bloody under those quaint artillery blades, it fell so easy, and the way was now made for the guns to roll into position.

Despite what this act made of John Brown, nothing suggests that he ever found a way to live with that night. It was something he kept close to himself, a devil on his back to add to his fatal gravity. His father would never know how right his letter to Florella had been; Squire Owen had died back on May 8, wondering about his son's fate in Kansas. And from that moment forward, it mattered little what life John Brown intended to live, or what his dreams were for his final years, because now he was something much more, and something far less. Everything changed after Pottawatomie. Everything came to weeping.

11

Skirmishes of an Untimely Man

> *What if you shall come to discern that the play and playground of all this pompous history are radiations from yourself, and that the sun borrows his beams? What terrible questions we are learning to ask! The former men believed in magic, by which temples, cities, and men were swallowed up, and all trace of them gone. We are coming on the secret of a magic which sweeps out of men's minds all vestige of theism and beliefs which they and their fathers held and were framed upon.*
> —Ralph Waldo Emerson, *Illusions*

Nothing was ever the same for the Browns. The fear that gripped the region and the rumors of the five mangled bodies reached John, Jr., Jason, and the Rifles on the lips of a messenger, who told them most ominously that the survivors claimed, "old John Brown did it."[1]

The Rifles spurred their horses towards home in alarm, fearing reprisals, and cursed the Old Man over the thunder of hooves. John, Jr.'s grip on his command was already shaky after an incident the day before, when he had attempted to lead the Rifles in the liberation of some slaves. His men had balked, most of them agreeing that freeing black slaves was not their goal. Still fragile from that challenge to his leadership, John, Jr., struggled to cope with becoming the focus of the Rifles' hostility because of his father's deeds. As the day went by he faded from satisfaction at the "good news" into emotional incoherence. But gentle Jason took the news the hardest, stating that "the thought that it might be true, that my father and his company could do such a thing" was the most terrible shock of his life.[2]

That night the Old Man himself came to the Rifles' camp, seeking his sons. He was evasive in the face of angry inquiries about the killings. John, Jr., however, recognized the horses that the Old Man brought to their camp, horses that were known to belong to the slain, and he resigned his command and retreated into emotional turmoil. They left the next day in silence, just the Old Man with his family and personally loyal company. Eventually it was Jason who confronted their father, troubling the quiet morning with angry questions. "I did not do it," Brown replied, "but I approved of it."[3] His peaceful son condemned the act as a wicked thing, at which a stung Brown hissed back: "God is my judge ... we were justified under the circumstances."

From there the family split. Owen, Oliver and Frederick, as was always their fate, followed their father. John, Jr., and Jason sought shelter in Osawatomie, where they found their families safe at the Adair home. However, after only a couple of days Jason set out alone to find federal troops so he could surrender, declare his innocence, and request protection. John, Jr., fell apart when he realized all of his friends had abandoned him, from the Rifles to his political allies. Even Samuel Adair was hostile. A delicate ego, John, Jr., became "crazed ... deranged," and retreated into isolation in the nearby trees to live like an animal. Both he and Jason were captured by an alliance of pro-slavery militia, U.S. soldiers from Leavenworth, and Missouri ruffians in the subsequent manhunt for the Brown family.

Nothing was ever the same for the free-state men. Though they had cast out John, Jr., and swiftly drafted a resolution condemning the murders and pledging support for the pro-slavery men, this was little more than a fearful reflex. The deeply divided representatives achieved a unanimous vote only by not specifically naming Brown, though they all knew who was responsible. Some viewed the killing as unforgiveable, inexcusable, and some were starting to see it as a necessary evil. As James Hanway reflected in his journal on the blame that was due the pro-slavery party, "They advocate assassination and now that 5 persons have been murdered on their side perhaps they will learn that such hellish sentiments when carried into effect, will work equally to the destruction of pro-slavery men."[4]

Nothing was ever the same for the pro-slavery men. The content of their press did not seem greatly altered, but ecstatic new highs of outrage and cries for war were reached, while slyly forgetting any of their partisans' crimes. This was the expression of a fearful culture made of bellicose imagery and chivalrous myths, but in which the narrative was but a means to try to keep the fear at bay. And Brown, a hunted man, took to the Kansas wilderness and became a ghost, became fear itself. As the pro-slavery faction lashed out in desperation, the free-state men came to see that they had to fight. The Old Man's voice echoed in the violence, though they tried to shut out the creeping awfulness that a ghost should be so practical.

John, Jr., and Jason were being held in Paola by Buford's men, who intended to kill the brothers, when a terrified messenger delivered a scrap of paper inscribed with a terse message: "I am aware that you hold my two sons, John and Jason, prisoners.— John Brown." No demands, no threats, just that, and the messenger's that he had been informed that his life depended on the successful delivery of that parchment. The note was a whisper of the "omnipresent dread" that Brown had become, and may have saved his sons' lives. That night, a pair of would-be assassins ran in terror when a dog outside started barking. The next morning John, Jr., and Jason were taken on a forced march to Osawatomie.[5]

Nothing was ever the same for John Brown, but his damnation lay in the fact that he upset the established order. People don't fear when events happen according to their preconceptions, no matter how horrifying those preconceptions may be. Free-state men had been dying for some time in varied ways, and all sides accepted that as the nature of the conflict. The Pottawatomie assault seemingly forced people to re-evaluate the situation and choose a side, and the men who rushed to Kansas with their Sharps rifles found the territory in the midst of a war inaugurated by John Brown. Afterwards, armed bands roamed the Kansas prairie, shooting and looting in a guerrilla campaign for the future of the state.

The thread of John Brown's narrative ran out into the plains and that tangled skein. He wandered the aftermath, searching for direction, attracting an increasingly diverse set of followers, men subtly different from the majority of free-staters in the territory. They gravitated to this supposedly inflexible and dogmatic Calvinist. But men change as time works upon them, and Brown wasn't the same as when he was younger and the world seemingly simpler.

He travelled with men like Theodore Weiner, a Polish Jew and Pottawatomie shopkeeper, a wheezing rotund man ill-suited for adventure who nonetheless had remained with the Old Man since that terrible night, their fates woven together. Weiner's business partner, August Bondi, also joined Brown. The struggle was upon them, and Bondi wanted to fight.

Bondi was an Austrian Jew who had been a member of the Academic Student Legion during Europe's 1848 revolutions. As those movements were individually crushed, Bondi's family was forced to flee Vienna for New Orleans, where he first saw the slave trade. They moved up the Mississippi river to St. Louis, and he tried his hand at a variety of trades, including working on a small freighter travelling up and down the Mississippi and around the Gulf of Mexico coast. In December of 1850, he made port in Galveston, Texas, where "the howlings of the slaves receiving their morning ration of cowhiding waked me at 4 o'clock a.m."[6] Too many experiences like that in Texas drove him back to St. Louis, and in 1854 he, like Brown's sons, read an article urging freedom loving men "to hurry out to Kansas to help save the state from the curse of slavery."[7] Doubly threatened as both a Jew and a free-state man, Bondi saw in Brown a chance to be faithful to the principles of the 1848 revolutions.

Another member of the 1848 European diaspora, a Hungarian named Charles Kaiser, joined Camp Brown on Ottawa Creek. Kaiser met Brown during the Wakarusa War, and after Pottawatomie decided that if war was coming to Kansas, he would travel with the Old Man. His face was a craggy map of sorrows, scarred by sword cuts suffered while fighting in Hungary's failed revolution. But his smile and inner joy shone easily through his pain-filled past, and his jokes brought a camp of men living on creek water and old bread to tear-filled mirth. The Old Man never laughed anymore though.[8]

There were men like John Cook, born in Connecticut in 1830. A garrulous and handsome son of privilege, he had studied law for a time in New York before determining to fight slavery

Aaron D. "Captain Whipple" Stevens (Library of Congress).

in Kansas. When Lawrence burned, and the pro-slavery army had been on the march, he was among the first to join the fight. Now he brought his deadly aim to Brown's camp, awaiting another opportunity.[9]

The Old Man's new followers did not share his faith, but his faith no longer required them to. They would all fight soon enough.

Initially Brown had taken to the countryside as a matter of practical self-preservation; the Missourians were hunting him after Pottawatomie, and there was no shelter with free-state men. Brown became a fighter after free-state men found him and asked him to fight back against a general campaign of retaliation.

Still, he was lost, his family split, and slavery supporters and some free-staters hunted him. Musing on the path ahead, he proposed one evening to his men that "if the cowardice and indifference of the free-state people compel us to leave Kansas, what do you say, men, if we start South, for instance to Louisiana, and get up a negro insurrection, and thereby compel them to let go their grip on Kansas?"[10] It was the first time he had mentioned anything like this to anyone outside of his immediate family, save Frederick Douglass. His followers demurred, swayed by Bondi's wise and worldly counsel, and a restless Brown contented himself to wait for developments at the end of the planting season.

The best illustration, though, of Brown's lost place in history happened after May 30. An enterprising and brave writer for the northeast papers named James Redpath had decided to wander about the Pottawatomie region to find the man behind the stories crackling from territory to coast and back. Lost by Ottawa Creek, he had a chance encounter with a wild looking man, his beard and hair unkempt, wearing red-topped boots and armed with six revolvers and a vicious knife. "Hullo," this figure said simply, standing there with a water bucket, "you're in our camp!" He smiled a wide and simple grin.

Frightened, Redpath drew his gun, but the strange disheveled figure cheerfully announced, "I think I know you!" and introduced himself as Frederick Brown. He offered to lead Redpath to his father's camp, and the entire way rattled on like a "maniac," denying the Pottawatomie murders. Redpath could not have known what a terrible trauma that night had been for Frederick, and it was even possible that Frederick believed his own words.

Redpath believed. He found Brown in person as impressive as the Old Man from Wakarusa War stories, though "he was poorly clad, and his toes protruded from his boots." Brown "respectfully but firmly forbade conversation on the Pottawatomie affair," so Redpath was only too happy to fill the silence with the story he wished. He was writing historically already, canonizing Brown as "the pre-destined leader of the second and the holier American Revolution."[11] But Brown never explicitly claimed to be innocent; Redpath needed him to be, because for his history to be comprehensible, deeds like Brown's at Pottawatomie should have never happened, and ought never happen again, and if he suggested the "the Old Hero" had taken the only action that could have started the conflict, then the ethical sureties of past and future seemed suddenly as fragile as paper.

And maybe, deep down inside a place where they never looked, those free-staters had wanted Brown to do something terrible. The truth that he had acted on was merely oracular in nature; as it turned out, Lawrence was not burned down. Only the Free State Hotel and Robinson's house had suffered that fate, and the presses were wrecked. Buford had actually acted to stop the Missourians from causing wider destruction.[12] But a messenger—the plains seemed to be filled with these omnipresent men—happened to bring his news to a man that everyone knew had a wagon of weapons and was looking for war. Lawrence was teeming with Sharps rifles, the Free State Hotel was a fortress; they all knew how they wanted it to end. But neither they, nor Redpath—Brown's first chronicler—could have accepted the Brown who killed at Pottawatomie any easier than eastern abolitionists could. There would be no parades for his bloody act, nor should there be. This story is a tragedy.

As the conflict escalated, Brown stubbornly and characteristically refused to coordinate his efforts with the other free-state militias. He was visited twice in May by Captain Samuel T. Shore, leader of a band of about 15 fighters. Shore had news of an invading Missourian group near Black Jack Springs, and to secure Brown's cooperation he appealed to the Old Man's pride, making an offer of alliance and humble request for aid. Would Brown join Shore's Prairie City volunteers, and aid them? Of course he would help, and the two rode out together on the 1st of June.

Upon arriving in Prairie City, the free-state militia captured a pair of Missourians wandering into town from their camp at Black Jack. The two captives served under Henry Clay Pate, a Missourian who led a militia into Kansas after the Pottawatomie killings. It was a fortunate find for the Old Man, since Pate had custody of John, Jr., and Jason, and was scouring the area for the rest of the "damn Browns." The Old Man decided to help Pate in this endeavor, but not until nightfall, after which he and his company would steal out to Pate's camp to surprise them at dawn.[13]

Brown and Shore arrived near Black Jack just prior to sunrise. Leaving Frederick in the trees to mind the horses, the men crept towards Pate's camp, but were spied by sentries. Staccato gunfire tore the morning as Brown and Shore led their men forward at a run to firing positions. It was a pandemonium of men deserting whenever the gunfire paused. Brown, followed by Weiner and Bondi, crawled low, hiding in last year's tall dead grass while exhorting the volunteers to continue the fight. Weiner, 57 years old and 250 pounds heavy, was struggling, huffing and puffing as bullets whistled above them. "Nu, was meinen Sie jetzt?" Bondi called to him. "Was soll ich meinen?" Weiner answered amiably. "Sof odom moves."[14]

The fight looked lost until a most remarkable event. Frederick, on a horse, galloped into the fray, waving one of the heavy Pottawatomie swords above his head, yelling "Father, we have them surrounded and have cut off their communications!" before disappearing back into the trees. It was inscrutable, perhaps a clever ploy, but likely the result of tremendous confusion. Poor Frederick, prone to mental troubles, had dealt poorly with the world in the days since Pottawatomie. In the confusion and din of gunfire he may have believed, or even hoped, that it was true. But the boy's charge was so dramatic, and so convincing, that Pate believed it; he actually thought he saw reinforcements just behind, and surrendered in order to buy time.[15]

Pate dispatched a white flag to Brown, and the Old Man quickly transitioned from near defeat to command of the situation. He sent the messenger back and demanded Captain Pate himself, who came and began to explain his official duties to Brown.

Pate was working under the delusion that he was in control. Coldly interrupting him, Brown said, "I understand exactly what you are, and do not wish to hear any more about it." Brown demanded complete surrender on the spot, but Pate asked for fifteen minutes—hoping that would be enough time for his own reinforcements to arrive— but Brown simply pointed his revolver at Pate, drew back the hammer, and stated "you are my prisoner." With that, the Old Man marched Pate back to his own men, with a gun held to his back, to order them to lay down their weapons. Pate again attempted to stall, but Brown put the gun to the side of his head and gave him exactly two minutes.[16]

Shore had also left for reinforcements when the battle seemed lost, and he returned with J.B. Abbott's Lawrence volunteers to find Brown and his small company inconceivably in possession of twenty-five prisoners, not to mention the horses and arms. Brown later wrote a summary account of the fight's volunteers and wounded for the committee in Lawrence. He listed Shore first, but omitted his own name save as the signatory on the report.[17]

Upon returning to Ottawa Creek, Brown drafted a proposal to the authorities for a prisoner exchange, specifically Pate and his lieutenant for John, Jr., and Jason.[18] The trade never happened though. Three days later 50 U.S. cavalrymen based in Fort Leavenworth under the command of Colonel Edwin Sumner converged on Camp Brown. The Old Man had little choice but to surrender his prisoners, protesting all the while about exchange terms. Brown viewed the event as proof of the "cruel & unjust course of the administration & its tools throughout this whole Kansas difficulty," but Sumner, enigmatically, did not arrest Brown.[19] Sumner had been directed to disperse *all* the combatants, and Brown was widely recognized with a uniquely famous warrant on his head, which Sumner must have known about.

The Old Man subsequently decided it was time to break camp and separate. Henry Thompson, nursing a gunshot wound from Black Jack, was sent to recuperate with cousins. Salmon joined him, having accidentally shot himself while packing up. Bondi was given a special mission; he was to go to Osawatomie to find word of Brown's family. Two days later, Bondi returned to report that John, Jr., and Jason were being held "in Irons" at a U.S. cavalry camp, while the women were safe with a neighbor. From there, Bondi set out for Fort Leavenworth while the Old Man, Owen, and Frederick retreated into the wilderness to live "like David of old … dwelling with the serpants of the Rock, & wild beasts of the wilderness."[20]

By July of 1857 Lawrence militias were making regular and coordinated raids against the slave-power redoubts in Franklin, Atchison, and Lecompton which surrounded them. Charles Robinson was a political prisoner, and James Lane, who had been at Robinson's side during the Wakarusa War, was stumping for support in the east. Prominent abolitionists like Samuel Cabot and Amos A. Lawrence responded with thousands of dollars in weapons and equipment.

Brown was frequently on the move for most of June, only peripherally connected to events. He eventually wrote Mary a detailed letter about the burning of Lawrence, the capture of Jason and John, Jr., and an exhilarated account of Black Jack. He was, however, coy about the terrible event that had led to the capture of his two sons, merely noting he had been "accused of murdering five men at Pottawatomie." He assured her that he and his sons were "not disheartened" despite primitive living conditions and being "nearly destitute of food, Clothing, & money." And his faith in the "God who had not given us over to the will of our enemies but has moreover delivered them into our hands" was steadfast. His request to Mary was that somehow his account of events in Kansas reached Gerrit Smith.[21]

On July 1, Brown re-entered the public eye, riding into Lawrence on the way to aid the free-state legislature assembly in Topeka on the 4th. It was widespread knowledge that President Franklin Pierce had no intention of letting this happen, and was dispatching Sumner and the federal soldiers to break up the meeting. The Old Man was ready.

But first, he needed to write to the newspapers. In the month since Black Jack, events had taken on unforeseen meaning within the broader struggle, and Pate, covering his ignoble defeat, had already provided his version to St. Louis and New York newspapers anxious for Kansas stories. So on the 2nd Brown called upon William A. Phillips, a journalist for the New York *Tribune*, which had carried Pate's story and would later print Brown's as well. Phillips had intended to leave that day for Topeka to report on events, but Brown suggested that he wait and travel by night with him. It was an opportunity that Phillips could not refuse.

Phillips had only briefly met Brown before. He had found the Old Man to be "always an enigma, a strange compound of enthusiasm and cold, methodic stolidity,—a volcano beneath a mountain of snow."[22] Now was his chance to find out who John Brown was, underneath the events and the necessities.

As the sun fell, Brown took Phillips to the top of Mt. Oread and looked down at Lawrence, and the land all about. The Kaw River sparkled in the setting sun through the trees tracing the web of creeks and rivulets that fed into it, becoming a dense sylvan grove where it met the Wakarusa. In between were broad pale grassy fields, dotted with woods and mounds. "What a magnificent scene," Phillips exclaimed to Brown.

"Yes," the Old Man replied, in his quiet and steady manner, "a great country for a free State." All the while, his men had been making a line towards them, riding by twos. There were no words passed. Brown merely fell into place at the head of the column, and gave the signal to ride forward on the California Road towards Topeka as molten dusk fell.

Later, after a dinner Phillips could barely eat of dried beef and corn balls cooked in the fire's ashes, the two spoke on the dewy grass under the mightily wheeling sky, which dominates everything under those open dark spaces. It surprised Phillips that in those quiet moments, the "rigid, stern, and unimpressible" Brown revealed a "poetic and impulsive nature" underneath. Brown did most of their talking, pointing at the stars and speaking about the constellations, and their movements, and marking the hours by their choreography.

It was in those kinds of moments that Brown heard God's whisper. "How admirable is the symmetry of the heavens," he said, "how grand and beautiful. Everything moves in sublime harmony in the government of God." Then a shadow crossed his eyes, obscuring the reflected light. "Not so with us poor creatures," he rumbled. "If one star is more brilliant than others, it is continually shooting in some erratic way into space." He went on to impugn the methods of oppression, the parceling of land, the current political order. His musings on the heavens were more than mere poetry.

The American founders named their insurrection after the preceding Glorious Revolution, which had adopted the term from Copernicus into the political lexicon when King James II of England was overthrown by a group of Parliamentarians, who installed William and Mary of Orange on the throne. Jefferson's Declaration of Independence did not spring fully formed from his brow like Athena but rather from the 1689 Declaration of Rights, which checked absolutism by uniting astronomy with political theory. Not coincidentally, the first public reading of the U.S. Constitution was not on a battlefield, or at a seat of government—it was at an observatory.[23]

Any form of social realism must be justified both epistemologically and ethically.[24] But it is not a balanced dialectic. Even people who believe in free will are willing to countenance nearly any ethical horror in the name of narrative fate, a belief in cause and effect that excuses them from overcoming narrative assumptions. For centuries the Catholic Church was the dominant storyteller, and the source of its power was in convincing people to die and kill in the name of the past the church owned, the future it wrote from that, and the supposed will of God as narrative voice and first cause.

Just prior to the age, Europeans embroiled in the church's latest ethical shortcoming—the Thirty Years' War—were starting to question their social realism. It remains one of the most destructive conflicts, in terms of per-capita deaths and overall duration, to ever have been waged in Europe. But what finally exposed the ridiculous nature of the dominant order was the Scientific Revolution, named retroactively for the book that held its inception: Copernicus's *On the Revolutions of the Celestial Spheres*. The church's favored Ptolemaic universe had endured for centuries with the aid of complex corrections, each patching up the theory's increasingly doubtful predictive utility. Copernicus eliminated the need for further corrections by casually moving the sun to the center of the earth's immediate neighborhood. With that, the church's claims to epistemological truth fractured, a problem exacerbated when Catholic priests lied about the demonstrable proof in Galileo's telescope, and replaced epistemological surety with power and silence.[25]

The efforts to patch up the social model multiplied in intensity and absurdity, and the secular princes of Europe realized that the blood, treasure, and deaths were not part of a destined story, but a long-dead narrative will to power. They called a conference, and in October 1648 social order was removed from God's keeping for reasons of exceedingly poor stewardship and given instead to a new system of states, vouchsafed by a mechanically modeled balance of sovereignty.[26] It was the founding of the modern world order and the source of the most dominant narrative metaphors.

They replaced divine fate with the physics of the gracefully wheeling heavens, drawing from them the new linguistic tools for understanding time and cause in the creation of history. Cosmology, along with the new mechanical clocks, formed the basis of Thomas Hobbes' metaphor of man as clock as Leviathan in a harmoniously linked society.

Eighteenth century thinkers wrote cosmologically derived narratives about the epistemology of power and the unfolding of history because very few people can transvaluate narrative and authority to live courageously as more than an automaton. Prior to the Scientific Revolution, the script that people acted out was the Heavenly City, but it was losing legitimacy, built from discomfiting words like "sin" and "salvation." So it was rebuilt in narrative with words like "future state," or by the felicitous translation of "grace" into a "virtue" with historical implications of meaning.[27] Once that ethical migration was complete, "god" could be made incarnate in "natural law" as described by David Hume, who knew better than anyone that it was an illusion.

As Cleanthes described the world in Hume's *Dialogues Concerning Natural Religion*:

> You will find it to be nothing but one great machine, subdivided into an infinite number of lesser machines.... All these various machines, and even their most minute parts, are adjusted to each other with an accuracy, which ravishes into admiration all men, who have ever contemplated them. The curious adapting of means to ends, throughout all nature, resembles exactly, though it much exceeds, the productions of human ... intelligence. Since therefore the effects resemble each other, we are led to infer ... that the causes also resemble; and that the Author of Nature is somewhat similar to the mind of man; though possessed of much larger faculties, proportioned to the grandeur of the work, which he has executed.[28]

Nature was once assumed rational because God was eternal reason. Now God was an engineer because nature is a machine.[29] From this ephemeris was charted varied systems of liberation and systems of oppression, crafted by men who claimed scientific fact similar to the Author of Nature. But their factual world was only a translation of miraculous beliefs, and they rivaled the deposed theologies in conjuring horrors. The line of division between the powerful and the weak was imagined in the space between where man, and man alone, controlled his daily life, yet was subject to ineluctable laws.

But no longer in John Brown's world. Despite his stern religious outlook, rigidly narrow schematization had once been alien to Christian reality, at least before the church became not only the steward of social order but also of its own dogmatic power. This is not a simple contradiction regarding Brown's supposedly antiquated religious beliefs pitted against the new "secular" order and some of its attendant ills, but about the comprehension of the representation of reality. Must people follow psychologically crude and rigidly schematized laws?

Despite the benefits to humanity, Brown believed something had been lost when society had been reorganized to believe in rational progress. Society needed to be re-imagined on a less selfish basis; this was the nature of all great reforms. Perhaps this was the revelation that Phillips sought when he followed Brown into the Kansas night. Or perhaps he wanted to document a revolution. And maybe the Old Man just wanted Phillips to tell him what he wanted him to say. He knew that Phillips believed in the order of things, as he once had, and that Phillips would turn away from Brown's darkest deeds. For such poor creatures, Revolution is a social platitude. There is only resolution, awful resolution, in blood.

For some reason, Brown camped outside of Topeka with his men but did not interfere with Colonel Sumner. He later returned to camp to care for Owen, who was terribly ill. The rest of his men were suffering from wounds, sickness, and poor nutrition, and were ready to simply go home. Brown decided the time was right to end his Kansas journey. Where his vision led is impossible to say with certainty, but wherever it was, John, Jr., knew. He replied to his father from prison that he was "very glad that you have started ... as all things considered I am convinced you can be of more use where you contemplate going than here."[30] Later that July, Brown loaded his sick and wounded into a wagon and left for Nebraska. Jason alone remained to dream of orchards on the land where his son lay buried.

When Samuel Reader and a group of free-state partisans happened upon Brown's party riding north, they didn't recognize the shabby and ill group. They spoke for a while, but Reader was skeptical of shooting tips from such a bedraggled man. Brown merely replied in his measured way: "Maybe you think me a little free in offering advice, but I am somewhat older than you, and that ought to be taken in account." Frederick simply stared at Reader with a broad and vacant grin.[31] Upon returning to his own camp, Reader was informed that he had just met the famous John Brown.

The next day Reader and his companions overtook Brown's slowly moving wagon— "There he is!"—they called in excitement, with great cheering. Brown did not react, and only occasionally looked about.[32] He was escorted all the way to Nebraska City by Captain Samuel Walker, who invited him to a meeting with James Lane, and a man going by the name of "Captain Whipple."

Whipple's real name was Aaron D. Stevens. He was a phenomenal physical specimen: tall, muscular, and darkly handsome. In early 1856 he escaped from Fort Leavenworth's prison, where he had been sentenced for nearly killing an officer while fighting in the Mexican War. The officer had been an abusive martinet, and his conduct finally caused the temperamental Stevens to draw a pistol on him. After escaping, Stevens hid among the Delaware, then assumed the name "Whipple" and became a free-state fighter. He was a deadly swordsman with a lovely baritone singing voice, and was a spiritualist agnostic who had turned from Christianity because it "never looked consistent" to him.[33] Now, having joined James Lane, he led a group of free-state partisans.

Lane and Whipple discussed their plans to reinforce Lawrence, which apparently changed Brown's mind about leaving Kansas right away. He sent his war-weary sons to Iowa, where Owen stayed to recover while the rest continued east. The Old Man turned back to Kansas, faithful Frederick at his side, with Whipple's group. Whipple was under orders by the Emigrant Aid Societies to not cross the border displaying arms and otherwise agitating for combat, but the obdurate Whipple wished to be provocative.

Near the Kansas border Whipple was in a heated argument with his superior regarding their instructions from Boston. As the confrontation escalated, an irritated Brown fixed Whipple with his level gaze. "Do as they wish," he said icily. "This train is to enter Kansas as a peaceable emigrant train.... Let us all stay together. Your services may be needed."[34]

Whipple jabbed his sword at the dirt and scowled like a sullen school-boy.

"Perhaps," rumbled Brown, "you don't know me; you don't know who I am?"

"Yes I do," Whipple replied, "I know who you are, well enough; but all the same, we are not going to part with our arms. We came armed, and we're going back armed."

Brown whirled his horse in anger and rode away. Whipple's lieutenant, a man named John Kagi, watched the mysterious stranger with admiration.

Brown went to Topeka alone while Whipple and Lane made good on their own plans, launching raids from Lawrence against the surrounding pro-slavery camps. Lane's proposal to help free both John, Jr., and Charles Robinson, residing as prisoners together in Lecompton, probably persuaded the Old Man to return. Lane likely had the manpower to make a good attempt of it, and Brown wrote Jason that "God still lives; & blessed be his great & holy name. The boys may go on farther East; & may hold on for me to join them."[35]

But John, Jr., advised strongly against any rash moves. It was probable that he would either be acquitted locally or sent to the United States for a likely acquittal. With no rescue in the works, Brown waited for, John, Jr.'s predicted release; apparently he had now decided he would not leave the territory without his oldest son. And so he had nothing to do but raise another armed company and join the fight. By late August he was on his way to meet up with Lawrence forces in Osawatomie, riding through the Kansas wastelands with his new "Kansas Regulars," passing burned homes and abandoned settlements.

Over the next week, Lawrence companies raided the region. Brown's "Regulars" were returning to Osawatomie one day with a lucrative haul of 150 cattle taken from pro-slavery Sugar Creek settlements when a resident "playfully asked" Brown "where he got those cattle." Brown shook his head with a grin, and replied that "they were good Free-State cattle now."[36] Despite his own poverty and the privations suffered by his family back home, he made no profit from the eventual sale of the livestock. He gave Mary only sympathy for her sufferings, and continued to live in dire need while the cattle sale supported the free-state cause.

Around that time he received a letter from Ruth, and a glimpse into the narrative significance of events he had played a role in. Ruth mentioned Brown's previous correspondence about Pottawatomie (indirectly) and Black Jack, remarking wryly that he "must have had very exciting times," but she had also read about Brown in the New York *Weekly Times*, which had even reported his death at one point. Ruth was very concerned about John, Jr.'s imprisonment, stories of which had galvanized the abolitionist community. Gerrit Smith himself "had his name put down for ten thousand dollars towards starting a company of one thousand men to Kansas."[37]

The Old Man did not have a lot of time to reflect on Ruth's message. After seeing his free-state cattle safely to camp, the exhausted Brown turned in for the night. On the other side of the river, a mail carrier informed the Lawrence men in Osawatomie that a force of Missourians had massed nearby and were on their way.

Politics in Kansas had been on the move during August. Governor Shannon had attempted to resign over his failure to contain the violence, but had been fired instead, and John W. Geary was appointed in his place. But until Geary arrived, Lieutenant-Governor Woodson was in charge, and that pro-slavery functionary intended to use his brief tenure as executive to make a name for himself in the South and exact revenge. On August 25 he declared that the free-state men had started an insurrection. The effect was the same as the previous summons to assault Lawrence, and while Brown was liberating cattle, nearly 500 Missourians gathered to exterminate the abolitionist base in Osawatomie.

Frederick Brown stayed in Lawrence while his father was raiding Sugar Creek, but he was dispatched to Osawatomie to alert the free-state partisans and recall them to Lawrence. The message was passed, and by August 29 the men camped in Osawatomie were on the move to their stronghold, but Frederick was exhausted and stayed the night with a friend near the Adair home.

The next morning, Frederick was walking up the road to his uncle's home, unaware that Missourian advance scouts were already in the area. Martin White happened to be nearby searching for some of his cattle. When Frederick saw him he called out "Good morning!" White approached, and Frederick, guileless as always and squinting in the dawn said, "I think I know you." Indeed he did. It was the Martin White who had once been a conflicted, anti–Negro free-state man, who had argued at the inception of the Free State party that obedience to the slave-power laws was the best solution, and who had left the party's meeting in anger after the Old Man had crystallized opinion around resistance.

White smiled and drew his gun, saying, "I know you, & we are foes." The bullet tore through Frederick's heart and the frangible morning calm. Samuel Adair ran to his nephew, but it was far too late. In a panic, Adair sent his son to raise the alarm, and as the townspeople of Osawatomie scrambled to arm themselves or seek shelter, one of them had the sense to ford the river to find the Old Man. The Old Man's own legend had finally found him, and had walked into Osawatomie with violence and death in its hands. The Old Man's legend had stalked down poor Frederick.

12

The Return Home

As for the famous "struggle for existence," so far it seems to me to be asserted rather than proved. It occurs, but as an exception; the total appearance of life is not the extremity, not starvation, but rather riches, profusion, even absurd squandering—and where there is struggle, it is a struggle for power. One should not mistake Malthus for nature ... the weak prevail over the strong again and again, for they are the great majority—and they are more intelligent.
　　　　　　　　　　　　—Friedrich Nietzsche, *Twilight of the Idols*

Brown was making breakfast when he learned that Frederick had been murdered and the town was under attack. Grabbing his gun, he roared, "Men, *come on!*" and rushed towards Osawatomie, which was in chaos when he arrived. He took up a position in the tree-line by the river with his thirty defenders, and with well placed shots was able to halt the Missouri charge. But the attackers regrouped and brought their cannon to bear on the timber.[1]

They brought grapeshot, the weapon by which the emperor had liquidated *La Révolution*. A fearsome munition, it allowed a cannon to fire a cluster of lethal projectiles against infantry, and it was exploding in the trees around the Old Man. Brown moved among his men, urging them to hold their ground. He stubbornly refused to give up his position until he was almost overrun, when the only option left was a desperate flight across the river, closely pursued by his enemies. At some point as the Old Man waded to the opposite shore, he cried out and stumbled, nearly immersing himself but holding his guns above his head.

He was later reported dead, fallen after being struck in the back by grapeshot.[2] But it was a glancing, low-velocity ricochet, and miraculously he suffered only superficial injuries. Those who witnessed him crossing alive recall him wading the river while Osawatomie crumbled in fire behind him, revolvers held high from the water, the tails of his linen duster floating gently upon it, his old broad hat on his head. After getting a safe distance from the town, he turned with Jason to watch the pillar of smoke rise into the air.

"God sees it," he said to his son, jaw trembling as he choked back the hot tears in his eyes. "I have only a short time to live—only one death to die, and I will die fighting for this cause. There will be no more peace in this land until slavery is done for. I will give them something else to do than to extend slave territory. I will carry this war into Africa."[3] He walked off into the prairie, taking only Frederick's hat with him as he fled. Somewhere during the crossing—perhaps when he was shot—he had lost his own.[4]

After about a week, on the morning of September 7, a lone rider on a pale gray horse came to Lawrence. He appeared dazed, slouched in his saddle, gun low and ready across it. He was a widely recognized figure, despite how much he had changed. But most did not truly know him. They merely knew the ghost-like figure of legend that appeared in a daguerreotype taken during this time of his life. Gaunt, worn from privations and strife, with his terrible, stern, unflinching stare.

Having devoted himself to an ideal, Brown had become something else in the minds of his enemies, even his friends. He was more than just a man, and less. His powerful will to act, and his utter devotion, had transformed him into a legend. He was fear.

Sen. Charles Sumner, around 1855 (Library of Congress).

They saw him everywhere. They said he defended Osawatomie with 1150 men. Colonel Atchison—Sumner's replacement—compiled reports of Brown raiding a settlement on the 6th of August leading 300 men, killing 225 of the settlers, one-third of whom were women, children, and slaves. On the 12th the Old Man was with an army, killing and burning and stealing a Mexican War trophy cannon. His captured icon spit fire at the head of an even larger army on the 15th, and of course none of those stories were true.[5] His defeat at Osawatomie was, however, very much true. Though he had been driven from the town, his bravery while standing with a mere thirty men while grossly outnumbered and outgunned only fed his legend.

The people of Lawrence cheered for the Old Man, "as loudly as if the President had come to town, but John Brown seemed not to hear it."[6] They told him that there were more war councils planned, and that James Lane wanted the Old Man to help. But Brown was not interested and rode on in silence. He stopped at some point to pen a detached letter to his wife, telling her about Frederick and the Battle of Osawatomie, embellishing his story at least as badly as his enemies did. He wrote about his brush with death, but said, "'Hitherto the Lord hath helped me,' notwithstanding my afflictions." He also prepared a second account for public release about "the Fight of Osawatomie" to refute the highly exaggerated rumors of his own death, though he grimly noted that "old Preacher White, I hear, boasts of having killed my son."[7]

The Old Man greatly admired Jason's bravery, but Jason later said, "I care nothing for the honors of war. It matters little whether the battles of Black Jack and Osawatomie are looked upon as victories or defeats. I was at the latter engagement, but I do not know whether I had the honor of *killing* (as it is looked upon by some persons) anybody at Osawatomie or not. If I did, I would gladly transfer the honor of the whole slaughtering part of it to the Rev. David N. Utter, and to his brother in divinity, the Rev. Martin White."[8]

After Osawatomie, Brown plotted, and signed new recruits to his Kansas Regulars, but it was time to go. On September 10 he was finally able to see his oldest son, released from prison on bail. John, Jr., was in terrible shape. He had been marched 9 miles to Osawatomie in the heat, his arms cruelly bound the entire distance, and was kept bound for two more days, so that when the ropes were removed his arms were swollen and black, and he was near blind with pain. That ordeal, along with his fragile state after Pottawatomie, had resulted in a mental collapse during captivity. The scars in his mind were invisible, but his wrists forever bore what he called "slavery's bracelet," made when the rope stripped his flesh as it was peeled away.[9]

His captors had suffered too, though not necessarily in kind. The scars of fear in the changing Kansas territory had inexorably driven most of Buford's men back to Alabama. A few subsisted for a while off sympathetic donations, or from raids of their own, but it couldn't last. By autumn few remained, only some isolated homesteads or those who had joined the U.S. Army. Some even became free-state partisans themselves. Buford was not seen in the territory again after the new year.[10]

Kansas was becoming no place for John Brown. Governor Geary intended to end the struggle, and he pledged to protect Lawrence if the residents would in turn support him. To truly stop the war, Geary needed to arrest Brown, along with any other combatant leader he could find. Charles Robinson, for his part, believed Geary was staging a farce and would show his true colors as soon as he had neutralized the free-state fighters. Robinson sent a letter to Brown asking for a meeting, but John, Jr., attached a cryptic note to it, both warning his father that Geary intended to arrest him, and also begging him not to enter some "secret refugee plan as talked of by Robinson."[11] Brown met with Robinson, who had been making arrangements to have more armed immigrants sent to the Kansas territory. The Old Man hinted that he might help Robinson, but only in exchange for two letters of introduction that would gain him admission to the best connected northeast abolitionists.

Brown's chief business at this time was evacuating his family, a task delayed by illness until October. First he sent the women to Ohio, then John, Jr., Jason, and Owen escorted him to Nebraska, while he slumped in the wagon, burning with fever. Along the way Owen returned to Iowa to set up a new secret headquarters in Tabor. Brown recovered and travelled on to Chicago, where he met with a chapter of the National Kansas Committee, and he secured yet another letter of introduction from Governor Chase of Ohio.

Why did the John Brown that emerged from Kansas become a memory made immortal by blood? Why not, perhaps, James Lane? Lane commanded many men, and his propensity for violence was so notorious that Samuel Gridley Howe of the National Kansas Committee eventually removed the "troublemaking" Lane from command.[12] Lane sacked the town of Osceola in 1861, and during the raid, he carried off a princely

12. The Return Home

amount of plunder as his 1,200 soldiers looted and burned. Nine pro-slavery men were executed in a military mockery of a trial.[13]

Or perhaps Charles Jennison could have been the figure of legend? Jennison was a brutal and unscrupulous man who plundered widely and often and exclusively for personal gain.[14] The siren call of violence drew him to Osawatomie in 1858, and he served as a territorial free-state officer before turning to banditry. During the U.S. Civil War he was an officer in the 15th Kansas Cavalry, a role that, under him, was indistinguishable from brigandry. He was later rewarded for looting and murder with a seat on the Kansas legislature.[15]

A man may be known by his friends. Lane and Jennison collected hundreds of men as eager to rid Kansas of slavery as they were to rid it of black people and to loot and fight; men behaved like religious crusaders with their new, nationalist, even synthesizing faith. But Brown, the old Calvinist, found a small, unique group constellating around him, drawn both by the religious power he exuded and by his odd post-religious appropriation of quasi-liberal language. He conducted his enterprise with a curious attention to the status quo, and yet utterly rejected its limits, and thus gathered a paradoxically devoted group. His disparate followers would represent aggregate roots in Judaism, spiritualism, agnosticism, and Protestantism.[16] They would be sons of pro-slavery people, and sons of anti-slavery, sons of wealth and sons of poverty. All worked together as mutually exclusive yet cooperating absolutisms. They followed him because of his unalterable conviction of the rightness of his actions. He was seemingly willing to go to any physical or financial hardship for justice. Oddly enough, Brown even found himself on friendly terms, in his own way, with men like Charles Robinson, who represented the established political order.

But perhaps more can be known of a man by his enemies, and the Old Man's enemies feared him like they feared no one else. Lane and Jennison were foes that they understood, but Brown was the knife, the stone, the lion prowling the desert of the numb black past underneath the beliefs of Americans. And as time went on and he transvaluated historical narrative, he gained more prominent foes. Charles Robinson even became one. But before that happened, Brown had farther to journey. He boarded a train in Ohio that whisked him away to Boston, letters in hand. Charles Robinson had served his purpose; those letters would get Brown the resources he needed, but not for any plan of Robinson's design.

It was a cold day just after the new year of 1857 when the train pulled into the station in Boston, arrhythmic percussive breaths of steam and mechanical ticking from the coal fired engine within. John Brown stepped onto the platform, fresh from a visit with his former brother-in-law. He crunched boot prints in his wake as he walked through the snow to keep an appointment.

The locomotive was becoming the dominant metaphor of a transforming world. It was "the only sure topic for conversation" in those days, the "work of art which agitates & drives mad the whole people." Days became hours, and Brown's old journeys were as nothing.[17] The decade had witnessed both inexorable and explosive railroad expansion, fueled by substantial investments in speculative railroad securities.

In 1850, most lines were either localized eastern networks serving established communities, or older western routes dedicated to material distribution. But by 1857 new western trunk lines were decimating their competition while providing near boundless speculative opportunities with their aggressive land-purchasing strategies and soaring trans-continental ambitions. The Chicago and Rock Island Railroad, a north-south regional connection, signaled their ambitions in April of 1856 by becoming the first line to cross the river, opening the way to the west.[18] As soon as any new frontier settlement was established, the people clamored for a railroad, the "breath of life ... an instant market for the wheat." And when one line went in they demanded a second, "because the first charges its own rates for freight which takes half the price out of their crop, or as much money as it costs to get it from Chicago to New York."[19]

Brown crisscrossed the northeast during a spring of market euphoria. The map of Kansas was an epidemic of land speculation, one which gained momentum as the papers not only ran articles asking for free-state men, but also narrated steady free-state success since May of 1856. Northeasterners were selling homes, leaving jobs, and borrowing money at interest rates up to 10 percent to move to Kansas. By April, nearly 1,000 settlers per day were arriving.[20] Passage rates plummeted as the railroads sought to expand their investments, and by 1857 even men as poor as Brown could afford railroad travel.

Brown's appointment was with the secretary of the Massachusetts State Kansas Committee, a handsome Harvard graduate and Concord schoolmaster named Franklin B. Sanborn. He was academically gifted and politically radical, and figured prominently in both Massachusetts' combative abolitionist community and in Emerson's intellectual circle; he was connected with all the men whose support Brown required. So Brown had sought him out, bearing letters from Robinson, Chase, and George Walker—Sanborn's former brother-in-law and an acquaintance of Brown's from his Springfield wool merchant days.

Sanborn was entranced when the old gunslinger walked into his office, tall and lean and right off the pages of Kansas abolitionism.[21] Brown, seldom one to banter when he wanted something accomplished, got directly to his purpose; he needed money—$30,000—and guns, hundreds of them, to complete his mission. As a blind, he suggested that he was collecting for Kansas based vigilance guards as Robinson had conceived them, which were needed to provide the protection that the federal government would not. Brown also knew that the most outspoken abolitionists had reached the point of advocating disunion, and should be primed to support such vigilance guards. Would Sanborn introduce him to those abolitionists, and help him arrange speaking engagements?[22]

Of course Sanborn would. How could he not? A great legend of his life's most important cause, with his bombardier eyes and his steady, "deep and metallic" voice had suddenly appeared, worn from the stories and with all the stories to tell. Sanborn wrote first on January 5 to the man he knew who most closely resembled Brown—the fierce minister Thomas Wentworth Higginson. He then took Brown to meet Theodore Parker, a highly controversial Unitarian minister fond of preaching apocalyptic oratory about slavery. Parker instantly warmed to Brown, and held a reception for the Old Man in his home.

Even the *Liberator*'s editor and ostensible voice of the abolitionist movement came to Parker's house to meet the celebrated John Brown. Garrison, however, could not countenance Brown's plans, and the meeting became an abrasive confrontation between the Kansas warrior and the peaceful perfectionist. Garrison thought Brown foolishly and even unethically bellicose, though still oddly impressive, while Brown scorned Garrison's pacifism. The two men never overcame their antipathy, despite the early significant influence of Garrison's *Liberator* on Brown.

From there, Sanborn escorted his storybook figure to meet Dr. Samuel Gridley Howe and George Luther Stearns. Dr. Howe was an adventurer who almost naturally formed a friendship with Brown. As a young man, Howe was knighted for heroism fighting in the 1824 Greek Revolution against the Turks. He wrote a memoir of the insurrection titled *Historical Sketch of the Greek Revolution.* At home, he worked tirelessly on behalf of the blind and the mentally ill, and he and his wife, Julia Ward Howe, were members of the Kansas Committee. He had visited the border during summer of 1856, and so understood the territory enough to see through Brown's over-generalizing and partisan exaggerations. He also believed that Kansas was all but assured of free-state status by this point, yet decided to endorse Brown's plans anyway, almost as insurance. Had they been closer friends, Dr. Howe may have found that Brown did not entirely disagree with him about the fate of Kansas.

Stearns, the big, generous, wealthy chair of the committee, was just as taken with Brown, just as skeptical as Dr. Howe, and just as prepared to endorse Brown as all of them. On January 7, Stearns introduced Brown to the entire committee as a man of "sagacity, courage, and stern integrity" and helped Brown persuade them to pledge to him their cache of weapons in Tabor, Iowa—where Owen had already established a base of operations—in addition to $1,000 for his expenses and return travel.[23]

Amos Lawrence had a "long talk" with "the old partisan hero of Kansas warfare" and found him "a calm, temperate and pious man," who when roused was "a dreadful foe." He appeared "about sixty years old." In time Lawrence would turn on Brown, but long after Brown was placed beyond caring. Yet when they met, Lawrence could only describe Brown as the "Miles Standish of Kansas," a man of "determined energy ... heroic courage ... all based on a deep religious faith ... a true representative of the Puritanic warrior." Eager to claim friendship, Lawrence bragged on an acquaintanceship that dated back to Brown's failed Springfield wool depot, and said he "should esteem the loss of his service, from poverty, or any other cause, almost irreparable."[24] Brown might have been amused to know that back when his life had unraveled such august benefactors had been so very concerned.

Thomas Wentworth Higginson finally had the chance to meet the Old Man in Boston after returning from Kansas on January 9. Higginson, 34 years old, was a truculent preacher, whose favorite social pastime seemed to be verbally abusing people for being foolish. Once a quiet and bookish youth, he became an active man and fiery speaker. He bore a scar on his chin from a saber cut suffered when he led the failed attempt to rescue Anthony Burns, a scar not remotely as celebrated as Andrew Jackson's similar wound. Higginson had indifferent memories of his first meeting with Brown, but he nonetheless collected pledges of support as he toured area disunion conventions.[25]

Before seeing Brown off, Stearns invited him to spend an evening at his luxurious mansion in Medford. After a sumptuous meal, Brown entertained the Stearns family and their guests with tales from Kansas filled with implausible victories, crushing defeats and the hungry children of war. Mr. Stearns was mesmerized, and asked Brown to tell him what kind of sound the bullet of a Sharps rifle made.

"It makes a very ugly noise, Mr. Stearns," replied the Old Man, solemnly.

Miss Augusta King attempted to rudder the tense conversation back to placid waters with a seemingly more positive and non-controversial comment. "We read a good deal in the newspapers about General Pomeroy," she said, "who seems to be an important man in Kansas. Is he a very good general?"

At that, John Brown laughed in his curious way, rocking and smiling in silence, mirth in his eyes. "I wish the ladies of Massachusetts would make a large military cocked hat," he said after collecting himself, "about three feet in length, and a foot and a half in height; and put the tail-feathers of three roosters in it, and send it with their compliments to General Pomeroy." Then, his expression becoming serious, he added, "As a rule, Miss King, the higher the officer the less of a soldier. Now I am but a plain captain, and yet I am always ready to fight the enemy. Jim Lane is a colonel, but I have no doubt he would fight if Governor Robinson would let him. Pomeroy is a general, and there is no fight in him at all."[26]

Mary, George Stearns' argumentative and well-meaning wife, was utterly charmed by Brown. His son, twelve-year-old Henry, was moved to donate his entire life savings—all thirty cents—to Brown that it might help at least one suffering child. And then Henry, attempting to understand the specious present and his own future becoming in terms of Brown's past, asked the first historical question that had ever been asked about John Brown. He asked: "Captain Brown, will you sometime write me a letter, and tell me what sort of little boy you were?" Everyone laughed, but not Brown. The Old Man smiled at Henry very seriously, and promised that he would, as soon as he finished the business of his travels. Then with a grin and a wink to the boy, he said the story had to wait because "it would weary the ladies."[27]

Before leaving Boston, the Old Man had a special request. He wished to meet one of George Stearns's close friends. Back in 1856, as Lawrence burned, Senator Charles Sumner of Massachusetts gave a spirited oration on the Senate floor known as his "Crime against Kansas" speech. For two days' worth of Senate proceedings, Sumner mined the depths of the Western historical and literary consciousness, from Greece to Rome to Britain to the formation of the American state, from Martin Luther to Machiavelli to Cervantes, from Norse mythology to Christian conscience. He expounded on legal arrangements, and historical precedent, and recent events. It was a devastating condemnation of the Kansas-Nebraska Act and the Slave Power, and Sumner advocated the immediate admission of Kansas to the Union as a free state. Faced with such a delivery, representatives of the slave power could only focus on the insulting sexual language in the speech.

His intended targets were incensed, as they should have been. Sumner was a gifted orator, and the colorfully recurrent sexual imagery was quite deliberate.[28] At the most superficial level, he intended to provoke men who had chosen a culture of honor over one of dignity by making a public denunciation of the manifestly true—but hardly ever spoken of—Southern custom of keeping slaves for sexual predation.

A culture of rape not only lurked underneath the South's slave-supported façade of gentility, it supported Southern society and by extension risk and credit from New

York to Liverpool. The letters of Isaac Franklin and Rice Ballard were littered with references to the farming out of "fancy maids," and during economic turmoil, when the "pirates" and "robbers" were at their doorstep, they had confidence that some singularly focused "one-eyed men"—a southern "gentleman's" way of referring to the phallus—would overcome mundane concerns like cotton prices in order to satisfy sexual desires, since certain of the "stock" carried "her funds in her lovers purse" rather than in her capacity for field labor.

Franklin often sampled the wares, and wrote boastful sham apologies like, "She has been used & that smartly by a one-eyed man about my size and age, *excuse my foolishness.*"[29] It was the bondholder's final indemnity, the bottom-most threshold for the losses of the powerful, held above penurious oblivion by the rape, over and over, of black women. It is the truest words that cut the deepest, particularly when they cut to the most monstrous lies behind the myths.

The myths fell under Sumner's verbal wrath as well, artfully bound to imagery of a lecherous and vile society. "The senator from South Carolina has read many books of chivalry, and believes himself a chivalrous knight with sentiments of honor and courage. Of course he has chosen a mistress to whom he has made his vows, and who, though ugly to others, is always lovely to him; though polluted in the sight of the world, is chaste in his sight—I mean the harlot, slavery. For her his tongue is always profuse in words."[30] Best, in Sumner's opinion, that the entire history of South Carolina be obliterated, and something be done for Kansas forthwith, since the territory—and the future—was plagued by men who were little more than "hirelings, picked from the drunken spew and vomit of an uneasy civilization."[31]

Representative Preston Brooks of South Carolina was upset. Any possible deeper awareness of the shameful truth was buried under superficial notions of a vicious personal attack on his honor, which also characterized the potted histories of what followed. Initially, Brooks wished to duel Sumner, but (conveniently) a fellow South Carolinian advised him that dueling was reserved for gentlemen of equal social standing, and that Sumner's crude language—employed with such intelligent purpose—had marked him as little better than a drunkard.[32]

Southerners had other means of violence against those they secretly feared were their betters. Late afternoon on May 22, Brooks approached Sumner at his desk in the Senate chamber. "Mr. Sumner," he said, "I have read your speech twice over carefully. It is a libel on South Carolina, and Mr. Butler, who is a relative of mine."[33] Sumner started to rise, but before he could make a barbed comment about the fact that it had required *two* readings, Brooks struck him as hard as he could with a thick, gold-headed cane. Sumner was pinned by the heavy desk bolted to the floor and was beaten savagely until he managed to rip the desk free.

He staggered up the aisle like a wounded beast, blinded by and choking on his blood before collapsing a few yards later. Brooks pursued, and rained down flesh and bone crushing savagery until the cane broke. South Carolina Representative Laurence Keitt had advised Sumner against a duel, but made certain to bring a pistol of his own to brandish at anyone who tried to help Sumner. The reaction across the North was clamorous, as thousands rallied for Sumner. As always, Emerson summarized the situation best:

Life has not parity of value in the free state and in the slave state. In one, it is adorned with education, with skilful labor, with arts, with long prospective interests, with sacred family ties, with honor and justice. In the other, life is a fever; man is an animal, given to pleasure, frivolous, irritable, spending his days in hunting and practising with deadly weapons to defend himself against his slaves and against his companions brought up in the same idle and dangerous way. Such people live for the moment, they have properly no future, and readily risk on every passion a life which is of small value to themselves or to others.... It is the best whom they desire to kill. It is only when they cannot answer your reasons, that they wish to knock you down. If, therefore, Massachusetts could send to the Senate a better man than Mr. Sumner, his death would be only so much the more quick and certain. Now, as men's bodily strength, or skill with knives and guns, is not usually in proportion to their knowledge and mother-wit, but oftener in the inverse ratio, it will only do to send foolish persons to Washington, if you wish them to be safe.[34]

In the South, Preston Brooks was a hero. Cheering crowds gave him canes to replace his broken one. The gifts were engraved with charming sentiments like "hit him again" and "use knockdown arguments."[35] As for Sumner, his allies could not gather enough votes in the House of Representatives to expel Brooks, who was tried and convicted in the District of Columbia, but was never made to serve a prison term. His punishment for nearly killing Sumner was a minor monetary fine.[36]

On the day that Brown visited, Sumner was still struggling to recover. Quietly, even fearfully, Brown asked if he could see the coat that Sumner wore when he was assaulted. Sumner limped gingerly to retrieve it from the closet, an artifact as frozen in memory as it was petrified with deep dried bloodstains. Brown held it in wordless contemplation, "his lips compressed and his eyes ... like polished steel."[37]

Behind those eyes was a night of terrible deeds in Pottawatomie. This was why he had killed those men, wasn't it? That's how Salmon remembered it years later, that after the burning of Lawrence one of those horseback messengers had a printed telegraph message in his boot detailing the barbaric assault on Sumner.[38] It would have been a remarkable feat of communication. Telegraph penetration into Kansas was exceedingly sparse; Leavenworth was not connected until 1859, though Jackson County to the east had possessed a telegraph office since 1851. The news would have needed to reach Westport and then traveled 30 miles more by horseback to intercept Brown.

That bloody coat was Brown's historical fate, if only because of those on whose behalf he killed. It is to the eternal credit of most Northern abolitionists that they deplored violence so much; such a noble sentiment cannot be condemned, despite the fact that the time to throw up the barricades had come. A violent society like the South would have celebrated a pro-slavery Brown as it did Brooks.

Reaction to Pottawatomie could have divided the Northern abolitionists as it did free-state men in Kansas, and cost Brown his support, save for that bloody coat. The attack on Sumner dominated public consciousness at the time of the Pottawatomie killings, and the perception was created, as awareness of both events merged, that Brown had retaliated for it. And while it is theoretically possible to outline a causal relationship linked by telegraph and swift hooves, it might be said either way that the bloody coat in Brown's hands was why he killed at Pottawatomie. As Annie Brown wrote in later years:

12. The Return Home

Moral suasion and non-resistance are excellent doctrines to preach in times of peace. But often in troublous times, some one has to fight for peace—and fight hard too. And then endure the remarks that are made by the carpet knights and quill-drivers who were not in the fray but stayed peacefully at home enjoying the after benefits derived from other's exertions. I am not trying to apologize for my father or his friends (followers is a better word) but to show you what, from their point of view, led on to Pottawatomie.[39]

Brown knew he and Sumner lived in a world where the crime against Kansas only had one answer, and that the connection was indelibly strong and completely acausal.

Next, Sanborn escorted Brown by train to the National Kansas Convention in New York, where his interrogators were far less inclined to unquestioningly accept his tales, and yet where he delivered a commanding performance that netted $5,000 in pledges, along with promises of more weaponry. Then it was time to part ways with Sanborn, the guide and facilitator of a seeming successful eastern tour. Shaking Sanborn's hand in gratitude, Brown boarded a train for Peterboro, New York, to see an old acquaintance.

Upon arriving, Brown found Gerrit Smith to be oddly cool. It was puzzling that Smith, who by all reports had recently pledged $10,000 in support of the Kansas cause, and who had known Brown longer than all the other abolitionists, should be so aloof. And yet, Smith demurred, saying that his contribution of $1,000 a year had already caused him some discomfiture, though he did not elaborate. Brown left disappointed, without the aid of the man who he thought would be his most generous and reliable supporter, and still far short of his goal.[40]

So he took his disappointed heart and his bag full of promises to North Elba, the most important visit of his northeast tour. After streaking brilliantly across the headlines, after carrying the burden for over a year and a half, he came home like a dull burnt stone, to fall heavily into Mary's arms. Among the snow and the towering mountains, he took solace, if only for a while, in his family's embrace. Owen, Oliver, and Watson had already made it safely back from Kansas, as had Henry Thompson, who was reunited with Ruth. He hugged them all and tearfully confided in Ruth, "If I had my life to live over again, I should do very differently with my children. I meant to do right, but I can see now where I failed."[41]

The food was meager, his family poorly clothed. The time Brown had been gone was a time of privation for Mary and the children. But he was home. He held his children that were still small and sang to them his favorite hymn by the fire that night. By the end of the evening there was only one he had not held. He beckoned tiny Ellen, now two, over to him, but she drew away from the strange stern man whom she did not know.

It might have stung a little. Not knowing what else to do and separated from his youngest by time and terrible events, Brown looked to his precious Annie for help and asked her to bring Ellen and reassure her. Holding both of them, he sang, and imagined laying down his burdens, days of tribulation at an end. There at home he found forgiveness, but never forgetfulness, for all that he had seen and done.[42]

13

The Child with the Mirror

If you have no faith in beneficent power above you, but see only an adamantine fate coiling its folds about Nature and man, then reflect that the best use of fate is to teach us courage, if only because baseness cannot change the appointed event. If you accept your thoughts as inspirations from the Supreme Intelligence, obey them when they prescribe difficult duties, because they come only so long as they are used; or, if your skepticism reaches to the last verge, and you have no confidence in any foreign mind, then be brave, because there is one good opinion which must always be of consequence to you, namely, your own.
—Ralph Waldo Emerson, *Courage*

Brown spent the remainder of February 1857 rumbling around New England on poorly networked and inefficient rails, hobbled as they were by parochial interests and "state's rights" proponents who barely comprehended the powers of Federalism. This infrastructure would not reach its potential until the great centralizing project of the Reconstruction. Americans had taken "to the little contrivance as if it were the cradle in which they were born." As a form of travel, it was "dreamlike," passing through towns which left no "distinct impression ... like pictures on a wall."[1]

Brown returned to the business of telling the story of pro-slavery hordes poised to take over Kansas, angrily displaying the iron manacles (or at least a set of iron manacles) that had bound John, Jr., when he was put on a forced march from Osawatomie to Tecumseh. He spoke at the conventions as the most prominent veteran of the stories, the man who had sacrificed his life's prospects for the struggle only to watch one son lose his sanity while leaving another in the Kansas dirt.[2]

But news from the territory was placidly silent. When questioned about that, Brown attributed the peace to the bitter Kansas winter—not unreasonable, given his own experiences.[3] He may or may not have believed his excuses, but he had no intention of returning to Kansas anyway. No one was buying Brown's story though. If the steadily rising value of Kansas land warrants since the new year was any indication, they were buying land in Kansas.[4] The few liquid contributions to Brown seemed to be donated out of nothing more than respect for the Old Man, and a desire to defray his personal expenses.[5]

He had a speaking engagement in Concord, Massachusetts, and a chance to reconnect with Sanborn, who was ebullient when he met Brown at the station. Sanborn had been waiting all spring for the opportunity to show Brown around Concord, and rushed him off to meet Henry David Thoreau. As all three ate lunch and traded stories, none other than the Sage of Concord—Ralph Waldo Emerson—called on Thoreau's house while out running errands. Emerson and Thoreau both invited Brown to stay with them during his visit.

That evening a beaming Sanborn took the Old Man to the crowded Town House, which was cheered by dancing lanterns and a warm oven fire. Brown the storyteller began his well-rehearsed Kansas tale, filled with pro-slavery killers, heroic free-state stands, and the looming helplessness against the powerful South and its allies in Washington. He told them of his family's sufferings, both in the territory and back at North Elba. Significantly, he did not tell them about Pottawatomie, or at least about his involvement.[6] Though Pottawatomie may have been the beginning of so much that had happened, Brown never seemed proud of that night. Furthermore, he would have known—especially after his confrontation with Garrison and his meetings with so many abolitionists—that the same crowds who cheered his resolve to fight to the bitter end would have turned on him the moment they knew the truth.

Brown hoped that James Buchanan's impending inauguration as president would serve to boost contributions. The territorial governor, John Geary, may have pacified Kansas in the Old Man's absence, but Geary was no free-stater, and had been appointed by a slavery friendly government. Despite Brown's scorn for Geary, the governor had vowed to administer impartial justice and, true to his word, he actually halted the violence, a fact that caused the Massachusetts legislature to pledge exactly zero dollars to Brown's cause. Geary was in fact so very fair that he was severely criticized by President Franklin Pierce for arresting Missouri Border Ruffians. But the surprisingly just and responsible governorship of John Geary would mean little, since Buchanan had made his intent to override a popular vote for Kansas as a free-state quite clear. Though a slavery supporter, Geary resigned in controversy on inauguration day rather than violate his own sense of justice.[7]

Abolitionists derisively referred to Buchanan as "dough-face," a broad derogatory term for northern politicians who were merely compliant puppets of southern slave-holding oligarchs. On the day of Buchanan's inauguration, the New York *Tribune* ran a letter from Brown "TO THE FRIENDS OF FREEDOM" in which Brown asked "all honest lovers of Liberty and Human Rights, both male and female, to hold up my hands by contributions and pecuniary aid, either as counties, cities, towns, villages, societies, churches

Ralph Waldo Emerson, by Southworth and Hawes, 1856 (public domain image).

or individuals."[8] Once in office, Buchanan appointed Robert Walker of Mississippi as Kansas territorial governor.

Back on the train again, the Old Man toured Connecticut, hoping that his home state would treat him well given recent developments. But three speaking stops yielded a disappointing $80. "I was told," he said to his home-state audience, "that the newspapers in a certain city were dressed in mourning on hearing that I was killed and scalped in Kansas, but I did not know of it until I reached the place. Much good it did me. In the same place I met a more cool reception than in any other place where I have stopped. If my friends will hold up my hands while I live, I will freely absolve them from any expense over me when I am dead."[9]

He did, however, collect something of far greater value. Visiting the graves of his grandparents, he retrieved the gravestone of his grandfather, John Brown. This he intended to "be faced and inscribed in memory of our poor Fredk who sleeps in Kansas." On the move constantly, he had not had the opportunity to memorialize his fallen son. Now he could do so properly, as he wrote John, Jr., "I value the old relic, much more for its age, & homeliness; & it is of sufficient size to contain more *brief* inscriptions. One hundred years from 1856 should it then be in the possession of the same posterity: it will be a great curiosity."[10] A proper memorial, with perhaps enough room for his own name when he rejoined Frederick, never to leave him alone again.

Before leaving Connecticut, he contracted a blacksmith named Chas Blair for 1,000 pikes, with blade-ends modeled on a vicious Bowie knife he had captured from Captain Pate at Black Jack. It was odd, to have an East Coast smith supply him with such primitive weapons to ship to a faraway territory where apparently every resident was already armed with a Sharps rifle. Equally intriguing was the contract he signed with an itinerant adventurer named Hugh Forbes.

Forbes was a curious man, a former merchant and veteran of the 1848 revolutions in Italy. He was also a casual associate of Higginson, and authored a tactics manual that Brown had read with approval. The Old Man perhaps wanted someone with 1848 expertise for his plan, someone who could speak the language of military adventurism and revolution to his young men, so he found Forbes in New York.

After listening to the Old Man's pitch, Forbes said he was interested, but not "merely to get Kansas for free white people."[11] Brown assured him that such was not the case. He revealed to Forbes an outline of his true plan to raise an insurrection in the South itself, and he wanted Forbes to write a manual for his men, and to serve as their instructor. Mercenary work writing so-called military "science" and instructing was a popular pursuit for the officer class of the West at that time, and apparently even for ambitious revolutionaries. Forbes jumped at the chance for such work, while dreaming that history might remember him as "the Garibaldi of a revolution against slavery."[12]

Then he was back on the train to Springfield, where he received a letter from Mary informing him that his sons would no longer fight. That is, except Owen, who from boyhood had lived with the expectation that his fate was to ever follow his father in pursuit of this cause. Already wrestling with disappointment over his fundraising tour, a hurt Brown scrawled a terse reply, reminding his family that "I have only to say as regards the resolution of the boys to 'learn & practice war no more'; that it was not at my solicitation that they engaged in it at the first: & that while I may perhaps feel no more love of the business than they do; still I think there may be *possibly* in their day that which is more to be demanded."[13] He was right. They may have forgotten, but they had called him to Kansas, and just as he had little choice in the matter, if he judged their character right then they should prepare themselves for the day when they too could do nothing but fight.

He couldn't dwell on these disappointments. Jason sent word that a U.S. marshal was hunting him, forcing Brown to seek refuge in the home of an abolitionist judge named Thomas Russell. While in hiding, Brown had time to dwell on his setbacks. His occasional streak of black pessimism pushed the thousands of dollars of pledges from his mind as well as the funds that Lawrence friends were raising to support his family. A man melancholy over his inability to attain his goal, magnified by the desertion of his sons, drew from his pen a querulous essay entitled "Old Browns Farewell to the Plymouth Rocks, Bunker Hill Monuments, Charter Oaks, and Uncle Thomas Cabbins." He had "left for Kansas" as the missive declared, and had

> been trying since he came out of the territory to secure an outfit or in other words; the means of arming and thoroughly equipping his regular Minuet men, who are mixed up *with the people* of Kansas, and *he leaves* the States, *with a feeling of deepest sadness:* that after having exhausted his own small means and *with his family and his brave men;* suffered hunger, cold, nakedness, *and some* of them sickness, wounds, imprisonment in *irons*; with extreme cruel treatment, *and others death:* that … after all this; in order to sustain a cause which every citizen of this *"glorious Republic,"* is under equal moral obligation to do.[14]

A visit from Mary Stearns a few days later cheered him immensely; she was a visible reminder of the faith and generosity of the Stearns family. Mrs. Stearns, for her part, was so moved by Brown's "farewell" that she asked her husband to sell their horses and carriage in support of the Old Man. George Stearns was equally moved, and gave Brown a draft note for $7,000. When Brown wrote John, Jr., next, he had a brighter outlook on the world, and ebulliently relayed that he had secured "the assistance, & instruction; of a distinguished Scotch officer [Forbes]; & *author* quite popular *in this country.* I am quite sanguine of my success in the matter. My collections I may safely put down at $13,000, & think I have got matters in such a train that it will soon reach $30,000." He added, "I have had a good deal of discouragement; *& have often felt* quite depressed; *but 'hither to God hath helped me.'* About the *last* of last Week, I gave vent to those feelings in a short piece (which you may yet see in the prints,) headed Old Browns Farewell." He also mentioned the collection in Lawrence "for my Wife, & little Girls in my *absence; & in case I never return to them.*" But Brown admonished his son to say nothing of "these things," as he was still pursued.[15]

Brown, ever wary, destroyed his correspondence to hide his movements, but the half that survived in John, Jr.'s care provide a sketchy outline. After stopping briefly in North Elba, he and Owen travelled to Iowa. In Hudson a cryptic letter from John, Jr., said, "It seems as though if you return to Kansas this Spring I should never see you again. But I will not look on the dark side. You have gone safely through a thousand perils and hairbreadth escapes…. Do you not intend to visit Canada before long? That school can be established there, if not elsewhere."[16] Whatever Brown planned, it involved more meetings, including one with Gerrit Smith in Wisconsin. Something had roused

Smith from his latest ennui and he was out supporting protests against the Fugitive Slave Law.

On July 15, the Old Man and Owen stopped at a place called Red Rock, outside of the brand-new town of Des Moines. Brown had made a promise to young Henry Stearns, and he kept it with a letter titled "A boy named John."

The narrative beginning of this story is here. There among the poplars, John wrote his story, and of the memory of wonderment and a world of unlimited possibilities, and also of incomprehensible pain, and the end of peace. Of a cattle drive and a slave boy, of the powerful and their armies. And after his long journeys, and the years of darkness and the improbable struggles, how much of his fifty-six years were infused into that autobiography? One might wonder if it was "true."

Brown was the product of his past. His letter was effectively true in that it shaped who he was, even as his present shaped his memory of what those events meant. By most accounts, he was scrupulously honest, sometimes given to exaggeration, but not to essential falsehoods. For that story he had already broken all ethical securities and every hope of a tranquil life with his family because his tormentors required harmony. The man writing to Henry Stearns may have been performing a written metamorphosis on the page, discovering in that child the true extent of what is possible.

That autobiographical letter was the only account of Brown's boyhood and the soil of his dreams. It has served as the biographical foundation of most of the histories on John Brown, and has attained the status of fact. Factual veracity is a product of the *consensus omnium*—that enough people have believed in its plausibility and possibility from what was known and witnessed of the man who wrote it, not the boy he was.

The criterion for what is possible in any age is derived from that age's rationalistic assumptions. There are no "natural laws" which support one's prejudices, and yet much of history has been imagined on the belief that there are. In counterpoint, the story that began this narrative is also a working critique of social philosophy that identifies individually all three types of people defined by the Constitution in its appeal to "natural law." If Brown's letter is a "true" memory, it is a remarkable portrait of subconscious narrative awareness. If it is a parable, it is an equally remarkable story illuminating the falsehoods of the age.

As a charter of collective identity, the Constitution was a statement of paranoiac malevolence, one that damaged the identities of all concerned. Blacks and Indians were an "other," defined by their exclusion. The black in America, made into a commodity, was stripped of his history; Haitians could trace their lineage back to Africa, but not American slaves. Unique among all slaves in history, American slaves were deprived of their identity by whites who wished to imagine that natural law and history dictated that they could never wrest their freedom from their masters. Their past was taken from them with terrible swiftness. Their history was only as a piece of (the present) civilization, which was the notional creation of white men. They had no name, and this had dreadful and recurrent moral implications. Unique among the civilizations of the age, Americans were notoriously shrill and brutal in their insistence on the idea of white supremacy, a narrative idea that rests entirely on a particular historical formulation of civilization.

One wonders what stories the first slave mother even told her children, or what the first "American" mothers said to their children about that slave mother. The abstract black slave was the defining feature of white narrative identity, the white man himself an abstraction by extension. The "Negro problem" in America was a form of insanity in white men, brought about by the necessity of collectively trying to find a way to live with the Negro and thus with themselves. As the nameless black man struggled to create an identity, the white man became less while nurturing an identity based on being not-black. Fear, and a frighteningly weak grasp on reality maintained the moral high-mindedness of white men and the separation between them and the Negroes and natives on the continent they felt destined to conquer. But living in a state of cruel innocence, eyes closed to reality, was to invite destruction.

Tocqueville posited that choices about culture and law were the foundations of "race" and the source of the limits of freedom in Jacksonian America when he discussed the "Three Races" in *Democracy in America.* And Brown, fully aware of the monstrosity of the contract, might have been willing to raze that false edifice to its foundation that he might never forget that motherless child, and to be happy for its destruction and the dashing of its children against the stones. And no matter what anyone else believed, John Brown "habitually expected to Succeed in his undertakings. With this feeling should be coupled the consciousness that our plans are right in themselves."

Brown's causally assertive and self-reliant statement was worthy of Emerson, whose ability to break through and even resolve the contradictions of the age's dogmas to arrive at a certain unity of citizenship marked him as the foremost philosopher of the modern liberal democracy. In fact, in his early career up to 1844 he nearly perfectly embodied the broader Western philosophical effort since 1648 to substitute natural law and civil society for covenantal grace and dispensation.

And yet, while he was capable of transcending ideas and identifying folly, the answers sometimes eluded, so he also settled into an intellectual ennui, entirely disenchanted (perhaps rightfully so) with his fellow man. His early writings showed a shiftless unwillingness to either commit to or confront the apparent contradictions of his constantly evolving beliefs, as well as the insouciance that led him to have misgivings about social action his entire life. Like the broader metaphors it tracked and critiqued, his early writings dissolved much that was meaningful into a tepid broth incapable of sustaining real dissent. It is from this period that some have drawn the statements most appealing to them, since his ideas about power, carried to a logical extreme and deprived of intellectual context, seem to prescribe little more than overriding self-interest, an ironically ineffective critique of the nascent commodification of man and the mechanical atomization of social philosophy.

Emerson's commitment to causes like abolitionism lagged significantly behind his social circle. The ministers he spurned had carried that fight and helped abolitionism retain its moral authority, while Emerson maintained a careful detachment, having absolved himself of all concerns, even abolitionism. Perhaps remaining aloof from his community's chosen cause was just one more way to demonstrate the sheer radicalism of his individualism. But he felt that abolitionists belonged to the "great class of the Vanity-stricken. And inordinate thirst for notice can not be gratified until it has found in its gropings what is called a Cause that men will bow; tying himself fast to that, the small man is then at liberty to consider all objections made to him as proofs of folly &

the devil in the objector, & under that screen, if he gets a rotten egg or two, yet his name sounds through the world & he is praised & praised."[17] Suffice it to say that Concord's most eminent philosopher made no public statements about slavery—*the* defining moral struggle of the day—prior to 1844. "I know nothing of the source of my being but I will not soil my nest," he wrote.[18] But he would change, as time and experience and even Goethe worked upon him.

The change was non-linear, and certainly not simple, and in his journals he was seemingly of at least two minds on everything. His most profound change arguably started in 1842, a year after the publication of the famous *Self-Reliance*, when his son Waldo died of scarlet fever. He discovered that true self-reliance and his willingness to unravel as meaningless even the most sentimental personal attachments in the name of a higher calling (in this case genius) had not protected him against bitter loss.

Emerson opened his essay *Experience* by asking, "Where do we find ourselves?" He delved into the familiar ground of *Self-Reliance* and convoluted attempts to convince himself that his innermost being could not be touched by the personal or political traumas of the day, eventually arriving at the horrid conclusion that little Waldo's death could not actually touch him. But this was a lie.

He truly felt empty desolation over the loss of his son: "What he looked upon is better, what he looked not upon is insignificant.... It seems as if I ought to call upon the winds to describe my boy, my fast receding boy, a child of so large & generous a nature that I cannot paint him by specialties, as I might another."[19] It would be years before he could meaningfully translate that part of life, but the journal of that year was filled with Waldo written in the present-tense, as if Emerson hoped to look up from the page to see his son there before his eyes, just as he had been written. This grief, after the broader trauma of 1837 and the continuously present evil of slavery, began the waking from his harmonious secular-universalist dream. He wrestled with religious and historical connections waiting just through a door in his mind, and he woke up one morning to find "the old world, wife, babes, and mother, Concord and Boston, the dear old spiritual world, and even the dear old devil not far off." The notion appeared in *Experience* as well.[20]

By the time he turned his pen on the Compromise of 1850 his journals had taken on a darker religious and prophetic tone, as in his charge that "it is not to be disguised that all our contemporaries, scholars as well as merchants, feel the great Despair, are mere Whigs, and believe in nothing. Repent ye, for the Kingdom of Heaven is at hand."[21] The Fugitive Slave Law and the re-enslavement of Anthony Burns in Boston in 1854 shredded what remained of his serene detachment from the world.

Emerson's uncharacteristic aggressiveness, passion, and theological oratory were conceptually nurtured in distant Kansas. The escalating violence, vague details about events like the Pottawatomie killings, the attack upon Charles Sumner after his "Crime Against Kansas" oration, and the growing legend of John Brown all led Emerson to remark in a speech in September of 1856 to the Kansas Relief Society that "there is this peculiarity about the case of Kansas, that all the right is on one side."[22]

"The revolutions that impend over society are not now from ambition & rapacity," he had written in 1842, "from impatience of one or another form of government, but from new modes of thinking which shall recompose society after a new order, which shall destroy the value of many kinds of property."[23] The entry immediately following it was on the subject of "Heroes." When Sanborn brought Brown to Concord to speak, Emerson made certain to be in the audience that night, and America's foremost intellectual recorded in his journal: "Captain John Brown of Kansas gave a good account of himself in the Town Hall, last night, to a meeting of citizens. One of his good points was, the folly of the peace party in Kansas, who believed that their strength lay in the greatness of their wrongs, and so discountenanced resistance. He wished to know if their wrong was greater than the negro's, and what kind of strength that gave the negro?"[24]

Emerson had ever had a mild disdain for abolitionists despite their noble ideals, and a contempt for slave-holders (save for a grudging acknowledgment that they were at least honest in their mendacity and evil). But when he hosted John Brown at his home after the speech, he saw a kind of truth that overcame most of his arguments and doubts. Brown was different; he was deeply involved with the plight of those who were victims of, above all else, the foolish appeals to natural law and the imagined communities that Emerson so despised. Significantly for Emerson, Brown had sacrificed and fought not out of any formulated program—not even out of abolitionism—but merely from an inner core of belief, a story of human wrong and a desire to see justice done. He was a "representative man" like Emerson had never before seen, a self-reliant, post-secular individual, devoid of the modern poisons of racism, possessing bravery and *Wille zur Macht,* who against all logic had extracted from grim orthodoxy and from heterodox revolution the power to fight for the value of man, invoking both the Golden Rule and the Declaration of Independence without apparent contradiction.

Self-Reliance had been Emerson's rough early effort to write a noble and life-affirming philosophy in an age that had witnessed knowledge's power to overthrow oppressive religious orders, but had merely crafted systems only superficially different. This was a nihilistic effort to overcome the brutalizing and disfiguring orthodoxy of conservative faiths, while harnessing the heterodoxy of the age to something more meaningful than the cold, contrived systems of power, prestige, and profit. But his formulation was incomplete; he was not searching for value that could be assembled and shopped from different pieces, despite his studies of global faiths. "Faith makes us, and not we it, and faith makes its own forms." Eventually his self-reliant isolation became hollow and privative, like cold or nonentity, very like his formulation of the evil of the age.[25]

Then there was John Brown, a man who appeared deeply rooted in the suffocating and ignorant soil Emerson had washed himself of, and yet who had grown from it anew. He stood in Emerson's parlor, tall, dark, and awful, and declared matter-of-factly that he should rather see "a whole generation of men, women, and children ... pass away by a violent death than that one word of either should be violated in this country."[26] Emerson, a man fond of shocking metaphor, nodded in approval. He would come to revel in Brown's words, and his writings would never be the same.

The fact that Brown apparently intended every word he said made a deep impression on Emerson, who had never said anything quite so brazen, and whose beliefs regarding the words he had only ever used as abstractions had been shaken. Brown was different from abolitionists, who were "not better men for their zeal. They have neither abolished slavery in Carolina, nor in me. If they cannot break one fetter of mine, I cannot hope they will of any negro. They are bitter sterile people, whom I flee from, to the unpretentious whom they disparage."[27]

By August of 1857, Brown was settled at his new base of operations in Tabor, Iowa. Hugh Forbes joined him; that man had made all haste to draw the funds authorized him, but had shown considerably less urgency when it came to doing the contracted work. To complicate things, he and Brown clashed over the particulars of the plan; Forbes advocated something like Brown's older "Subterranean Pass Way" scheme, and felt that anything bigger was lunacy.[28] To placate him, Brown agreed—or feigned agreement—on a plan for a quick raid and escape called the "Well Matured Plan."

While the Old Man waited on Forbes's manual, his health was failing. He distracted himself from his painful fever by reading about Toussaint and about Arthur Wellesley, who had aided the Spaniards in grinding up Napoleon's *Grand Armée* over a nearly eight year span, after which they disgorged its mangled pieces across the pages of histories that the West's military class would do anything possible to forget. Part of Wellington's success was arming Spanish insurgents with 80,000 steel bladed pikes. Brown also made lists in his notebook of federal arsenal locations either within or bordering the South.[29] Whatever he planned, it didn't appear to be Underground Railroad business.

Aside from illness, Brown was vexed by numerous problems, not the least of which was an ill-timed apparent outbreak of peace in Kansas. If President Buchanan had possessed a cogently articulated pro-slavery plot for Kansas' political fate when he appointed Mississippi's Robert Walker to be the territorial governor, it backfired. Walker surprised everyone involved by being a scrupulously honest executive, as forthright as Geary before him. Most suspected that Walker was appointed to rig the Kansas elections, but he ensured that there was no Missouri interference, nor were fraudulent returns counted. The free-state side won overwhelmingly, complicating Brown's fundraising pitch.

Maybe he had seen it coming; prior to the elections he had shifted his narrative away from Kansas to "secret service & no questions asked."[30] To be fair, while touring the northeast his rousing Kansas stories had always been spare on details concerning his plans. He mostly let his audiences fill in the blanks with conjecture. On one rare occasion someone caught on to this and queried him directly about invading Missouri or the South, and Brown firmly replied, "You all know me. You are acquainted with my history. You know what I have done in Kansas. I do not expose my plans. No one knows them but myself, except perhaps one. I will not be interrogated; if you wish to give me anything I want you to give it freely. I have no other purpose but to serve the cause of liberty."[31]

The peace dividend in Kansas emptied Brown's coffers and voided his pledge notes; he could barely afford food. Stearns to cancelled his own generous authorization for $7,000, and to complicate matters Brown's drill-master was increasingly discontented and mutinous. To be certain, Forbes had reason to doubt Brown, if for no other reason than he found himself training a class of one—Owen—at his new school in Tabor. That was inauspicious enough, but it was the lack of money that troubled Forbes, whose primary motivation in life appeared to be mercenary.

Franklin Sanborn explained the shortfalls to Brown with dismay and embarrassment, writing, "There has been no such pressure since 1837, if things were as bad then."

Things really were quite worse then, but Sanborn was a young man, and may be forgiven his lack of perspective for an event that happened when he was six. All told though, things were quite bad.

Something had caused an abrupt, unexpected implosion of the booming speculative securities market racing along the railroad lines. In this case, cause of the newest panic seemed to be the spectacular failure of Ohio Life, a large mortgage-holding bank, on August 24, 1857. Most commercial bank suspensions occurred in the wake of that event.[32] Panic really is the best descriptor for (economic) crises, since they essentially happen when the pseudo-scientific oracular predictions of the social model don't fulfill the tautologies that people desperately crave. Fear fills in the rest.

But Ohio Life was merely a symptom. The engines of growth, exploitation and optimism were the locomotives, and they steamed in one direction: Kansas. Between April and June, Kansas land warrants shed 10 percent of their previously dizzying value, beginning a downward trajectory that would continue for the next two years. The stock of the major westward trunk lines followed predictably, plummeting anywhere from 15 percent to 50 percent, and foundered there for two more years as well. And as the railroad went, so did the increasingly networked economy—to a degree. A number of banks not involved in the mortgage business, or ones that were connected strongly with cotton and the slave trade, fared reasonably well during this period.[33]

This story did not start with Ohio Life, but around 1800 when a man named Dred Scott was born into slavery. In 1820 with the passage of the Missouri Compromise his owner, Peter Blow, relocated him to Missouri. After Blow's death, Scott was purchased in 1833 by a U.S. Army surgeon named John Emerson, and taken to Fort Armstrong in the free state of Illinois. Another move followed in 1836 to Fort Snelling in the Wisconsin territory, specifically designated "free" under the Wisconsin Enabling Act. Technically, John Emerson was in violation of the law, but the law came from a social paradigm that was never equipped to deal with an increasingly mobile society. The territory-based statutes regarding the subjugation of human beings were based on antiquated assumptions that involved landed gentry and a slow permanence of map and place.

The situation became more complicated when Scott married Harriet Robinson. Under Southern statutes, slaves couldn't legally marry because, as non-persons, they could not enter into contracts. Then in 1837, John Emerson was relocated to Missouri, but he left Scott behind to be hired out for labor, an arrangement that was—on a micro scale—an example of an illegal interstate slave economy.

After John Emerson married Eliza Sanford and relocated to Louisiana, he summoned Scott back, and during the journey Harriet Scott gave birth to a daughter on a steamboat along the Iowa border, which made the child legally free. John Emerson's family and the Scotts returned to the Wisconsin Territory again in 1838, and in 1840 while John Emerson fought in the Second Seminole War, his wife and child moved to St. Louis while hiring Scott out in Wisconsin.[34]

The Seminole War was yet another artifact, in a way, of Andrew Jackson's rising star after 1812. During the war, English soldiers on the Florida peninsula built an armed fort at Prospect Bluff, intending to recruit allies among the natives and the enslaved to help continue their campaign. Jackson's men thwarted their one incursion north prior to the conflict's end, shortly after the treaty was signed. Under the terms of the Treaty of Ghent the English gave the fort to their allies, and it was soon the sole property of the fugitive slaves; the Seminole had no interest in it. The whispers of a fort at Prospect Bluff controlled by escaped slaves terrified the South. They feared it would become a magnet for other fugitives, or worse.[35]

Worse happened, and after a group from the fort killed some U.S. sailors, Andrew Jackson determined to destroy the outpost. He faced a problem, however, in that it was technically in Spanish territory, and Spain's territorial governor either lacked the resources or the inclination to have the place destroyed. So as the U.S. Army built a regional network of outposts, they routed their supply lines in a way that would enable them to keep a watchful eye on the so-called "Negro Fort," all while presenting an omnipresent target in the hopes of creating a pretext. It didn't take long, and in July of 1816 the two sides exchanged fire. A chance shot hit the fort's gunpowder stores, causing an explosion that killed nearly all the occupants, mostly families and fearful escapees.[36]

Mission complete, the Army withdrew its line of outposts and the void was filled with thieving and murderous settlers. The Seminole retaliated in kind, and hostilities escalated into the First Seminole War. That conflict became one more chapter of the Andrew Jackson legend, ultimately resulting in the cession of Florida by Spain. During the war, Jackson conducted himself in a questionable and highly autocratic manner, to include summarily executing two British subjects, but his popularity was such that Congressional inquiries were mere formalities. The Seminole were resettled onto a reservation, and their eventual resistance to subsequent resettlement under Jackson's "solution" to the Indian problem led to the Second Seminole War in 1836.

John Emerson returned home from that war and died in the Iowa territory in 1843, whereupon Scott attempted to purchase his freedom from Eliza Emerson. She refused, and Scott sued in Missouri for his freedom in 1846. Missouri was the logical choice, since as recently as 1834 the Missouri Supreme Court had ruled in *Rachel v. Walker* that an Army officer taking his slave to a free territory forfeited the ownership of that slave. For Scott, however, the decision came out differently. Paradoxically, since Scott wasn't a "person" by law, he could not give witness testimony regarding his ownership, and since he failed to produce a witness who was a real person, a lower court dismissed the case regarding his personhood.

He was eventually granted a new trial, and in 1850 a court ruled that Scott was, indeed, free. But Eliza Emerson appealed the decision all the way to the Missouri Supreme Court; after all, aside from the loss of his liquid value, her continued life of relative leisure depended upon his present and future labor. In 1852, the Supreme Court of Missouri issued a decision which reflected the increasingly powerful regime of oppression of black people in America. The court's opinion read:

> Times are not now as they were when the former decisions on this subject were made. Since then not only individuals but States have been possessed with a dark and fell spirit in relation to slavery, whose gratification is sought in the pursuit of measures, whose inevitable consequences must be the overthrow and destruction of our government. Under such circumstances it does not behoove the State of Missouri to show the least countenance to any measure which might gratify this spirit. She is willing to assume her full responsibility for the existence of slavery within her limits, nor does she seek to share or divide it with others.[37]

13. The Child with the Mirror

This had always been an interstate legal contest, and the new executor of John Emerson's estate, John Sanford, was a native of New York, so Scott sued again in federal court. The court unfortunately followed the (new) Missouri precedent, and so *Scott v. Sanford* was appealed to the United States Supreme Court.

By the fall of 1856, the issue had become literally bloody, if not potentially explosive. After "doughface" James Buchanan's electoral victory, he started exerting pressure on the Supreme Court to render a decision that would place the issue forever beyond any further political debates.[38] Prior to the inauguration, Justice Taney assured Buchanan that the decision would be favorable, so when the newly sworn president gave his first speech, he addressed the slavery divide by plumly declaring it was "happily, a matter of but little practical importance." Besides, as a judicial question, it legitimately belonged to the Supreme Court of the United States, before whom it was pending, and would, he understood, be "speedily and finally settled." He went on to utter words that were at the time the statements of an insulated and petty plutocrat, and are in retrospect grotesquely ironic: "Most happy will it be for the country when the public mind shall be diverted from this question to others of more pressing and practical importance. Throughout the whole progress of this agitation, which has scarcely known any intermission for more than twenty years, whilst it has been productive of no positive good to any human being it has been the prolific source of great evils to the master, to the slave, and to the whole country."

To create the appearance of a court not divided on sectional lines, he persuaded a northern justice to side with the southern majority, and on March 6, 1857, the Taney Court delivered the expected ruling. According to Taney, the drafters of the Constitution regarded black people as "beings of an inferior order, and altogether unfit to associate with the white race, either in social or political relations, and so far inferior that they had no rights which the white man was bound to respect."

Taney was sadly incorrect; that was the very problem. However, lest anyone give Justice Taney too much credit for engineering a legal reckoning, his justification was based at least in part on fearful racist hyperbole: "It would give to persons of the negro race ... the right to enter every other State whenever they pleased, ... to sojourn there as long as they pleased, to go where they pleased ... the full liberty of speech in public and in private upon all subjects upon which its own citizens might speak; to hold public meetings upon political affairs, and to keep and carry arms wherever they went."

Officially ruling that Dred Scott was a commodity rather than a person implied that declaring the territories of the Louisiana Purchase "free" was beyond the federal government's power. This ruling voided the Missouri Compromise and also set the stage for the expansion of the slave-power, potentially repeating the Kansas conflict in territory after territory. The value of heretofore profitable land speculations in Kansas was decimated as the future of the entire western frontier was thrown into turmoil. The wave of immigration suddenly choked off, and the fortunes of the railroad followed.

The Old Man's operational budget tracked the economy's glum trajectory, making it impossible to pay Forbes, who saw it all as a deliberate attempt to personally wrong him. Forbes wrote a shrilly angry letter to Howe, claiming that his wife and daughter in Paris were starving, and that Howe and his associates were "guilty of perfidy and barbarity, to which may be added stupidity.... You must be worse than insane—you must be depraved."[39]

Brown needed something to reinvigorate his cause, and Forbes's verbal abuse of his benefactors, despite the fading support, was certainly not it. Then, unexpectedly, Kansas beckoned again when he received funds from James Lane along with a request to bring his weaponry to Lawrence. That November, Brown decided to go to Lawrence to "see how the land lies."[40] The Old Man left his weapons in Tabor, however, deeming it unwise to give them over to James Lane, much to the latter's disappointment. Forbes went with Brown, but did not complete the journey. He mysteriously disappeared after they crossed the Iowa border in Nebraska City.

14

Preparatory Men

> *There are men, who, by their sympathetic attractions, carry nations with them, and lead the activity of the human race. And if there be such a tie, that, wherever the mind of man goes, nature will accompany him, perhaps there are men whose magnetisms are of that force to draw material and elemental powers, and, where they appear, immense instrumentalities organize around them.*
> —Ralph Waldo Emerson, *Power*

On a snowy Sunday morning in Lawrence, William Phillips heard that the "old man" wished to see him again. Brown was concerned that the free state politicians in Lawrence had sacrificed their principles and their cause for their recent power, and thus their usefulness was coming to an end. He made dire accusations about some individuals in particular, and about compromises with the slave-power, but Phillips assured him that such was not the case; the free state leaders were true.

Brown fixed Phillips in his terrible gaze, then took his surveying compass from his pocket and placed it on the table. "You see that needle," he said, never taking his eyes from Phillips, "it wabbles about and is mighty unsteady, but *it wants to point to the north.* Is he like that needle?" Phillips was at a loss for words.

So Brown went on to describe his fundraising, and the men he was gathering, and wondered where Phillips thought would be an opportune place to strike. Missouri, perhaps? Phillips had never regarded the imperious Brown as the type to heed advice, but thought that maybe things were different this time, and so he suggested that the Old Man should instead lay down his burdens, and settle on a plot of land by Salina—Phillips would, in fact, give him the title. Brown could stay there and start a prosperous community, and also be ever ready for Missourian mischief. But Brown would not hear of it. He informed Phillips he would be returning to Tabor to continue his fight.

Since arriving in Lawrence, Brown had collected a $500 bequest from George Stearns, and had set about gathering his troops. First he had asked John Cook if he would like to join a "company for the purpose of putting a stop to the aggressions of the pro Slavery men," and furthermore if he knew anyone else who would join.[1] Cook eagerly signed up, and was soon joined by another old acquaintance—Aaron D. "Captain Whipple" Stevens—as well as Whipple's compatriot John Kagi.

Stevens would become Brown's warrior, but Kagi was the group's intellectual and mentor, an articulate man who was never without a small satchel of his own essays, even while fighting in Kansas. He was educated in law, logic, and mathematics, and had taught school for a time in Virginia before he returned to his native Ohio as an outspoken opponent of slavery. In the summer of 1856 he went to Kansas as a newspaper correspondent but became part of the story, fighting in "Captain Whipple's" company before being captured and jailed. Religion and God were "useless problems" to the atheist Kagi, whose hatred of slavery nonetheless came from a place just as passionate as Brown's.[2]

After his meeting with Phillips, the Old Man left for Tabor with nine men. Along the journey he considered his options and reflected on his dreams, and one evening he gathered his recruits around the campfire to explain his plans. If it wasn't apparent already, Brown pointed out that Kansas was far too peaceful now for them to act. And the Kansas winter, as everyone was certain to recall, was never conducive to guerrilla warfare anyway. But Brown had a plan; this new adventure would involve something quite different. He looked at each of them, the crackling fire glinting in his eyes and throwing sparks into the chill autumn air. His words coiled in his fogged breath as he said, "Our ultimate destination is Virginia."[3]

It seemed the height of folly—it *was* the height of folly—and many of the men were opposed. It was also the beginning of a prickly relationship between Brown and Cook. Some believed in later days that Brown harbored a mistrust of Cook merely due to his garrulous tongue. Cook was a man who may have understood that it was possible for people to pass moments in silence, but simply didn't understand why they would, while Brown was of a more reticent character. But, when Brown told his Kansas refugees their destination, it was Cook who quarreled the longest, and the two men wrangled over the issue for days, setting the domineering Brown on edge with everyone, including Owen.

Hugh Forbes (Library of Congress).

The war in Kansas was over. Everyone probably knew it, and they had been told to lay down their weapons. Yet each man knew that the war was only just beginning, if they could survive the journey there. Kansas may have become a free state, but Brown's men had gone for the liberation of the slave, and that task was not yet done, so they would keep their weapons and their valor, and by the former somehow make use of the latter. The debate tested Brown's nerves, but the only true question was not whether they would continue this journey or stay behind, but rather how best to conduct the journey, and where the destination would be. And since each had, for private reasons, elected to follow the strange

Old Man with his dreams of lightning and fire, they followed him still when he announced that they were going to Ohio to train closer to their goal.

On the road in December Brown gradually revealed the details of his plan. They listened closely, though Kagi and Stevens didn't care so much for Brown's more oracular "Bible talk," nor did Owen, an agnostic who had grown up with it. But their respect for the Old Man's ideas and for the man himself carried them along and kept their excitement high.

Evening campfire conversations were sketched out in Owen's journal, like on December 7 when gentle snow fell beautifully on a discussion about theories regarding moral killing and the sexual exploitation of slaves: "the inconsistency of the Slave-holder mingling in breed etc. with the Africans at the same time calling them brutes." On the 8th they had an apparently rousing debate about some of the Bible's pricklier issues, like polygamy, infidelity, and war, and speculated about the economic and political consequences of abolition for the southern and northern states. They discussed the philosophical origins of civilization, while forming their own little polity around these questions, journeying from danger into danger, attempting to gain relief from the biting vermin while the snow blew and the wolves howled in the distance.[4]

Funds exhausted, Brown was compelled to leave his men in Springdale, Iowa, for the rest of the winter while he went east in search of at least a small portion of his pledges. He stopped briefly in Ohio to visit with John, Jr., then continued to the home of Frederick Douglass on January 28, 1858. They spoke in greater detail about Brown's Subterranean Pass Way, now transformed into a much more expansive vision. "The horrors" that Brown intended to visit on the South made Douglass shudder ever so slightly, but it was "the shudder one feels at the execution of a murderer," the confusing feeling of an awareness of evil, a sense of justice, and a visceral satisfaction wholly separated from logics. Ultimately, Douglass believed it was a foolishly doomed gesture, and also found that Brown's singular focus had become "something of a bore" to him.[5] Douglass was not interested in helping, but introduced Brown to a friend of his named Shields Green who potentially was.

The Old Man started formalizing his polity during the lonely hours in the spare bedroom in Douglass's home, drafting a "Provisional Constitution" for implementation in a fugitive state in the Alleghenies. He also began a letter writing campaign to all his closest backers, like Stearns, Parker, and Sanborn, and wrote as well to Mary, expressing his regrets that though he was in New York, he would likely be unable to see her, despite how much he wished to. "But, courage, courage, courage!—the great work of my life ... I may yet see accomplished (God helping), and be permitted to return and 'rest at evening.'" He pleaded with Ruth to allow Henry to join him, and to inquire as well with Salmon, Oliver, and Watson. But, he cautioned her to be discreet about his presence in the East, and to address any correspondence to "N. Hawkins, care of Frederick Douglass."[6]

When his supporters replied, Brown discovered that Hugh Forbes had been roundly abusing them, even turning his temper on Charles Sumner in letters that lived somewhere between "insult and lunacy." An exasperated Franklin Sanborn wished Brown would do something about Forbes, who "might be hanged" for all he cared.[7] Brown refused to communicate directly with Forbes, and instead used John, Jr., to convey his displeasure, reminding Forbes of the considerable funds already given him, for which little had been received in return. The Old Man made sure Forbes understood that he did not take kindly to "highly offensive and insulting" letters to either his friends, or himself.[8]

By and large Brown's friends responded positively, though not with money. Gerrit Smith summoned everyone to Peterboro to discuss matters further, while Stearns, though ambivalent, was willing to at least listen more in Boston. Higginson, the fiery cleric, wrote cheerfully that he was "always ready to invest in treason, but at present have none to invest. As for my friends, those who are able are not quite willing, and those who are willing are at present bankrupt."[9] But Higginson decided not to meet with Brown, since he felt that the Old Man's explanations about "Rail Road business on a *somewhat extended* scale" were far too vague.[10] Sanborn was on the fence, given the drama involving Forbes and rumors about Brown from some in Kansas (who were upset that Brown had not given his money and weapons to them), but was persuaded by a friend to rendezvous at Smith's Peterboro home.[11]

The previous March, Sanborn had proudly announced to a Concord audience that should there be war over slavery, freedom would need men like John Brown. Now he questioned his sanity while Brown outlined his Provisional Constitution, and the necessity of it for the general insurrection he intended to ignite in the South. "It is an amazing proposition," Sanborn told him cautiously, as Smith looked on. He likely meant "amazing" as a euphemism for desperate, and certainly fantastic.

To Brown it seemed simple; the earliest stages would of course be the longest, and the most dangerous, as he attempted to put as much space as possible between his freed slaves and the South's armies. But once he and his armed fugitives reached the mountains his small state would never be overtaken. The South would not dare attack with just a small army, and a large and heavily equipped army would lack the ability to march quickly, and might even suffer from supply exhaustion. There, said he, "if God be for us, who can be against us?" He intended to proceed with or without their support, and was prepared to die, if necessary.

Sanborn and Smith took a walk outside among skeletal trees and powder-crusted pines to talk and clear their heads while Brown waited inside. Sanborn was dizzy with the difficult and impossible position he found himself in. But it was Smith who got to the heart of the matter. It mattered little whether they believed Brown's plan was possible; did they believe in Brown the man, and in the man's will? Because if they believed he meant every word, then this was a human question about John Brown the man, not about the end of the South, or even the Union. "You see how it is," Smith said, "our dear old friend has made up his mind to this course, and cannot be turned from it. We cannot give him up to die alone; we must support him. I will raise so many hundred dollars for him; you must lay the case before your friends in Massachusetts, and ask them to do as much. I see no other way." Sanborn had come to the very same conclusion: a choice between betrayal or support.[12]

Sanborn, who had done more than anyone to make all of these developments possible, left the next day for Boston to try to arrange more fundraisers, and the Old Man wrote him a letter of gratitude. Maybe Brown felt he deserved not only heartfelt thanks for overcoming doubt, but also something close to confessed truth about the mission, so that when it was over, no matter what the outcome, Sanborn would not have to live with the burden.

"My dear Friend," Brown wrote, "Mr. Morton has taken the liberty of saying to me that you felt half inclined to make a common cause with me. I greatly rejoice at this....

> You will feel that you are out of your element until you find you are in it, an entire unit. What an inconceivable amount of good you might so effect by your counsel, your example, your encouragement, your natural and acquired ability for active service! ... Certainly the cause is enough to *live* for, if not to—for. I have only had this one opportunity, in a life of nearly sixty years; and could I be continued ten times as long again, I might not again have another equal opportunity.... I expect nothing but to "endure hardness"; but I expect to effect a mighty conquest, even though it be *like the last victory of Samson*. I felt for a number of years, in earlier life, a steady, strong desire to die; but since I saw any prospect of becoming a "reaper" in the great harvest, I have not only felt quite willing to live, but have enjoyed life much; and am now rather anxious to live for a few years more.[13]

That March of 1858, Sanborn's Boston friends were far more supportive than perhaps Brown anticipated. President Buchanan was helping by threatening to override the vote in Kansas, and he was pressuring the pro-slavery Senate to admit Kansas as a slave state based on the fraudulent Lecompton Constitution. Howe and Parker were preparing for conflict, and Higginson started asking the Old Man whether he was going to make some spectacular disunionist move, or if he was merely talk.

By this point, even the peaceful Stearns and Sanborn were starting to believe, again, that the conspiracy could only end in war. Howe put the remaining doubts about Brown's plan to rest, drawing on his experience in the Greek rebellion to pronounce the plan feasible, even if it was a long shot. But as Sanborn recalled, the endorsement was reassuring but unnecessary. Since his walk with Smith they had already decided to support him even "without accepting [the] plans as reasonable ... we were prepared to second them merely because they were his."[14]

The group in Boston wrote to Smith to inform him of their commitment. Smith, so tepid and distant only a year prior, gleefully wrote to Joshua Giddings that "the slave will be delivered by the shedding of blood, and the signs are multiplying that his deliverance is at hand."[15] It seemed that everyone in the Committee of Six was paraphrasing the Old Man.

Assured of the backing of the Committee of Six, Brown went to work gathering his fighters. He knew that most abolitionists would not join him—they were of Garrison's mold—and even if they weren't, they were certainly not going to undertake a truly dangerous expedition for something that was to them an abstract social ill. So he and John, Jr., canvassed the black churches and the homes of prominent black leaders in Philadelphia in the hopes that they would prepare recruits for the coming invasion and the convulsions to follow.[16]

From there it was back to North Elba to see if his sons had experienced a change of heart. Henry Thompson—or at least Ruth—was firm in his resolve to no longer fight the Old Man's war, but after a long argument Watson and Oliver came around. Brown did not try to recruit Jason, but not because of any ill will towards his son. Rather, even if Brown could persuade Jason, it would have been a terrible evil against that gentle soul.

John, Jr., had come out of Kansas a broken man, and the Old Man seemed unwilling to ask his most militant son to come on his final mission. John, Jr., was given other, less demanding tasks. While Brown canvassed the free black communities at the Underground Railroad's Canadian terminus, John, Jr., remained behind to continue networking in New York's free black settlements. In Canada, Brown met the legendary Harriet Tubman, who promised to spread the word, and provided all the information she could about the Virginia terrain from her frequent and dangerous travels. The Old Man, for his part, was overwhelmed by his impressions of that brave woman.[17] After dozens of new supporters agreed to meet in May in Chatham, Ontario, Brown hastened back to Iowa to see how his men had fared during the winter.

He found his men in Springdale restless but well, having managed to survive the winter without being shot by angry fathers for being too popular with some daughters, particularly C.P. Tidd and the ever charming Cook. Owen and Stevens had kept them busy doing "military maneuvers" around the small farm, and between that and the boys' odd mock legislature meetings, their Quaker neighbors were half convinced that they harbored Mormon spies. But the Abolitionist Quakers had sheltered Brown's young party, as promised, through the winter.

New recruits had joined in Brown's absence. Two were local Quakers: Barclay and Edwin Coppoc. Another was George B. Gill, who had known Brown in Kansas and who had introduced the Old Man to Stewart Taylor, a young Canadian who also joined them in Springdale in the increasingly cramped farmhouse. Brown gathered all his recruits from their winter hideout, wrote to his sons to expect to be "called on before the middle of May," and set out for Chatham.

It was supremely ironic that the May 8 Chatham Convention where Brown presented his Provisional Constitution and recruited to overthrow the social order was disguised as the opening of a Masonic lodge. The Old Man circulated through the Chatham schoolhouse shaking hands and smiling despite his disappointment at the small turnout among black supporters from the States, and Underground Railroad passengers. The absence of his most influential backers was near deafening. Nevertheless, Brown would not be deterred from telling those who had troubled to show up about his breathtaking goal.

As he told it, he had harbored this dream for nearly thirty years. It was born emotionally of lifelong sympathies and intellectually from the 1848 European revolutions. If enough men followed him, it would be a story to add to an arc that spanned from the Spanish uprising against Rome, to Napoleon's defeat in that same land, to Toussaint L'Ouverture. As Brown explained to the delegates, he had only gone to Kansas "to gain a footing for the furtherance of this matter." Maybe that was merely how he comprehended the original journey, or how he wanted to tell it, but it was essentially true that all of these things had set him irrevocably on the path where he had "devoted his whole being, mental, moral, and physical, all that he had and was to the extinction of slavery."[18]

After swearing all present to secrecy, he revealed his proposed constitution. As the preamble read:

> Whereas slavery, throughout its entire existence in the United States, is none other than a most barbarous, unprovoked, and unjustifiable war of one portion of its citizens upon another portion—the only conditions of which are perpetual imprisonment and hopeless servitude or absolute extermination—in utter disregard and violation of those eternal and self-evident truths set forth in our Declaration of Independence:

14. Preparatory Men

Therefore we, citizens of the United States, and the oppressed people who, by a recent decision of the Supreme Court, are declared to have no rights which the white man is bound to respect, together with all other people degraded by the laws thereof, do, for the time being, ordain and establish for ourselves the following Provisional Constitution and Ordinances, the better to protect our persons, property, lives, and liberties, and to govern our actions.

The remainder of the document, forty-eight articles in all, wasn't the most elegant political charter ever drafted—a curiously unstructured combination of administration with the personal, domestic, and mundane. It was also an appropriation of the cultural forms of the program of nationalism, a clever historical scripting in the manner of the narrative plot that had been accepted as social vector: cause, convention, constitution, convulsion, and thence civilization.[19]

Article 46 was a candid admission of the document's derivative character and its intentionally temporary scope: "These articles not for the overthrow of government," it reads. "The foregoing articles shall not be construed so as in any way to encourage the overthrow of any State government, or of the general government of the United States, and look to no dissolution of the Union, but simply to amendment and repeal. And our flag shall be the same that our fathers fought under in the Revolution."[20]

That mitigating article was the only point of contention in the document, but in the end the constitution was unanimously approved. Support was less than unanimous for the Old Man's dangerous proposal though. Some were willing to go, but most who were there had already risked death escaping north on the Underground Railroad, and the thought of returning to the South to possibly die in a likely futile insurrection against the South's garrison state was simply horrifying. But as Brown saw it, he had already come out of Kansas unscathed, and: "Did not my Master Jesus Christ come down from Heaven and sacrifice Himself upon the altar for the salvation of the race, and should I, a worm, not worthy to crawl under His feet, refuse to sacrifice myself?"[21]

The convention was intended to have been the start of the movement South, but Brown had almost no fighters, and couldn't even finance his travel. As he wrote Mary, he was "completely nailed down at present" and "may be obliged to remain inactive for months yet."[22] When Brown did finally obtain funds, they arrived with troubling news about the expanding mischief of Hugh Forbes.

No longer content to merely abuse Sanborn and his friends, Forbes had decided to write to Senator William H. Seward of New York and Senator Henry Wilson of Massachusetts to partially expose the plan and denounce Brown as a "very bad man."[23] Forbes went so far as to allege a grand conspiracy concocted by Amos Lawrence, who supposedly wished to reinvigorate his private fortune by speculation on a post-insurrection cotton trade.[24] Tellingly, Forbes chose to contact Abolitionist Senators who had supported the various Kansas Committees, and not Southern representatives who would have swiftly acted to crush the plot. Forbes made certain to highlight his differences with Brown, positioning himself as being aligned with the Kansas Committee's true intentions. What he wanted was to assume leadership of the effort, and to have access to what he believed would be a comfortable flow of income and, most importantly, historical glory.

What he achieved was absolute panic on the part of Sanborn, Smith, Parker, and

Stearns. Senator Wilson contacted them with awkward questions, and gave instructions to see that the weapons pledged to Brown were placed in the hands of more "reliable men."[25] Most importantly, he wanted assurances that nothing like what Forbes claimed was being planned.

It was a splash of chilling reality to the Committee of Six, who feared possible accusations of treason, and wanted to call off Brown's mission. But not Higginson; that worthy was furious about his friends' timidity. If not now, then when? Higginson felt that if they waited, Forbes, or someone else, would just throw another wrinkle into the arrangements, but if they started now, it wouldn't matter what anyone said. Nonetheless, an emergency meeting was called, with all attending save Higginson, and they decided to postpone the plan. Ever a pendulum of sentiment, Gerrit Smith insisted that he "never was convinced of the wisdom of [the] scheme."[26]

Lavishly spending some of his few remaining dollars, Brown travelled the rails to Boston to reassure the Six. But they were adamant, and insisted Brown return to Kansas in order to throw Forbes off the trail and convince all who were watching that he intended—as he had said all along—to dedicate his arms to matters there. Brown reluctantly agreed, "but the sly old veteran," Higginson recalled, "had appeared to acquiesce far more than he really did; it was essential that they should not think him reckless."[27] The crafty Brown then granted his backers plausible deniability by reaching an agreement that henceforth they would know nothing of his plans, and by personally taking possession of all the weaponry.

He departed on June 3 to rejoin his little group and disperse them. Richard Realf was assigned to mark Forbes in New York and ensure that he did nothing rash. Stevens and Gill were to continue fundraising and then rendezvous with the Old Man in Kansas. Cook insisted on going to Harpers Ferry as an advance scout, and surprisingly Brown consented, despite the fact that Cook had done little but run his mouth recently about his "secret expedition." Realf believed that Cook was at least as much a threat as Forbes to the secrecy of the scheme, with his incurable "tongue malady."[28] Allowing Cook, his silver tongued trickster, to prepare the way at Harpers Ferry would turn out to be one of the most inspired decisions Brown ever made. In the meanwhile he had to return to Lawrence one last time.

15

The Convalescent Wanderer

God is dead. God remains dead. And we have killed him.... Who will wipe this blood off us? ... Here the madman fell silent and looked again at his listeners; and they too were silent and stared at him in astonishment. At last he threw his lantern on the ground, and it broke and went out. "I have come too early," he said then: "my time has not come yet. This tremendous event is still on its way, still wandering—it has not yet reached the ears of man. Lightning and thunder require time, the light of the stars requires time, deeds require time even after they are done, before they can be seen and heard. This deed is still more distant from them than the most distant stars—and yet they have done it themselves."
—Friedrich Nietzsche, *The Gay Science*

The Old Man travelled under the alias Shubel Morgan with Tidd and Kagi. He built a small house on Eli Snyder's claim, which had a commanding view of all the terrain, including the scene of the Marais des Cygnes killings. Later that summer Stevens and Gill rejoined him. Kansas was restless, but certainly not the violent place he wrote about to Sanborn.[1] Brown may have believed in rumors, or may have been leading his audience, but the most nervous event in the territory was the August 2 vote, and even that went smoothly.

Mississippi's Walker became the second territorial governor to resign in protest over President Buchanan's attempt to override the Kansas vote. After his resignation a new election was called, resulting in an overwhelming 6 to 1 margin in favor of admitting Kansas to the Union as a free state. This outcome made Brown's purported mission unnecessary, and extinguished any abolitionist zeal for supporting him. Chas Blair, who had been forging Brown's pikes, was far more understanding than Hugh Forbes had been about payment. He understood that financial times were hard, and he certainly "did not know but things would take such a turn in Kansas, that they would not be needed."[2]

Any troubles in Kansas seemed centered on the Old Man. The "Shubel Morgan" cover was remarkably transparent, and word spread that John Brown was improving a claim right on the border. As a consequence, hostile visitors gravitated to the property. Brown accosted one trespasser by reciting the litany of Ruffian wrongs, and informing the man that Missourians in the region "might have perfect quiet if they honestly desired it, and further, that if they chose *War* they would soon have all they might *any of them* care for." The man did not doubt the fearsome old abolitionist with the flowing white beard and those hard eyes. Brown related that he then "gave him the most powerful

Abolition lecture of which I am capable, having an unusual gift of utterance for me." But before sending him home to warn others, Brown fed the man dinner.[3]

A few days later, Brown was in Missouri along with Kagi, Tidd, and Eli Snyder. Spying a cabin in a grove, Snyder took a closer look through Brown's field glass and exclaimed in surprise, "I declare that is Martin White, reading a book in a chair in the shade of a tree." Amazed that fate had delivered them an opportunity to avenge Frederick, he turned to Brown and said, "Suppose you and I go down and see the old man and have a talk with him." Old Man knew what kind of "talk" Snyder meant, but also he knew revenge for Frederick could not be in this manner.

"No, no," he told Snyder, "I can't do that," as Kagi's jaw dropped in disbelief. "Let Snyder and me go," Kagi pleaded with menace. "Go if you wish" Brown replied, "but don't you hurt a hair on his head; but if he has any slaves take the last one of them." Kagi grudgingly relented.[4] Brown would later express a similar sentiment to James Hanway. "People mistake my objects.... I would not hurt one hair on [White's] head. I would not go one inch to take his life; I do not harbor feelings of revenge. *I act from a principle. My aim and object is to restore human rights.*"[5] He wouldn't be able to visit Hanway for a month though, as he fell frightfully ill—an increasingly common occurrence—and spent the time recovering at Samuel Adair's home, wracked by fever and malarial or typhoid-like symptoms. Kagi and Florella Adair nursed him to health, and by September Brown could write to his wife that though he was still feeble, he would be able to move soon.[6]

The tragedy of getting away with something is that you must live with yourself, and Brown's tragedy was that those he helped and those he hurt hated and feared him the same. When Brown was well enough to visit Hanway, he was overjoyed when Hanway told him that, by and large, the killings were regarded as justifiable. "Oh, I knew the time would come when people who understood the circumstances ... would endorse it," he said, transformed from the sickly, feeble man he had been just days prior into nervous, pacing energy. "I tell you, Mr. Hanway," he said, spinning around after a moment of contemplation, "that it is infinitely better that this generation should be swept away from the face of the earth, than that slavery shall continue to exist."[7]

Judge Hanway would conclude, in time, that the Pottawatomie killings "prevented the ruffian hordes from carrying out their programme of expelling the Free-State men from this portion of the Territory of Kansas ... 'for God only knows what our fate and condition would have been, if old John Brown had not driven terror and consternation into the ranks of the proslavery party.'"[8]

Brown went to Lawrence as another autumn fell on Kansas, and the air quickened with crisp rattling breezes. While there, he dispatched Kagi to find William Phillips, who was still writing stories about the territory. Since their last meeting, Phillips had heard many rumors about the Old Man; he was in New England, then Canada, perhaps in the Ohio valley. So he was quite surprised when John Kagi knocked on his door to tell him that Brown was there—in Lawrence—and wished to speak with him.

Phillips refused, and sent Kagi back to tell the Old Man that he felt it was a futile exercise to speak with him, since Brown never listened to advice and was unlikely to start. Phillips declared that he intended to write no more about John Brown. Kagi soon returned and told Phillips that the Old Man was going away soon, and would likely never see him again. He wished to speak one last time. Unable to contain his curiosity and fascination, Phillips finally agreed.

Kagi led him to the Whitney House, a Lawrence hotel by the Kaw River. The Old Man looked up from his page as the two entered, and Phillips was struck by how much he had changed. Older, to be sure, but somehow a more dignified man than the feral guerrilla Phillips had met merely three years prior. He had a long, flowing, white beard, and his eyes seemed brighter, maybe even a bit feverish, and lit by thoughts within once held behind a contemplative repose.

The Old Man had apparently summoned Phillips in order to give the correspondent a history lecture. He began describing the myriad evils of slavery, remembered and forgotten, and emphatically declared that the republic's founders had all been opposed to slavery, and that it was antithetical to the American Constitution. But, he said, as it became increasingly lucrative, good intentions were thrown to the wind and men of avarice came to control the machinery of government. The result was that the country had

John H. Kagi (Library of Congress).

> reached a point where nothing but war can settle the question. Had they succeeded in Kansas, they would have gained a power that would have given them permanently the upper hand, and it would have been the death-knell of republicanism in America. They are checked, but not beaten. They never intend to relinquish the machinery of this government into the hands of the opponents of slavery. It has taken them more than half a century to get it, and they know its significance too well to give it up. If the republican party elects its president next year, there will be war.[9]

Why "they" hadn't succeeded in Kansas hung unspoken between them, silent pretext for the Old Man's plot. Phillips later remembered the exposition as "strangely prophetic," but do prophets see the future, or do they cause it, or is there a difference? Brown had chosen Phillips to be his witness one last time, in this case for his secret future dreams, that he might have a voice when all was said and done, no matter how it might end. Prophesies are only so in memory.

Phillips regarded Brown as having great mental powers, but Brown's prophecy seemed an improbable fantasy if for no other reason than the odds that the next president would be a Republican were slender indeed. The new Republican Party was just confused and lost Whig remnants. Nonetheless, Brown outlined a broad ongoing conspiracy to fortify the South against that eventuality. Most of his claims of soldier and naval movements were unfounded paranoia. But, the movements he described would be entirely logical for a southern society that also saw and feared the war he predicted. The South might not have been afraid enough yet, but when they were, would they move exactly the way Brown described? It seemed farfetched though, given their political dominance, and Phillips was certain that Brown saw monsters where there were none.

Brown's claim that the founders were categorically opposed to slavery was erroneous, yet as a broad statement it was largely in harmony with a certain kind of truth that formed the future-past of histories like Bancroft's, which had difficulty reconciling the founder-mythology, slavery, and the fact that black people were becoming *less* free with every mile west manifest destiny moved. Ultimately, Brown's speech sounded prophetic because he had carefully reconstructed the narrative of the nation's animating principles to re-orient pseudo-religious historical realism so that after the fact people would countenance a war that had not happened yet, a war that was happening every day in Brown's world. It's a pity that the worth of people was not enough.

Brown shook his head. "No," he said, "no, the war is not over. It is a treacherous lull before the storm. We are on the eve of one of the greatest wars in history, and I fear slavery will triumph, and there will be an end of all aspirations for human freedom. For my part, I drew my sword in Kansas when they attacked us, and I will never sheathe it until this war is over. Our best people do not understand the danger. They are besotted. They have compromised so long that they think principles of right and wrong have no more any power on this earth."

At this point, Phillips—a clever man—started to sense what Brown intended, and tried to persuade him that the system could and would sort this out. But Brown would not hear it anymore; too many fearful wrongs had been carried out in the name of that institution. Instead, Brown invoked the slave uprising of Spartacus, and Phillips rebutted with the racist stereotype of the black slave as a "peaceful, domestic, inoffensive race … incapable of resentment or reprisal."

Eyes flashing, Brown retorted, "You have not studied them right, and you have not studied them long enough. Human nature is the same everywhere." Ever conscious of the slipping years, he was beautifully ignorant of just how young he could be, and would be. Brown had a certain innocence in never really understanding just how unique he was in even regarding black slaves as human, which was why he felt they had a common human nature. Phillips didn't understand him because they weren't even speaking the same language.

As the Old Man went on to describe how Spartacus might have triumphed, Phillips became horrified that he was going to lead a group of unsuspecting and idealistic young men on a fool's quest, one which could only end tragically. Brown rose to his feet. "Well," he said, "I thought I could get you to understand this. I do not wonder at it. The world is very pleasant to you, but when your household gods are broken, as mine have been, you will see all this more clearly."

Offended, Phillips turned to leave, but Brown restrained him with a gentle hand, tears shining on his cheeks. "No," he said, "we must not part thus. I wanted to see you and tell you how it appeared to me. With the help of God, I will do what I believe to be best." He grasped Phillips's hands firmly, kissed him on the cheek, and sent him on his way. It was the last time William Phillips ever saw John Brown, but not the last he heard of him.

The Old Man spent the fall attempting mischief in southeast Kansas, where a low-level guerrilla campaign still existed. He was anxious; at 58 years old, his bouts of sickness were getting worse, and he felt that as time passed what little support he had rallied in Chatham was slipping through his fingers. So he roamed, and argued constantly with faithful Stevens, who was impishly pleased to raise "merry hell" whenever Brown became overly querulous. His men patrolled the border, and Brown hoped daily that God "would provide him a basis of action."[10]

Fate provided. Gill was out on scout duty one day when a mulatto man approached, pleading for help. He introduced himself as Jim Daniels and explained that his family all belonged to a Vernon County slave-owner, but the owner intended to break up the family and sell them soon. Gill dashed to their base with the news, and when the Old Man heard it, he leapt to his feet, exuberant for the "heaven-sent" opportunity to possibly begin his war. On the night of December 20, with little time to lose before the sale, Brown and Stevens each led a small group of fighters into Missouri.[11]

The Old Man only had a small personal retinue, so he asked James Montgomery's fighters for help. Thus augmented, Stevens led a party of eight that included Tidd and Hazlett, while Brown was in charge of approximately ten men, among them Gill and Kagi, as well as brutal and less scrupulous men like Charles Jennison, who was in a piratical hiatus between more "official" military appointments.

Brown's column went to the home of Harvey Hicklan, Daniels's master, and forced the door. The expedition was perhaps a little too fruitful. Gill recalled that he "soon discovered that watches and other articles were being taken; some of our number proved to be mere adventurers, ready to take from friend or foe as opportunity offered."[12] Hicklan later pinned the looting on Brown, claiming he said that he "defied [them] and the whole United States to follow him" in order to get their property back. But Brown wasn't talking about the watches and silver.[13] The Old Man referred to the Daniels family, and he successfully rode away with all of them. From there, he went to the home of John Larue, freeing five more slaves and taking Larue and his guest, Dr. Ervin, as prisoners.

Stevens did not fare so well. He was to visit the outlying homesteads, freeing any who wished to come with him. But at the first house he panicked when he thought the home's owner was reaching for a weapon. Stevens shot him and fled with one slave. The incident weighed heavily on the bold and impetuous Stevens, and months later he would tell his friends, "You might call it a case of self-defence ... or you might also say that I had no business in there, and that the old man was right."[14]

Locals on the Kansas side were less than pleased about the freed slaves, for despite the brigandry of men like Montgomery and Jennison, they had achieved an uneasy peace and Kansas's political status was no longer in doubt. Freeing slaves was not, and had never been, their concern. Brown was accused of making trouble that could only come back to people trying to make homes there, and he grumbled vaguely that he too had suffered hardships, an old and sick man, far from home and family, in order to fight for this cause.[15]

The pro-slavery press reacted as Brown wanted, but their shrieks were hollow noise and little else. Samuel Medary, the new territorial governor, kept the peace, and the raid's only political results were some irate people and a $250 bounty on Brown's head, issued by none other than President Buchanan.

On January 7, 1859, Brown was visiting Augustus Wattles, an old friend who had once run a Cincinnati school for Negroes and was now the associate editor of the Lawrence *Herald of Freedom*. Brown was arguing fiercely with Wattles and Montgomery about the recent raid. At his side, Kagi was eloquent as always in the Old Man's defense. An exasperated Brown finally left Kagi to finish the argument while he sat down to compose a short essay titled "Old Brown's Parallels."

The essay justified his little raid into Missouri by juxtaposition (and a hinted causal connection) with the Marais des Cygnes massacre. He felt it rationally preposterous that people who were barely stirred by the Marais des Cygnes killings were suddenly filled with terror at the fact that he had "forcibly restored" eleven human beings to freedom.[16] But fear is not rational.

Brown may have hoped that his "Parallels" would restore philosophical perspective to what he had done, thereby forcing the parties concerned to choose sides that would lead to war, but he had known for a long time that his next step would not happen in Kansas. His new allies had little moral capital, and his local enemies were only minor slaveholders, removed from the core of the institution. The territory's fate was decided, perhaps back in 1856. The potential of terror could not be realized in Kansas anymore.

Brown told Wattles, "I considered the matter well; you will have no more attacks from Missouri; I shall now leave Kansas; probably you will never see me again; I consider it my duty to draw the scene of the excitement to some other part of the country."[17]

It was time, no matter what his backers said, to cross over the river and move on with his plan. But first he needed to deliver to freedom on Canadian soil the eleven slaves he had liberated and who were now in his care. One last pilgrimage before carrying his fight into the great below, and on the 20th of January the Old Man moved northeast with his charges and his men, evading bounty hunters and lawmen. Though not fully recovered from his fever, he drove them at a murderous pace, summoning all of his hellish endurance and fierce determination.[18]

Rumors spread along the mysterious conduits of the Underground Railroad. "Mother, John Brown has started for Canada with the Missouri slaves," wrote Daniel Sheridan, a poor New England settler who lived in a tiny earthen home outside of Topeka, barely large enough for a family of two. He had only one concern when heard that the Old Man was on his way: "Are there plenty of provisions in the house?" In the gray early dawn on January 28, a pounding on the door roused Sheridan. "Who's there?" he asked nervously. "Friends," came the reply. "Are you ready to receive visitors?" It was George Gill, who had ridden ahead of Brown, the wagon, and his eleven refugees. When they all arrived, they were shivering with cold.[19]

Mrs. Sheridan started a fire, and the refugees, many shoeless and shirtless, warmed themselves while Brown paced nervously. After a quick breakfast, the eleven were hidden with neighbors to get some sleep, while Gill and Sheridan went in to Topeka to find warmer clothes. The Old Man hid in the house for everyone's safety; his face was too well known. When Mrs. Sheridan politely inquired how long they would be staying,

Brown answered, "We must be gone to-night.... There is a great work before me—greater than I can tell, and you may never see me again, but you will hear."[20] At dusk the animals were saddled, and Kagi and Stevens rejoined the party. January had been mild, but snow swirled on the winds.

They were accompanied to the Kansas River crossing by Sheridan's neighbor, Jacob Willits, and as the fugitives boarded the ferry and the cold winds sliced across the water, Willits saw the Old Man shivering. "I don't believe that you have enough clothes for this weather," he said with concern. "Do not bother about me," Brown replied. "There are others not so well supplied." Impulsively, and on a hunch, Willits grabbed the Old Man's trousers and found only a single threadbare layer of material. With nothing better to offer, he stripped down right there and removed his own woolen undergarments and offered them. Brown accepted with gratitude.[21]

The next day found them north of Topeka at the home of Albert Fuller, awaiting final re-supply and resting their horses, who were weary and temperamental from dragging their burden through the cold sticky roads. The hunt for Brown and the "property" he had absconded with was in full swing, and two youthful deputies found Stevens while he was watering the horses at nearby Straight Creek. They asked, "Have you seen any slaves around here?" Stevens, the proud fighter, was unarmed; he could have simply waved back and feigned ignorance. Instead, he gave them a friendly smile and answered, "Yes, there are some over there at the cabin now," pointing to the building where his gun and his friends were. With a twinkle in his eye, he helpfully offered to go with them.[22]

After spending an inordinate amount of time fussing with his horse in order to ensure that his friends saw who accompanied him, Stevens walked to the door with one of the deputies in tow. He threw it open, saying, "There they are. Go and take them." The deputy blinked for a moment at the cabin's dark interior, but eventually his eyes focused on gun barrels. "Come in here" a gravelly voice commanded, "and be quick about it." The young man complied as Stevens claimed his own gun. The other deputy, who had remained with the horses, fled to report to Sheriff John P. Wood of Lecompton that they had discovered John Brown. The fugitives were certain that their recapture, and all the subsequent horrors, was imminent. "You won't be caught," Brown said. "We will take care of you."

Soon Wood's men, who remained cautiously beyond rifle range, surrounded the cabin. Inside, sentries peered warily out through small rifle holes knocked in the walls; Stevens prowled about with his gun, anxious to start fighting, but the Old Man restrained him by force of will and argument.[23] When night fell, Brown dispatched one of his men under cover of darkness to Topeka to summon Col. John Ritchie to his aid. Then he began preparing his departure.

Ritchie and a small force of mounted free-state men arrived on the afternoon of the 31st to the sight of Kagi, Stevens, and Gill hitching up their refreshed horses to the wagon while Brown loaded the fugitives into the back. A mere 100 yards across the rain swollen and swift creek, they could make out hurriedly constructed rifle pits dug by Wood's men, in perfect position for ambush. "What do you propose to do, captain?" asked one of the men. What he meant was: which way shall we detour around the enemy position and the high water?

He was certainly not prepared for the Old Man to set his mouth in a grim line and reply, "Cross the creek and move north," as if any other suggestion was lunacy.

"But, captain," said another, "the water is high and the Fuller crossing is very bad. I doubt if we can get through. There is a much better ford five miles up the creek."

"I have set out on the Jim Lane road," Brown coolly replied, eyes narrowing, "and I intend to travel it straight through, and there is no use to talk of turning aside. Those who are afraid may go back, but I will cross at the Fuller crossing. The Lord has marked out a path for me and I intend to follow it. We are ready to move." He mounted his horse to ride into the teeth of what appeared to be a kind of suicide. If the waters did not pull them under, snipers would make quick work of them. And everyone followed anyway. He lined up his armed escort, twenty-three in total now, in double file ahead of the wagon. "Now go straight at 'em, boys!" he said. "They'll be sure to run." The Old Man sat easy in his saddle, ignoring the men across the creek as he rode to the fording site. No shots were fired.[24]

As the water damped the hooves of the Old Man's horse, there was a commotion on the opposite bank as men fled in terror. One or two of them startled their horses and were dragged across the prairie hanging onto the animals' tails. The fear of John Brown, that ghost that had haunted Kansas since May of 1856, had laid its icy touch upon them. Only four remained to show that they were not as cowardly as their companions, but those four had thrown down their weapons.

Col. Ritchie was incredulous, but he did the best he could to make some order out of the scene. "Do you surrender?" he shouted at them as he made the crossing. Richard Hinton later named the episode the "Battle of the Spurs," since any blood drawn that day was by the spurs of Wood's men on their horses. Now Brown was burdened with four new prisoners. He couldn't take the chance of letting them retain their mounts, for fear they would cause violence, or flee for more reinforcements. So he ordered them to give up their horses to some of his fugitives. They would walk behind the wagon to the border.

Ever polite and magnanimous, even to his enemies, Brown also dismounted in order to walk with them. While they walked he lectured them on the evils of slavery and on matters of faith. Noticing what a devout man he was, his captives attempted to antagonize him with loud, profane swearing. "Tut, tut," the Old Man said, smiling and shaking his head, "you are not doing right, for if there is a God, it is wrong to speak His name in that way; if there is none, it is certainly very foolish." He also kept them safe from the more vindictive among their Topeka escort.[25]

After they bid farewell to Col. Ritchie at the border, Kagi advised hanging the prisoners, but Brown demurred, and insisted that they would be freed to return home. The prisoners demanded their weapons and animals back as well, but on that point the Old Man's generosity was at an end. Wryly amused, he told them, "No, your legs will carry you as fast as you want to run; you won't find any more Old Browns between this and Atchison."[26]

The story of the raid and their journey to freedom preceded Brown's party at every step, but the meaning of this would change the farther east they travelled. Wood's men made one final, unsuccessful attempt to capture Kagi at his sister's home in Nebraska, then the group reached Tabor on February 5. Kagi wrote back to William Phillips two days later,

15. The Convalescent Wanderer

> We are here with the fugitives. After I joined J.B. we started North. The possee thought we were going to attack them in their quarters, and took to the crossing of Spring Creek & hitched horses. We came on, and they left, and took up another position, and still another. Finally, finding that we still came on in utter disregard broke and ran for Mo. We caught five of them and took from them their horses and revolvers, and kept the men until the next day. They thought there had been advantages on both sides—we getting some good horses and arms; and they some valuable experience.[27]

Brown was not permitted to speak publicly at his former base of operations, but this was partly because town leaders would not countenance horse thieves of any kind, no matter the motive. So the Old Man and his company decided to speed the pace, and though hunted, boldly travelled by day. Des Moines was different though; there the editor of the *Register* personally paid for his passage across the river. In Grinnell, Iowa, three ministers and the town's founder offered support, money, and supplies on behalf of the citizens.

East of Des Moines in Iowa City, a man had gathered a sizeable crowd on a street corner and was loudly denouncing John Brown as a villain, a murderer in the dark, a reckless outlaw who owed his success to his unwillingness to fight honestly. "If I could get sight of him," the speaker boldly declared, "I would shoot him on the spot; I would never give him a chance to steal any more slaves." At the edge of the agitated crowd, a quiet and worn countryman with a broad hat pulled low over his eyes listened in silence.

He walked forward then, drew two revolvers from his coat and offered one to the speaker. "My friend," he said steadily, "you talk very brave; and as you will never have a better opportunity to shoot Old Brown than right here and now, you can have a chance." The famous face framed by a flowing white beard, fierce blue-gray eyes over a hawk-like nose, looked up from under that hat. The street corner orator fled, and the Old Man re-holstered his pistols and moved on to Springdale. He and his men arrived on the 25th and were permitted a two week respite, guarded by normally peaceful Quakers who had vowed to fight to the death to defend them.[28]

On March 9 the Springdale Quakers helped them catch a train to Chicago, where Allan Pinkerton sheltered Brown and raised $500 for the refugee group before he got them on another train to Detroit.

The journey to Canada took 82 days, during which Gill had the time to observe the Old Man as never before. He was amazed at his energy, his will, and his humanity towards the freed slaves travelling with them. And yet Gill also noticed that Brown showed a vindictive streak and an intolerance of rivals. With every mile they traveled east, fame fed an ego that was convinced that only he could accomplish what needed to be done.[29]

A freed slave named Samuel Harper recorded an account of the journey full of near captures, stolen horses, and the Old Man's exceptional egalitarian spirit towards all in their marching republic. "What kind of man was Captain Brown?" Harper remembered him as "a great big man, over six feet tall, with great big shoulders, and long hair, white as snow. He was a very quiet man, awful quiet. He never even laughed ... we used to cut up all kinds of foolishness. But the captain would always look as solemn as a graveyard."[30]

Brown carried a note on his person; it may have been an outline for a speech to give to reluctant northeast backers, but it also reads, in the past-tense voice, like words in preparation for inevitable defeat.

> Vindication of the Invasion, Etc.
>
> The Denver Truce was broken; and (1) It was in accordance with my settled policy; (2) It was intended as a discriminating blow at slavery; (3) It was calculated to lessen the value of slaves; (4) It was (over and above all other motives) right.
>> Duty of all persons in regard to this matter.
>> Criminality of neglect in this matter.
>> Suppose a case.
>> Ask for further support.[31]

On the 12th of March 1859, Brown boarded a ferry in Detroit and crossed into Canada, delivering his fugitives to freedom. One of the women even named her child, born on the journey, after him. Having seen them to safety, he offered this prayer for them: "Lord, permit Thy servant to die in peace; for mine eyes have seen Thy salvation! I could not brook the thought that any ill should befall you,—least of all, that you should be taken back to slavery. The arm of Jehovah protected us."[32] The Great Lakes are not as majestic as the sea, but for this small group the feeling of justice flowing like water was as soul stilling as the unbounded ocean. *Thalatta, thalatta.*

Brown and his men scattered from there, promising to meet again at the appointed place and time. Eight of them went to Ashtabula County in Ohio, where John, Jr., had hidden their weapons, while Brown travelled with Kagi's group, giving occasional fundraising speeches. Two recruits joined them in Cleveland: John Anthony Copeland, an Oberlin College student, and Lewis Sheridan Leary, an Oberlin resident who lived there with his wife and six-month-old daughter.[33]

He pressed on grimly to Peterboro on the 11th of April, fighting through terrible fever and pain to visit the mercurial Gerrit Smith, who lavished Brown with praise and money on account of the Missouri raid and the flight to freedom. From there it was on to North Elba, to delight in the company of his family. Too ill to travel for nearly a month, he discussed his plans with his sons and occasionally strolled outside to gaze sadly on his grandfather's old tombstone, intended as a monument to Frederick.

By May he was strong enough to go to Concord to meet with the Six, though two were absent. Parker had departed for more pleasant climes in an effort to relieve his consumption, while Higginson stayed away in an effort to relieve his disgust with the timidity of the other five. He had "perfect confidence" in Brown, but longed to see him "set free from timid advisers & able to act" in his own way.[34]

When the Old Man spoke in Concord Town Hall, he was more striking than ever: an iconic figure with his flowing white beard and grave mien. Bronson Alcott was among the audience, and wrote that he thought Brown "equal to anything he dares—the man to do the deed, if it must be done, and with the martyr's temper and purpose.... I think him about the manliest man I have ever seen—the type and synonym of the Just." As for what "the deed" might be, or what the "purpose" might entail, Alcott confessed that Brown had left them "much in the dark concerning his destination and designs."[35]

Though not one of the Six, Alcott's impression probably summarized their thoughts and understanding of Brown and his plan at this point. The darkness concerning his designs was important, and not merely as a fallback position for legal defense. For instance, it was the only way that the dashing adventurer Howe would countenance the destruction that he feared would come and yet did not wish to contemplate, and the others—save Higginson—shared his civic-minded ambivalence. At the same time they also blinded themselves to their own inability to conjure forth from the wondrous metaphors of their age the means to solve its evils.

Thus, rather than attempting to relate to Brown as a product of the collective historical identity, they viewed him as an archetype of sorts, and paraded him about proudly as an idealized and honest example of some "Puritan militant order," a "Cromwellian warrior," a "Miles Standish of Kansas," a backwoods force of history sprung from the page to somehow correct the narrative. In their haste to solve history for themselves they rhetorically elevated the Old Man to Olympian stature, while vocally and overtly denying the chthonic nature of that which they created, and that which they spurned.

By the end of his Concord visit, the Six had raised nearly $4,000 for the Old Man. He collected another $2,000 in several speaking engagements, and then decided to call once more on the family of Judge Russell. This time he was not the harried, hunted, and despondent man who had hid in their attic some two years prior. Now he was calm, resolute, and full of grim, sardonic humor. That evening he gave the Russell's new baby daughter a gift of maple candy, and then held her against his chest with her tiny feet standing on his palm. "Now," he mused with a smile, "when you are a young lady and I am hanged, you can say that you stood on the hand of Old Brown."[36]

Practically retracing the path of his first eastern tour, he stopped by the workshop of Chas Blair with money for his pikes, if they were finished. Having kept up with the news out of Kansas, Blair did not understand why Brown would even still want them, but the Old Man brusquely dismissed Blair's concerns, stating that he could find a better use for them than sitting in Blair's smithy.

On June 11 Brown came home. It was the last time on his march towards history that he would break his step, his last chance to breathe and lay down his burdens, if only for a moment.

The family was getting by as well as they could; the boys were working to support the homestead, and Brown had managed to send home a portion of the funds from the horses he had "liberated." Little Ellen had also received the inscribed Bible that this stranger—her father—had sent to her as an expression of loving remembrance and moral concern.

> This Bible, presented to my dearly beloved daughter Ellen Brown, is not intended for common use, but to be carefully preserved *for her* and *by her*, in remembrance of her father (of whose care and attentions she was deprived in her infancy), he being absent in the territory of Kansas from the summer of 1855.
>
> May the Holy Spirit of God incline your heart, *in earliest childhood*, "to receive the truth in the love of it," and to form your thoughts, words, and actions by its wise and holy precepts, is *my best wish* and *most earnest* prayer to Him in whose care I leave you. Amen.
>
> From your affectionate father,
> John Brown[37]

When the time came to leave, he found that Salmon had decided to join with Henry and Jason in refusing to fight any longer. Salmon was nearly as stubborn as his father, and though they argued bitterly there was no moving him. On June 16, Brown accepted that he had run out of time to persuade his boys, so he pushed aside his hurt over the betrayal, bid Mary and his children a tearful goodbye, and rode south to Harpers Ferry, Virginia.

Opposite: **John Brown being led to his execution. This scene never took place; Brown was led in isolation from his cell to a wagon. But the image is true enough (Library of Congress).**

Part Three:
Dies Irae, Dies Illa

But thus saith the Lord, Even the captives of the mighty shall be taken away, and the prey of the terrible shall be delivered: for I will contend with him that contendeth with thee, and I will save thy children.

And I will feed them that oppress thee with their own flesh; and they shall be drunken with their own blood, as with sweet wine: and all flesh shall know that I the Lord am thy Saviour and thy Redeemer, the mighty One of Jacob.

—Isaiah 49: 25–26

16

The Means to Real Peace

The great moments of history are the facilities of performance through the strength of ideas, as the works of genius and religion. "A man," said Oliver Cromwell, "never rises so high as when he knows not whither he is going." Dreams and drunkenness, the use of opium and alcohol are the semblance and counterfeit of this oracular genius, and hence their dangerous attraction for men. For the like reason, they ask the aid of wild passions, as in gaming and war, to ape in some manner these flames and generosities of the heart.

—Ralph Waldo Emerson, *Circles*

The Old Man first saw Harpers Ferry on July 3, 1859, accompanied by Owen, Oliver, and Jeremiah Anderson, grandson of Revolutionary War slaveholders who had joined Brown on his 1858 Missouri raid. Anderson would write that they went to Harpers Ferry because "millions of fellow-beings require it of us; their cries for help go out to the universe daily and hourly. Whose duty is it to help them? Is it yours? Is it mine? It is every man's, but how few there are to help. But there are a few who dare to answer this call and dare to answer it in a manner that will make this land of liberty and equality shake to the centre."[1]

Thomas Jefferson described Harpers Ferry as a place where the Shenandoah and Potomac rivers, "in the moment of their junction ... rush together against the mountain, rend it asunder, and pass off to the sea ... monuments of a war between rivers and mountains which must have shaken the earth itself to its centre."[2] Surrounded thus by rivers and high terrain, the town would be an indefensible trap if Brown could not quickly escape as his "Well Matured Plan"—the one he had arrived at with Hugh Forbes—required.

It was a smallish town of 2,500 people, nearly a third of whom were "foreigners," a southern term for skilled white workers from the North. There were also 1,251 "free coloreds" and 88 slaves. There were no cotton plantations here which held the armies John Brown hoped to raise; the climate and the terrain were inhospitable to them.

Travelling as "Isaac Smith," a cattle buyer from New York, the Old Man hurried to find Cook in order to both get a report on the town and to ensure that his sociable and loquacious scout had not given them away. It had been a busy year for John Cook, who used his own name. He had managed to seduce and wed a lovely plump blonde named Mary Kennedy, but he had not slipped a whisper of the plan, not even to his bride. He had worked in Harpers Ferry variously as a teacher, a canal lock keeper, and a bookseller. He published original poetry in the local newspaper, and a number of prominent townspeople were his friends. By now nothing would have aroused suspicion like removing Cook from his new community, so Brown left him in place and set about securing lodging. He rented the Kennedy Farm, a worn, two-story farmhouse seven miles away on the Maryland side of the Potomac.

The town was packed tightly into the mountainous river confluence. From the Maryland side of the river the Old Man could gaze upon the future, just making out the homes, shops, and the cluster of buildings that formed the armory. In 1859 the American nation had so far managed to prevent the military class from re-creating the burdens of the standing Continental armies. And yet, in Harpers Ferry along the west bank of the Potomac River was an armory housing nearly 100,000 of the world's most advanced rifles, perhaps the largest concentration of firearms per capita in the country, if not the world. And one-half mile to the west on the north bank of the Shenandoah River was Hall's Rifle Works, an industrial facility capable of producing, via precisely made and infinitely interchangeable parts, nearly 10,000 weapons per year for a country at peace with no standing armies.

The factory was named for John H. Hall, the inventor of the breech-loading weapons it produced, and of the methods by which they were produced. The military's short-sighted and ritual-bound officers had a cultural preference for muzzle loaders, so that soldiers could stand up and be shot in orderly lines during the choreography of reloading, but even they could be forced to recognize utility, and once they did their initial order was so large that Hall had to refuse; individual craftsmen could never produce such numbers in such a short time. So Hall changed the methods of production. It was the shape of things to come, whereby he could "make every similar part of every gun so much alike that ... if a thousand guns were taken apart & the limbs thrown promiscuously together in one heap they may be taken promiscuously from the heap & will all come right."[3]

After perfecting his process on a small scale, Hall started a lobby to pressure the secretary of war to award him a contract that would dwarf the one he had refused. When the new

Annie Brown, around 16 years old (Library of Congress).

contract was delivered, he built his factory at Harpers Ferry. It succeeded beyond anyone's wildest dreams; his rivals resorted to lobbying their own political patrons to form a commission to report (negatively) on Hall's operation and shut it down. Instead, the commission delivered an amazed report on the machines, and of weapons that had "never been made so exactly similar to each other by any other process ... the machines we have examined, effect this with a certainty & precision, we should not have believed, till we witnessed their operations."[4]

The federal armory was a tidy complex that included a fire-engine house, a machine shop, and the arsenal storehouse. The only place like it in the United States was the armory near Springfield, Ohio, the home of Brown's failed wool depot. The armory was the Old Man's target; its arsenal would arm the slaves when they rushed to his standard.

In the meantime, he pored over maps and waited for his men to arrive. Before long he decided he also needed women to help him maintain his facade, to stand between him and the outside world and cover his movements as an "outside guard." Oliver was dispatched back to North Elba to fetch Mary, but she refused. Instead, Oliver's sixteen-year old girl wife, Martha, came along with Annie, and the two ran social interference while doing domestic chores. Watson Brown along with Henry Thompson's brothers William and Dauphin followed soon after. Watson didn't want to go, but had decided it was his duty to replace Salmon at his father's side. He left behind a wife and a three-month-old baby.

In early August, Stevens, Tidd, Leeman, Barclay and Edwin Coppoc, and Hazlett arrived at the little farmhouse. Stewart Taylor, a Canadian spiritualist who may have been the only actual fanatic among them, joined them before the month's end.[5]

Despite the living conditions, it was a kind of joy for Oliver and Martha to be together again. Oliver was a sensitive, handsome man who had once hoped to study natural philosophy in New York City, and Martha had married him over the strenuous objections of her family, who disliked abolitionists in general and perhaps the Browns in particular. The young lovers shared a room with Annie, and she heard them in the night "stirring and beating" their coarse, straw-filled bed. She would ask, either innocently or mischievously, exactly what they were doing, and Martha simply answered that they were "trying to stir a little soft into our bed."[6]

Annie and Martha had their hands full maintaining the conspiracy as the farmhouse grew more crowded. Annie, more socially gifted than Martha, was the public face and lookout, and mistress of the house whenever prying guests visited. She relished being an "outlaw girl," explaining to neighbors that her mother had remained in New York to sell their property. As boxes of guns arrived from Ohio—dispatched by John Kagi—she marked them "furniture" and told visitors that the boxes must stay packed because her mother was quite particular, and only she could unpack them. All the while she maintained watch through the window while washing dishes, or while sewing on the porch. In the evening she could relax there and watch the fireflies flit around the yard while the boys told stories. The men could only move freely after dark, and during thunderstorms they felt it was safe to play, as Annie said they did, "making all kinds of noise ... as they thought no one could hear them."[7]

Annie played her role brilliantly. Though only fifteen, she had grown into a clever, headstrong, and intelligent young lady, the most capable of Brown's lieutenants along with Kagi and Stevens. Fitting, since abolitionism had benefited incalculably from the intellectual contributions of women, and women had powerfully employed the language of slavery in the name of feminism, or "the Woman Question," as Annie called it.

Brown encouraged educational debates, and one day Oliver was disputing the idea that women were the intellectual equals of men. Brown's final word on the subject was his daughters. "I think my girls are quite as smart and intelligent as my boys," he said. "Ruth can write a letter quite as good, and perhaps better, than any of her brothers; and Anne here succeeds quite well in holding her own in a dispute with any of you boys."[8]

Annie was naturally argumentative, and amused herself while vexing her brothers by having spirited quarrels with the young men she kept safe. She also delighted in their attention, and variously described them as "gentlemanly," "tall," "very attractive," or "really handsome."[9] It was a magical summer, hiding her "invisibles" as she called them, from the ever-present danger while deftly managing movements and alibis behind a breezy façade.[10]

It wasn't always so easy. A poor family had rented a small plot near the farmhouse to use as a garden. Consequently, Mrs. Huffmaster and her children, barefoot all, "had a good excuse for coming at all times to look at the garden—and at us," Annie recalled. As the house filled and it became difficult to hide the men, Mrs. Huffmaster's visits became the "plague and torment" of Annie's days.[11]

She and Martha alone carried the exhausting burden of hiding them for the entire summer; the slightest mistake, and all would be lost. Annie was strong, but she was only 16, and the pressure bowed her shoulders. "What's the matter, Annie?" her father asked after she let out a weary sigh while clearing dishes. "Are you homesick?"

She angrily retorted, "Yes—homesick and sick of living this life, where I have to live a lie—going by another name, and telling so many lies—or, what is the same, acting them. I wish you would hurry and get through with me, and let me go home." Brown flinched in pain and dropped his head, but Stevens came to the rescue; with a grin and a wink he said, "Annie, let me give you a piece of advice: Always tell the truth, the whole truth, and nothing but the truth; but if ever you *do* have to tell a lie, tell a whopper." All hurt was forgotten as they burst out laughing.[12]

The men lived in crowded isolation, hidden by Annie and Martha, and to a degree unknowing of Brown's designs. Most had followed out of faith in the Old Man and had not inquired too deeply. Annie later claimed that her father had confided to her when she was a young girl of 11 that his mind was on Harpers Ferry.[13] Whatever she and her brothers knew, they assumed that Brown intended to steal the weapons, stir up a slave exodus, and retreat to the mountains. Kagi had said as much to the Kansas veterans on their last Missouri raid in December 1858. It was their impression, Annie wrote, "that they had come there to make another such raid, only on a larger scale."[14]

Neither she nor her brothers knew of Brown's intent to seize the future at Harpers Ferry, hold it, and only then rouse the slaves. The Old Man's sons were the vocal leaders of a near mutiny when he revealed his plan. Charles Tidd, who had followed him out of Kansas to Tabor and beyond, left the farmhouse in outrage and went into town to stay with John Cook. Owen compared the idea to Napoleon's seizure of Moscow, to which his father could only reply, "We have here only one life to live, and once to die;

and if we lose our lives it will perhaps do more for the cause than our lives could be worth in any other way."[15]

The group had once nearly fractured over the idea of going to Virginia. Now they were there, but the little fellowship was pulling apart over the Old Man's latest audacity. He had brought them far, but time was short; there were no more long journeys to weld them to his cause. So he summoned Kagi from Chambersburg and called an emergency meeting in late August. Kagi and Cook together carried the debate in the Old Man's favor; Kagi may have been surprised as well, but no less eloquent in his support, while Cook—typically Brown's most vocal skeptic—gave an optimistic assessment based on his comparatively deep local knowledge.

Brown turned the debate into a test of loyalty, offering to resign as commander so the position could be voted on. It may have been the savviest political gesture he ever made, or it may have been a guileless act of validation. Whichever it was, within five minutes the Old Man was reconfirmed as their leader. Who else were they going to follow, after how far they had come? Owen, who had the unfortunate position of intermediary between the men and his father, drafted the formal endorsement, writing: "We have all agreed to sustain your decisions, untill you have *proved incompetent,* & many of us will adhere to your decisions as long as you will."[16]

His position as leader was tenuous, the boys clearly had reservations, and as the days rolled closer to his improbable plan, it probably frightened him as much as it stung. "The trouble is," Watson told him with a sigh, "you want your boys to be brave as tigers, and still afraid of you."[17]

None of them realized that the original plan had just become impossible. In Titusville, Pennsylvania, near Brown's old Randolph home and his planned Allegheny fugitive stronghold, something remarkable happened. An unemployed railroad conductor named Edwin Drake had been using an old steam engine to drill for "carbon oil," a little-utilized substitute for whale oil in lamps. On August 27, the day before he would run out of money, Drake struck a bed of oil at a depth of 69 feet; it began an industry in the commercial extraction of petroleum and forever reshaped society's energy consumption. Soon newly formed oil companies claimed the previously valueless land, and drill teams flooded the area. Maybe Brown and some fugitives could have held the land against southern slave-hunters for a while. He would never have held it against the scramble for oil. The Old Man's refuge was gone.

As August neared its end, Brown was still trying to find black leadership for his uprising. He believed that the liberation of the slaves depended on the innate capability and intelligence within them. In southern narratives, black slaves had no such potential, which meant the South had turned itself into an armed camp out of fear of the impossible. Contemporary people had come to base their ethical humanity on philosophically crude ideas about free will, and had invoked "natural law" to demonstrate that free will was impossible for black slaves. In other words, Negroes were not human.

Brown, a Calvinist who found modern notions of free will wanting, believed that black people deserved a chance to exercise their will as humans. Osborne Anderson, one of the attendees of the Chatham convention, wrote, there was "no offensive contempt for the negro, while working in his cause.... In John Brown's house, and in John Brown's presence, men from widely different parts of the continent met and united in one company, wherein no hateful prejudice dared intrude its ugly self—no ghost of a distinction found space to enter."[18]

Brown wrote to Frederick Douglass for help, and Douglass agreed to meet him along with "Emperor" Shields Green. Rendezvousing in Chambersburg with some of Kagi's associates, Douglass was directed to an abandoned quarry outside of town. The Old Man waited there, dressed in gray and leaning against a fishing pole, his face "anxious ... much worn by thought and exposure," partially hidden by his broad hat. He was perplexed that despite his wide canvassing of black communities he had so few black recruits. There "among the rocks" Brown and Douglass resumed their debate from years ago in Springfield.

Douglass was aghast at Brown's evolving designs. But the Old Man explained that the attack was now as much symbolic as practical. But Douglass wondered, if so, why a federal facility? A wholly southern target would be symbolically appropriate, while attacking Harpers Ferry could "array the whole country" against them. Brown nonchalantly dismissed this rational argument by simply stating that "it seemed to him that something startling was just what the nation needed." Of course, the Old Man had never regarded slavery as purely a southern problem; the South's was simply the ugliest expression of a systemic evil. What he hoped was that something so drastic, so visible, would "instantly rouse the country," while boldly announcing "to the slaves that their friends had come."[19]

Douglass tried to dissuade Brown from this course, but Brown would not be moved, and eventually ended the debate with a friendly arm around Douglass while saying, "Come with me ... I want you for a special purpose. When I strike the bees will begin to swarm, and I shall want you to help hive them." Douglass was equally unmoved and would have nothing of it.

It was suicide, the entire situation a "perfect steel trap," from which the celebrity Douglass could not hope to emerge alive. Douglass later admitted, "My discretion or my cowardice made me proof against the dear old man's eloquence—perhaps it was something of both which determined my course." As he rose to leave, he asked Green what he had decided. To Douglass's surprise, Green coolly said, "I b'leve I'll go wid de ole man."[20]

Brown's second black recruit arrived about a week later. His name was Dangerfield Newby, and he was on a personal quest. He was a former slave freed after his owner moved to Ohio; unfortunately his wife and children remained in bondage in Virginia. Newby had labored for years to save the money to purchase their freedom, but every time he saved enough the owner either raised the price or refused to sell. His wife, Harriet, wrote broken-hearted letters to him saying that all she wanted in the world was to see him, regardless of money or freedom. Their infant daughter was just beginning to crawl. By that summer her letters were more frantic; they were going to be sold to anyone but Dangerfield Newby.[21] One more for Brown's mission. In September, Osborne Anderson arrived from Canada, then Kagi came with the pikes from Chas Blair. Counting Martha and Annie this brought the Old Man's company to nineteen.

While at the farmhouse, the two ladies had served as friends and confidantes to the men hidden within, and had kept them safe from the outside and arguably from each other. All were particularly close to Annie, in whom they confided their hopes and fears. In late September, the Old Man determined that it was time for them to leave. On the day before her departure, Annie gave a final parting gift to Mrs. Huffmaster, explaining as she did that she would be gone for a couple of weeks and it would be best if no one called at the house, which would be unfortunately dominated by bachelors.[22]

On their last night, the men serenaded Martha and Annie with an a cappella chorus of "Home Again," and the next morning the Old Man took them to the railroad station. With tears in his eyes, he hugged Annie for the last time in this life, and as the train pulled away she looked back for as long as she could at her father smiling in the sun, and prayed that she would see him that way again. When he woke up the following day, John Brown wrote a letter home, with special words for Annie, the little girl who had brought light in his darkest hour, and who had kept his dreams safe on the Kennedy Farm.

> I parted with Martha and Anne at Harrisburg, yesterday, in company with Oliver, on their way home. I trust before this reaches you the women will have arrived safe. I have encouragement of having fifty dollars or more sent you soon, to help you to get through the winter; and I shall certainly do all in my power for you, and try to commend you always to the God of my fathers.
>
> I sent along four pairs blankets, with directions for Martha to have the first choice.... My reason is that I think Martha fairly entitled to *particular* notice.
>
> To my other daughters I can only send my blessing just now. Anne, I want you, first of all, to become a sincere, humble, earnest, and consistent Christian; and then acquire good and efficient business habits. Save this letter to remember your father by, Anne.[23]

It would seem John Brown suspected that Martha bore Oliver's unborn child home.

17

Upon These Stones

Confronted with a world of "modern ideas," which would banish everybody into a corner and a "specialty," a philosopher—if there could be any philosophers today—would be forced to define the greatness of man, the concept of "greatness," in terms precisely of man's comprehensiveness and multiplicity, his wholeness in manifoldness: he would even determine worth and rank according to how much and how many things a person could bear and take upon himself, how far a person could extend his responsibility. Today the taste and virtue of the time weaken and thin out the will; nothing is more timely than weakness of the will.
—Friedrich Nietzsche, *Beyond Good and Evil*

The men were anxious to change history, if for no other reason than to break the tedium; Brown had restricted their communications after their pens had proven loose with information to family and lovers, and there was only so much diversion to be found in quietly playing chess in the loft, or reading Thomas Paine's *Age of Reason*.[1] And they were getting anxious with their two protectors gone; it meant that secrecy would soon be irrelevant, and the Old Man intended to move soon. The impulse to change history largely defined the age. Thomas Paine—the most Jacobite of the American revolutionaries—wrote in the exceedingly popular *Common Sense*, "We have it in our power to begin the world over again."[2] There had been a profound feeling that the "revolution" represented an historical discontinuity.

Every break with history in the age was announced by a declaration to assert narrative control, the most recent example being the feminist declaration from the 1848 Seneca Falls Convention. Brown spent hours in the farmhouse appropriating the language of the age to draft a companion to his provisional constitution entitled "A Declaration of Liberty by the Representatives of the Slave Population of the United States of America." In fiery language it proclaimed a new revolution. In structure it was identical to the American Declaration of Independence, beginning with an introduction and an appeal to "natural law," quoting from Jefferson's original instrument. Then followed the preamble, outlining the intent, but where the original closed with the proposal "To prove this, let Facts be submitted to a candid world." Brown stated that "facts innumerable have been submitted to the People, and have rec'd the verdict and condemnation of a candid and Impartial World."

Specific grievances and injustices were next, framed in the nascent language of class and social division, and spanning the short history of the age. The indictment encompassed historically undifferentiated daily horrors to historically specific events such as Judge Taney, literacy laws, and the attack on "Blount's Fort"—the Negro fort in Florida—which had begun the First Seminole War. And according to Brown's declaration, a war was being waged upon black people, and had been for a long time. He would later be mocked for this notion and for his provisional constitution, but words were losing their meanings, and mockery was merely civilization's balm for burning ignorance and inadequate ideas.

The only way John Locke had been able to logically countenance slavery in a supposedly enlightened world was to define it as a kind of warfare, an extension of violence on a conquered people. But, as Thucydides knew, grasping power and war disfigures civilizations; the kinesis without brings about kinesis within. The greatness of Greek civilization was a culture where people no longer carried weapons in their cities, but the poison of slavery and war changed that and made collapse inevitable. Brown's enemies glorified generals and a certain form of history so much that they failed to realize that organized social violence exists beyond the absurd ritual sacrifices of battlefields. American wasn't a culture, just abstract power ... a myth covering a war. Brown would translate the violence to a cultural form that Americans recognized; enemies, be they equal, have the right to fight back. If Brown alone among white men believed the black slave equal, so be it.

Additionally, within the grievances was a philosophical secularization of certain karmic religious ideas similar to those in Emerson's essay "Compensation." It was a subtle idea, the notion that there are no returns-to-scale, and that even the smallest of transgressions may contain the beginning of remarkable things: "Any Tribe, Rulers, or People, who Rob and cruelly oppress their faithful Laboring Citizens, have within themselves the Germ, of their own certain and fearful overthrow; *It is one of Nature's Immutable Laws....* For in Nature the Principle of Reciprocity is Great."[3]

And, like Jefferson's original, Brown's declaration closed with a conclusion that the argu-

Oliver and Martha Brown (Library of Congress).

ments had left the signatories no choice but to seek violent redress and change. The final sentence of Jefferson's declaration was: "With a firm reliance on the protection of divine Providence, we mutually pledge to each other our Lives, our Fortunes and our sacred Honor." This was the second to last statement in Brown's, for he added an addendum, a final departure from collective language to assertive *Ich,* an invocation for postsecular violence: "Indeed; I tremble for my Country, when I reflect; 'that God is Just; And that his Justice; will not sleep forever' &c. &c. Nature is mourning for its murdered, and Afflicted Children. Hung be the Heavins in Scarlet."

The Old Man and Owen labored for days hand-scribing copies. Kagi busied himself drafting "General Order 1," dated October 10, 1859, intended to organize the people in the chaos following the raid. The men readied rifles and assembled the pikes. When preparations were nearly complete, copies of the declaration, along with numerous (and incriminating) letters from the Six, as well as from John, Jr., and Frederick Douglass, were stored in a trunk in the farmhouse.

Kagi wrote one final message to John, Jr., explaining that it was "just the right time" to attack. The slaves were "discontented at this season more than at any other" after a grueling harvest—which would also provide food—and the traditional autumn religious revivals were sure to nurture an appropriately incendiary mood. Most importantly, "We have not $5 left," Kagi wrote, "and the men must be given work or they will find it themselves."[4] He and the Old Man were still short of the twenty-five men they reckoned they needed, and Harpers Ferry did not even house the 288 slaves that the organizational plan of General Order 1 called for, but time grew short, and Brown's fever had returned. In the meantime, Sanborn assured Higginson that it would begin soon, for "though the mills of *John* grind slowly, yet they grind exceedingly small."[5]

Brown hesitated as the hour approached; too few men and insufficient funds troubled his normally resolute confidence. But on the 15th of October, some last minute help arrived in the form of John Copeland and Lewis Leary, the two Oberlin "rescuers" whom Brown had met after taking the Missouri fugitives to Canada. Additionally, a stranger came to the Kennedy farm that day: a frail, one-eyed, emotionally unbalanced man named Francis Meriam, with a syphilis scarred face. Higginson described him as "half-crazy" and ill-suited to help Brown with his operation. But Merriam had doggedly sought out Brown after touring Haiti with James Redpath, and he made up for his shortcomings with the $600 in gold he carried.[6]

The men loaded the wagon on the evening of Sunday, the 16th of October. Brown explained the plan to the newest arrivals; Stevens read aloud the provisional constitution in his rich baritone voice, and all were sworn to secrecy. It was determined that Owen, with his crippled arm, Barclay Coppoc, who had bad lungs, and Meriam, for perhaps uncomfortably obvious reasons, would remain behind guarding the farmhouse. As the embers of the sun smoldered low on the horizon, Brown said a few final words to them. "You all know how dear life is to you, and how dear your life is to your friends. Do not, therefore, take the life of any one if you can possibly avoid it; but if it is necessary to take life in order to save your own, then make sure work of it."

Darkness fell, and Brown forced his feverish and pain wracked body into the wagon for one last ride, calling, "Men, get on your arms; we will proceed to the Ferry," as he "put on his old Kansas cap" and prepared to face destiny. The nineteen men moved "as solemnly as a funeral procession" towards the river. Though it was a chilly, drizzly night, from the Old Man's black coat came an awful, fevered heat.[7]

They moved in silken darkness, drifting like gathered leaves, steps rustling and wagon creaking toward the lanterns of Harpers Ferry. Through the trees they could see the few home lights of the town and the blackness of the mountains against the starry sky. They soon reached the canal by the Potomac and turned towards the bridge. As they neared, Brown gave the signal.

Night watchman Bill Williams' shift had less than two hours remaining when Kagi and Stevens captured him without struggle. Seventeen more men emerged from the shadows and he started to panic until he saw affable John Cook with them, along with that odd Isaac Smith, who had been seen looking for cattle around town. This was obviously an elaborate joke concocted by the impish Cook, who had once worked a nearby canal lock. Williams thought he ought to play along with it for a while.

Brown then dispatched Cook and Tidd on a priority mission to cut the telegraph lines. Oliver, Newby, and Thompson were left to guard the bridge, thus securing primary lines of communication. With the bridge secure, Brown moved with the rest of his men and his prisoner to the armory and sent a man up to the wrought iron and granite gate to break open the lock.

A few simple fences, a wall and some unskilled workers who didn't even carry guns protected one of the most advanced weapons facilities in the world. A sentry named Daniel Whelan heard the commotion at the gate and came to help. It was not unlikely that during the tedious watch a fellow sentry had forgotten his keys. But Whelan saw a stranger at the other side who demanded the door be opened. Whelan refused, but his courage faded fast when he found several guns trained on him. The men made quick work of the lock with a pry-bar, and rushed in.

Whelan was as confused as the bridge guard; here with these men was John Cook, who had visited the facility before. But Cook's tours were how the fierce old man with him knew that only a few poorly armed men stood guard. Whelan watched the Old Man give orders, and his men swiftly left in groups to secure the rifle works, the arsenal, and the bridge across the Shenandoah, thereby securing all remaining access points to Harpers Ferry.

Now in possession of perhaps 100,000 weapons, the rail lines, and electronically disconnected from distant listeners, the Old Man turned with satisfaction to his captured audience of two and finally spoke.

"I came here from Kansas" he said matter-of-factly, "and this is a slave state; I want to free all the negroes in this State; I have possession now of the United States armory, and if the citizens interfere with me I must only burn the town and have blood."[8]

Brown commonly spoke this way, but that was an extravagant statement, and despite Brown's reputed gravitas and earnest presence, it would be a stretch to believe this even of him, and especially of unknown Isaac Smith. But he said, "I came here from Kansas," which was both metaphor and a statement about the meaning of ideas. Brown, of course, did not come from Kansas in the conventional sense, or even most recently. "Kansas" was more—and less—than the political boundary near the center of the east-west continental span. It meant something else, something that made his threat believable. It was a place that forever has no history of its own, no identity; it was an abstraction, an empty cartographic representation of eastern U.S. ethical struggles, a tangible manifestation of a system. He may as well have said that he came from the end of the modern order, the shores of nightmare, the stasis and the sickness in the West that was slowly crumbling apart the conceptual pillars of society.

In the meantime, Cook and Stevens had been dispatched on a mostly symbolic errand, which owed its authorship to Cook. While living in town, Cook had learned about a prominent resident named Lewis Washington, great-grandnephew of the first president and owner of a 670 acre estate, one of the few in the area complete with slaves and an overseer. Washington was also a close friend of Governor Henry Wise, and an "honorary" colonel.

In early autumn of 1859, a young stranger approached Washington and said, "I believe you have a great many interesting relics at your house." The stranger introduced himself as John Cook, and he was extraordinarily eager to actually view Washington's collection of important historical artifacts. Washington was happy to oblige and the two spent the afternoon at Beallair, where Washington took a liking to the young man.

He was therefore quite surprised to find Cook at his door well past midnight on the 17th in the company of armed men. The fearsome Aaron Stevens held a torch in one hand and a revolver in the other. He pointed it at Washington and declared, "You are our prisoner." Cook led Stevens to the gun cabinet, which held a sword supposedly given to George Washington by Frederick the Great of Prussia, and a pistol given by Lafayette. Most of Washington's slaves were away, as it was Sunday evening and the harvest was complete, so Brown's men freed seven from a nearby estate and then returned with them and the prisoners to the armory.

Once inside, Washington met the leader of this midnight brigandry, a care-worn fierce old man with a white beard. The stranger greeted him and said, "You will find a fire in here, sir," while guiding him to a stove in the engine house. "It is rather cool this evening."

Later, in the pre-dawn hours, the Old Man would explain to Washington why he had been among the first taken. "I wanted you particularly for the moral effect it would give our cause, having one of your name as a prisoner."[9] He presented Frederick the Great's sword with as much ceremony as circumstances allowed to Osborne Anderson, a black man, as a symbolic lesson to the South on the meaning of property and history.

It was a charged and even contemporary gesture. After all, Washington had only crossed the Delaware in the public consciousness in 1851, when a painting captured the birth of the American *Geist* nearly 75 years after the fact. The painting is still famous; the North Star shines in the background as Washington gazes to the left (west) of the frame with purpose, his men pulling with ponderous unity, plying their boats across the ice-choked river on Christmas Night in 1776.

The actual attack on the Hessian barracks at Trenton was an act of desperation, an effort to achieve a symbolic victory so people would believe in—and thereby fight and die for—a revolutionary cause that was on its last legs. It did insignificant harm, and yet captured the imagination. Without that bold raid the American Revolution might have simply died of widespread apathy. Who was to say that Brown couldn't attempt something analogous? But his effort at narrative inception served only to terrify, declaring him as the most fundamentally dangerous kind of revolutionary: an eddy in historical consciousness.

The whole spectacle probably seemed a contrived farce to Washington at first, but he soon saw just how quickly his certainties could change, and how serious Brown was. As the cold pre-dawn wore on, his neighbor's slaves came in occasionally to warm themselves by the stove. The bladed pikes in their hands had transformed the relationship between master and servant, and while southerners professed to believe such a thing beyond the nature of the black bondsman, their greatest fear was the deep knowledge that their belief was false.

When Patrick Higgins arrived to relieve Bill Williams at the bridge, he narrowly escaped Brown's sentries and fled to the Wager House Hotel while bullets smashed into trees and buildings. Breathlessly, he warned night clerk William Throckmorton that robbers were on the bridge, but Throckmorton decided that Higgins had merely been overly alarmed by "some rowdies."[10] He went to warn the night porter at the railroad platform adjacent to the hotel about the mischief. But as Throckmorton peered out at the B&O Bridge, east of the hotel and depot, he saw the dim outlines of men with rifles. Maybe, he thought as he quickened his pace back, there was something to this, after all.

At 1:25 a.m. as Cook and Stevens were rounding up Lewis Washington, Throckmorton and Higgins warned the crew of the Baltimore-bound express train that there were armed bandits ahead on the bridge. Conductor Andrew Phelps was not going to be delayed by hooligans, and figured that Throckmorton was surely mistaken. Deciding to personally clear the way for his locomotive, he walked ahead of the slowly moving train onto the covered bridge.

He had walked about 150 feet across the 1,000 foot span when a voice called, "Stand and deliver!" Peering beyond the light of his companion's lantern, Phelps could just make out rifle barrels before the lantern was suddenly extinguished. He ran, heart pounding, shouting for the engineer to reverse the train off the bridge. Then, over the screeching of steel and the puffing of the mighty engines, he heard gunshots, and a black man stumbled out from the bridge clutching at his chest.[11]

The man was Heyward Shepherd, a rare free black Virginian and the night depot baggage master for the B&O railroad. He had apparently ventured onto the bridge by the other fork to investigate the disturbance, and when he ran after being hailed in the same manner as Phelps, had been shot in the back by one of Brown's nervous sentries. The bullet exited his chest, a wound pronounced fatal by the doctor; it was only a matter of waiting. That single bullet left no doubts about the lethal intent of the unknown adversaries on the bridge, and when one of them was seen leaving to go to the armory, bullets flew.[12]

After that, it was bedlam on the train platform. The passengers were running every which way and screaming echoed from the cars. With the train stuck for the moment, they sought shelter in the Wager House. From the upstairs windows, observers could see armed men prowling the armory yard that stretched to the northwest just across the street. The immediate assumption was that they were exceptionally brazen robbers, but when a young doctor named John Starry saw a wagon leaving to cross the Potomac bridge to Maryland bearing pike wielding men and guarded by others with rifles, he decided to leave just before dawn to spread the alarm across town. Inside the engine house the Old Man had just broken his silence and informed his first two captives that he had come to them from Kansas.

As the sun rose on Harpers Ferry on October 17, the air hummed with tension while wary eyes watched the captive armory. It was a silent morning, since the man who normally rang the bell to start the workday was a prisoner, along with nearly 40 other employees and passersby who had been caught too close. Magnanimous as always, even to his enemies, Brown ordered breakfast for all of his captives from the nearby Wager House, from the very man who had traded gunfire with his raiders in the middle of the night. After that, Phelps met with "Isaac Smith" about allowing the train to move on with its passengers.

Inexplicably, the Old Man agreed, and to assure Phelps that it was safe, he left the armory and walked ahead of the train across the Potomac River bridge. "You no doubt wonder that a man of my age should be here with a band of armed men," he said once he had seen Phelps safely across, "but if you knew my past history you would not wonder at it so much." Phelps and everyone else only knew the Old Man as Isaac Smith, or simply "the Captain" if they had overheard his men during the raid, and though his past remained a mystery for the moment, Smith revealed his plan to liberate the slaves. And there was no idea more frightening, more dangerous to the United States than that liberation.

At 7:04 a.m. the little town of Harpers Ferry was fairly certain that a few robbers held the armory. At 7:05 a.m. because of Brown's curious decision, the telegraph connection at the B&O central office chattered to life. At that moment the railroad, with its coordinating communications network, knew that a large group of abolitionists had taken over the armory. They intended to "free the slaves ... at all hazards," and no more trains would be allowed to pass. Phelps added that it might be advisable to "notify the Secretary of War at once."

Brown was not ignorant of Phelps's access as a railroad man to the most advanced communication systems of the day. Furthermore, he had primed Phelps with the additional information—perhaps hopeful, perhaps for effect—that he expected 1,500 reinforcements, which Phelps dutifully passed on. Brown kept the people in and around Harpers Ferry in a constant state of uncertainty regarding his actual numbers by regularly moving his men and keeping them masked. Observers estimated his force in the hundreds.[13]

As Phelps's train steamed north, passengers flung written notes from the windows while the telegraph lines flickered the news across the Eastern Seaboard. When the train arrived in Baltimore, the newspaper headlines were proclaiming a widespread slave insurrection in Harpers Ferry. The passengers were veritable celebrities and a crowd of reporters eagerly waited to interview them.

In twelve hours, nineteen men had captured the attention of a nation. Millions had gone to bed one night with one idea of the world around them, and had awoken to an entirely different one. One of the unique features of the European 1848 revolutions was that via the telegraph people across great spaces could be united in the experience of the barricades. They coordinated a resistance without tightly coupled social linkages or elite driven mandates. Similarly, people across the United States and beyond could conceptually live Brown's Harpers Ferry insurrection as a part of their world, though to them it had all the attributes of illusion.

Releasing the train seemed like an artful suicide, but Brown figured that time—for the moment—was on his side. The overwhelming majority of the U.S. Army, almost 20,000 strong, was west of the Mississippi, busy being exceptionally poor at fighting an asymmetric conflict against Native Americans. The rest were holed up in their forts, occupying the day with ritual and drill, stuck in the tightly coupled system of military command, and hardly capable of rapidly moving to engage an armed insurrection. As Brown likely saw it, he had time to wait for the slaves to throw down their plows and come to him to take up the sword; the telegraph would get word to them, too.

Brown didn't yet know that no slaves were flocking to his barricade, and as the morning wore on he had trouble on his hands. Harpers Ferry, like many southern communities, was home to a militia ever watchful for slave uprisings. With "Smith's" men in control of the armory, the militia figured they were sorely outgunned and, for all they knew, outnumbered. James Starry galloped off to Charleston for reinforcements, but eventually some of the militia-men remembered that during the previous flood season a number of rifles had been taken to an alternate storage facility on a part of the armory not controlled by the raiders. They retrieved the rifles, and the townspeople melted any lead they could find for bullets. Soon, Brown's men were taking cover from sporadic sniper fire.[14] John Kagi, perceptive as always, sent a messenger from his position at the Rifle Works across town urging an immediate withdrawal. Brown did not send a reply.

Militia reinforcements from Charles Town arrived to face sporadic gunfire just as Phelps's northbound train was pulling up to the platform in Baltimore to the din of reporters and the strained hush of the collectively held breath of the Northeast. The reinforcements were terrified, mostly inexperienced recruits nurtured on Mexican War stories from the handful of veterans who led them. A deep fog obscured the riverbank as they flanked the armory, crossing the Potomac in flatboats to reach the B&O railroad bridge on the Maryland side. They had no reason not to believe they potentially faced hundreds of men, who counted among their number "armed bands of maddened blacks." Imagination conjured fearsome adversaries in the mist-shrouded cliffs of Maryland Heights. Their terror burst forward from them in a charge across the bridge, surprising and overwhelming the Old Man's lookouts, who swiftly retreated to the armory.[15]

One didn't make it. A crude homemade bullet from a high window tore through Dangerfield Newby's neck, felling him on Shenandoah Street in the middle of downtown. In his pocket, a letter from his enslaved wife read: "If I thought I shoul never see you this earth would have no charms for me…. Do all you Can for me, witch I have no doubt you will." She was only 50 miles away.[16]

18

Like Ashes in the Fall

> *Man is the cruelest animal. At tragedies, bullfights, and crucifixions he has so far felt best on earth; and when he invented hell for himself, behold, that was his heaven on earth. When the great man screams, the small man comes running with his tongue hanging from lasciviousness. But he calls it his "pity."*
> —Friedrich Nietzsche, *Thus Spake Zarathustra*

By the afternoon, Brown's armory and rifle works outposts were isolated from each other by a steady rain of bullets. Exhibiting all of the preternatural cool he had shown in Kansas under fire, the Old Man selected ten prisoners, among them prominent armory officials and local wealthy slave-owners—including Lewis Washington—to take to his fallback position in the large fire engine bay. As the gunfire intensified, crashing into the walls and through the windows, the hostages offered to help broker a ceasefire. One was sent with William Thompson to negotiate.

Earlier that morning, the Old Man had walked across the B&O Bridge and back to his position. Now the crowd was no longer inclined to allow such things, nor did they wish to negotiate, and Thompson was seized and dragged across the street to the Wager House. Bound to a chair to be interrogated, he would only tell his captors what Brown had already said; they had come to free the slaves, and they believed a mass of slaves and ordinary white laborers would join them shortly. Brown was counting on the fact that since 1800 the world was dividing largely along class lines, but he never fully appreciated the narrative of racial superiority that overcame class divides to unite the South and helped keep the slaves under control. Ordinary white laborers in the South would never join his cause.

The Old Man and Stevens watched through sniper holes they had knocked in the walls, and when Thompson was captured, Stevens flew into a rage. He prowled the engine house like a caged beast, vowing violence against Thompson's captors. He may have acted, had not the acting superintendent of the armory, Archibald Kitzmiller, made an offer to "possibly accommodate matters."[1] Kitzmiller offered his services as ambassador; he proposed to go outside—escorted by Stevens—to end the standoff.

Almost comically, given Thompson's capture, the Old Man agreed, and for added insurance Watson went along. Kitzmiller, Stevens and Watson walked gingerly down the street between the armory and the buildings sheltering the siege force. They hadn't made it far before someone smashed out an upper story window and bullets raked the street. Watson doubled over and fell to the street. Stevens was hit next, but refused to fall, roaring in defiance and returning fire as fast as he could. Bullet after bullet tore through his body, and only after six of them did he finally drop to the pavement.

The rain—the real rain—was now drilling down, and since most of the onlookers were gazing in horror at Stevens, they didn't notice Watson crawling back to the armory, vomiting blood and clutching at an oozing stomach wound. His father could do little for him, and Watson lay in agony. Gut wounds are a slow, painful way to die; victims linger for days as sepsis, blood-loss and malnutrition claim them. Brown paced nervously, his icy exterior splintering enough to reveal the rushing turbulence beneath. He told one of his hostages—perhaps wishfully—that "he had it in his power to destroy that place in half an hour."[2] Then he and the townspeople saw Stevens attempt to rise to his feet again.

Brown was desperate to help, but could not afford to send another of his men into the line of fire. Curiously, a hostage named Joseph Brua offered to aid Stevens and return afterward. Brown had little choice but to open the door for him, and Brua ran to help lift the wounded Stevens and supported him to shelter in the Wager House. Then, true to his word, Brua returned to the armory.

During all this confusion, William Leeman decided he had stayed long enough and fled the armory unnoticed, slipping between the buildings for shelter before crossing the tracks and attempting to swim the Potomac. He was eventually spotted and, when he realized he could not shake his pursuers, raised his hands in surrender. One of the gunmen calmly walked up to Leeman, and the bang and flash from a point blank shot to the face ended his life. Leeman's body remained on the rocks in the shallow water, visible from the buildings and the bridge nearby. It served as target practice until the current finally caught him up and bore him mercifully away.[3]

Meanwhile, by early afternoon, John Kagi spied attackers taking up position in the buildings surrounding the rifle works, and decided he could no longer wait on the Old Man; he ordered the evacuation. He and the four men with him fled south across the Shenandoah River. But as they plunged into the river, unseen gunmen emerged from the trees on the opposite shore and began shooting, while others pursued the fleeing raiders into the water.

Kagi took the first bullet, falling under only to be lifted from the current to have his skull smashed in by a club before his body was dragged ashore. Lewis Leary and John Copeland, the two Oberlin rescuers, were close behind. Leary was shot in the back after attempting to climb ashore; he died twelve hours later. Copeland was spared a lynching by the omnipresent John Starry, who was racing around coordinating the town's response. Additionally, Ben, a slave from a nearby estate, was captured. One of Washington's slaves was with them too, but unable to swim, he drowned in the river.[4]

The remaining pocket of resistance at the armory was drawing to it a volatile mix of organized militia, infuriated partisans and toughs fueled by drink and delusion. The situation started to spiral violently beyond control when a man named George Turner was shot through the neck while attempting to take aim at Brown's raiders. He fell in front of several onlookers and the crowd became darkly frenetic. Turner was a prominent local, a friend of Lewis Washington and a plantation owner who derived great prestige in the South from the perceived virtue of his Seminole War experience.

Then Heyward Shepherd, the night baggage master, died of his wounds. He was well-liked, but the death of a free black Virginian wasn't going to further stir up the militia. But B&O Agent Fontaine Beckham, the man who had sponsored Shepherd for employment in town, was very agitated and moved to a firing position behind a pumping station a mere thirty yards from the engine house. At that range he was accurate and dangerous, which drew Edwin Coppoc's attention. "If he keeps on peeking I'm going to shoot," said Coppoc. When Beckham looked around the corner to fire again, Coppoc fired two shots. After the second, Brown reported, "That man is down."[5]

Neither knew the man's connection to poor Heyward Shepherd, nor that Beckham was the popular mayor of Harpers Ferry. With his death the mob outside became seething and frantic, and a pair of men went inside the Wager House where Thompson was still tied to a chair. After some arguing about Thompson's fate, they dragged him outside, shot him multiple times, and dumped his body in the river. They returned for Stevens, who regarded them with undisguised contempt in his proud eyes. Deciding that he was nearly dead anyway, the men decided to let Stevens suffer from his wounds.[6]

Watson Brown (Library of Congress).

Reinforcements were trickling steadily in, but not for Brown. By mid-afternoon the militia from Martinsburg, Virginia, began assaulting the engine house. They might have ended the affair then but John Cook, who was supposed to be a mile away guarding a stash of weapons at a Maryland schoolhouse, had become anxious about the escalating sounds of battle. From a ridge above the Potomac River, he saw Brown's position was hopelessly encircled. Not knowing what else to do, he tried to cause a distraction by firing on the militia, who returned fire but also retreated from the armory in alarm. They feared that a larger force had arrived to help the men inside.

The raiders had inflicted casualties on the militia, but had purchased them dearly. Stewart Taylor was shot, and as Edwin Coppoc recalled, before Taylor died "he suffered very much and begged us to kill him."[7] Oliver Brown was also hit, but instead of crying out he sat alone with his thoughts, his days of following his father at an end, before closing his eyes forever.

As sunset drew near, the shooting dwindled and negotiations resumed. Colonel Baylor was nominally in command, so Brown sent him the demands that Thompson and Stevens had failed to deliver: he wanted horses, and a head start across the Potomac.

Baylor would not—and probably could not—accede to this proposal. "In command" meant that he had tenuous control of his own men, a local militia, and a motley assortment of other partisans. But four-fifths of the whole did not answer to him and prowled the evening drunk, shooting into the air and randomly at the engine house.[8]

Twilight fell. In the street, pigs rooted Dangerfield Newby's corpse, while the occasional townsperson wandered by to cut a trophy from the body: a button, a scrap of cloth, the contents of his pockets, a finger, an ear. Within, Watson begged someone to kill him. His brother lay just across the room. Brown tried to comfort his son, saying, "No, my son, have patience; I think you will get well." As the night wore on, Brown confessed to Washington that he knew escape was impossible, and that he would soon die. He implored Watson to "endure a little longer" so that "he might die as befitted a man."[9]

Tuesday morning revealed federal soldiers under the command of Colonel Robert E. Lee arrayed outside the armory. Before the shooting started again, Lee sent Lt. Jeb Stuart to the engine house to demand the surrender of the insurrection's mysterious leader. No one knew for certain who it was, though there were rumors about cattle trader Isaac Smith from up the road. Stuart blinked in surprise when the door cracked open for him. "You are Osawatomie Brown, of Kansas?" Stuart, who had served under Colonel Edwin Sumner during the "Bleeding Kansas" saga as territorial enforcer and genocidaire, distinctly remembered the Old Man.

"Well, they do call me that sometimes, Lieutenant." Brown replied.

Regaining his composure, Stuart said, "This is a bad business you are engaged in, Captain. The United States troops have arrived, and I am sent to demand your surrender."

"Upon what terms?" Brown asked querulously, hope and maybe irritation in his pinched, rough voice. Stuart delivered Lee's message, promising to protect Brown from the townsfolk and to place his fate in the hands of the president. Brown replied with his previous request, asking for horses and a head start. When Stuart indicated that he had no authority to grant such a request, Brown informed him coolly that he preferred to die fighting, and that he intended to "sell his life as dearly as possible."[10]

With that, Stuart gave the signal, and the Marines rushed to batter down the heavily barricaded doors with hammers and, eventually, the heavy ladder in the yard. Each thunderous blow echoed off the mountains.[11] Brown's men returned fire, but they had been caught off guard by the speed of the assault.

The doors came in and smoke and noise came out as both sides traded gunshots. Two Marines fell, but as more rushed in, most of Brown's men surrendered. Only the Old Man continued to fight. And why not? His enemies only had bullets, and the hope that when they were done shooting he and his dreams might be dead.

Israel Green, a Marine lieutenant, had been the first through the door. Inside, he peered through the smoke for his quarry, then Lewis Washington got his attention and pointed to a fierce old man with a long white beard crouched on one knee, calmly reloading his gun amid the screams of the dying. Green raced towards him, drew his saber, and delivered a killing attack, one slash with all his strength to Brown's head to disorient or incapacitate, and then a stab to his chest, intended to pierce heart, lungs, or both.

But the sword bent in half as it hit the Old Man's chest.

Brown was wounded, his head bled profusely, but he lived. Green frantically slashed with his broken and ineffective weapon, keeping the Old Man down by the speed and ferocity of the blows. But he found that he could not mortally wound this superman.

It was one of history's finest wrinkles. That morning, Green had reached for the weapon most appropriate for his dreams of glory and decoration—his ceremonial sword. It was a weapon as beautiful as it was useless, made of delicate steel alloy unsuited for actual weaponry. Therefore, the blow to Brown's head had superficially wounded, and when he struck at Brown's heart he hit a buckle. A real sword would have broken through, but the ornamental blade bent upon the homely little device.[12]

Dauphin Thompson and James Anderson were bayoneted, the latter so aggressively that his attacker's charging momentum carried Anderson across the room and pinned him to the wall, where he remained hanging, alive, until he was finally brought out with the other prisoners. In the bedlam outside, people were howling for the execution of all the prisoners. A man came by and spat tobacco into Anderson's face, and returned a few minutes later to drawl, "Well, it takes you a hell of a long time to die."[13]

Watson eventually died the death his father had envisioned; after his captors took him for medical care, they asked why he had done this. He replied, "Duty, sir. I did my duty as I saw it."[14] The next day he succumbed to his wounds.

Brown was taken into the room where Stevens lay. His face and beard were matted with blood; it dripped in small puddles on the floor. Most believed he would soon be dead, but after they cleaned him up they realized that perhaps he would live to face trial after all. A reporter asked to interview the Old Man, and Colonel Lee acquiesced, so long as the wounded were not pained or taxed by the interview. The reporter found that quite to the contrary, Brown was eager "to be able to make himself and his motives clearly understood."[15]

Governor Henry Wise soon joined the reporters. Wise was a man of nearly bottomless political ambition, a ruthless social climber who had intended to use the Harpers Ferry situation to script heroics for himself. He had dispatched the Richmond militia and had planned to "lead" the capture, but was delayed. He was therefore considerably irritated when he arrived to find that Lee had already ended the standoff. Nonetheless, he intended to take center stage by confronting the man who had brought all this trouble. Hopefully he could do so in front of reporters.

Brown, despite his wounds and the circumstances, did not act like a man facing interrogation from the state's highest elected official, but received the governor into his presence with the utmost composure. "Well, Governor," he said wryly, "I suppose you think me a depraved criminal. Well sir, we have our opinions of each other." He freely informed Wise of his failed plans, and also where to find the incriminating documents hidden at the Kennedy Farm. The two conversed at length, and Wise eventually left, bemusedly commenting that Brown was "the gamest man I ever saw."[16]

It was soon time to move Brown from the Wager House to a proper jail. An angry and inquisitive crowd waited outside, along with a number of the state's dignitaries. Lee and Stuart were still present, as were Washington, Wise, and several Congressmen. One of them, Senator James Mason of Virginia—the author of the Fugitive Slave Law—walked forward to question Brown for the benefit of the reporters and voters present.

"How do you justify your acts?" Mason asked.

Brown stared at him from the stretcher, covered in blood but oddly dignified. "I think, my friend, you are guilty of a great wrong against God and humanity. I say that without wishing to be offensive. It would be perfectly right for any one to interfere with you, so far as to free those you willfully and wickedly hold in bondage. I do not say this insultingly."

Perhaps not knowing what else to say, Mason said, "I understand that."

"I think I did right," Brown continued, musing out loud, "and that others will do right who interfere with you at any time, and all times. I hold that the golden rule, do unto others as you would that others should do unto you, applies to all who would help others to gain their liberty."

A voice shouted from the crowd: "I think you are fanatical!" Brown did not deny this, but merely replied, "And I think you are fanatical. 'Whom the gods would destroy they first make mad.'" It was as accurate a judgment as any on all of them, himself included. It sounded like one of his usual biblical quotes, the words of a prophet, but he had actually chosen an aphorism from Greek tragedy.[17]

Before he was finally moved away, Brown looked to the crowd and the reporters and said, "You had better—all you people at the South—prepare yourselves for a settlement of that question that must come up. You may dispose of me very easily; I am nearly disposed of now; but this question is still to be settled—this Negro question I mean—the end of that is not yet."[18]

Back across the river, Owen hung his head as he began to realize how things had gone with his father's great work. He had followed his father all of these years, but would not follow him on his final journey. John Brown would have wanted it that way.

19

The Revelation of John Brown

> *Whom shall he accuse?*
> *Nobody, and everybody.*
> *The imperfect age in which we live....*
> *It is impossible for us not to admire, successful or not, the glorious combatants of the future, the professors of Utopia. Even when they fail, they are venerable, and it is perhaps in failure that they have the greater majesty. Victory, when it is according to progress, deserves the applause of the peoples; but a heroic defeat deserves their compassion. One is magnificent, the other is sublime. For ourselves, we prefer martyrdom to success, John Brown is greater than Washington, and Pisacane is greater than Garibaldi.*
> *Surely some must be on the side of the vanquished.*
> —Victor Hugo, *Les Misérables*

On October 18, blood stained the streets of Harpers Ferry and the Potomac Bridge, and bodies floated in the Shenandoah River. A dog lapped at Dangerfield Newby's blood while pigs rooted in his guts.[1] Jeremiah Anderson finally died of his gruesome impaling, and his body, along with Watson's, was sent to a medical school in Winchester for dissection. The remaining of Brown's dead were dumped in an unmarked grave one-half mile west of town along the Shenandoah, and people in Harpers Ferry and beyond breathed deeply with relief that Nat Turner's ghost had not succeeded, and they convinced themselves that the shared rails of social reality were intact. "The work is done," W.P. Smith, the B&O master of transportation, telegraphed to the company president. "No difficulties have attended our trains, except their slight irregularity by the interruption."[2]

And yet, the *New York Herald* wrote that with every "shaking of a tree on the mountain" the townspeople trembled with fear that more guerrillas were "throwing up entrenchments." On the night of the 19, a lone rider galloped through town, his steed's hooves thundering in the bloody dust as he cried, "To arms! To arms! They are murdering women and children!" Once the immediate panic subsided, it turned out that the man believed he had heard screams and gunshots from a neighbor's home in Pleasant Valley, Maryland, and had seen slaves running to the mountains. Nothing was actually happening, but citizens from Sandy Hook, across the Potomac, were flooding into Harpers Ferry seeking refuge.[3]

The house where Albert Hazlett and Osborne Anderson had been hiding with their Sharps rifles was discovered, but the men escaped. Additionally, the popular John Cook was missing, and it was feared that he was regrouping with other insurgents for a re-attack. Those fears multiplied when Robert E. Lee's men discovered Brown's trunk of letters, declarations, and provisional constitutions, along with thousands of pistols and rifles, a heavy swivel gun, and enough ammunition, clothing, and other supplies to equip a small army. There was even a letter from the Ordnance Department, addressed to "Isaac Smith," regarding "inquiries as to the disposition of the United States troops."[4]

He obviously expected more men. A massive manhunt began, and innocent black people predictably suffered. In the meantime, Gov. Wise ordered all of the documents found in Brown's safehouse transcribed into the state's archives, while he delivered two days' worth of thunderous orations rousing the "Sons of Virginia" to be vigilant against what he portrayed as a vast northern conspiracy.[5] Wise was Brown's new best ally, a man rendered witless by his fear and his desire for celebrity.

Wise was attempting to define the narrative as one of Virginian moral superiority, his own role central to events. At the same time, a trial was necessary to reassure people that their conception of social reality held true. There may have been only a slight irregularity in the trains when all was complete, but history and memory are curious things: "It is quite essential to the locomotive, that it should be able to reverse its movement, & run backwards & forwards with equal celerity. Is it less needful to the mind that it should have this retroaction, & command its past act & deed?"[6]

The great innovation of the rise of the absolutist state was the establishment of narrative regarding the nature of justice and historic cause written in metaphors. Nations, as social systems, maintained order through an agreed upon form of law considered impartially applicable (at least for those included as equals in the system), and predicated upon appeals to com-

John Brown, 1859 (Library of Congress).

monly held conventions regarding cause and effect and moral culpability. It was furthermore based on geographically defined polities—an innovation of the state system—and relied on precedent, such that tomorrow should of necessity resemble yesterday.

A telegraph line had been run to Charles Town exclusively for communicating the proceedings of the trial, which was swiftly becoming not only a defining experience, but also one of the first shared collectively beyond the limits of immediate human perception. Brown's trial commenced with alacrity, and on the 25 of October he found himself in yet another courtroom, this time in Charles Town, Virginia. The stakes were only subtly higher than in the court that had once shorn him of his worldly possessions, a decision which arguably precipitated the conditions leading to the loss of three of his precious children. As for this trial, if the speed did not indicate what was really taking place, then the location did. It was in a *Virginia* court, across the street from the prison which held Brown, Stevens, and Edwin Coppoc, along with Cook and Hazlett, who had been captured and brought to join their leader.

The presiding judge, Richard Parker, was a slave owner and the former paymaster at the Harpers Ferry armory. He opened by addressing the jury with a contradictory and legally dubious statement, declaring that he would not permit himself "to give expression to those feelings which at once spring up in every breast when reflecting on the enormity of the guilt." Rather, he wanted a fair trial granted to the men who had invaded "our common country" and had slain Virginians "without mercy." If the jury had any doubts about what was on trial, Judge Parker counseled them: "It would seem, gentlemen, and yet I speak from no evidence, but upon vague rumors which have reached me, that these men, who have thrown themselves upon us, confidently expected to be joined by our slaves and free negroes, and unfurled the banner of insurrection, and invited this class of our citizens to rally under it." Interesting that he chose to identify them as a "class of ... citizens," but he smugly reassured his southern audience, saying, "And yet, I am told, they are unable to obtain a single recruit."[7]

President Buchanan had informed Governor Wise that jurisdiction was "a matter quite indifferent to me," but by definition his indifference shouldn't have mattered, if the law was, in fact, the law.[8] But with a craven shrug and perhaps a fearful tremble, he blithely cast aside the epistemological and ethical foundation of the state. In different circumstances, it might have been just the foolish utterings of an inept politician, but this directly involved matters of life, and death, and one man's attack upon the social order itself, so his apathy was a terrible portent. Virginians, for their part, cared little for which law should govern the case; they had baser needs to fulfill. And while bowing to the shrill demands of Southern states had become a regular political hobby in Washington, D.C., the charges against Brown were the next indication that the language of state served as masquerade for a deeper struggle.

The charges ran seventeen pages, and the wounded defendants were made to stand for the reading. Stevens eventually was allowed to lie down after nearly passing out. While crimes were certainly committed, the sweeping, grandiose indictment charged Brown with murder, conspiracy to incite a slave insurrection, and treason against the State of Virginia. His provisional constitution was presented as evidence not that he acted against the United States, but that he had committed the apparently more dire crime of attempting to overthrow Virginia's laws, and that the accused did so "not having the fear of God before their eyes, but being moved and seduced by the false and malignant counsel of other evil and traitorous persons and the instigations of the devil."[9]

Dubious charges, but given that the nature of the system is in question, the legal conventions deserve an examination that they were not granted at the time, beyond the plainly obvious ethical and logical arguments against. Two specific points speak to a seven-decade struggle over the relationship of the states with the federal government. The first—though crimes had been committed, by what right did Virginia try them? The second, a subtext of the first—what exactly is the relationship between man and state such that there existed a prerequisite for the charge of treason against Virginia?

Brown's lawyers contested the treason charge first, raising the obvious objection that he was neither a citizen of the state, nor a resident, nor had he even briefly domiciled there. The Kennedy Farm was located in Maryland. Judge Parker dismissed the objection of the attorneys out of hand, and by allowing the charge to stand, he indicated a perceived supremacy of Virginia law, and also implied that treason only required presence on the soil, as opposed to more broadly understood prerequisites.

Provided that words mean anything, nearly anyone with a working understanding of the English language and shared culture would agree that a form of allegiance is a prerequisite for treason, whether that allegiance stems from birth, residency, domicile, or citizenship. Brown was, however, being tried in Virginia, and technically Judge Parker could invent definitions *sui generis* since Virginia statute in 1859 was silent on the subject. In such instances though, it is generally acceptable to appeal to a shared heritage of English common law for reference, if not clarification.

The most analogous precedent was the case of Thomas Howard, the 4th Duke of Norfolk, in 1571. In collusion with a Spanish banker and several northern (Scottish) nobles, he staged a raid in which, as the indictment indicated, he "conspired to depose the Queen and to compass her death ... to spread civil war, make insurrection and rebellion ... and to make public war within the realm against the Queen and her Government, to endeavor to change the worship of God as established in the kingdom ... and to induce foreigners to invade the realm."[10] The justices held that the Scottish lords involved could not be guilty of treason, because they were not residents. Norfolk, being English, was not so fortunate. Lord Hale corroborated this ruling in 1847 when he wrote, "And hence it is if an alien enemy comes into this kingdom hostilely to invade it, if he be taken, he shall be dealt with as an enemy, but not as a traitor."[11] Residence is requisite for treason, "and this allegiance is either natural from all that are subjects born within the king's allegiance or local which obligeth all that are resident within the king's dominion."[12]

While the trial of Lord Norfolk most closely resembled John Brown's raid, the 1781 Pennsylvania case *Respublica v. Chapman* was more proximal. Samuel Chapman was tried for treason as a result of his actions during the recent war/rebellion. Chapman, however, asserted that a subject of the Crown could not be guilty of treason against a polity that hadn't even existed when he had been born in Pennsylvania. The judge agreed on all the technical points.[13]

Judge Parker exceeded any definition of treason that had stood since the Peace of Westphalia, beyond any framework established under Henry VIII or even George III. U.S. case law after Brown's trial would revert to form, mitigating common law regarding treason. And even if Judge Parker had applied an exceptionally loose interpretation of the term "residence," he would be forced to appeal to the single night that Brown spent in the armory.

The armory, technically, wasn't even Virginia soil, and Brown merely traversed a few hundred Virginia yards en route to it. In fact, Brown committed exactly zero crimes on Virginia soil; Hayward Shepherd was shot on the Potomac Bridge somewhere between two states. The rest were felled on federal lands, to include slain mayor Fontaine Beckham. Brown only left the armory to escort the B&O railroad conductor across the Potomac Bridge, and no one was killed then, though the conductor may have been his instrument for broadcasting the insurrection. If so, their conversation took place in Maryland, making this an interstate, and thus a federal, crime.

As few as three days before the trial began, most people assumed that Brown might be tried in Virginia for murder, but certainly in United States courts for treason. On October 22, *The Baltimore Sun* had informed readers following the trial that Federal court would be in session "next Monday." The *Sun* did note the curious fact that the federal district attorney for the Western District of Virginia was in conference with President Buchanan, and commented, "The sending of the prisoners to Charles Town is believed to be a concession to the views of Governor Wise who claims to try them by the laws of Virginia." At that date though, the editors thought this notion mildly nonsensical, and furthermore, criminal justice had never been the place for such "concessions."[14]

Everyone involved knew that a federal trial would likely give a more clement verdict than a Virginia court. Therefore, Brown's attorneys appealed the jurisdiction, but were again rebuffed by Judge Parker, who cited an obscure decision of his own which allowed him to maintain jurisdiction for Virginia. None of this obviates the fact that no "concession" or decision by a provincial Virginia judge could take precedence over Article I, Section 8, of the United States Constitution, provided that the Constitution was indeed the recognized law. Despite the fact that Brown ultimately mollified the Virginians in the court by accepting the trial as fair, the law does not allow the accused to waive jurisdiction either.

Andrew Hunter, the prosecutor, was another slave-owner, related by marriage to the slain mayor. Hunter's son Henry arguably should have been on trial as well, since he had been one of the men who had executed William Thompson in retaliation for Beckham's death. Andrew Hunter was also a close friend of the governor and shared Wise's political desire to achieve "not only the destruction of these men whom we have in confinement," but also "higher and wickeder game."[15]

In 1909, George F. Caskie claimed that Virginians were not trying to make a mockery of justice; they simply did not have access to the in-depth legal precedents required to bring more appropriate charges and make correct jurisdiction determinations.[16] He argued that they merely proceeded from southern interpretations of state's rights. Fundamentally though, that meant the trial was either a caricature of justice, or a deliberate attack upon federal power that had begun with the Dred Scott decision. The only other alternative was that Brown's accusers were legally incompetent and poorly educated imbeciles who had no right to try him.

On the one hand, there was the obvious scheming of the governor and the prosecutor. On the other was the spectacle of a prosecutor with his face bruised from a brawl the night prior, wads of tobacco dripping from his mouth onto the courtroom floor that was "inches deep, in places, with nut shells."[17] One puzzles as to whether ambitious scheming or imbecility characterized the trial more.

When the trial officially began on October 27, Brown stood for the beginning of his finest days and passed his judgment on the proceedings. "Virginians," he said softly, still struggling with his wounds, "I did not ask for any quarter at the time I was taken. I did not ask to have my life spared. The Governor of the State of Virginia tendered me his assurance that I should have a fair trial; but, under no circumstances whatever, will I be able to have a fair trial. If you seek my blood, you can have it at any moment, without this mockery of a trial." He protested his lack of counsel, his obvious wounds and poor health, and his inability to confer with his friends. "But if we are to be forced with a mere form—a trial for execution—you might spare yourselves the trouble. I am ready for my fate.... I beg for no mockery of a trial—no insults—nothing but that which conscience gives, or cowardice would drive to practice.... I have no little further to ask, other than that I may not be foolishly insulted, only as cowardly barbarians insult those who fall into their power."[18]

Defense attorneys appealed to psychology and attempted the new but increasingly accepted plea of insanity for their client. Brown would not countenance this defense though. Virginians were tickled when he voided what appeared to be his lawyer's last gambit, rising with difficulty from the cot he rested on for most of the trial to announce, "I look upon it as a miserable artifice and pre-text of those who ought to take a different course in regard to me. I am perfectly unconscious of insanity, and I reject, so far as I am capable, any attempt to interfere on my behalf on that score."[19] He would not accept an acquittal that called his will and intellect into question. An insanity defense is, at the root of it, an effort to mitigate moral judgment upon the accused by arguing a lack of rational, free will. It was both an irony, and yet worthy of consideration on at least one level; Brown's will was not rational by the prevailing climate of opinion, and sanity is to a degree a social convention.

The verdict on Brown in the public was faring poorly both in the North and in the South. Desperate to distance the entire population from him, the northern press dubbed him "a fanatic; *sui generis*," a "wild and absurd freak," and he and his men a collection of "Nigger-Worshipping Insurrectionists." Even abolitionist publications condemned him; the *New York Tribune* concluded the raid was "deplorable" and "the work of a madman." Garrison's *Liberator*, maybe predictably, called it "misguided, wild, and apparently insane."[20]

But there was a faint signal that maybe fear would not have the last word. On the 30th of October, Emerson's close friend Henry David Thoreau announced a lecture in support of the Old Man. He did so over the strident objections of Concord abolitionists, and walked by himself to summon the people by ringing the Town Hall bell. His talk was published as "A Plea for Captain John Brown"; it was the beginning of something extraordinary. He contrasted Brown's singular heroism, his relentless moral authority and causal *Ich* against the "cackling of political conventions" and the mindless "herd" who condemned Brown or pronounced him insane. Southerners did not suffer his most scathing condemnation; they were behaving rather as expected. But he was harsh to a northern culture in which life was seen in terms of financial utility. Their seemingly rational judgment was that Brown had wasted his life. "No doubt," Thoreau said, "you can get more in your market for a quart of milk than for a quart of blood, but that is not the market that heroes carry their blood to."[21]

In Thoreau's estimation, no antislavery speech had ever matched Brown's words to Senator Mason, which reporters had dutifully broadcast across the country. The Old Man may have been wounded, bleeding, and defeated, yet "he could afford to lose his Sharpe's rifles, while he retained his faculty of speech,—a Sharpe's rifle of infinitely surer and longer range."

The trial's closing arguments were conducted on Monday, October 31. The courtroom was packed beyond capacity as people crammed in to hear the verdict they knew would come, and though it may seem odd that a verdict foreordained would draw such a large crowd, mankind has built his histories around reassuring himself that all will happen as it *should*. The herd flocked there for psychological relief and to witness history.

"Gentlemen of the Jury," the clerk asked after the jury returned from forty-five minutes of deliberation, "what say you, is the prisoner at the bar, John Brown, guilty or not guilty?"

"Guilty."

"Guilty of treason, and conspiring and advising with slaves and others to rebel and murder in the first degree?"

"Yes."

The courtroom was silent. Brown "said not a word, but, as on any previous day, turned to adjust his pallet, and then composedly stretched himself upon it."[22]

When sentencing came three days later, Brown was healthy enough to walk and to sit in court rather than lie prone on a cot. The defense went through the requisite motions, Judge Parker overruled all objections, and during those procedures Brown "was like a block of stone."[23] Finally, he was told to rise, and the clerk asked him if he could state any reason "why sentence should not be pronounced upon him."[24]

The Old Man straightened his jacket and took a hesitant step forward. Resting his hands on a table for support, he paused for a moment, seeming "wholly unprepared to speak at this time."[25] But then he did, and those present fell silent to listen to their fears in the echo of that steady voice, flinty, pinched, and weary, as he addressed what he knew was his imminent death.

> I have, may it please the court, a few words to say. In the first place, I deny everything but what I have all along admitted—the design on my part to free the slaves. I intended certainly to have made a clean thing of that matter, as I did last winter when I went into Missouri and there took slaves without the snapping of a gun on either side, moved them through the country, and finally left them in Canada. I designed to have done the same thing again on a larger scale. That was all I intended. I never did intend murder, or treason, or the destruction of property, or to excite or incite slaves to rebellion, or to make insurrection.
>
> I have another objection; and that is, it is unjust that I should suffer such a penalty. Had I interfered in the manner which I admit, and which I admit has been fairly proved (for I admire the truthfulness and candor of the greater portion of the witnesses who have testified in this case)—had I so interfered in behalf of the rich, the powerful, the intelligent, the so-called great, or in behalf of any of their friends—either

father, mother, brother, sister, wife, or children, or any of that class—and suffered and sacrificed what I have in this interference, it would have been all right; and every man in this court would have deemed it an act worthy of reward rather than punishment.

This court acknowledges, as I suppose, the validity of the law of God. I see a book kissed here which I suppose to be the Bible, or at least the New Testament. That teaches me that all things whatsoever I would that men should do to me, I should do even so to them. It teaches me, further, to "remember them that are in bonds, as bound with them." I endeavored to act up to that instruction. I say I am yet too young to understand that God is any respecter of persons. I believe that to have interfered as I have done—as I have always freely admitted I have done—in behalf of His despised poor was not wrong, but right. Now, if it is deemed necessary that I should forfeit my life for the furtherance of the ends of justice, and mingle my blood further with the blood of my children and with the blood of millions in this slave country whose rights are disregarded by wicked, cruel, and unjust enactments—I submit; so let it be done!

Let me say one word further.

I feel entirely satisfied with the treatment I have received on my trial. Considering all the circumstances it has been more generous than I expected. But I feel no consciousness of guilt. I have stated that from the first what was my intention and what was not. I never had any design against the life of any person, nor any disposition to commit treason, or excite slaves to rebel, or make any general insurrection. I never encouraged any man to do so, but always discouraged any idea of that kind.

Let me say also a word in regard to the statements made by some of those connected with me. I hear it has been stated by some of them that I have induced them to join me. But the contrary is true. I do not say this to injure them, but as regretting their weakness. There is not one of them but joined me of his own accord, and the greater part of them at their own expense. A number of them I never saw, and never had a word of conversation with till the day they came to me; and that was for the purpose I have stated.

Now I have done.[26]

The courtroom clerk did not record his words, but thankfully northern journalists were present. He dissembled a bit concerning his innocent intentions in Virginia, and the benign nature of events in Missouri, yet it was a remarkable speech. It had none of the collective historical language of Lincoln's later Gettysburg Address, none of the dissolving of ethics into aggregate vision. Brown's oration was suffused with the same causal assertive *Ich* heard in the writings of Thoreau and Emerson. It was one of the finest and most aware political speeches of the era. Lincoln's address was an affirmation of historical consciousness; his invocation of *nation* was conceptually new, yet might have been delivered in 1800 just as easily as in 1863. Conversely, Brown's courtroom address would have been impossible to deliver when he was a young man.

Identifying hierarchical social divisions with class-based language had only recently surged into mainstream consciousness with the writings of Karl Marx and Max Weber. It was a way of recognizing that though the Age of Revolution had largely removed the older forms of hierarchy and predation, it had not removed those phenomena from human civilization, despite the fond imaginings of the architects of nations. In other words, the idyllic imaginings of a happy and classless proto–America were only possible because there was a gap in linguistic concepts capable of portraying the new forms of power.

Brown felt "no consciousness of guilt," but only regarding what he had been charged with. He knew that he was guilty; he had interfered with the desperately witless acceptance of established order. That knowledge was held up to his audience like a mirror that revealed that no matter how they hid from the truth behind rational language and orderly forms, what they really needed was a human sacrifice to their beliefs, and to the Leviathan as they understood it. Given that, he certainly had been treated generously, "considering all the circumstances."

Finally, Judge Parker intoned: "The sentence of the law is that you, John Brown, be hanged by the neck until you are dead," and almost as if underscoring Brown's point, "for the sake of the example" the execution would be public, rather than in the confines of a prison yard.[27] One man applauded, but was promptly hushed by the crowd. They had howled for the Old Man's blood all the way to Charles Town, had opened court that day by shouting at him, gleefully calling him a "damned black-hearted villain," but now they were silent, and averted their eyes. They would have their sacrifice, but Brown had taken away their ability to pretend it meant anything other than what it was.[28]

Brown peacefully accepted these events, but he had always known that God was no "respecter of persons," and that the pretensions of men were as frivolous as Emerson knew them to be, albeit for different reasons. Inside, he had perhaps always known the caricature of justice in that Virginia court was irrelevant. He would die for the murder of five men in Kansas, no matter what anyone present thought. He would die for the slaves, and he would die for the fear of everyone in that room.

He would die for a social order that had already ended; no one had admitted it yet, but if the ethical and epistemological foundation of the nation rested upon conventions that were arbitrarily discarded so that a man could be killed in order to pretend they were still in force, then the nation technically didn't exist anymore. He would die because few sins are darker than those that oppose what people believe is the unfolding of history.

20

The Metaphysics of the Hangman

> "Peace of soul" can be, for one, the gentle radiation of a rich animality into the moral (or religious) sphere. Or the beginning of weariness, the first shadow of evening, of any kind of evening.... Or the attainment of calm by a convalescent who feels a new relish in all things and waits ... or the emergence of certainty, even a dreadful certainty, after long tension and torture by uncertainty. Or the expression of maturity and mastery in the midst of doing, creating, working, and willing—calm breathing, attained "freedom of the will." Twilight of the Idols—who knows? Perhaps also only a kind of "peace of soul."
>
> —Friedrich Nietzsche, *Twilight of the Idols*

Perhaps because Judge Parker was conscious of the negative impression of Virginia that the speedy trial had created, he granted Brown an entire month before execution. That would, in theory, allow time to file futile appeals which would create at least the perception of due process.

When the reprieve became a month long vigil, Thoreau said of it that, "No theatrical manager could have arranged things so wisely" to give Brown a stage.[1] His pen indefatigably scrawled out letters to family and friends through every waking hour. Northeast intellectuals employed their own pens to help him create a narrative that had been growing steadily since Thoreau walked alone to ring the Town Hall bell in Concord.

Victory and defeat are merely functions of cultural choices and social philosophy, as Brown said when he wrote to Mary that though he may be defeated "as the saying *is*," he was certain to "recover all the lost capital occasioned by that disaster; by only hanging a few moments by the neck." He felt equally determined "to make the utmost possible out of defeat" and was "dayly & hourly striving to gather up" what he could from circumstances.[2]

The Old Man had been prepared for some time for martyrdom, at least since when he wrote in his confessional letter to Franklin Sanborn in 1858 that his quest might end like the story of Samson. Dying as a criminal bothered Brown not in the slightest, since Jesus of Nazareth had done no less. Pragmatically, his execution was likely to do "vastly more toward advancing the cause I have earnestly endeavored to promote, than all I have done in my life before."[3] It was, in most respects, a summation of all he had done in his life, and as he phrased it more wryly to his brother, once that life was financially summed up he was "worth inconceivably more to hang than for any other purpose."[4]

The fierce warrior and defiant defendant transformed to sage and reflective prisoner, using every hour of his brief conscious existence as a ghost to add depth and meaning to the metaphor he had become. He sought refuge and vindication in a stoic apprehension of the meaning of events, filling his letters with words about justice, courage, wisdom, and temperance.

On insurrection:

> I do not feel conscious of guilt in taking up arms; and had it been in behalf of the rich and powerful, the intelligent, the great (as men count greatness), or those who form enactments to suit themselves and corrupt others, or some of their friends, that I interfered, suffered, sacrificed, and fell, it would have been doing very well.[5]

On the connections between people:

> I have often passed under the rod of him whom I call my Father; & certainly no son ever needed it oftener; & yet I have enjoyed very much of life, as I was enabled to discover the secret of this; somewhat early. It has been in making the prosperity, & the happiness of others *my own:* so that really I have had a great deal of prosperity. I am very prosperous still; & looking forward to a time when "peace on Earth & good will to *men* shall every where prevail."[6]

On perspectives:

> You cannot have forgotten *how; & where our Grandfather* (Capt. John Brown) fell in 1776; *& that he too* might have perished on the scaffold had circumstances been but *very little* different. *The fact* that a man dies under the hand of an executioner (or other wise) has but little to do with his true character, as I suppose. John Rogers perished at the stake *a great & good* man as I suppose: but *his being* so does *not prove* that any other man who has died in the same way was *good or otherwise.*[7]

On social realism:

> The great bulk of mankind estimate each other's actions *and motives* by the measure of success or *otherwise* that attends them through life. By that rule I have been one of the *worst,* and one of the *best* of men. I *do* not claim to have been one of the latter; and I leave it to an impartial tribunal to decide whether the world has been the *worse* or the better of my *living* and *dying* in it.... My *whole* life *before* had not afforded me one half the opportunity to plead *for the right. In this,* also, *I find* much to reconcile me to both my present condition and my immediate prospect. I may be *very insane,* (and I *am* so, if insane at all.) But if that be so, *insanity* is like a very pleasant dream to me.[8]

To find peace, and to maintain his own courage, he did not hate, nor display anger towards his tormentors. But it was love, perhaps, that he feared most of all as the end neared. Higginson was accompanying Mary on her way to her husband when a telegram from Brown's attorneys finally reached him, reading, "Mr. Brown says for gods sake dont let Mrs. Brown come." Brown had another one of his attorneys write to her that he feared a visit from her might "unman and unfit him for the last great sacrifice" and would "disturb the great serenity and firmness which he wills to have accompany him to the gallows."[9] Brown also wrote Higginson, "Her presence *here* will deepen my affliction a thousand fold. I beg of her to be *calm, & submissive; &* not to go *wild* on my account." He wished as well to save his wife from the indignity of being a spectacle for crowds in Charles Town.[10] Mary was finally persuaded to end her journey in Baltimore.

"In this world," Brown finally wrote her, in a letter of gratitude and of sorrowful consolation, "we must have tribulation: but the *cords* that have bound *you* as well as I;

to Earth: have been many of them severed already." The severing had been painful, having lost so many of their children, and he knew the fear of severing his dearest tie would cause him the anguish of wishing to live just a bit longer. His one request to her was that "if after Virginia has applied the finishing stroke to the picture already made of me, you can afford to meet the expense & trouble of coming on here to gather up the bones of our beloved sons, & of your husband; and the people here will suffer you to do so; I should be entirely willing."[11]

Among the visitors Brown did receive was Lydia Maria Child, a prominent abolitionist and the first New England intellectual to come to Brown's defense. While the rest of the North had kept a fearful distance, she wrote Gov. Wise the day after the trial commenced, requesting permission to visit and tend to Brown's wounds. Wise wrote a lengthy, cordial, and perhaps overly supercilious reply in light of the farce his court and prosecutor were orchestrating. He guaranteed her safety by virtue of his and his state's fervent embrace of "the Constitution which unites them [Massachusetts and Virginia] in one confederacy" which he was "sworn to support," and was, therefore, "bound to protect [Child's] privileges and immunities." And though he abhorred her abolitionism, and blamed Brown's raid largely on the philosophy of her circle, she was welcome to visit.[12]

Sheriff James Campbell, Brown's executioner (Library of Congress).

Child would not tolerate being pandered to, though she accepted the invitation. She replied at length, detailing the ways in which southern states had freely trampled the Constitutional rights which they claimed to hold dear, often merely to punish apostasy against the "peculiar institution." "With these," Child wrote, "and a multitude of other examples before your eyes, it would seem as if the less that was said about respect for constitutional obligations at the South, the better. Slavery is, in fact, an infringement of all law, and adheres to no law, save for its own purposes of oppression."

By way of illustrating the depths of Wise's hypocrisy, she quoted a vitriol-filled speech he had delivered in Congress in 1842 in defense of the various filibustering societies infiltrating Mexico. The societies caused so many problems that the federal government had considered trying to restrain them. In response, Wise had treasonously boasted that if he were in charge of a filibustering group, he would overrun the troops of the United States should they try to stop him. He also declared his goal, thinly veiled in euphemism and heroic rhetoric, to gain wealth and glory by robbing churches, and by wholesale murder. And, as Child pointed out, he intended to do so not out of a desire "to right the wrongs of any oppressed class; not to sustain any great principles of justice, or of freedom; but merely to enable 'Slavery to pour itself forth without restraint.'"

Surely, Child lectured, if John Brown were truly as evil as Wise portrayed him, it was only because Brown was as evil as Wise, and she reminded him of the words of Macbeth:

> "We but teach
> Bloody instructions, which, being taught, return
> To plague the inventor: This even-handed justice
> Commends the ingredients of our poisoned chalice
> To our own lips."

As Child told Wise, she and hers were certainly *not* responsible for Brown's actions, but they were quite closely related, having grown of a slave state social order that the entire intelligent world looked upon with shame. "By fillibustering and fraud, they dismembered Mexico, and having thus obtained the soil of Texas, they tried to introduce it as a Slave State into the Union. Failing to effect their purpose by constitutional means, they accomplished it by a most open and palpable violation of the Constitution, and by obtaining the votes of Senators on the false pretences." In time, their terrible hunger had taken them to Kansas. And there, "they literally tied the stones, and let loose the mad dogs. This was the state of things when the hero of Osawatomie and his brave sons went to the rescue. It was he who first turned the tide of Border-Ruffian triumph, by showing them that blows were to be taken as well as given."

"You may believe it or not, Gov. Wise, but it is certainly the truth that, because slaveholders so recklessly sowed the wind in Kansas, they reaped a whirlwind at Harper's Ferry."[13]

Senator Mason's wife decided to write to Child and attempt to bring the combative and expansive debate to a close by the exceptionally banal practice of quoting Bible verses at her, as if that settled the matter. Such justifications might have had weight in Mrs. Mason's social circle, but Child was far too intelligent. She replied with her own choice biblical quotes, illustrating the silliness of the exercise. But she also contributed a detailed exposition on southern law, revealing slavery as justified only upon a foundation of absurdity, contradictions, and willful ignorance. The correspondence was eventually published in the abolitionist press.

Gov. Wise, to his credit, spent hours writing replies to the swelling stream of letters, many of them pleas to spare Brown's life. As the month passed, more of the letters came from prominent southerners who had gauged changing public sentiments and were becoming worried that they were about to complete a martyrdom. Prudent advice, but Wise had ambitions beyond the hanging of a single man, and when he addressed the legislature on the subject, he claimed that if the North would truly make of Brown a martyr, "then it is time indeed … that we should prepare for the 'irrepressible conflict.'"[14] Fundamentally, his rhetoric had changed little since 1842, and his greatest mistake was that he comically believed that he was in control. But then again, so did everyone else. Martyrs can be made, but can also make themselves out of the absurd voids in the narrative.

Brown's imprisonment provided him opportunities to speak personally with pro-slavery people in very unique circumstances. He wrote about "daily" visits, and endeavored "to improve them *faithfully, plainly, and kindly*. I do not think I ever enjoyed life better than since my confinement here." It was like vivid memories from a lifetime ago, of ministering to people in Randolph, Pennsylvania, before the world moved on. However, the support of the southern clergy for slavery was a heresy he could not countenance, and he would not so cheerfully welcome those who wished to minister to him. "No," he wrote to a friend, "There are no ministers of *Christ* here. These ministers who profess to be Christian, and hold slaves or advocate slavery, I cannot abide them. My knees will not bend in prayer with them while their hands are stained with the blood of souls."[15]

Brown's distance from the organized church is difficult to measure. From the earliest to his final hour, the language of faith filled his writings and was the foundation of his moral philosophy. And yet, in his later years he did not seem so dogmatic, nor as active in churches as he had been. Strict Sabbatarianism had once led to a deep rift with his brother-in-law and childhood friend Milton Lusk over Lusk's casual adherence to church dogma. But when Lusk was feuding with his Hudson, Ohio, church, Brown visited to both show support and to apologize in a way, confiding that Lusk was perhaps "nearer right than he had thought."[16] He may have been devoted to the church as a young man, but by the time he wrote his autobiography to Henry Stearns, he was only "to some extent a convert to Christianity."

He never turned from faith, and agonized over the agnosticism of his children to the end, but faith and religion are different. Brown would never, and could never, be the ferociously clever apostate that Emerson was, but there was a tenuous kinship between the two men in their attempts to philosophically reconcile the age.

The Old Man always welcomed reporters to his cell, and the press was filled with his words, the impressions of him, and the words of an intellectual circle in Emerson's orbit. By mid-month the translation of John Brown was nearly complete. Northerners increasingly admired him, and Charles Town became an armed camp in reaction to rumors of rescue plots and fears of slave insurrections. There were so many southern soldiers in town that all normal activity ground to a halt, and as military institutions always demand, the inhabitants of Charles Town were able to do "nothing but make efforts to provide for the military," taxing their infrastructure to the breaking point.[17]

John Brown realized as his execution drew near that ideals alone would not lift him from fear. He knew at last that he needed love, though it may hurt. Besides, Mary was growing anguished. "You have nursed and taken care of me a great deal; but I cannot even come and look at you," she wrote, and was indignant that other women, like Child, had been allowed to "minister to your wants, which I am deprived of doing."[18] Brown finally wrote Mary a soft plea for help:

20. The Metaphysics of the Hangman

Life is made up of a series of changes: & let us try to meet them in the best manner possible ... the near aproach of my great change is not the occasion of any particular dread. I trust that God who has sustained me so long; will not forsake me when I most feel my need of *Fatherly aid; & support.* Should he hide his face; my spirit will droop, & die: *but not otherwise:* be assured.

If you *now feel* that you are *equal* to the undertaking do *exactly as* you FEEL *disposed to do* about coming to see me before I suffer. I *am entirely willing.*

Your affectionate Husband
John Brown.[19]

She left immediately with Higginson and arrived on December 1. The place had been under martial law for some while, and the soldiers occupying their time with parades and parasitism equaled the civilian population.[20] Robert E. Lee had returned to command the military, and a group of cadets had been sent to Charles Town from the Virginia Military Institute under the command of Major Thomas J. Jackson. This military assembly, preening with bayonet and cannon, greeted Mary, and the *Baltimore American* noted, "There seemed to be an evident intention to appall the poor woman with the military majesty of the Commonwealth of Virginia."[21]

Nevertheless, she went to the prison with the same steely fortitude shown by her husband, and impatiently endured nearly fifteen minutes of formalities, "stiff platitudes," and sanctimonious mouthing about "Southern hospitality."[22] Then, after a search, she was led in to see John.

She ran to him and they embraced, and stood there speechless with mutual wonder, her head resting on his chest and her arms wrapped fiercely around his neck, as if she could hold him to this world. Finally, Brown composed himself enough to speak.

"Wife, I am glad to see you," he said. They passed some time speaking of their children, his wishes regarding their education, and the disposition of their estate. He also gave her instructions regarding his dead body, should she be allowed to leave with it.

His final bequests were poetic. John, Jr., who led him to Kansas, would receive the compass and surveying tools that the two had used to scout Buford's camp and the victims at Pottawatomie. Owen, ever faithful of vision and brave in support was given an opera glass, rifle, and $50, "in consideration of his terrible sufferings in Kansas: & his crippled condition from his childhood." Peaceful Jason, with his shining, constant morality was left with a silver watch, and his family Bible was for Ruth. With nothing left but a meager sum of money, he asked Mary to purchase a small Bible for each of the others. He had once sworn to make things right with George Kellogg, from time to time, as divine providence would allow, so he willed $50 more in one final payment.[23]

That evening the couple ate with Brown's jailer, John Avis, and Avis's family. After, though it was against policy, Avis gave them some privacy before returning to tell Mary it was time to leave. This was the only time that Brown's serenity during his imprisonment cracked, and he "showed a good deal of temper."[24] So long so far from home, and now she was here when he needed a sea to his shore, before letting go into darkness. It was too late. He didn't know how to let her go, but at some point anything said could only hurt them more. He did what he had to do and bid her a tearful farewell, and Mary returned to the Wager House to await the dawn.

In his final letter to his family, John Brown wrote:

I am writing the hour of my public *murder* with great composure of mind, & cheerfulness; feeling the strongest assurance that in no other possible way could I be used to so much advance that cause of God; & of humanity; & that nothing that either I or all my family have sacrifised or suffered; *will be lost....* So my dear *shattered; & broken* family; be of good cheer; & believe and trust in God.... Do not feel ashamed on my account; nor *for one moment* despair of the cause; or grow *weary* of *well doing*.

Circumstances like my own; for more than a month past; convince me beyound *all doubt* of our great need: of something more to rest our hopes on; than merely our own vague theories framed up, while our *prejudices* are excited; *or* our *Vanity* worked up to its highest pitch. Oh do not trust your eternal all uppon the boisterous Ocean, without even *a Helm;* or *Compass* to *aid* you in steering. I do *not ask any* of you; to throw *away your reason:* I only *ask* you, to make a candid, & sober *use of your reason....* Be determined to know by experience *as soon as may be:* whether bible instruction is of *Divine origin* or not; which says; "Owe no man anything but to love one another."[25]

The next morning, December 2, the Old Man's arms were bound and he was led from the building to a waiting wagon. On his way out, he bid farewell to his fellow prisoners and conspirators, saving his final farewell for Stevens, his cell-mate, his lion, his loyal lieutenant to the bitter end. They clasped hands firmly, and smiled. "I feel it in my soul Captain that you are going to a better world," Stevens said. Brown nodded, and replied, "Stand up like a man—no flinching now. Farewell." He passed a note to Stevens upon which he had quoted Proverbs: "He that is slow to anger; is better than the mighty; and that ruleth his spirit, than he, that taketh a city."[26] Brown passed another note to Avis before being seated on the black walnut coffin in the back.

It was a weirdly clement December day, warm and vibrant with honeybees and the chirping of birds. The wagon rolled laboriously towards a field at the edge of town, flanked by two lines of riflemen and Brown perched upon a coffin. He breathed deep, looked around with eyes that savored eternity in each slipping moment, and said wistfully, "This is a beautiful country. I never had the pleasure of seeing it before."[27]

Wise tried to ensure that the execution would fortify the authority of the state. Furthermore, he finally realized the damage that had been done by Brown's celebrity, and abruptly reversed his permissive attitude regarding access. A reporter noted that on execution day, Wise had decreed that only military men were permitted "within hearing of what Brown may say," and went on to speculate, "Why this jealous caution? Can it be that it is feared this old man's sturdy truths and simple eloquence will stir a fever in the blood of all who listen, that shall break down the barriers of prejudice, and shatter their feeble principles like glass?"[28] Wise certainly wanted to avoid a repeat performance of Brown's courtroom address, but his ban was doing just as much damage, so he eventually allowed a few reporters a position near the major-general's staff, to witness the death in the shadow of Virginia's military might, unable to accuse the state of fear-based censorship. Besides, the spectacle needed witnesses, other than the one.

And it was a massive spectacle, the largest ceremonial death in the history of the United States before or since. Brown was led to the gallows through what Major Preston recalled as "the greatest array of disciplined forces ever seen in Virginia, infantry, cavalry, and artillery combined, composed of the old Commonwealth's choicest sons, and commanded by her best officers, and the great canopy of the sky, overarching all, came to add its sublimity."[29] He swiftly ascended the scaffold with "the same imperturbable, wooden composure which had distinguished him at every step of his progress."[30] Brown was a man who had futilely tried to carry all of humanity and its longings within himself. From that platform he saw the men in their tidy geometric blocks, the expression of a people who reassured themselves by wishing humanity to become a single individual, the same, duplicated to the end of number. Then a coarse hood was drawn over his face.

Only executioner William Campbell accompanied the Old Man. In a way, the demands of executioner and historian are not so different; charged with culturally translating death into social narrative, those executioners are subject to many of the same demands. There are the prerogatives of the powerful, who wish the symbols and ceremony to be just so, and the howls of the sanguinary, who wish it to be shameful agony. Attention is due those who demand a humane death, either out of blessed compassion or the desire to preserve the illusion of logic. And finally there is the victim, who must be guided competently through it all. Campbell asked Brown to step to the trap door, but Brown said calmly, "You must lead me, I cannot see." The executioner quietly asked if it would help if he were to give some signal, like the drop of a handkerchief, so that Brown could be ready. "No," the Old Man replied, "but do not detain me any longer than is absolutely necessary."[31]

Despite his request, it was not swift. He waited, unseeing, alone with thought and memory before the eyes of hundreds arranged in their meaningless ritual, connected to the world by only the platform beneath his feet and the single, final cord around his neck. He was delayed because it was apparently necessary that his armed escort be incorporated properly into the blocks and columns; no person could be out of place. He could not see this foolishness though, so he waited, breathing in each last moment.

Close your eyes, John Brown. Lay down your burdens; it is only in the light of civilization that we are different. One is the beginning.

Breathe.

Smells of grass, the fluttering of birds.

Breathe.

Uncomfortable and embarrassed fidgeting of the executioner.

Breathe.

Clattering boots and rifles.

Breathe.

Memories. Loved ones lost, loved ones left. Days long ago when everything in the world was possible.

Breathe.

So many regrets, and all that could have been.

Breathe.

Warm sunshine, forgiving and out of place in December, beaming through the rough hood.

How did he not break under the awful apprehension? Much of the history of the age had been the quest to mechanically compel men to behave just as Brown did on the gallows for causes that had far less meaning. The arrangements of the men there not only enabled their simple-minded officers to impose theory on violence, but also to mask fear in faceless geometry and social reinforcement. With none of their foolish devices, Brown stood still as a stone, as if at the end of that rope someone would smile and simply say, "Take my hand, John Brown." It was a long way down, and the thread to those gallows as straight as the cord wrapped around his neck.

There may be only one relevant idea in this narrative. Close your eyes, and imagine for a moment standing there, impossibly alone, while everything inside you cried "save me now." Ask yourself if you've ever believed in anything so deeply, or loved so much.

Finally, they were ready. You know what this is, what came next. There is a word for it, when during the story a person or some other contrivance is lowered by a rope onto the stage. It refers to a causal force, personified, and brought in during the last act. Some say that it is an archaic contrivance for poor playwrights, but that unfairly ignores the need it fulfills. Many good playwrights, ancient and modern, have understood well the audience's need for reassurances that their assumptions were correct all along, and that this constitutes a good ending. They provide it by whatever means it amuses their audience to believe, so that they will have a play that ends well rather than face the sins of their hands and the sins of their tongues.

There hung the frail broken body of John Brown, all too human. He thrashed for five minutes, and clung to life for thirty more—the rope had been cut too short for gravity to deliver swift mercy—before he finally swayed at rest, no life in eyes gone cold and gray on that warm winter day. It had been so much to demand of one man.

In the years to follow, Lincoln would refer to "our forefathers" in his Gettysburg Address, which conceptually solidified a nation that was proxy for the families it had compelled into a westward diaspora. And most of his audience would be so much younger than Brown, and would not remember an age before destiny, before history.

Those forefathers were clever men given to divinely elegant machinations and also an inscrutable cosmic legerdemain, out of which the United States of America was perhaps their grandest joke, home of a mechanical people arrayed before Brown, drawn up in the geometries of ritual sacrifice to the machine. But there was only awful silence as they, uncomprehending, regarded that dead, cast off, and wretched son of a dying age. He had come from Kansas, he had come from history, and from that he was nothing. He would become the emblem of their darkest fears, but he would also give people an ideal to strive for.

Though Gov. Wise had mostly allowed only soldiers—whose minds he felt best insulated against wisdom—to view the death, some of them might have wondered about the events. An ordinary man had risen up behind an ideal, and had stumbled and fallen and done some evil things, and it would be tempting to say that he died because of them. But you know why he died. He died because he tried to change history, in more ways than one.

Sometime afterwards, a soldier named John Wilkes Booth wrote in his journal that he was "proud of my little part in the transaction" and happy to have seen the traitor hanged.[32] Sometime afterwards, John Avis unfolded a crumpled up note. It was the final revelation of John Brown, a sentence on injustice. The good Lord whispers like the Kansas thunder. At the time, it must have seemed a quaint curiosity. Who knew how the years would change the meaning of those words, and how far thought and memory would fly? But something about them stuck with Avis, who felt a need to save them for later reflection: "I, John Brown am now quite certain that the crimes of this guilty land: will never be purged away; but with Blood. I had as I now think; vainly flattered myself that without verry much bloodshed; it might be done."[33]

21

Where Faith Is Needed

Our age is proud of its historical sense; How could it ever make itself believe the nonsense that at the beginning of Christianity there stands the crude fable of the miracle worker and the Redeemer—and that everything spiritual and symbolical represents only a later development? On the contrary: the history of Christianity, beginning with the death on the cross, is the history of the misunderstanding, growing cruder with every step, of an original symbolism.... The destiny of Christianity lies in the necessity that its faith had to become as diseased, as base and vulgar, as the needs it was meant to satisfy were diseased, base, and vulgar.
—Friedrich Nietzsche, The Antichrist

Prophets live between interpretation and tradition, reason and revelation, cause and effect. They challenge people to know that their certainties are an expression of chance, choice, and history, and they speak for justice and mankind's highest ideals. Their words, ominous predictions, are an interpretation of the moral failures of their age and a bridge to the human consequences. Understanding and truth, renouncement and reflection, even reconciliation, are the roles of the sage.[1] Emerson may have best understood this story—that of a powerful will shaped and brought forth by a fundamentally grotesque society and fated to, perhaps, end the same.

Emerson the wise sage was also a perceptive student of the Bard, and of Goethe, who offered a profoundly beautiful and convincing formulation of Hamlet's tragedy as the end result of the collapse of the youthful social reality. Hamlet was the strongest character in his story, bold and cunning, with a driving will, and an aura that inspired respect and fear. In a world of cause-and-effect and free will such an individual could craft a destiny out of choice and accomplishment. But Goethe countered that the play has its own will, and a nature so demonically gifted, so fiercely strong as Hamlet's eventually comes to be bound by the doubts and weariness of life, and the story could only unwind as it did. "A horrid deed is done; it rolls along with all its consequences, dragging with it even the guiltless: the guilty perpetrator would, as it seems, evade the abyss made ready for him; yet he plunges in, at the very point by which he thinks he shall escape, and happily complete his course."[2]

Now Brown was only a ghost. But he had masterfully performed his enemies' script, and his crimes would only multiply after his death. Emerson's initial reaction to the Harper's Ferry raid drama is unknown. His copious journals walked the length and breadth of the intellectual landscape, yet were utterly silent on John Brown in the days immediately after. But on October 23, he did write his son that "we are all very well, in spite of the sad Harpers Ferry business, which interests us all who had Brown for our guest twice.... He is a true hero, but lost his head there."³ That simple expression of puzzled concern for the person that he had, in fact, only met twice, and truly only conversed with once, were Emerson's last words about a mere man named John Brown. But Brown's daring raid and sacrifice was the most incredibly irrational act that he had ever had the privilege of witnessing outside of literature. And upon reflection, it was a summation of wisdom and courage, as if to say: "If not I for myself, who then? And being for myself, what am I? And if not now, when?"⁴

When Emerson had previously written about John Brown, he had never written about John Brown; he had written about a story walking incarnate. At their first meeting Brown and Thoreau had conversed in his parlor, and Brown had asserted that with a

Mary Brown (Library of Congress).

dozen good, peaceable, respectful fighters he could oppose a hundred of Buford's ruffians. That at least was how Thoreau recalled it.⁵ Emerson's recollection was nearly identical, save for a more epic twenty thousand ruffians.⁶

Zarathustra "had a line saying, 'that violent deaths are friendliest to the health of the soul.'"⁷ After John Brown's narrative was set loose in the world by that death, it kept ramifying. It was oddly verifiably true and yet hardly connected with any shared form of history. At the same time, it was deeply connected with things that people—like Emerson—felt about their real, shared experience. "Inspiration is that," he wrote of Brown, "to be so quick as truth; to drop the load of Memory & of Futurity, Memory & Care, & let the moment suffice to us: then one discovers that the first thought is related to all thought & carries power & fate in its womb."⁸

By the 26th of October, blithe statements about a man he barely knew were gone, replaced by a narrative metamorphosis: "For Captain Brown, he is a hero of romance, & seems to have made this fatal blunder only to bring out his virtues. I must hope for his escape to the last moment."⁹ He attended Thoreau's bold speech of October 30 and wrote a brief essay summarizing Thoreau's "Plea." His commentary on the speech: "The man is so transparent that all can see through him, that he had no second thought, but was the rarest of heroes, a pure idealist, with no by-ends of his own"¹⁰ would resurface nearly verbatim in a November 18 speech in Boston.

Brown was becoming one of Emerson's "representative men," but the nature of cause and effect and the edge of truth blurs as the story ramifies. Brown witnessed his own apotheosis from his prison cell, watched his ghost begin to walk the world, and he performed marvelously for that ghost in correspondence and in the press. An act or not, a lesser man would have lacked the vision, courage, and philosophical fortitude to vindicate Emerson with his final days.

As usual Emerson saw better than any what could be occurring. On November 7, during his first speech on Brown, titled "Courage," he made a remark that he later omitted from the published version: "The Saint," he said, "whose fate yet hangs in suspense, but whose martyrdom, if it shall be perfected, will make the gallows as glorious as the cross."[11] When he said it, the blasphemous statement provoked a collective inhalation of shock. Some consoled themselves that it was a careless phrase by a man attempting to make a point.

One person even sought out Emerson to verify that the sage had not, in fact, said anything so scandalous. Emerson asked the man to repeat for him—just to be certain—what apostasy he was reported to have said. Upon hearing it read back to him, he nodded: "That's about what I said."

"Surely," his interlocutor stammered in shock, "you do not approve the bloody raid of John Brown upon the families of Virginia."

Emerson, so beautifully and gently offensive, could only wryly reply, "If I should tell you why I disapproved, you might not like it any better."[12]

That poor man, like all the others, had chosen to merely look at the surface of Emerson's words, particularly the superficial Christ comparison, and understood Emerson as poorly as he understood himself. Of course, the surface comparison was there for effect, desperately begging for offense, but it was hardly fair to the age's finest philosophical mind and apostate to think he was saying something as hideously simple as John Brown is like Jesus Christ.

The line was likely deleted when he realized (which he should have all along) that people were far too cloistered to read his meaning beyond their ideas of literal biblical truth. But Emerson meant there was absolutely no historical evidence that Jesus Christ died for *our* sins. Despite the fact that somehow, after nearly two millennia, Christ became associated with what people regarded as "good" and "just," that holy anarchist had rebelled not against some abstract concept but against all that was considered "good" and "just," against hierarchy, against privilege. Against the "good" people of society. He brought up people from the bottom using language that, in Emerson's day, would have sent him to the gallows as it had John Brown. Jesus Christ was a political criminal, and he died for *his* guilt. But the Christ that most believed they knew was the product of apostolic hermeneutics, an act of literary interpretation for which the objective was the crafting of history from words of Old Testament prophets to demonstrate that Jesus was the Messiah.

Twenty-one years prior, Emerson caused a stir with an address to the six graduating seniors of Harvard's divinity school. He said that in this age man had become "an appendage, a nuisance," and where history acknowledged the divine nature, it was only so that it could attribute it to the few and deny it to all the rest "with fury." Christ had taught that our lives are not our own, and that the knowledge of the divinity in him as a man could serve as a mirror to see the divine in ourselves, connected to each other by each spark of grace. It only took a generation for that idea to become "This was Jehovah come down out of heaven. I will kill you, if you say he was a man." This, Emerson said, became the historical essence of Christianity, usurped by formalists who built the church upon "an exaggeration of the personal, the positive, the ritual. It has dwelt, it dwells, with noxious exaggeration about the person of Jesus." He wrote, "He spoke of miracles; for he felt that man's life was a miracle, and all that man doth, and he knew that this daily miracle shines, as the character ascends. But the word Miracle, as pronounced by Christian churches, gives a false impression; it is Monster."

The tyranny and power of the church in the age had been broken by reason, and it was clinging to the superstitious and the uneducated. But Emerson was not speaking of the church exclusively. He was speaking of a humanity that believed the world was the product of "manifold power," rather than "of one will, of one mind." Specifically, he was skeptical of the efforts to translate the same old sins of the City of God onto the Newtonian Universe, and recalled the grotesque spectacle of Citizen Robespierre, torch in hand, inaugurating a "new worship introduced by the French to the goddess of Reason," and declaring the end of history and the beginning of Year One of *La Révolution* on September 22, 1792. "Today, pasteboard and fillagree, and ending tomorrow in madness and murder."

He had been waiting to find a kind of overman with the capacity for "bold benevolence, an independence of friends," who would resist "for truth's sake the freest flow of kindness, and appeal to sympathies far in advance," and who would above all have a "certain solidarity of merit, that has nothing to do with opinion, and which is so essentially and manifestly virtue, that it is taken for granted, that the right, the brave, the generous step will be taken by it, and nobody thinks of commending it."[13]

Emerson wasn't really speaking about Christ at all; he was speaking about everyone else, and about what memory might make of it all when people eventually tried to absolve their nation, in the historical sense, of the original sin of slavery. As usual, they were too dim to understand that if history does rhyme, the possibility was that, properly told, the story of John Brown could be transformative, even lacking a divine element. And the Roman Empire had foundered on Christianity.

The "Secret Six," who supported Brown's insurrection, were wanted in Virginia as "witnesses" after the discovery of the letters at the Kennedy Farm, so Sanborn fled to Canada. After all, "is any man in Massachusetts so simple as to believe that when a United States Court in Virginia, now, in its present reign of terror, sends to Connecticut, or New York, or Massachusetts, for a witness, it wants him for a witness?"

Emerson had discovered the extent of the "conspiracy," though Sanborn was the only member of the Six that he counted as a friend. As for the others, Gerritt Smith avoided questioning by committing himself to an asylum—appropriate, since the strain of being linked with Harpers Ferry took a terrible mental toll on him. Howe and Stearns sought refuge in Canada as well, at least until Emerson, disdainfully unperturbed, calmly refuted Virginia's power and persuaded all to return. His practical advice was to simply avoid Virginia and otherwise seek legal counsel. He also gave Sanborn a terse admonishment to kindly remember his responsibilities as a schoolmaster.[14] Of the Six, only Higginson had stayed, cursing his peers for their cowardice and vowing to rescue the Old Man. He was a figure of support by Mary's side.

Emerson briefly entertained the idea of trying to somehow influence Gov. Wise on behalf of Captain Brown, but nothing ever came of it.[15] Maybe he divined Wise's deeper intent, or maybe he realized that a philosopher who had never been invited to speak in the South probably had little influence there. So he devoted his attention to the story, and waited for the end, as he wrote to Lydia Julia Child: "Thanks thanks for your letter to Captain Brown:—and his reply will stand instead of all letters to you. I cherish to the last, hope for his brave life. He is one of those on whom miracles wait. I do not much think I shall go to Boston on the 2d December. We are talking of a little ceremony here, which Thoreau has projected, for that day."[16]

Church bells across the North rang on the appointed hour of Brown's execution (though not the actual time, due to ceremonial silliness). The bells heralded how different Mary's return journey with her husband's body would be. She had gone to Charles Town anonymously, while the country damned Brown as a maniac, and she feared a life as pariahs for herself and her children. But the world had changed dramatically by December 3.

To her fell the task of bearing his body, the task of waking. Gov. Wise had given his word that she would have the body, unharmed, and would be given safe and unmolested passage. He was true to his word, but was in no position to make her journey uneventful. In Philadelphia the crowds waiting to meet her train were so large that the mayor feared a riot. To distract the crowds on Brown's final road home, multiple John Browns left Philadelphia in decoy hearses, a physical metaphor for trajectory of the idea of him.

The South's effort to mutilate the memory began at the trial, even though Wise did not deliberately allow the body to be desecrated. But the undertaker in New York discovered that no particular care had been paid either. Brown had been slung in the coffin with the rope still around his neck, head crumpled under his shoulder, which had turned his face into a swollen, black, unrecognizable mess. The undertaker's office was surrounded by the crowds who followed the body as it and the memory were delivered into more compassionate hands. After the undertaker had done what he could for the body, a lock of hair and pieces of the rope became prized relics for someone among the penitents.[17]

On December 7 the wagon rumbled through snow and sticky slush in North Elba; they buried Brown the next day. It was a wake for widows, four of whom stood their lonely vigil as the man who had led their husbands into death was lowered into the frozen ground. The Old Man's neighbor and friend Lyman Epps sang his favorite hymn—"Blow Ye Trumpet, Blow"—after which Wendell Phillips delivered the oration. "History," he said, having witnessed the story's tangled growth for a month, "will date Virginia's Emancipation from Harpers Ferry. True, the slave is still there. So, when the tempest uproots a pine on your hills, it looks green for months—a year or two. Still, it is timber, not a tree. John Brown has loosened the roots of the slave system; it only breathes,—it does not live,—hereafter."[18]

The Old Man was not the last casualty. The other prisoners were tried and hanged with just as much legal propriety, which is to say that one human sacrifice somehow makes the others less shocking. Their hangings were not attended by so much ceremony, though the executioners did try to ensure that the ropes were of the proper length and strength, with varying degrees of success. Stevens endured a long and painful death; that lion was simply too strong for mere gravity to finish, despite the hangman's best intentions.

Mary became history's casualty. While John's body was fed to his waking dreams, Mary's business was the actual waking to responsibility. She had a family to care for, and no means of support save for men with a political cause, so she fed herself to history's silent forgetting in order to feed her children. If the Mary of memory reads like a stereotype written by nineteenth century white men, it's because she was. The men who nurtured the John Brown story crafted the only role they could imagine for her; they even wrote some of her correspondence. The woman who listened to feminist speakers and tried to passively resist the raid is still depicted as complacent and simple, characterized by "primitive stoicism."[19]

Her love for John and his in return were genuine. John Avis remembered clearly the couple's last meeting, and he—a slave-trader—had no motivation to make of her other than what she was. Her correspondence with John had been both tender and terse long before Higginson and Sanborn took charge of it. The final mutiny of the Old Man's sons was likely as much her doing as theirs; she had already given the life of one to that cause, and the health and peace of mind of others. When Brown dispatched Oliver to fetch her to Harpers Ferry, she had attempted further resistance by refusing; perhaps she thought that if he needed her so much, then without her the endeavor must end.

But she hadn't counted on her headstrong, moody, rebellious fifteen-year-old daughter, nor that girl's abiding love for her father and her desire for adventure. She was a lot like her father. And Martha, so deeply in love with Oliver, was not going to let him return alone either. Annie obliquely covered her mother's refusal with mundane excuses, but they seemed like petty subterfuges given everything at stake, especially if Mary truly was such a subservient woman. Her quiet effort to save her husband and sons failed when brave Annie and devoted Martha saved the Kennedy Farm façade and made the raid possible.

Martha was the next of the insurrectionists to die, after the men. Her daughter, conceived in a little farmhouse on a faraway adventure, was born early the next year. The baby was not well, and Martha—already despondent with grief—told Annie that if it lived she should try to live to care for it, "but if it dies I shall die too, as I shall have nothing to live for, then." The baby, named Olive in memory of her dead father, died two days later. Martha did as she said she would, and joined her baby and husband within the month.[20]

The memories killed Annie too, in their own way. For months afterwards, though she kept a brave public face, she often locked herself in a room and rolled on the floor "in the agony of a tearless grief for hours at a time." Others may have found inspiration in the "honor and glory" of the memories, but not her; they were pitiful substitutes for the "aching void that was left in [her] heart, losing so many loved ones."[21] She learned that one day you find that death has taken people until there is nothing there to keep you anymore: little deaths killing you a piece at a time. Those dead and lost outnumber the living in every realm of human endeavor. Most wise men and fair women, most cowards and heroes, most beautiful children; they are all dead. They stay with us, in a way, and through history people try to understand the ways they haunt the silent spaces between what we see, what we think, and what we say.

Annie was mourning her father, but most were awaiting the New Year and a presidential election that would show them if they should also be mourning a particular point of view, and hopeful candidates were already positioning themselves in the face of the most inflammatory subject of the day. As 1859 neared its close, the predicted winner was Sen. Stephen A. Douglas of Illinois. He was a quasi–Northerner; but as a Democrat, a proponent of "popular sovereignty," and as the author of the Kansas-Nebraska Act, he should carry the South. Portions of the North should be his by identity-association and for opposing President Buchanan's efforts to bring Kansas into the Union under the Lecompton Constitution. And no one would truly find him palatable due to his efforts to tack to a non-committal position on the Dred Scott decision, making his other legal efforts potentially irrelevant. He was the perfect kind of prefigured non-choice for the polls.

Douglas's likely opponent from the new Republican Party was Sen. William H. Seward, a New York Whig and a staunch opponent of slavery. Despite being—oddly for a Whig—a manifest destiny expansionist, his efforts to ban slavery in the new territories were certain to earn zero Southern votes. Additionally, he was unlikely to carry most of the North, since many Northerners feared that the politically powerful South would make good on its secessionist histrionics if a candidate like Seward attempted to advance an abolitionist agenda.

Seward's candidacy was effectively over when Gov. Wise essentially declared that it was necessary to hang John Brown in order to politically dare the "irrepressible conflict." That phrase came from a speech Seward gave in Rochester, New York, on October 25, 1858, when he predicted that the forces of history were gathering to a point where the United States would become entirely a slave state, unless the people acted "to confound and overthrow, by one decisive blow, the betrayers of the constitution and freedom forever."

His candidacy would not survive his foresight, or events. In 1858, the speech angered Southerners but was not quite a crippling political liability. But following Brown's raid, the words were returning to haunt him—and everyone—thereby casting a shadow over Seward's electoral viability. Adoring or fascinated crowds followed John Brown's body and gathered to hear Emerson and Thoreau speak, but this did not represent a majority of sentiment. The North was splitting on the issue, with a growing minority supporting abolitionism, but a significant majority unwilling to dare disunion, particularly over black people. The Republican Party predicted an overwhelming Douglas victory the following year if Seward was their candidate.

On a bitterly cold 30th of November, a little-known prairie lawyer who had lost an Illinois Senate race to Stephen Douglas crossed the Missouri River into Elwood, Kansas, and gave a brief speech, heard by few, in which he declared slavery to be "evil" and, reliving his 1858 debates with Douglas, pinned the recent troubles in Kansas on Douglas's endorsement of "popular sovereignty" and the Kansas-Nebraska Act.[22] The speech was a sparsely attended I-told-you-so epilogue to those old debates and made little press. After he spoke, Abraham Lincoln moved on to Atchison.

He was there on December 2 when John Brown's execution was the most popular topic of conversation in Kansas. Reflecting on the best, perhaps most politic way to address it, Lincoln said to another small crowd that Brown had "shown great courage, rare unselfishness." But that was as far as he would go, and in concert with much of Northern opinion, and the entire South, he made the legally dubious statement: "Old John Brown has just been executed for treason against the state. We cannot object." He also reasoned, "Even though he agreed with us in thinking slavery wrong. That cannot excuse violence, bloodshed, and treason. It could avail him nothing that he might think himself right."

The quote, in isolation, conveys one meaning. And yet, carefully and delicately balancing the competing needs of memory and philosophy, Lincoln went on to give the dire warning to the South that if "you undertake to destroy the Union, it will be our duty to deal with you as old John Brown has been dealt with. We shall try to do our duty. We hope and believe that in no section will a majority so act as to render such extreme measures necessary." Lincoln was adroit at navigating the social currents with capable ambiguity, and his warning to the South must not be read through the lens of the Emancipation Proclamation nor of John Brown's death on the altar of slavery. It was not an abolitionist statement, but a nationalist one, perhaps the first meaningful effort to subvert the John Brown story to the service of a hollow philosophy that was serving as proxy for all it had replaced, rather than as signal symbol of the flaws in that philosophy.

The next day Lincoln was speaking in Leavenworth, revisiting old debates again, telling his audience that Douglas's Kansas-Nebraska Act had been "based on the idea that slavery is not wrong" and therefore could not bring about an end to slavery, despite what the act's proponents said. What was needed was a policy that had no internal ambiguities. However, Lincoln insisted, "We are not trying to destroy it [slavery]. The peace of society, and the structure of our government both require that we should let it alone" where it already existed.[23]

Lincoln's speeches were insignificant until the 8th of December, when Mississippi Senator Jefferson Davis spoke on the Senate floor. Davis was one of the most outspoken of the Senate's fire-eaters, a man whom Sam Houston once described being "as ambitious as Lucifer and cold as a lizard."[24] Davis proposed to demonstrate that "Seward, by his own declaration, knew of the Harpers Ferry affair. If I succeed in showing that, then he, like John Brown, deserves, I think, the gallows, for his participation in it." There was great applause for this novelty, and probably some nervous fidgeting.[25] He compared Seward's "irrepressible conflict" speech, so hated in the South, with many of Brown's own words in Harpers Ferry and Charles Town. His conclusion was:

> That is exactly what John Brown said. He said if we would allow him to take our niggers off without making any fuss about it, he would not kill anybody. [Laughter.] Brown said he did not mean to kill anybody; Seward says, it is harmless and beneficent to us if we yield to their just demands. But if we do not yield, what then? Why, Brown said he would kill our people, butcher our women and children. What does Seward say? "Whether that consummation shall be allowed to take effect and with needful and wise precautions against sudden change and disaster, or be hurried on by violence, is all that remains for you [the people of the South] to decide."
> That is the very language of John Brown. Whether we will allow them to do it quietly or not, is the only question for the South to decide. Virginia has decided it, and has

hung the traitor Brown; and may, if she can get a chance, hang the traitor Seward. [Laughter.] We have repeatedly refused to yield, and you have sought to force us to yield by violence, and Virginia has met it with violence, and has hung the man; and Virginia has had twenty five hundred men under arms, and has defied all your efforts to rescue him.

The public statements of politicians may be full of rhetoric and artifice and have little in the way of "truth," but they must of necessity reflect some shared idea of truth; otherwise, the calculating politician would not say them. Even electoral failure following such statements does not necessarily discount them, but given Davis's eventual prominence, he can with some confidence be regarded as representative of the South's climate of opinion.

It might have been rude to deprive Davis of his chance to preen by mentioning that no one had attempted to rescue Brown. However, it was becoming clear to at least a faction of the Republican Party that William Seward was an impossible candidate, despite the fact that he did not believe that slavery would end the way John Brown foretold. Seward was much like Lincoln, though less cautious with his words; he was a centrist who inexplicably believed that slavery would peacefully expire.

At the same time, the seemingly impervious Douglas ticket was being threatened from within the South. The "moderate" Illinois Democrat simply did not have the ideological purity regarding slavery required in the post–Harpers Ferry South. Kentucky went so far as to exile six men on December 31, 1859, for the crime of believing that slavery was a sin. Committees gathered signatures on loyalty oaths to the perpetuation of slavery, and Southern state governments ordered their post offices to destroy copies of the *New York Tribune* (an abolition friendly paper that printed John Brown's speeches verbatim) instead of delivering them to subscribers.[26]

Conservative Southern newspapers portrayed the raid as emblematic of Northern society and its designs upon the South. "The spirit of the effort to wrest Kansas from slavery ... is manifest enough from the dead and captured agents of the bloody design at Harpers Ferry."[27] "This affair at Harpers Ferry is ... the presage of the future storm.... Brown and his followers are but the advance column of the partisan disciples of Seward and Chase."[28] "The 'irrepressible conflict' between the North and the South then, has already commenced; to this complexion it must come at last. It is useless to talk of the conservatism of the North. Where has there been any evidence of it?"[29]

The Democratic Convention of May 1860 split in this reign of terror. Douglas received the most votes, but not enough to carry the nomination, and a delegation of Southern fire-eaters withdrew from the convention, thus ending it without a nominee. The fire-eaters, led by men like Jefferson Davis and William Yancey of Alabama, denounced Douglas as a traitor to the party and advocated an explicit pro-slavery platform.[30] This seems dubious as a winning political strategy for a national election; if Seward was the presumptive Republican nominee, a Douglas Democratic ticket was surely a path to victory. But it appeared they decided to split their party in order to nominate a candidate that would be so repugnant to the North that Seward could actually win the election, thus hastening the secessionist crisis within the South.[31]

It's not entirely implausible; indeed, hazarding the implicit counterfactuals it becomes a logical—though ethically repugnant—course of action. It's difficult to say how effective the fire-eaters at the convention would have been without the overriding fear in the wake of John Brown's raid. But without that raid, Seward would not have appeared to be such a damaged candidate, damage that was ironically inflicted by the Southern separatists.

At the time though, Southern fire-eaters still foresaw a Seward nomination, and after Harpers Ferry they intended to use his words against him to exacerbate an electoral and even a sectional split. In the best case scenario, Northerners might even be so frightened of voting for Seward that a true Southern patriot and zealous crusader for slavery would be elevated to the presidency, rather than a compromise candidate like Douglas. Conversely, a Seward presidency would have then been used to rally the Southern populace to support the slave-holding oligarchy in secession. Feeling confident that northerners were not about to dissolve the union, fire-eaters gambled that they could elect a hard-line pro-slavery candidate who would allow Southern oligarchs to write the national identity.

But Seward was not the nominee—not yet—and he discovered at his party's convention that a faction opposed his nomination in the interest of beating Douglas and staving off a sectional division. Despite the Democratic split, prudent politicians still anticipated a Douglas nomination. Even on a split Democratic ticket, many believed Douglas could still win against a supposed abolitionist on one side and a hard-line Southern fire-eater on the other. Should Douglas not emerge from the nominating process at all, a candidate other than Seward, tarred by spurious association with John Brown, would be necessary. Seward carried the convention's first two rounds of voting, but his margin was insufficient to secure the nomination and never increased. However, during the second round of voting the prairie lawyer who had once lost the Illinois Senate election to Douglas made a dramatic leap in vote totals, enough to threaten Seward with a near tie.

It was a swing in Lincoln's fortunes that had as much to do with Seward's presidential hopes being dragged into John Brown's grave as it had to do with the new shape of society. There was as yet no political voice for the new laboring class born of the industrial revolution. In the U.S., workers' choices at the polls amounted to Whigs and Know-Nothings on one side, who were all too happy to turn soldiers and police on them—particularly on the foreign-born—and slave-holding or slavery-supporting Democrats on the other, who were concerned with Southern power and had little concern for the plight of labor. While the pro-slavery sentiments of Democrats may not have troubled many workers in the north, a growing number of the laboring class were German Socialists, who were not as easy about slavery as their U.S.-born peers.

"The act of John Brown," proclaimed the German Socialist Ohio Social Working-Men's Association, "has powerfully contributed to bring out the hidden consciousness of the majority of the people." The new Republican Party, searching for a political base that could carry it through the current crisis and a possible split in Democratic power, had not overlooked how significantly those German Socialists were affecting electoral dynamics in the North.

Workers had accepted the fact that Seward—their preferred candidate—was unlikely to emerge the nominee of a party in the convulsions of a conservative backlash. So two months prior to the convention, to bring clarity to the issue, the workers announced their "determined opposition to all efforts for the extension and perpetuation of slavery," and swore to support only candidates that stood with them on this sentiment.[32] The records of the convention are vaguely silent about German Socialists' influence, but the rapid decline of insider favorite Simon Cameron—a former Democrat, Know-Nothing, and railroad and banking tycoon—along with the surprising emergence of a vaguely pro-labor party platform under Lincoln suggests that the influence was powerful.

In the meantime the Democrats reconvened in Baltimore—minus the walkouts—and easily nominated Stephen Douglas. The fire-eaters in the South separately nominated incumbent Vice President John C. Breckinridge of Kentucky. This split ticket challenged Abraham Lincoln in the November 1860 election. Lincoln won 40 percent of the popular vote but carried the electoral vote on Northern states alone. Douglas won in turn 30 percent of the popular vote, and Breckinridge the 18 percent that likely would have been Douglas's had he been his party's single candidate. Not one pro-slavery state voted for Lincoln.[33]

It was the first campaign to actively appeal to the new working class. Republicans promoted themselves as the party of labor, and southern Democrats perceived their new electoral enemy, if their scare-tactics were any evidence. A notice ran in the *New York Herald* on November 1, 1860, which warned, "If Lincoln is elected you will have to compete with the labor of four million emancipated negroes. His election is but the forerunner of an ultimate dissolution of the Union. The North will be flooded with free negroes and the labor of the white man will be depreciated and degraded." Northern employers and the wealthy also attempted to intimidate workers into abandoning Lincoln, telling them that if the status quo were to be preserved, they would be able "to take care of yourself and your family. But if the Republican candidate ... is elected the South will withdraw its custom from us and you will get little work and bad prices."[34]

But many German Socialists were 1848 revolutionaries and were not going to be cowed by petty and amateur threats. They rallied in support of Lincoln, who, one year prior at the State Fair Agricultural Society in Wisconsin had said it was labor, not capital, which was "the source from which human wants are mainly supplied ... that labor is prior to, and independent of capital; that, in fact, capital is the fruit of labor, and could never have existed if labor had not first existed; that labor can exist without capital, but that capital could never have existed without labor. Hence ... labor is the superior ... greatly superior to capital."[35]

The secession of the states that would form the Confederacy began on December 20, 1860, with South Carolina, and the majority joined in January of 1861. On the surface, without Seward to lampoon as the ruination of the country and the Southern way of life, seceding over a Lincoln presidency looks patently ridiculous. It was even sillier given the fact that Southerners opted to secede before Lincoln was even inaugurated and had the opportunity to demonstrate the falsity of fire-eater rhetoric. What they hoped was that he would react just as he had threatened back in Atchison. So at levels of consciousness poorly articulated, the fear that attended John Brown's lengthening shadow made secession entirely realistic to the people of the South. After those states began to splinter off, on January 29, 1861, Kansas was admitted to the Union as a free state, and black people in the former territory lost the right to vote.

21. Where Faith Is Needed

On April 12, less than two years after the revelation of John Brown, cannon fired on Fort Sumter, South Carolina, and most were probably dizzy trying to understand how the situation had come about. Gov. Wise, however, was endlessly irritated by the fact that Virginia—the central stage of the drama and the heart of the slave system—was not yet a member of the Confederacy. So while the state government in Richmond debated secession, Gov. Wise decided that he would do something to accelerate the process.

On April 18, he dramatically interrupted the secession debate, brandishing a pistol and announcing: "Blood will be flowing at Harpers Ferry before night." That evening, he and a small group of conspirators seized the federal armory at Harpers Ferry over the strident protestations of the townspeople, who were not altogether eager to secede. The Richmond government approved secession the very next day, and sent Virginia soldiers to Wise's aid before the U.S. Army could respond. The result of the raid was a generous bequest to the new Confederate Army in the form of thousands of weapons and the marvelous machines at Hall's Rifle Works, which were removed and taken to Richmond.

As for the outcomes, draw the lines wherever it amuses you to do so. But we ought to preface our sentences with the words *true,* or *apparent,* to indicate whether we intend to write that which is, or that which merely seems to be. If a nation is a thing of laws and nothing more, then *apparently* the United States, despite weathering a terrible storm, has existed continuously since its providential founding in 1776, or maybe 1787. But *truly,* if law means anything, the founder's Constitution failed and the republic ended on the gallows with John Brown.[36] Our illusions are maintained by the successful rewriting of the Constitution after the war. But before people were desperate to believe in historical unity, many in Kansas received news of the shots on Fort Sumter with relative aplomb. This was particularly true for violent and predatory men like Charles Jennison; when hostilities and war became more-or-less "official," Jennison could once again find uniformed glory doing what he had been doing all along anyway—killing people from Missouri.

22

The History of an Error

How slowly how slowly we learn that witchcraft & ghostcraft, palmistry, & magic and all the other so called superstitions, which, with so much police, boastful skepticism & scientific committees, we had finally dismissed to the moon as nonsense, are really no nonsense at all, but subtle & valid influences, always starting up, mowing, muttering in our path & shading our day. The things are real, only they have shed their skin which with much insult we have gibbeted & buried.
—Ralph Waldo Emerson, *Journals*

Where do the barricades go up? The quaint idea of using a map as a metaphor for human power makes it seem believable that the war began with a Southern rebellion. Southern oligarchs, for their part, actively manufactured a "revolution" in the minds of their Confederate countrymen along these lines, and Northerners claiming the sanction of history, union and natural law were all too willing to abet this story, since within the borders of the United States was the Capitol and a house in a shockingly amnesiac white.

But the error in writing narrative on space is that those boundaries are mere conventions, and space is the simplest and most malleable of mediums. What endures in civilization is time, the place where ghosts whisper in the interstices of human memory and belief.

There is also an error in defining history by battles, which are mankind's grossest tautologies. They are a ritual whereby miracle is metamorphosed into fact via the incontrovertible truth of death. An effort to impose historical patterns on violent change, the only place they have meaning is in ideas or hopes about how they will be remembered. Thus, implausibly, the end is made to satisfy the blood, and the blood transubstantiates the idea. In other words, they have no substance, no truth beyond a concept imposed upon them. They are a cultural reaction to dynamic forces already at work, and they preserve above all else the illusion of control. They have every attribute of non-existence.

Illusions are often intended to persuade, and persuading other people to die is the central problem of the illusion of control. Dying for concepts and culture is a supernatural kind of death, even if steel in flesh is painfully biological. For millennia, the sharpest persuasive edge had belonged to religion, which was always about death. It thrived on the desire for life's most defining aspect to mean something, and was a stunning and enduring technique for getting people to die for ideas about death. But dying for death eventually became unfulfilling when the institutions built around it proved woeful at narrating the specious present. However, the basic notions had been translated into a new secular form, and people could now die for history, to help history along towards its destined shape, and by doing so assure themselves a place as an immortal word in a story.

The American Civil War is just a story, an illusion written on six hundred thousand dead and Southern propaganda and a map. You can write the story on those dead, on the visible convention of geographic representations of human information, and on Southern fictions, or you can write it on the death of one man, and the subsequent vortex collapse of the age's ideas into absurd mass sacrifice. The former is an emergent property of millions of individual choices to believe, and a need to satisfy returns-to-scale. But, beyond the criteria of miracle, those six hundred thousand don't necessarily mean more than a murder of one.

Where do the barricades go up? They had been forming for years, like a web through the city, every moment of loss, every cruel oppression, every act of love adding to their presence. They came from the earth, they came like thunder from the sky, a criticality that organized around a terrible focal point of human will, when a man named John Brown climbed the barricades with gun, and sword and pike. He waved a banner emblazoned with "Subterranean Pass Way," dipped in the language of revolution and the words of prophets and the blood of millions. Was Brown a murderer in this butchery? Charles Robinson wrote:

> I think not. He worshipped the God of Joshua and David, who ordered all the enemies of his people slaughtered, including non-combatants, women, and children, flocks and herds, and "everything that breathed." John Brown seemed to believe he was the special messenger and servant of God; and he may have been as sincere as was Abraham when he stretched forth his hand to take the knife to slay his own son, or as Joshua when he slaughtered all that breathed of his enemies.[1]

Emerson reflected, during the war, that events had been perilously close to being apparently different from what they truly were. More intelligent choices by Southerners could have resulted in their using the army of the Union to carry slavery north, "& it is not easy to see how the ardent abolitionists—always a minority hated by the rich class—could have successfully resisted. The effect however would have been to put the *onus* of resistance on the North."[2]

But instead the complacently powerful South awoke in 1860 to the fact that the barricades had advanced through the sinuous streets to challenge the power they had held since the ratification of the Constitution. And so they decided that the time had come to destroy the barricades, to disperse the revolutionaries, to assert the "natural" order. They were the powerful, gathering their might by withdrawing from the social contract, an act that could be sold as rebellion by virtue of geographic convenience and the sudden conceptual strength of the barricades of abolition.

From the war narrative of Southern rebellion and the eventual defeat came the ugly and disingenuous "Lost Cause" trope of American history, a consequence of wanting desperately to believe in a nation, and allowing too many Southerners to dominate postbellum history writing. "Lost Cause" narratives are a form of military history predicated on effusive and astonished praise for the heroic and doomed Southern rebellion against the supposedly powerful North. But the only astonishing thing about the duration of the Southern war effort was the rapid collapse, given the Confederacy's considerable resources and astounding political capital.³

The Confederacy was a "lost cause," though for reasons entirely contrary to the mythologizing of Southern historians and conciliatory nationalists. The *becoming* of John Brown, from gallows to ghost, was part of the fatally flawed genesis of the Confederacy, and also of its undoing. If not for the iconic attempt of a Northern white man to set up an insurrection, and his subsequent Northern canonization, poor working whites in the South would have been unlikely to make war on poor working whites in the North, all to support an exceptionally wealthy few.

Secessionists utilized the terror of poor Southern whites to launch the Civil War. After the attack on Fort Sumter, patriotic Southern whites rushed to join the Confederate Army, convinced that abolitionists had translated "their hated theories into direct action, and that the Brown raid heralded the opening of the abolitionist offensive."⁴ That was the centrally convincing narrative supporting a dangerous idea held by Southern martial oligarchs; security depended on and was defined by a strong escalation of threats and action. Threats were broadly defined not simply as direct forces acting upon their interests, but anything that might call into question their resolve. John Brown helped convince the mass of poor Southern whites to believe this recondite notion.

The domestic South had long been a garrison state peopled by idle poor white militias. Now those fighters were compelled to leave their communities to fight a war against the United States. The problem was, of course, that they were already engaged in a war, and if they were not at home to fight it, who would prevent the fate that they were in theory fighting the United States about? Southern elites, if they failed to recognize this, were entirely guilty of believing their own history. John Brown knew, but John Brown was dead.

Even if they had not overlooked the conundrum, Confederate elites expected to swiftly

Salmon Brown (Library of Congress).

demolish the barricades once they had gathered their strength and built their armies on racist populism. Attacking Fort Sumter was arrogance, but the formula appeared rather simple to them: their longstanding superior military tradition, capacity to quickly mobilize large armies, and a culture that glorified the soldier would give their young white men victory over a hapless United States. Control of the cotton trade would compel recognition from the powers of Europe, and all the while the slaves toiling on the plantation would be the economic engine that fed the war effort.

After the First Battle of Bull Run, on July 21, 1861, it appeared as if Confederate elites had predicted accurately. It was a humiliating rout for the United States Army, after which the capital of the United States was defenseless before the Confederate Army. Southern victory was imminent, yet they didn't advance.

The generals of the Confederacy had good reason to question if their armies were strong enough to attack Washington. They had multitudinous volunteers on paper, but the Confederate Army could only field about half of them, and half of the gap was due merely to a lack of guns.[5] Early in the war, the Confederacy actually had a lot of guns, far more than were given to the army. The problem was that Confederate state governors held tightly to weapons that their new national government needed. This may have been the "me first" political ideology underlying "state's rights," but the governors were also keenly aware that they might need those weapons; as early as May of 1861 an English observer noted that since the war began there had "been very alarming disturbances among the blacks; on more than one plantation, the assistance of the authorities has been called to overcome the open resistance of the slaves."[6]

Wealthy slave owners kept men home to hold the rifles kept by the state governors. In the first summer of the war, slaves were planning demonstrations to coincide with Abraham Lincoln's inauguration, and were openly speculating that Lincoln intended to free them. At the time, Lincoln had no such intent, but unfortunately their primary source of news was the fear mongering of Southern secessionists. Nonetheless, wealthy planters were forced to try to bring their overseers home in order to remedy the startling erosion in the architecture of plantation control.[7] With poor white enforcers gone, the slaves became deliberately unproductive and entirely unresponsive to the commands of the women left behind; many of those women could only make silly threats about what would happen "after the war," when the men came home.

Absent a quick victory, the internal contradictions and class divisions eventually came to the fore. Even during that first summer, Confederate generals faced near endless petitions from the wives of poor whites who needed their husbands home for the planting season. As summer faded to autumn, their plight grew increasingly desperate, and widespread starvation threatened the poor. By spring of 1862, volunteerism was evaporating, and the Confederacy resorted to universal conscription, except the definition of "universal" did not encompass the sons of wealthy planters. Far be it that those who had crafted the Southern martial myth might actually have to go die for it.

If the Confederacy's elites completely overlooked the need to provide for poor families in order to sustain their armies, those isolated plutocrats in Richmond were very attentive to the need for plantation discipline. Poor whites in the Confederacy grew increasingly suspicious of the wealthy planters' deceitful motives, but popular conviction in the cause was still enough to sustain it until the autumn of 1862.

By that time Jefferson Davis was growing desperate. Despite the Confederacy's initial battlefield victories, battles are meaningless rituals, and the inability to pursue a more meaningful goal had given the United States the needed respite to regroup and counterattack. The Confederacy was enduring losses and a U.S. occupation in a number of states. The domestic situation was also anxious; labor was still unreliable, and widespread drought had crippled crop yields.[8] During this time of troubles, Abraham Lincoln allowed his Preliminary Emancipation Proclamation to circulate.

The great virtue of the proclamation, Emerson wrote, was that "it works when men are sleeping, when the Army goes into winter quarters, when generals are treacherous or imbecile."[9] The initial attack by the Confederacy was enough to spur some military enlistment in the United States, but not the kind of overwhelming patriotic mobilization enjoyed by Confederate leaders. Many Northerners were content to see the Southern states leave—so long and good riddance—and a push for disunion had long been popular with certain segments of the abolitionist movement.

But with war a reality, abolitionists like Wendell Phillips and prominent former slaves like Frederick Douglass hounded the president. Lincoln was a colonizationist—a position he inherited from his political idol, Henry Clay—as well as a supporter of the Fugitive Slave Law, a supporter of measures which barred black people from public office, and a man who was wont to use the word "nigger" in private conversation. Why the South should have been so afraid of him defies reason, save for its own internal logics. He once described slavery as a "monstrous injustice," but in the very same speech advocated sending the slaves "to their own native land."[10] All this too ignores the fact that in Lincoln's famous "fiery trial" speech to Congress in December of 1862 he first used the ominous word "deportation" in place of the more antique "colonization."

But Lincoln found that Union soldiers did not march off to kill or be killed with the cry of "nationalism" or "union" or even a hymn to revolution like *La Marseillaise* ringing in their throats. Certainly not with a "national anthem" on their tongues; that particular foolishness was the creation of Europe's military class, and paeans to nationalism had not quite taken hold in America. Instead, they sang the song "John Brown's Body." It soon became apparent that John Brown's war might be the key to breaking the Confederacy; Lincoln and his planners knew the effect that domestic fears were having on the Confederate war machine, and his own soldiers needed an explicit cause to believe in.

Shortly after the release of the Preliminary Emancipation Proclamation, General Daniel Ruggles wrote to the Confederate chief of staff with his concerns:

> Voluntary enlistment and conscription have taken into the military service of the country such a large proportion of the active freemen of this district ... that many plantations with numerous slaves are being left without the ordinary and necessary control of the white man.... I am constrained to bring the subject to the attention of the War Department because of the large and grave interests at present and prospectively involved, especially should there be an opportunity for the execution to any extent of the recently enunciated purpose of the Federal Government with reference to our slaves.[11]

Jefferson Davis attempted to remedy the situation by passing the "Twenty Nigger Law." It was a simple piece of legislation: men attached to plantations with more than twenty slaves were exempt from military service in the interest of keeping the slave population under control. This law was the beginning of the end. The illusion of an egalitarian revolt against the United States was entirely shattered, at least until the Reconstruction, and with the passage of the law a large proportion of the Confederate army "pledged never to fight while the law remains in force and ... lay down their arms in the face of the enemy."[12]

On New Year's Day, 1863, the full Emancipation Proclamation was issued by Abraham Lincoln. It "had all the moral grandeur of a bill of lading" and somehow proposed to free every slave that Lincoln could not, in fact, free, while allowing any slave states who were actually in the United States to retain theirs.[13] What moral authority it did have was largely derived from the tireless work of men who had adopted as their symbol one lone insurrectionist on the gallows. It "defined every man's position." Just those "few words show at once the *animus* of the men, shows them friends of Slavery, shows us that the battleground is fast changing from Richmond to Boston. They unmask themselves, &, though we tried to think them freemen, they are not. Look where they rage, at Sumner. They find not Lincoln, for they do not think him really antislavery, but the abolitionist they can find is Sumner, and him they hate."[14]

Though no slaves were legally freed, from that moment forward a U.S. victory could only mean a sweeping social revolution in the South and the end of slave power. It also opened the way for black soldiers to serve in the U.S. Army and accelerated the disintegration of Confederate society and illusions. Emerson wrote of those soldiers and the proclamation, "It does mean liberty to you in the opinion of Jeff Davis for the South says, we fight to plant slavery as our foundation. And of course we who resist the South, are forced to make liberty of the negro our foundation.... Plainly we must have a worthy cause for such soldiers as we send to battle or they shall not go."[15] As Karl Marx approvingly observed, "Up to now, we have witnessed only the first act of the Civil War—the constitutional waging of war. The second act, the revolutionary waging of war, is at hand." It is entirely fair to Lincoln to say that he intended as such; the letters and circumstances surrounding the drafting are highly convoluted, and Lincoln was delicately balancing many contentious interests.[16]

Despite the army's fondness for its legacy as the instrument of liberation, it would have carried out, just as proudly, the program of spreading slavery to Massachusetts. So long as it was decorated and celebrated. But it was Abraham Lincoln who directed and shaped the army with a firm hand, and as he led the war, the generals that emerged were not the ones of the Army's choosing, but the choosing of Lincoln.[17]

U.S. generals celebrated themselves via the transitive property by helping Southerners institutionalize Confederate generals—graduates of West Point—as not only brilliant leaders of armies but also noble gentlemen of the first order, the kind that the doomed Southern culture had produced before the inexorable crushing momentum of the Lost Cause. And they were, indeed, true paragons of Southern morality, and perhaps even of the Army that West Point was crafting. As Emerson wrote:

> I charge the Southerner with starving prisoners of war; with massacring surrendered men; with the St Albans' raid; with plundering railroad passenger-trains in peaceful districts; with plots of burning cities; with advertising a price for the life of Lincoln, Butler, Garrison, & others; with assassination of the President, & of Seward; with

attempts to import the yellow fever into New York; with the cutting up the bones of our soldiers to make ornaments, & drinking cups of their skulls.[18]

And still, after the fact, it seems that all the paper in the world might be consumed to print patriotic hagiographies of racist traitors like Davis, and Lee, and Stuart, while Brown thrashes at the end of a narrative rope.

The social and economic wreckage of the Confederacy metastasized terminally from 1863 on, the denouement of a society doomed by its predations and worship of violent solutions. Recognition from Europe never came, and domestic failures made it impossible to purchase enough arms to overcome the U.S.; while the U.S. held the production advantage by that point, the Confederacy also required, conservatively, 50 percent more weaponry if it was to keep its slaves in check.

Europe was not going to loan money to the only countries of the revolutionary world that still held slaves. England in particular considered the bloodless emancipation of its slaves to be one of its signature political accomplishments. The fact that throughout the early nineteenth century slavery was vigorously expanding under English-speaking Americans despite the fact that England had dismantled their entire slave network was a subject of concern for English abolitionists.[19] Furthermore, the economic reputation and credit of the Southern states had never recovered from the Panic of 1837.

Not to discount the skillful diplomatic work of William H. Seward, but there were reasons of purely narrative significance as well. Though John Brown did not dominate the news in Europe, his story was still discussed—somewhat widely in England, less so on the Continent. Victor Hugo, one of Europe's most prominent intellectuals, had written to Virginia in the autumn of 1859 pleading for Brown's life to be spared.

> Politically speaking, the murder of John Brown would be an uncorrectable sin. It would create in the Union a latent fissure that would in the long run dislocate it. Brown's agony might perhaps consolidate slavery in Virginia, but it would certainly shake the whole American democracy. You save your shame, but you kill your glory. Morally speaking, it seems a part of the human light would put itself out, that the very notion of justice and injustice would hide itself in darkness, on that day where one would see the assassination of Emancipation by Liberty itself.... Let America know and ponder on this: there is something more frightening than Cain killing Abel, and that is Washington killing Spartacus.

But Washington did indeed kill Spartacus, who lived on as a kind of anachronistic and representative supra-historical vantage point in *Les Misérables*, an example against whom Hugo measured events. It might have appeared that Thenardier found prosperity as a slaver, but the Old Man's shadow loomed from the future of that book, waiting, though only as the hint or reverberation of an idea. Hugo's other writings on Brown—the only by a European celebrity—filled the pages of Garrison's *Liberator*.

In 1861, Victor Hugo was an exile living in England because of the hostility of Louis Napoleon's government. He wrote to ask his brother-in-law, Paul Chenay, to find his painting *Le Pendu (Ecce Lex)* (reproduced on the cover of the present work) and make an engraved version of it to publish under the title *John Brown*. In it, a gallows-tree rises from the murk, and from that beam a distorted body hangs with the weight of a lodestone. A slender ray of light from heaven touches it, but not enough to illuminate the face. The inscription echoed Emerson's words: "*Pro*

Christo—Sicit Christus, John Brown,—Charleston." M. Chenay's engraving was confiscated by the authorities after he unthinkingly published the image with the execution date—December 2—which also happened to be the date that Louis Napoleon seized power in 1851. There were rumors of a drama written by Hugo featuring Brown as the protagonist, but they remained rumors.[20]

European papers found Brown's goal of insurrection somewhat distasteful, but they viewed him as the victim of an inhumane institution because of his prison letters, his appeals to moral authority, and the narrative crafted by Emerson's circle. Europeans had never had anything but contempt for the South, and the Harpers Ferry drama deepened their disgust. They sneered at the South's self-proclaimed manliness and chivalric virtues while ridiculing the sad panic and massive mobilization in reaction to an event that, in Europe, would have been a minor disturbance. The hasty trial invited disgust as well, and with each report about Brown's dignified personal behavior, disdain for the South deepened.

It was the execution that solidified European opinion, particularly those final minutes when Brown stood unwavering on the edge of eternity. The *Belfast Banner of Ulster* had particular fun with this grim scene, contrasting Brown with a hypothetical "brave and noble captain" who after the hanging "prescribed a dose of arsenic" while "others suggested decapitation" because they were afraid the Old Man might return to life.[21]

The barbaric haste of the trial and the bizarre stinking fear of the months after prompted European commentators to adapt the overarching metaphor of the Terror to the American South, a theme picked up by Garrison and other abolitionists. Europeans indicted the United States far more ecumenically; many, particularly on the Continent, held the entire United States responsible for Brown's execution. To the monarchies that had endured the Age of Revolution, it was just another sad historical example of the affinity of republics for slavery.[22] The Confederacy could expect no help from Europeans, who felt that John Brown's execution had shredded the few tatters of legitimacy a slaveholding republic possessed.

When Lincoln's Emancipation Proclamation went into effect on January 1, 1863, the stately Sage of Concord was sipping drinks at the well-appointed home of George Stearns, who was hosting what he called his "John Brown Party" on Emancipation Day. Franklin Sanborn was there, as was William Lloyd Garrison and Wendell Phillips. So was feisty Julia Ward Howe, and Emerson's friend Bronson Alcott, accompanied by his daughter, Louisa May. It was most of the intellectual community that had carefully cultivated Brown's story.

They had gathered to celebrate the author of events that no one could have ever foreseen. Almost no one. Maybe they remembered, with the faintest shudder, that the Old Man had in fact foretold these events with terrifying clarity. But they sang songs and offered toasts, and such is often the sad reward of prophets; only their ghosts are welcomed in from the cold. Who knew that a ghost could be so practical? The highlight of the evening was the ceremonial unveiling of a marble bust of the Old Man, and perhaps as the gathering read aloud and conversed and remembered, young Henry Stearns looked at that sculpture with a letter clutched in his hands.

One of the readings that evening should have been a poem entitled "The Portent," written in December of 1859, after the hanging of John Brown, by a commercial failure of an author named Herman Melville. At the time, the Old Man was the only subject of intellectual harmony between Melville and Emerson. Melville was not at Stearns's party, and his poem was not published until 1866, but there were few better efforts to comprehend the troubling memory of John Brown, and the nature of civilization and history.

> Hanging from the beam,
> Slowly swaying (such the law),
> Gaunt the shadow on the green,
> Shenandoah!
> The cut is on the crown
> (Lo, John Brown),
> And the stabs shall heal no more.
>
> Hidden in the cap
> Is the anguish none can draw;
> So your future veils its face,
> Shenandoah!
> But the streaming beard is shown
> (Weird John Brown),
> The meteor of the war.

In fourteen elegant lines, Melville accomplished what historians labor for hundreds of pages to communicate. He subtly paired the powerful image of Brown's death with Emerson's Christ allusion, and with the language of natural law in the body's pendulum motion. The shadowy future veils a past full of wounds and grief, and the poem ends with a most powerful celestial metaphor. It is not merely about John Brown, but about the entire epistemology of the West. It is an expression of memory and philosophy, of the age as it was imagined, and of the illusions that John Brown was sacrificed to.

When Melville wrote of Brown's slowly swaying body—such the law—he was not referring to the legal absurdities of the Virginia court. The pendulum body was a metaphor about predatory social philosophies that had co-opted the language of Isaac Newton's laws of motion, and therefore claimed the same coercive predictive utility. But the language was an illusion hiding the same old primitive and arbitrary faiths, bloody rituals, and even human sacrifice.

The future would veil the story's face. Necessity in historical emplotment conveys legitimacy—realism—by circumscribing future possibilities with the metaphorical causal mechanisms underlying the present. As a method of approach, history is about philosophical realism, since no phenomenon can be described without reliance on its historical process. History in the age of Newton in particular was strongly marked by the desire to measure and master the world rather than understand it.[23] Newton's laws were predictive, manipulative, and portrayed a nature above all else law-abiding and fundamentally reversible. They were also a *revolutionary* novelty as claimed by the earliest positivist historians when they described how Newton alone had the courage to infer from the study of planetary motion and falling bodies the action of a universal law.[24] Of course, if the dominant metaphor of time was fundamentally non-ideographic, it would be difficult for a narrative art like history to achieve a meaningful representation of realism that would, no matter how truthful, ever attain a level of social achievement greater than the novel.

In the Age of Revolution no one had the poor taste to comment on the fact that eighteenth century rationalists had explicitly found favorable comparisons between Newton's laws and more ancient occult suppositions. Newton apparently believed that Chiron the Centaur had made the first astronomical tables, and behind his mechanical immaculata was an alchemist's passion: for three decades he had labored to transmute lead to gold and, unable to discern the "affinities" that formed, disrupted, and *animated* matter, he had turned his gaze to the heavens, where he assumed similar forces would be easier to observe.[25] When he separated sunlight in a prism, he named his discovery the "spectrum," from the Latin for "ghost."

The publication of Newton's *Principia* came about through one of history's unpredictable convergences. Edmund Halley had gone to Isaac Newton for help with some of the more frustrating problems in the Copernican model. Fortuitously, Newton had already solved the problem; from a few fundamental principles of motion, he could model most of Copernicus's universe. Halley published Newton's work, which could encompass future and past and reality in ways that only the church had ever claimed to be able to do. Unfortunately it didn't make men any better than when they blindly believed church authority.

Halley was also profoundly interested in historical process. Like most learned men of his day, he studied the philosophers of antiquity, particularly the thinkers of Rome and Greece, and also admired the astronomical insights of Byzantine and Arab science. Measurable, incremental data in the historical record was one of Halley's passions, and from narrative descriptions of astronomical and tidal observations, he painstakingly calculated the particulars of Julius Caesar's landing at Deal.

Newton struggled with one object in the heavens—comets—because of their seeming randomness. He also cared little about searching history for physical models, which is partially why the most famous comet in Western lore bears the name Halley.[26] Human civilization was built on understanding the steady rhythms of the stars, which mapped the future through harvests, migrations, and festivals. People had filled the heavens with their myths and legends. Comets were no less personal, and because of their startling irregularity, were viewed as a terrifying portent of doom. People panicked, they killed, and Halley the historian knew that a comet would figure prominently in recorded narrative. He speculated that, like the planets, they were actually regular visitors too.

He was right. The same comet he observed in 1682 had once shone in the dark for two months as William of Normandy convinced his army that, since it clearly signified awful tidings, those tidings may as well come to the shores of England and mean the death of Harold Godwinson. As a result a not insignificant portion of the words on this page are simply mangled and poorly pronounced French, and William of Normandy, now the Conqueror, had the apparition duly recorded in the newspaper of the day, where it can be seen in stunning prominence on the Bayeaux Tapestry.

The age began with the first true prophecy in human history. Halley calculated the orbit, and named the year in which the comet would appear as reliably as every other object in the gracefully wheeling sky. And though he didn't live to see it, the comet visited on cue, slightly delayed by an unforeseen sojourn through Jupiter's powerful gravitational field. In 1758, for the first time in human history, Aristotle's "long-haired" weird star did not enter the narrative as it had for thousands of years, sowing gossamer strands of discord from its silently shimmering hair, a golden apple tossed unceremoniously into the firmament. Nothing changed but narrative perception.

It also appeared, coincidentally, during a territorial and trade struggle that would become known as the Seven Years' War. From that contest came the 1763 Treaty of Paris, an agreement which resulted in England's becoming the mightiest colonial power in the world, which in turn led to monarchical transgressions on English liberty in the colonies, and the central event in the American historical identity. That identity depends on perceptions of what is and is not expected: setting the inception with the Revolution makes the imperial events and the insults to the colonies which followed seem like inevitable precursors to the Revolution itself. It casts the events following 1763 as pre–Revolutionary, a stellar conceit that can only occur after the fact, rather than depicting them as post-treaty, or the startling and random mess which it appeared to people living through those events. It's a narrative trick that depicts "an unfolding logic in history, a logic which is on the side of the [historians] and which makes them appear as co-operators with progress itself, but there is a concrete sense in which it might be said that [the historian] does not believe there is an historical process at all."[27]

The historians of the Age of Revolution filled their narratives with the philosophical transformation of old ghosts, like Michelet's light of revolution, and Ranke's Leviathan-legitimized essential truths. Tocqueville, the third of the long nineteenth-century's masters, alluded to it as well, when he claimed to have added something quite new to history in attempting to treat the future itself as his subject. He acknowledged that other historians had done so to a degree, but had been "busied for the morrow only" while he regarded "the whole future."[28] Tocqueville's narrative structure was comfortably at home with the dictates of science despite his ironic approach, and his division of historical events into typologies and categories—classes, philosophies, and political phenomena—fit nicely with a world viewed as interlocking systems.[29] Most significantly, Tocqueville recognized the sheer arbitrariness of his own narrative choices without reservation.

Tocqueville vaguely grasped that to write about an age epistemologically founded on "revolutions," he needed to adopt the age's linguistic assumptions, and he was a capable translator of the age. Michelet was born to French Huguenots, industrious Parisians elevated by the spirit of revolution. Ranke was a bourgeois German, classically educated with a love of Thucydides and Kant, and perhaps a desire to refute some of Hume's underlying nihilism. But wry Tocqueville was a child of Norman nobility, whose ancestors had once been convinced by an apparition to fight at Hastings in AD 1066. He alone did not attempt the unification of narrative time, but rather pitted tragedy and irony against the narratives of his peers, attempting to ascertain whether anything short of complete disaster could be salvaged from a human society crushed by irreconcilable forces.[30]

Having settled on two historical social definitions, Democratic and Aristocratic, Tocqueville noted that one's choice of historical language is entirely related to the present social structure. His initial quest in writing history began with the presupposition of laws, from which social forces could be derived and thence as suggested by Thucydides, the inevitable events of human progress could be brought about with a minimum of suffering.[31] But since he could not escape the very irrationality of humanity, either in the collective or the individual, he moved to a linguistically relativistic position:

22. The History of an Error

Two kinds of causes are always in operation; only their proportion varies. General facts serve to explain more things in democratic than in aristocratic ages, and fewer things are then assignable to individual influences. During periods of aristocracy the reverse takes place: special influences are stronger, general causes weaker; *unless, indeed, we consider as a general cause the fact itself of the inequality of condition, which allows some individuals to baffle the natural tendencies of all the rest.*[32]

Truth and cause, in other words, are entirely distinct. Too often "cause"—a word with magical connotations—is disguised as narrative truth by the powerful merely to sanctify their black hunger and their scarlet crimes. History can be the strongest chain of slavery, and the only standard of proof required is that asked of miracles. The powerful, out of their hunger, fought to maintain their version of realism, but the thousands of the least among men made it a cooperative crime from the same base instinct. "The poor and the low find some amends to their immense moral capacity, for their acquiescence in a political and social inferiority.... They sun themselves in the great man's light, and feel it to be their own element.... Men such as they are, very naturally seek money or power; and power because it is as good as money,—the 'spoils,' so called, 'of office.'"[33]

Tocqueville saw history as a mediative endeavor, making the thoughts of one era comprehendible to another, to impart perspective on the atmosphere of ideas. And though he remained committed to the search for causes by which he could explain his own age, he abandoned the search for general causes, which were merely plot choices. Furthermore, he viewed such a quest as morally debilitating for the society that consumed those histories and therefore wrote history as therapy rather than unity: the tragic counterpoint to the *consensus omnium* and the nature of fact.[34]

Among natural objects, man alone actually has a history. For all practical purposes, any historical process has humanity itself as its sole conceivable outcome. Melville's "The Portent" asks why people believe what they believe, and even whether man can be both a thinking and a knowing being, living in his own inquiry. The comet, which figures so prominently in human philosophy and historical events, is not "historical" in and of itself. It simply *is,* a visible herald of nothing more than its own *Ich*. It is only the human mind—desperately fearful, foolishly confident, or maybe even both—that gives over the meaning of human actions to that apparition.

The West's supposed rationality was merely a comfortable fantasy. Nineteenth century thinkers may have flattered themselves that they no longer had to be concerned with embarrassing, ghostly apparitions as the basis for their thoughts, but this was mere conceit. They were doing little but pursuing ghosts, and when confronted with this fact had sacrificed a man to those ghosts.

The laws that compel the fall, pendulum sway, and grim death of John Brown in "The Portent" might be imagined as having existed before Isaac Newton, waiting to be discovered. Similar assumptions underpinned the social narratives of class, slavery, race, and nation. But there was a time that natural law did not actually exist, just as there was a time in the void before sun and earth when the principles that Newton named did not exist. When people conceptualize the idea of natural law, what they actually believe is a narrative, in which the ideas were waiting in the void for the world to come into being and conform. Phrased this way, "natural law" has every single attribute of miracle. It is merely a construct of the human mind, which itself lacks mass or measure, yet is the only thing exerting absolute dominance over all that man does.

The laws and the world, like ghosts, have no meaningful existence outside of human imagination. The conceit lies in imagining that some ghosts are real, while others are not, when it is merely a matter of linguistic preference. Those ghosts whisper to us the words we require to see and order the world, those ghosts of Christ and Aristotle and Emerson and Hume and Lincoln. Ghosts like Sir Isaac give us words so powerful they may order entire worlds. Some, like the emperor, whisper the ways to manipulate those words for power and glory. Most of the time, so that people won't draw attention to themselves, they unthinkingly believe. How everyone came by these beliefs was another matter entirely.

> Do you see the kitten chasing so prettily her own tail. If you could see with her eyes you would see her surrounded with hundreds of figures performing complex dramas, with tragic & comic issues, long conversations, many characters, many ups & downs of fate, & meantime it is only puss & her own tail. How long before ... we shall suddenly find it was all a solitary performance.
>
> A subject & an object: it takes always so much to make the galvanic circuit complete; but magnitude is of no moment. What matters it whether it is Kepler & his sphere, Napoleon & Spain, Columbus & America, or a child with a doll or pussy with her tail.[35]

Once in a while someone like John Brown makes people question everything. Melville asked if man could honestly understand and question his past and his beliefs, and still live meaningfully. If not, the alternative is that man only lives in civilized peace by virtue of unquestioning belief in those "laws," and when confronted with the knowledge that they are merely an expression of will, attempt to validate them with the one incontrovertible aspect of human existence. Death may give life meaning, but ritual death gives narrative meaning; it creates ghosts. John Brown was killed in a ritual intended to join his ghost to the dominant pantheon—the climate of opinion—as a kind of scourge, warning the infidels. That ghost is also still wandering out there with the "lost cause" and other failed stories, but this is not the story of that ghost. From the beginning, this has been the story of the black, bloody, glad-of-war ghost that had other ideas entirely.

The poet Walt Whitman knew what kind of story this really was. In "Year of Meteors" he did not sing the anger or rage of Achilles, but instead wrote:

> I would sing how an old man, tall, with white hair, mounted the scaffold in Virginia,
> (I was at hand, silent I stood with teeth shut close, I watch'd,
> I stood very near you old man when cool and indifferent, but trembling with age and your unheal'd wounds you mounted the scaffold;)....[36]

Much like the comet (or even Achilles), who is to say that John Brown *caused* anything? If he did—if one man could act to end all that people believed, and the social order they held dear—then it suggests that defining laws are demonstrably false. If he did not, then people would have to confront the knowledge that they killed a man and ended their society in an orgy of violence simply because they saw a metaphorical comet, and realized that their beliefs were nothing more than a false tautology. Where one possibility leaves off and the other begins is quite impossible to see. The Old Man's ghost would continue to challenge beliefs and confront people with the knowledge that their nation had ended nearly as soon as it was written perpetual, and that perhaps before he hung, the gallows god had rightly said it would. It was a prophecy to end the age, and it immortalized the ghost of weird John Brown, instrument of fate, meteor of war.

23

The Last Witness

History is the group of the types or representative men of any age at only the distance of convenient vision. We can see the arrangement of masses, & distinguish the forms of the leaders. Mythology is the same group at another remove, now at a pictorial distance; the perspective of history.
—Ralph Waldo Emerson, *Journals*

Back in 1859, shortly after the execution, when Mary Stearns asked Emerson to write Brown's biography, he made an undated journal entry that read: "*John Brown;* He drew this notice and distinction from the people among whom he fell from the fact that this boy of twelve had conducted his drove of cattle a hundred miles alone."[1] But his pen stopped there, poised forever above the page with that beginning. Maybe he wondered who would believe such a tale about a mere child. Maybe he smiled as he set his pen down and walked away to muse. And maybe he simply felt that John Brown had suffered on the gibbet in full measure for his sins, and in death he deserved slightly better than Jesus Christ in this regard.

Hardly anyone knew that story save for—presumably—Brown's family, and anyone who had read Brown's letter to Henry Stearns. Emerson told the story in public only once, adapting the letter nearly verbatim for a speech in Salem on January 6, 1860. But after that, John Brown became a reference point for other people or ideas, like in an 1865 speech on Abraham Lincoln in which he weighed the just-slain president's Gettysburg Address against Brown's courtroom oration. Elements of that speech became part of the essay "Eloquence."[2] When he eulogized his friend Thoreau (in a eulogy that was otherwise a rather sweeping condemnation of the modern world) he numbered among Thoreau's signal few accomplishments his bold public defense of John Brown.

Though he never wrote the biography, nothing suggests that Emerson loved the story any less. After all, he had only ever related to John Brown through belief. He knew Brown, yet he never knew him, and what he seemed to see when that awful Kansas warrior walked into his life was an embodiment of the social strife that had been working upon him and society. He saw his need to find meaning in a world where his young son was dead. He saw an essay he had written over two decades prior to their meeting, titled "Heroism": "Heroism feels and never reasons, and therefore is always right; and although a different breeding, different religion and greater intellectual activity would have modified or even reversed the particular action, yet, for the hero, that thing he does is the highest deed, and is not open to the censure of philosophers or divines."[3]

Emerson oriented to the world in the manner that every person and every historian does, and if his interpretations of some of the most mundane and verifiable facts were

An 1866 print entitled "Pioneers of Freedom." Pictured, clockwise from the top: Charles Sumner, Wendell Phillips, Horace Greeley, Henry Wilson, Gerrit Smith, Henry Ward Beecher, and William Lloyd Garrison. In 1866, the year before Emerson's "Progress of Civilization" speech, who wanted to remember John Brown (Library of Congress)?

creative, he never claimed to be explicitly writing history with his few words on Brown. Perhaps the most serious historical offense the lapsed preacher might be accused of is that he told people what to believe about the story of John Brown, but he differs little from other historians in that regard. Emerson's John Brown was an archetype, a form of primitive, ideal, historical force. For him, Brown's autobiographical letter and his other speeches were just confirmation of the narrative he had been imagining since their first meeting, and Emerson crafted a character seemingly from some kind of American Eden, one who lived hardily with the animals, communicated secret knowledge with nature to draw forth a lucrative harvest of wool, and who shouldered the burden of prophet to strike down injustice.[4]

There was truth in the story: Brown did once raise sheep. His inexperience led at first to inadequate care for the flock of Simon Perkins, who seemingly kept that association alive out of simple loyalty, and regarded Brown as "a rough herdsman, but a nice judge of wool."[5] The story of the rough, flawed herdsman—and his dark road to Kansas—is more meaningful, in its own way, than Emerson's ahistorical archetype; but Emerson's narrative Brown was as much about his own doubts as about anything else.

His was a tormented belief. Once in a speech in Concord he had reveled in Brown's most violent sectarian words:

> He joins that perfect Puritan faith which brought his fifth ancestor to Plymouth Rock with his grandfather's ardor in the Revolution. He believes in two articles,—two instruments, shall I say?—the Golden Rule and the Declaration of Independence; and he used this expression in conversation here concerning them, "Better that a whole generation of men, women and children should pass away by a violent death than that one word of either should be violated in this country."

He earned a good deal of applause and laughter when he added, "There is a Unionist—there is a strict constructionist for you."[6]

Emerson appeared to cast Brown as a nationalist—with direct lineage to the founding English presence in North America—and his struggle as one of national ideologies: "He believes in the Union of the States, and he conceives that the only obstruction to the Union is Slavery, and for that reason, as a patriot, he works for its abolition."[7] But the laughter at Emerson's sly "Unionist" comment underscored what he, and everyone else present, admired the most—Brown's obvious and obdurate lack of patriotism, and the fact that he was waging a weirdly rational religious war against an incomprehensibly irrational and cruel secular order.

Emerson—the rational and secular apostate—knew well the hideous nature of religious violence, and many of his own writings stridently denounced those old dogmas. Yet he confronted the awareness that the Age of Revolution was disguising the banality and evil of a religion-dominated society in the language of science and reason. His writings after his 1857 meeting with Brown—like *The Conduct of Life*, written at the apogee of his fame—were daring contemplations on the epistemological and ethical foundations of the Western world. Brown's example had boldly demonstrated the nature of fate and power, of illusions and culture, and he struggled for the metaphors to describe the world. Brown's words, the language of the ministry he had spurned, were compromised, but so was his own revolutionary vocabulary.

A world shrunken by compass and wind, by coal and steel, was one in which Christianity was, blessedly, one faith among many. To write of justice he had the Islamic Turk and the Norse gods for examples, and he was powerfully drawn to Buddhists and the "Hindu, under the wheel" in order to contemplate the connections in the world. Brown's Calvinism was a similar example of religious fanaticism and selflessly indifferent resistance to the predations of the West. "Our Calvinists, in the last generation, had something of the same dignity. They felt that the weight of the Universe held them down to their place. What could they do? Wise men feel that there is something which cannot be talked or voted away,—strap or belt which girds the world."[8] This was less a nod to the old *doxa* he had rightly cast aside than it was to John Brown, who had shown him that even though "Calvinism was as injurious to the justice, as Greek myths were to the purity of the gods"—exemplars, respectively, of stifling religious orthodoxy and the inventors of Western rationality—"noble souls carried themselves nobly, & drew what treasures of character from that grim system."[9]

To Emerson, John Brown was courage, true courage in an age that desperately needed it, not the false courage of "the hurras, the placarding, the flags."[10] During this period, when the scientists, poets, and businessmen who populated Emerson's early writings faded, John Brown walked among Achilles and Hercules, Washington and Cromwell, Saladin and Napoleon. He walked as much in Kansas as he did in the pages of Xenophon and Shakespeare, of Homer and Thucydides. As Emerson pondered on courage in an empty age, he must have wondered more than ever who would believe that not only had a child courageously navigated a herd, but the inception of the fall of a republic was found on that journey.

And yet the story needed that beginning. Without it, vile and pathetic men like John Wilkes Booth could claim with no self-awareness that "John Brown was a man inspired, the grandest character of this century!"[11] Emerson surely knew though that after the blood of millions had soaked the earth and a president had been slain, no one wanted to remember, and people were probably no more prepared to ponder on a story like Brown's than Booth had been.

No one wanted to hear about John Brown, and no one wanted to hear what Emerson thought they should believe about the story. So when Emerson was invited to Cambridge on July 18, 1867, to address the Phi Beta Kappa society about progress and civilization, he was eager to do so, because that could only be done if he spoke about the stories we tell. The systems of science and state had indeed produced wonders aside from their material truths, but only because without those, men were merely animals.

After *The Conduct of Life* and the American Civil War, something in Emerson seemed to have burnt out, perhaps from a combination of age, disillusionment, and a smoldering hatred of the South that was more consuming than his earlier detachment. His speech began somewhat disappointingly, a Panglossian ode to an age that was, seemingly, the best of all possible worlds. This was not altogether disingenuous; the "age of steel, of gold, of coal, petroleum, cotton, steam, & electricity" was undeniably transformative. And, as he noted, many old social barriers were still being swept aside, allowing people to pursue their dreams and raise their voices as never before.[12]

Newton's work, Emerson instructed, had made all of this possible. "The correlation of forces and the polarization of light have carried us to sublime generalizations,—have affected an imaginative race like poetic inspirations." The triumph of the age was that "we have been taught to tread familiarly on giddy heights of thought, and to wont ourselves to daring conjectures. The narrow sectarian cannot read astronomy with impunity. The creeds of his church shrivel like dried leaves at the door of the observatory." This remarkable lens on reality had achieved not only material marvels but would soon result in political equality for women. And, he was certain the growing labor troubles would be sorted out shortly. If he seemed uncharacteristically optimistic, he was either wearily aloof, or genuinely hopeful, ever since "the war gave us the abolition of slavery."[13]

He of all people knew that war's end is evil, no matter the incidental good. It is murder and debt, and serves only the power and glory of the wealthy and "the only harlequin that has come down to us from the middle ages," the military class.[14] He had been a witness, and he knew that no one had intended to free the slaves. The war was about what everyone involved *knew* was going to happen. Fire-eater Edwin Ruffin *knew* that the North would never fight, but when he fired the first gun at Fort Sumter, he freed the slaves, something he also *knew* would never happen. And the North's armies became armies of emancipation by accident, for not a fraction of them at the beginning would have fought to free a people considered an unfortunate presence. They *knew* they were fighting a white man's war to preserve a nation, until that too rang hollow because it was just too dubious an idea.

Only John Brown knew how it would end and John Brown was dead. Did Emerson believe that slavery had ended because of what people *knew,* and because of the army—the human expression of historical mechanics? Emerson must be read thoroughly, and deeply, and certainly in context. Even to the end, he was a preacher, and a good one, and he lured his audience into agreement with platitudes and head-nodding common opinions before he sounded them with his hammer. "Progress of Culture" may be gentle as Emerson's speeches go, but he would not leave his audience, or his future students, with such a baffling conundrum.

Our lives, he knew, are not our own. "I find" he said, "the single mind equipollent to a multitude of minds, say to a nation of minds, as a drop of water balances the sea; and under this view the problem of culture assumes wonderful interest. Culture implies all which gives the mind possession of its own powers; as languages to the critic, telescope to the astronomer."[15] The collective culture, systems, and beliefs are invaluable to man, yet as beautifully necessary as the metaphors may be, Emerson cautioned us to never mistakenly believe that they mean anything. Civilization itself is a narrative act bound up in a web of historical faith. It is a miracle, an idea about yesterday, and a hope about tomorrow, translated in all the choices and moments between birth and death. It is what keeps us out of the void, and allows us to aspire to be more than what we are. But most are incapable of being more, of rising above and being a causal force. Most, if they tried, would be fooling themselves; their efforts would be pale imitations with no end other than their animal selfishness.

Sometimes men come around who are out of their time, and despite every intention of the powerful, they bend everyone's sense of the order of the world to their will. "If a theologian of deep convictions and strong understanding carries his country with him, like Luther, the state becomes Lutheran, in spite of the Emperor." This is real kingship, what kings believe to be their power is merely a title. "Literary history and all history is a record of the power of minorities, and of minorities of one. Every book is written with a constant secret reference to the few intelligent persons whom the writer believes to exist in the million.... How much more are men than nations! the wise and good souls, the stoics in Greece and Rome, Socrates in Athens, the saints in Judea, Alfred the king, Shakspeare the poet, Newton the philosopher, the perceiver, and obeyer of truth,—than the foolish and sensual millions around them!" Sometimes, he said, "the men were so great, so self-fed, that the recognition of them by others was not necessary to them.... I think I have seen two or three great men who, for that reason, were of no account among scholars." These men, the causal forces in the narrative of human civilization, stand apart from their time "as in a barbarous age; amidst insanity, to calm and guide it; amidst fools and blind, to see the right done."[16]

There was something wrong with the stories we told, perhaps something he knew people of the West would never accept, or understand. He had seen such a remarkable metamorphosis of his society in his lifetime, and knew that he could not explain it according to anyone's intentions, nor could he tell them the stories they wanted to hear, which were little more than confirmations of their beliefs. He had witnessed the inexplicably bizarre phenomenon of thousands dying singing Julia Ward Howe's "Battle Hymn of the Republic," a song repurposed from one about a man who had died as a sworn enemy of the state and the established order.

And as he spoke, the largest wealth reallocation program in the history of the United States to this day was underway, but black bondsmen were not the recipients of the fruits of their labor. They became a cautionary underclass, a goad to others to serve faithfully the capitalists of the North. Politically, Republicans expunged their "radical" members and attached themselves to more powerful masters, as surely as Democrats had once hewn to the slave-power. "Every interest is found as sectional & timorous as before. The Episcopal church is baser than ever ... the Southerner just the same Gambia negro chief,—addicted to crowing, garotting, & stealing, as ever: the Democrat as false & truckling; the Union party as timid & compromising, the scholars pale & expectant, never affirmative."[17] The end of the war seemed to only dramatize the failure of the system; the new wave of entrepreneurs was more voracious than the last, the public domain was given with greater abandon to railroad barons and swindlers, and demagoguery stood in place of politics.

To support Lincoln and the war, reformers and scholars like Emerson had set aside their questions about whether the nation was even worth salvaging. But after hundreds of thousands had died to redeem the sins of their fathers, nothing greater than merely saving the Union had been realized, and that particular end was the least of all the hoped for outcomes. In 1868, trying to bring about real change, Richard Henry Dana, Jr., had attempted to wrest a Massachusetts congressional seat from Benjamin F. Butler, symbol of the "unthinking, reckless ... portion of the community."[18] Dana, one of Massachusetts' own intellectual Brahmins, a voice of abolition reform in the state that had nurtured the movement, received only 10 percent of the vote. Not even Massachusetts was a place for John Brown's story, and little had changed since 1848, when Emerson, despite his conflicted intellectual relationship with revolutions, wrote, "People here expect a revolution. There will be no revolution, none that deserves to be called so.... When I see changed men, I shall look for a changed world."[19]

In fact, despite the changes that the war had brought about, there was one constant in American culture that remained remarkably resistant to progress—the idea that Negroes were a "base class." If there had been any progress at all during Brown's life, maybe it was only indicated in Emerson's heart. He made a long ethical journey to become the man who wrote, "Who makes & keeps the jew or negro base, who but you, who exclude them from the rights which others enjoy?"[20]

Most importantly, Emerson knew that the ideas in his "Progress" speech were all illusions, and that "we live by our imaginations, by our admirations, by our sentiments. The child walks amid heaps of illusions, which he does not like to have disturbed.... The man lives to other objects, but who dare affirm that they are more real?"[21] It was the old nihilism of Hume the arch-skeptic, whose *Enquiry Concerning Human Understanding* provided Emerson some of his greatest philosophical difficulties. "The constant appeal is to our feelings from the glozed lies of the deceiver but one would feel safer & prouder to see the victorious answer to these calumnies upon our nature set down in impregnable propositions."[22] The world of rational history had always been no more than a choice of belief. "Our ideas are nothing but copies of our impressions," Hume said, and it is "impossible for us to *think* of anything which we have not antecedently felt." Though we may have pretensions of seeing natural law manifest in human life and history, this too was an illusion. We merely perceive sequence, and we have chosen to substitute cause and effect, though we are not "able to comprehend any force or power by which the cause operates, or any connection between it and its supposed effect."

"Events seem conjoined," Hume wrote. "But as we can have no idea of anything which never appeared to our outward sense or inward sentiment, the necessary conclusion seems to be, that we have no idea of connection or power at all, and that the words are absolutely without any meaning."[23] The difficulty for Emerson was that he could not refute Hume's assertion that the rational world was a comforting illusion, as illusory as free will. But the real problem was the will to power. It was something that Emerson *knew* was real, yet power implies, by its nature, cause. His struggle with deeper cause, and his early decision regarding his academic studies, was akin to the thinking of Immanuel Kant, who felt that Hume had focused overly much on the easy problems, and that something more integrative lay behind events and will, a kind of "transcendental" consciousness.

Antecedents and cause in the physical world were one thing, but antecedents in culture and civilization something else entirely; when Emerson drew historical antecedents for John Brown, he was fond of parallels with Oliver Cromwell, a theme enthusiastically echoed by others. It was a fateful comparison, given Cromwell's broader historical significance in helping to bring about the English Civil War. But Emerson's Brown was not the Cromwell of Hume's *History of England,* which had fixed the Protector in the Western mind as an ambitious and violent fanatic, a conflation of political deceit and religious zealotry. He was the heroic Cromwell of Thomas Carlyle, who said things like: "A few honest men are better than numbers.... I had rather have a plain russet-coated Captain that knows what he fights for, and loves what he knows, than that which you call 'a Gentleman' and is nothing else."[24]

Emerson couldn't shy from the comparison when Brown *apparently* said things to him like "For a settler in a new country, one good, believing, strong-minded man is worth a hundred, nay, a thousand men without character; and that the right men will give a permanent direction to the fortunes of a state," or his other comments about men of character besting hordes of ruffians.[25] One wonders who Emerson was actually writing about, and Carlyle's *Cromwell* was one of Brown's favorite books as well.

It was all one great circle; man cannot cause himself *ex nihilo,* but his narrative antecedents exist in the present mind. "The world rolls, the din of life is never hushed. In London, in Paris, in Boston, in San Francisco, the carnival, the masquerade is at its height. Nobody drops his domino. The unities, the fictions of the piece it would be an impertinence to break."[26] But even if the rational world is an illusion of the mind, it doesn't make it any less *real,* unless the mind is, itself, nothing. The mind's will to power was the reality that Hume regarded as illusion, the reality that Emerson found in Goethe and in John Brown. Will, like life, could be of adamantine power and gossamer fragility. It existed only in the dynamic interactions between forces and mediums regarded as discreet and fundamental.

What of Brown's story, forever unfinished in the pages of Emerson's journals? His subtle silence might have been compelled as much by his verdict on the age as by anything else. "The key to the age may be this, or that, or the other, as the young orators describe;—the key to all ages is—Imbecility; imbecility in the vast majority of men, at all times, and, even in heroes, in all but certain eminent moments; victims of gravity, custom, and fear. This gives force to the strong,—that the multitude have no habit of self-reliance or original action."[27] He contented himself to elevate John Brown to the status of supra-historical overman, writing that genius "has a right and a duty to affront and amaze men by carrying out its perceptions defiantly, knowing well that time and fate will verify and explain what time and fate have through them said. We must not suggest to Michel Angelo, or Machiavel, or Rabelais, or Voltaire, or John Brown of Osawatomie (a great man), or Carlyle, how they shall suppress their paradoxes and check their huge gait to keep accurate step with the procession on the street sidewalk."[28]

Whether it was true or not, life had shown Emerson a man who could be rooted in history like a great ash tree, could *know* the strength of that sense of place, could with every flaw and transgression reach and grow to overcome and not be a slave to it but for the value of human life bring forward something as startlingly unexpected as a fragile flower. And Emerson knew what the fate of such people was. Brown had said it himself in the courtroom, when he told them how different things would be had he acted on the behalf of the powerful.

Men were mostly apelike homonculi who clung to any story, any idea, so long as it would deliver them from the abyssal horror of attempting to meaningfully comprehend the world, so long as it allowed them to pretend that banal avarice was an intelligent and courageous *Wille zur Macht.* God help him if John Brown became one of their stories. And in the years since Brown's death, his story made less sense in a world filled with new metaphors, and so much the better if those ideas crafted the illusion of reason and justice. John Brown in the minds of small men had perhaps inspired the death of Abraham Lincoln. Let them mouth, with all false and solemn profundity, ideas barely understood so long as it secured the web of civilization. Far better that than they should parrot John Brown.

Greatness does not come in a slavish imitation of the past, in a farce. Such a farce can be hailed as greatness though, as Brown had alluded to during his trial. And greatness cannot be achieved by destroying the past. Civilization requires an idea about yesterday from where tomorrow may grow anew. The unidirectional narrative of civilization—the state—that keeps people safe by checking the random predations on the vulnerable also causes war by becoming the conduit for those myriad evils. Yet maybe better that the mass of unthinking men kill and die for the state than imitate John Brown only to chaotically assault the vulnerable. Wise Emerson likely understood that this story had no place in civilization, no redemptive qualities. It is a tragedy that only has victims and villains, often indistinguishable. Brown might have been courage, but he was also civilization's monster. A victim. Aren't we all?

So he shrugged, left the history to others, and gave no easy answers. Abraham Lincoln freed the slaves, there is not enough paper in the world to print panegyrics to treasonous Southern generals, and Brown hangs forever on history's gibbet. And the easy answers came from Ivy League men of progress like Owen Wister and Teddy Roosevelt. Their mythic past was a resumption of an interrupted fable projected on the nothingness of the Midwest, a kind of Elysium of memory that could be spun into nearly literal modern gold. It was a sinister bequest to future Americans, a narrative landscape in which beatific images of the powerful smile on sun-dappled prairies (which look suspiciously like Kansas) and absurdly promise to reclaim the American past. In their counterfactual reality, does Ralph Waldo Emerson go to Washington while Preston Brooks goes to prison? Hardly. The future-past they actually imagine looks rather more like the catalog of horrors hidden under their idyllic simplifications.

What would people do to earn that future-past, in which the Oregon Trail was not littered with the bodies of babies and the victims of genocide, and murder was made forthrightly elegant by the beautiful slain lying in memoriam, who only ever had gory exit wounds on their hidden backs. A personalized mythology which called His wretched poor to exaltation in history's charnel house, where death was usually far less iconic; bodies broken by steel, ravaged by pox and disease, distorted by starvation, or mangled in the fires and gears of industry, but those were the voiceless. They were the silent price of "progress," the process of the beatification of the captains of finance and the clownishly festooned military class, the kind of men to whom Emerson addressed "Progress of Culture." And despite his mollifying conclusion that "I think their hands are strong enough to hold up the Republic. I read the promise of better times and of greater men," one gets the impression that Emerson held a private fear that because of those men the hour would come when again something awful would slouch towards Kansas to be born, but if it did then perhaps someday greater men truly would come along.

W.E.B. Du Bois observed that in the year of John Brown's execution, the ideas he tried to kill were gifted with new and powerful scientific metaphors with the publication of *On the Origin of Species* by Charles Darwin. The evils of the century to follow may not be laid at Darwin's feet; the West had not required his sanction to sustain nearly one century of predation, let alone another. But, in an era where people were suddenly losing faith in cosmological justifications for their historic destiny, it arrived just in time for appropriation, along with an entire social vocabulary of its own.[29]

It even re-cast Emersonian self-realization, passing it through the fires of scientific

Western nationalism along with everything else to create an idea in which "freedom" means an unbounded hunger, an historically imagined attainment of future demands. An eternal possibility of achievement stretching, physically immortal, into the void. And thanks to the monumental achievement of the Civil War, this idea was free forever of slavery. That word was frozen forever in the amber of history, conquered by anyone but John Brown, an idea either awkwardly ignored or allowed recognition only as the most sacred part of the African American experience and only insofar as it is part of the progress of history. But a word that once had many subtle gradations in order to contrast it with and attempt to understand the word "freedom" was all but forbidden. We had six hundred thousand dead to "prove" that slavery was no more.

Du Bois described Brown, or at least his story, as the riddle of the sphinx. That story is, of course, a tragedy. Oedipus certainly solved the riddle, using historical logic. He arrived at that point because of a journey he undertook—rationally—to avoid the fate the oracle foretold for him. He did everything he should have, and the triumph of his reason was the ruination of himself and a kingdom, and the coming to pass of all that the oracle foretold.

Simply learning what to overlook might be wisdom though, and Emerson the sage was very wise.[30] John Brown—driven like Hamlet, demonically aware of the crimes around him—was incapable of overlooking, and like Hamlet could only illuminate wisdom while his demons drove him to become, ultimately, his own doom. As an historical figure, more than human—or maybe less—the only place he had in the mind of Emerson's civilization was that of Nemesis, the un-wisdom of the Greek pantheon, the remorseless and inescapable scourge of hubris. Our guilt, our mortality, and our inability to just forgive.

Though Emerson chose in the end to overlook this story most of all, he was probably curious to see just how the memory of civilization would interact with John Brown as the narratives collapsed into each other. A young Emerson had sought to deal with Nemesis in the way of Goethe, cultivating our personal genius for others. And older Emerson found the iron of Brown's fate to occupy the place in his writings belonging to the lovelier but just as terrible Nemesis.

A better civilization would remove the power of Nemesis from her. A civilization that was rational, with rational histories, was supposed to be better than the myth-haunted one that killed Christ and abused him just as badly as a myth for centuries after. But Nemesis was the power of the John Brown myth, and he was almost as many things to storytellers as Christ had been. Was the story fact, or miracle? Nearly every quote, anecdote, recollection, tale—including the story that Emerson began but left unfinished—was remembered after Brown's execution, after his shadow from the gallows was larger than he. Events cannot always be perceived. The past is an illusion, and historians may only write about events as they revisit them and collapse them into the present.

Others wrote the story, and the stories themselves are interesting characters. The earliest writers, men like Sanborn, and James Redpath, were actually actors in the play. Their writings may have been hagiographic regarding a man they personally respected, but they were not dishonest men. And in a confused era they were joined by Europeans who wrote about predation and revolution, such as Richard D. Webb, an Irishman and anti-slavery activist who met Frederick Douglass in 1845, and Herman von Holst, a German historian whose principle work, *Verfassung und Demokratie der Vereinigten Staaten*, was preoccupied with the subject of slavery in a "free" republic.

Until 1910, most of the authors had actually met Brown. Then came Oswald Garrison Villard, the grandson of William Lloyd Garrison. Yet Villard's phenomenally well-researched yet mildly unfulfilling volume faded from print while W.E.B. Du Bois's lyrically powerful work endured. Du Bois's *John Brown* suffered more than most, surviving Villard's attempt to bury it, and later the purging of library shelves in order to correct our history during the McCarthy-ite inquisition, in an age when America collectively smiled at both its new hegemony and the realization of what nation-hood had long meant to European military powers, yet found that the smile caused the plastic face to crack, revealing a brittle façade over gray and rootless thoughts beneath.

Until 1910, as well, the most vituperative narratives were confined to Southern journals read by few, but the tragedies of Brown's life would continue to be acted out in the contest of words. When Villard did not prove capable enough at de-mythologizing Brown, Hill Peebles Wilson published a nearly unreadable work of character assassination at the bequest of Charles Robinson's widow, who was trying to purchase her dead husband's place as the most influential figure in Kansas history. And in 1929 poet laureate Robert Penn Warren wrote of an inept and warped Yankee businessman whose failures drove him to violent abolitionism. He asked readers to accept on faith that the key to understanding Brown was by taking every word as a lie and every friend as a dupe, fooled by Brown's ability to rationalize his actions by some "elaborate psychological mechanism for justification."[31] It might be rude to point out by way of elaborate psychological justifications that Warren wrote this book contemporaneously with authoring some rather unfortunate paeans to Southern white men and racial segregation.

In 1942, during the heart of a time out of Emerson's nightmares, James Malin of the University of Kansas—an institution first proposed by Territorial Governor Reeder, built on land donated by Charles Robinson as part of his quest to emerge from the Old Man's shadow with a grant from Amos Lawrence—wrote a 700 page "scientific" effort to demonstrate that Brown had "zero" causal power. Brown, a "parenthesis" in history, who had stood atop Mt. Oread and made it possible for those men to found the university, was in Malin's account a flagrantly dishonest individual, motivated by money and personal gain to the bitter end. Such a thing cannot be proven anymore than many other narratives, but if it was believable it says more about *us* than about John Brown, and the creative interpretation was exactly as scientific as Malin claimed.[32] From Malin's same sources, in 1970 Stephen Oates wrote a mildly sympathetic treatment, which made Brown acceptable by writing him as an incomprehensibly anachronistic theological creature. This was three years after most states repealed America's repulsive "one drop" laws demarcating racial purity. From those same sources David S. Reynolds was able to portray both a putative pilgrim progenitor and also a prototype progressive man-of-tomorrow, in an era when Gov. Tim Kaine of Virginia can absurdly pardon Gabriel Prosser.

If there is any one lesson to be derived from Emerson's journals, it is the capacity for man to grow, learn and change, and to become more than what he is and greater than his faults. Later in life Robert Penn Warren publicly and eloquently recanted his early views on race. He never forgave Emerson for John Brown though, and to the end of his days denounced Emerson as the Devil.[33]

This book is a character in the story too, albeit a minor one. Is this book any more about John Brown than the others? Addressing the past as collective prose discourse, I have drawn thematic inspiration from the stories that are our ghosts, much in the way Nietzsche drew on Herodotus when he wrote that "to speak the truth and to handle bow and arrow well" was important to those who gave Zarathustra his name. I would like to imagine that this work would earn a kind nod from Emerson, who argued that historical understanding requires fictional imagination. I never knew John Brown—John Brown is dead. I think we're still trying to figure a lot of that out.

Other biographers walked in the actual story. Emerson led the intellectual chorus. James Redpath and Franklin Sanborn were prominent actors, the former in Kansas, and the latter as history's catalyst. He spent thirty long years gathering family letters and the statements of friends, and corresponding with Brown's children. Shortly after the publication of Sanborn's *Life and Letters*, William Lloyd Garrison's grandson took on the task of writing the history. He disparaged W.E.B. Du Bois's use of Sanborn's old sources, but Du Bois lacked both Villard's resources and the technological offspring of the telegraph. Villard had the next best thing, perhaps better, in a phenomenal research assistant named Katherine Mayo, who travelled the breadth of the country on a web of steel rails and coal to visit the surviving children. She gained a form of immortality in the novel *Cloudsplitter*.

Those children she visited told the story that defined their lives, each within the limits of their abilities, each according to their own needs. Mary had moved with her remaining children to California not long after Emerson refused to take part in a subscription to help her and her family remain on the North Elba farm. She wanted to give her daughters "a chance to do something for themselves in a new country that they cannot have here." All she wrote of the parting itself was, "I very much regret that I ever spent a cent on that farm."[34] She lived in peace in California until her death in 1884; the only time the past came back to physically haunt her was in 1882, when a doctor returned the body of Watson to be buried at North Elba with Frederick and his father.

In the end the entire family had become stigmatics, burdened with carrying the Old Man's ghost. Sometimes the hauntings were unpleasant, like when the *Lawrence Daily Journal* published James Townsley's "confession" to the Pottawatomie killings in 1879, eliciting numerous letters from the otherwise silent sons in an effort to historically integrate the long ignored killings into the martyr's myth.

John, Jr., had been emboldened by the tragic end of the Harpers Ferry raid to overcome many of his private fears and misgivings. He proudly defended the cause thereafter, and after the U.S. defeat at Bull Run he recruited a group of antislavery men to fight for "the freedom of all" under the auspices of Senator James Lane of Kansas. His men later became part of Charles Jennison's Seventh Volunteer Cavalry, or "Jennison's Jayhawkers." John, Jr., was succeeded in his command by George Hoyt, one of his father's attorneys. In later years he sent packages to the Haymarket anarchists.[35]

He vigorously employed his pen to rebuke attacks on his father's character, and his home was filled with memorabilia of his father and of Kansas.[36] Occupying a commanding place in his parlor were two portraits—one of himself, one of his father—perhaps for guests to compare. One might almost forget that John, Jr., was not at Harpers Ferry. He had been at home, in Ohio, living a comfortable life with his wife and his friends, planting potatoes and starting a prosperous homestead. Back in Kansas, he had stayed with his own men the night his father had gone to Pottawatomie. He had been in prison during Black Jack and during the sack of Osawatomie.

Sarah, his sister, remarked that his brothers "found it conspicuous that he always managed to keep out of danger." He claimed in later years that he hadn't been at Harpers Ferry because the timing surprised him, but sometimes he insisted that he had been performing a kind of detached duty in Canada.[37]

It's true that his father had given him other tasks to perform, which he did entirely ineffectively. But when John, Jr., attempted to secure his place in the family story, did he remember that while his father was begging his sons to come to Harpers Ferry that the plea did not include him? Did he remember that he had not been there for any of the highly storied moments of his father's legend? He died of heart failure in 1895, and until that day he clung to his role supporting the "cause of truth" as his father's namesake.[38]

On the other hand, the Old Man had begged Salmon to join him, and Salmon had refused. He attempted to attribute his absence to a kind of precognition granted by special knowledge of his father's character—"You know father. You know he will dally till he is trapped."—and he even for a time claimed that other supporting duties had kept him. But in truth, his wife, Abbie Hinckley, had refused. Eventually, his memory came to involve shaking hands with his father, and in that fateful moment the ghost absolved him by saying, "I wish you could go along, but someone has to stay and take care of things at home."[39]

In 1919, at the age of 83, Salmon Brown celebrated his father's birthday one last time alone, then picked up his old Kansas pistol and killed himself. After that he was no longer the survivor who turned away.

Jason, who had tearfully condemned his father after Pottawatomie, maintained his moral constancy and also refused to go to Harpers Ferry. He withered in the very waters of memory that nurtured John, Jr., and found himself somewhat lost in the world and vaguely ashamed of his own place in the family. His internalization of his identity as a Brown was bound up in statements like "It is a Brown trait to be migratory, sanguine about what they think they can do, to speculate, to go into debt, and to make a good many failures…. If I hadn't inherited it, I might have been worth something more than nothing now."[40]

His reticence and turning away may have earned him the mistrust of his brothers, but that was not his true damnation. Jason's terrible cross was his father's forgiveness, love, and acceptance. From prison the Old Man wrote that Jason had always "underrated himself" and was not "(like his father) too much inclined to assume…. He never quarrels, and yet I know that he is both morally and physically brave." He was "a most tender, loving, and steadfast friend, and on the right side of things in general."[41] Jason, in the end, could only tell Katherine Mayo, "I have always considered myself the greatest coward, moral and physical, in our family."[42]

Owen had been there, and had escaped with his life. He may have even made the entire event possible, overcoming the internal frictions of the group to help his father form of them a cohesive whole. He held them together for nearly two years while his father travelled the continent in search of weapons and money. But then again, Owen had always been there, with his crippled arm, at his father's side. And when it was all over, he was still there, a living reminder to his brothers of their failures and inconstancy. Yet unlike them he was mostly silent, just a kindly man who drifted lost down the years, even living for a while in a little shack behind John, Jr.'s fine house. Later he became a lone hermit on "Brown's Peak" near Pasadena before he died in 1889.

Annie knew what she intended of the remembering. She refused for most of her adult life to write anything of those days, preferring instead to merely tend to her garden and care for her children, and shelter them from others' ghosts. When her father's broken body had made the long cold journey home, she never looked at him. She "preferred to remember him just as we parted."[43]

For a time after the Civil War she had been a student of Sanborn's, and had even briefly taught at a school for black children in the former home of Gov. Wise. But she found she needed to flee those ghosts, and in 1864 she moved to California with her mother. She eventually married and had a family, but she told them very little about the unbelievable past, or about that halcyon summer by Harpers Ferry in 1859. She had decided to live her new life, "not the old, sad one that was gone," so she simply "shut the past away."[44] She was sometimes invited to commemorative events, but refused those as well. "My work," she said, "like that of the rest was a freewill offering, not something to boast of or exhibit myself for. I may be a relic of John Brown's raid on Harper's Ferry, but I do not want to be placed on exhibition with other relics and curios, as such."[45]

She was the last witness, and as John, Jr., said, "born to suffer and yet endure."[46] As the years wore on, as she witnessed the progress of civilization, she returned to memory and contributed hers to the history of her father. Late in life she frequently corresponded with her old friend and mentor, Franklin Sanborn, and wrote some delightfully truculent replies to people who were attempting to claim the story—and therefore some fame—as their own.

> In regard to the pretended claims of a man who calls himself "Colonel Richard W. Howard, the last survivor of John Brown's Raid" ... Mr. Howard says, "I have never courted notoriety." I would like to know what he was courting, last February, when he had a long article ... claiming that he was with John Brown at Harper's Ferry and escaped. He further says that he was not known by his right name at Kennedy Farmhouse. Will he oblige me by giving the name he was known by there and also the key to the cipher he claims to possess? I was my father's housekeeper at Kennedy Farm and knew his men, and know that this man Howard was not there. Since Owen Brown's death, I am the only person who can honestly claim to be "the last survivor...."
>
> This man seems to have studied his lesson well, but neglected to make the acquaintance of the housekeepers at Kennedy Farm, one of them still survives, and is certain that he was not there. The number of men who claims to have slept with John Brown the last night he was in Kansas, are so numerous, that I have often wondered how wide that wonderful bed was. I have had men tell me that they used to know me, when I was a little girl in Kansas. I always reply that "I do not doubt it, as I never was there."[47]

She lived out the remainder of her days in Petrolia, California, at the western edge of destiny, a continent away from the beginning of the story. Poverty wrapped its tendrils around her too, though she bore it with a sad and awkward dignity, enmeshed in an unhappy marriage and a life of lost dreams. But she was blessed with daughters who were the joy of her days. By her later years she had sold every scrap of paper with her father's signature, and every artifact she possessed, to relic hunters. Early on these were not such cruel losses, but later as the world moved on the absence seemed to be a bit keener. Both to tell the story and to support herself, Annie tried her own hand at writing, but found no audience for her anonymously submitted narrative. Though she was self-deprecating when it came to her literary capacity and education, her letters show that she had a story to tell and a capable pen.

And her story was perhaps the best of them all. Unlike any of the others, mythical or monstrous, her story was human. Our lives are not our own, and we live as much as the product of our own memories as we do the memories of others, and they in turn are shaped by those memories, connected by every act of grace and cruelty. When they took up their work, the men had "hoped that they would come out alive. Some were more earnest in the work than others. They were all men. Heroes are made out of men. People who never did a heroic deed themselves are very particular as to how heroes behave." "They did not impress me as 'men who could do bloody deeds—the bloodier the better,' as was said at a public meeting; but as men who were earnest and true, kind and generous, warm-hearted and sympathetic; neither saints nor the worst of sinners."[48] Just human, all too human.

In 1918, the house that John Brown was born in burned to the ground—an unfortunate chimney fire accident. Then in 1926, the same year that Stephen Vincent Benét's *John Brown's Body* was published and sixty-seven years after her father's death, the last witness fell and broke her neck. During the twilight of a long life, after one final summer to live in the glow of her memories, Annie Brown died on October 3. Nothing much else uncommon happened that day.

Annie Brown-Adams, late in life (Library of Congress).

Chapter Notes

Preface

1. Emphasis added. However, in the reading of this book, the idiosyncrasies, misspellings, and emphasis of original correspondence has been reproduced as faithfully as possible in type. Following the convention of several preceding authors, I have used italics where Brown often underlined words. A transcript of the discussion can be found at: http://www.continuinged.ku.edu/kt/session3/discussion.html.
2. Genocide: A distinction that the United States had the proudest claim to in 1882. Those who claim that the Indian Removal was not an example of genocide are technically correct in that the word hadn't been invented yet; the use here is therefore an anachronism. One is free to make of that what one will.
3. Ernest Renan, Qu'est–Ce Qu'une Nation? Conférence Faite En Sorbonne, Le 11 Mars 1882 (Paris: Calmann Lévy, 1882), 9, http://books.google.com/books?id=IngGAAAAQAAJ&printsec=frontcover&source=gbs_ge_summary_r&cad=0#v=onepage&q&f=false (accessed March 6, 2012).
4. Benedict Anderson. *Imagined Communities: Reflections On the Origin and Spread of Nationalism.* Rev. and extended ed. (London: Verso, 1991) 6, 199–204.

Chapter 1

1. Owen Brown's autobiographical essay, qtd. in Franklin B. Sanborn, *The Life and Letters of John Brown, Liberator of Kansas and Martyr of Virginia* (Boston: Roberts Brothers, 1891), 7.
2. Ibid., 6.
3. Ibid., 4.
4. Owen Brown's Autobiography in Oswald Garrison Villard, *John Brown 1800–1859: A Biography Fifty Years After* (1859 reprint: New York: Kessinger Publishing, LLC, 2010), 13.
5. Letter, John Brown to Henry L. Stearns, July 15, 1857.
6. Owen Brown's Autobiography in Villard, *John Brown,* 13.
7. Lora Case, *Hudson of Long Ago: Progress of Hudson During the Past Century, Personal Reminiscences of an Aged Pioneer: Reminiscences, Written in 1897* (Hudson, OH: Hudson Library and Historical Society, 1963), 49.
8. Letter, John Brown to Henry L. Stearns, July 15, 1857.
9. Ralph Waldo Emerson, *Selected Journals 1841–1877,* ed. Lawrence Rosenwald (New York: Library of America, 2010), 727.
10. The earliest biography to reference this letter was Sanborn's *The Life and Letters of John Brown.* Villard began his volume with the same brief autobiography, as did DuBois. Louis Ruchames places it first in the order of letters written by John Brown, though written later in the chronology, since it is the single account of John Brown's boyhood. Emerson recounted the tale in a speech on Jan. 6, 1860, as did Frederick Douglass on May 30, 1881.
11. In his letter, Brown actually wondered if God was not "also the boy's father." The suggestion of the death of God is not merely for brazen effect though. As Nietzsche illustrated, a God that was not the boy's father would have philosophically been a God that was dead, killed by civilization.
12. Salmon Brown, *My Father, John Brown.* Reprinted in: *A John Brown Reader: The Story of John Brown in His Own Words, in the Words of Those Who Knew Him, and in the Poetry and Prose of the Literary Heritage* / Edited with Introduction and Commentary by Louis Ruchames (London: Abelard-Schuman, 1959), 184.
13. Katherine Mayo, interview with the wife of Judge Thomas Russell, reprinted ibid., 236. This description is placed here deliberately because the man that Mrs. Russell described for Miss Mayo is the one who—in the space-time juncture of that memory—wrote that autobiographical letter to young Henry Stearns. What you observe in the story of his boyhood and the memory of the man is, in a way, the exact same description.
14. Letter, George Gill to Richard Hinton, July 7, 1893, reprinted ibid., 231–232.
15. Katherine Mayo, interview with the wife of Judge Thomas Russell, reprinted ibid., 234. "Old Covenanter" is an ironic favorite; few interpreted Job with the mad genius of John Calvin, and the God who spoke to Job seemed a wickedly sarcastic being no longer much interested in Covenants at all.
16. To paraphrase John Jay Chapman, "Doctor Howe," in *Learning and Other Essays* (New York: Moffat, Yard, 1910), 131.
17. Mark Twain, *Letters from the Earth* (Kindle edition), loc 1848 Twain's argument parallels David Hume's famous essay on Miracles, or may be seen as a critique of the most common interpretation of Hume's treatment of the subject. Twain has merely neglected to name his fictitious Professor of "Comparative Science and Theology" "Professor Hume."
18. Ralph Waldo Emerson, *Selected Journals, 1820–*

1842, ed. Lawrence Rosenwald (New York: Library of America, 2010), 185. David Hume, Essay on Miracles, in *An Enquiry Concerning Human Understanding*.
 19. Ibid.
 20. Emerson, *Selected Journals 1841–1877*, 728. 1859 was a year that Emerson wrote a lot about the nature of illusion and belief.
 21. See Carl L. Becker, *The Heavenly City of the Eighteenth Century Philosophers* (New Haven, CT: Yale University Press, 1951), 119–121, and Emerson, *History*, published in 1841.
 22. Eric Hobsbawm, *The Age of Revolution 1789–1848*, (New York: Vintage, 1996), 1.

Chapter 2

 1. Emerson, *Selected Journals, 1820–1842*, 109.
 2. See Stanley Cavell, *Emerson's Transcendental Etudes* (Stanford, Calif.: Stanford University Press, 2003). It's a sentiment that I heartily agree with.
 3. Emerson, *Selected Journals 1841–1877*, 111–112.
 4. George Bancroft. *The History of the United States from the discovery of the American Continent* Volume VII (Boston: Little, Brown, 1858): 312, Making of America Collection.
 5. Richard Hofstadter, in *The Progressive Historians*. (New York: Alfred A Knopf, 1969) 17, expressed this opinion. Hofstadter was in my estimation nearly the greatest historian America has ever produced, and he was less than kind to America's 19th century body of historical work. See also Eileen Ka-May Cheng, *The Plain and Noble Garb of Truth: Nationalism and Impartiality in American Historical Writing, 1784–1860* (Athens: University of Georgia Press, 2008), 149–152.
 6. Eric Hobsbawm, *The Age of Revolution 1789–1848*, 74–5 and Alfred Vagts, *A History of Militarism* (Westport, CT: Greenwood Press Reprint, 1981), 120–2.
 7. Major L. Wilson, *Space, Time, and Freedom: The Quest for Nationality and the Irrepressible Conflict, 1815–1861* (Westport, CT: Greenwood Press, 1974), 107–112.
 8. Guy Godlewski, "Napoléon et Les-états-amis," *La Nouvelle Revue des Deux Mondes* (July–Sept. 1977): 320.
 9. David Brion Davis, *The Problem of Slavery in the Age of Revolution, 1770–1823* (New York: Oxford University Press, USA, 1999), 557.
 10. Owen Connelly, *Blundering to Glory: Napoleon's Military Campaigns* (Wilmington, Del.: Scholarly Resources, 1987), 72.
 11. Tim Matthesen, "Jefferson and Haiti," *Journal of Southern History* 61, no. 1 (May 1995): 209–48.
 12. For an excellent account of this brief and abortive uprising, see: Egerton, Douglas R. *Gabriel's Rebellion: The Virginia Slave Conspiracies of 1800 and 1802*. Chapel Hill: University of North Carolina Press, 1993.
 13. Qtd. in Eric Foner, *The Story of American Freedom* (New York: W. W. Norton, 1999), 35.
 14. Ibid., 36.
 15. Eric Foner. *Forever Free: The Story of Emancipation and Reconstruction*. (New York: Vintage Books, 2005) 11.
 16. Kevin Phillips. *Wealth and Democracy: A Political History of the American Rich*. (New York: Broadway Books, 2002), 21–22.
 17. Alexis de Tocqueville, *Democracy in America* (New York: Library of America, 2004), 350.
 18. As alluded to by Charles A. Beard, *An Economic Interpretation of the Constitution of the United States* (1913; repr., Mineola, NY: Dover Publications, 2004), 239–252.
 19. Emerson, *Selected Journals 1841–1877*, 745.
 20. Steven Watts, *The Republic Reborn: War and the Making of Liberal America, 1790–1820 (New Studies in American Intellectual and Cultural History)* (Baltimore: Johns Hopkins University Press, 1989), 239.
 21. Professor Michael H. Hunt, *Ideology and U.S Foreign Policy* (New Haven: Yale University Press, 1988), 26–8.
 22. Alison L. LaCroix, "A Singular and Awkward War: The Transatlantic Context of the Hartford Convention," *American Nineteenth Century History* 6, no. 1 (March 2005): 3–32.
 23. Russell F. Weigley, *The American Way of War: A History of United States Military Strategy and Policy*, Indiana University Press paperback ed. (Bloomington: Indiana University Press, 1977), 46.
 24. Daniel Walker Howe, *What Hath God Wrought: The Transformation of America, 1815–1848 (Oxford History of the United States)* (New York: Oxford University Press, USA, 2009), 64.
 25. Ralph Ketcham, *James Madison: A Biography*, 1st pbk. ed. (Charlottesville: University of Virginia Press, 1990), 579.
 26. Howe, *What Hath God Wrought*, 9.
 27. Bradford Perkins, *The Cambridge History of American Foreign Relations Vol. 1: The Creation of a Republican Empire, 1776–1865* (New York: Cambridge University Press, 1993), 146.
 28. Emerson, *Selected Journals, 1820–1842*, 148.
 29. According to Mary Brown as stated to Thomas Wentworth Higginson. Noted in Higginson, "A Visit to John Brown's Household in 1859," an essay first printed in James Redpath, *The Public Life of Capt. John Brown. With an Auto-Biography of His Childhood and Youth* (Freeport, NY: Ayer, 1901), and also reprinted in Ruchames, ed., *A John Brown Reader*, 229. The account of James Foreman written to James Redpath corroborates this story as well. See ibid., 167.
 30. Emerson, *Selected Journals, 1820–1842*, 768.
 31. Cheng, *The Plain and Noble Garb of Truth*, 18.
 32. Ibid., 36, 159–160, 162–4.
 33. Ibid.

Chapter 3

 1. Letter, Herman Hallock to Gerald Hallock, Dec. 1859; in Sanborn, *The Life and Letters of John Brown*, 32.
 2. The opinion of Boyd Stutler, qtd. in Ruchames, ed., *A John Brown Reader*, 16.
 3. Oswald Garrison Villard, *John Brown 1800–1859: A Biography Fifty Years After*, reprint (New York: Kessinger Publishing, LLC, 2010), 18.
 4. Account of James Foreman to James Redpath, in Ruchames, ed., *A John Brown Reader*, 167.
 5. The Rev. John S. Duncan, "John Brown in Penn–

sylvania," *Western Pennsylvania Historical Magazine* 11 (Jan. 1928).

6. Statement by James Foreman to James Redpath in Ruchames, ed., *A John Brown Reader*, 164.

7. Louis A. Decaro, Jr., *Fire from the Midst of You: A Religious Life of John Brown* (New York: NYU Press, 2005), loc. 2457, and ibid.

8. Statement of James Foreman in Ruchames, ed., *A John Brown Reader*.

9. Qtd. in Foner, *The Story of American Freedom*, 50.

10. Richard J. Hinton, *John Brown and His Men*, Vol. 1 of 2. (New York: Funk and Wagnall's, 1894), 419.

11. Charles A. Beard, *An Economic Interpretation of the Constitution of the United States*, 1913 reprint (Mineola, NY: Dover Publications, 2004), 24–25. Jefferson's private financial mess was the result of living well beyond his means, poorly considered debts and co-signing of business arrangements and an economic "panic" which preceded the far more calamitous "panic" of 1837. Jefferson also believed, based on the technology at the time, that it would take 1,000 years to spread across the continent.

12. Foner, *The Story of American Freedom*, 59.

13. David S. Reynolds, *John Brown, Abolitionist: The Man Who Killed Slavery, Sparked the Civil War, and Seeded Civil Rights* (New York: Vintage, 2006), 45.

14. Letter, John Brown to Seth Thompson, April 13, 1832. Photocopies of the Atlanta University Center Archives John Brown Letters at the Kansas State Historical Society, John Brown Papers. The Atlanta University Center Archives contain mostly Brown's business correspondence, to include nearly all of his correspondence with Seth Thompson.

15. Kenneth Pomeranz, *The Great Divergence: China, Europe, and the Making of the Modern World Economy*, revised ed. (Princeton University Press, 2001). The "cul-de-sac" is Pomeranz's description for the nearly insurmountable barrier that existed prior to American slavery. Historian Eric Hobsbawm has commented that when one says "industrial revolution," one is actually saying "cotton."

16. Emerson, *Selected Journals 1841–1877*, 448.

17. Ibid., 235.

18. Jessica Lepler, "1837: Anatomy of a Panic" (PhD diss., Brandeis University, 2007), 26. Also, Richard Holcombe Kilbourne, Jr., *Slave Agriculture And Financial Markets in Antebellum America: The Bank of the United States in Mississippi 1831–1852 (Financial History)* (London: Pickering & Chatto Ltd, 2006), examines the link between the fall of Biddle's bank and the rise of the slave and speculation system that created the crash of 1837. An interesting study in the economics—particularly the capitalist economics—of American slavery is Robert William Fogel and Stanley L. Engerman, *Time on the Cross: The Economics of American Slavery* (New York: W. W. Norton, 1995).

19. Letter, Isaac Franklin to Rice C. Ballard, Dec. 8, 1832. Folder 8, Series 1.1. Rice Ballard Papers, Southern Historical Collection, University of North Carolina, Chapel Hill, North Carolina.

20. Wendell Holmes Stephenson, *Isaac Franklin: Slave Trader and Planter of the Old South; With Plantation Records* (Baton Rouge: Louisiana State University Press, 1938), 11–12. Franklin's Mississippi plantation, called "Angola," later became the notorious prison by the same name, a fact which makes the prison's existence and purpose all the more troubling.

21. See Kilbourne, *Slave Agriculture And Financial Markets*, for the reverse analysis of the dependency of the banks on the output and even the existence of the slaves.

22. Drafts for payment drawn from a variety of these institutions can be seen in the Ballard Papers at http://dc.lib.unc.edu/cdm4/results.php?CISOOP1=exact&CISOFIELD1=descri&CISOROOT=/ead&CISOBOX1=04850.

23. Kilbourne, *Slave Agriculture And Financial Markets*, 81, 129.

24. Letter, Isaac Franklin to Rice C. Ballard, June 11, 1833, Folder 11, Ballard Papers.

25. R. Seymour Long, "Andrew Jackson and the National Bank," *The English Historical Review* 12, no. 45 (Jan. 1897): 85–99.

Chapter 4

1. *Liberator*, Jan. 1, 1831.

2. Emerson, *Selected Journals, 1820–1842*, 711.

3. Ibid., 425.

4. Ralph Waldo Emerson, *Selected Journals 1841–1877*, ed. Lawrence Rosenwald (New York: Library of America, 2010), 615.

5. *Journals and Miscellaneous Notebooks of Ralph Waldo Emerson, Volume II: 1822–1826* (Boston: Belknap Press of Harvard University Press, 1961), 43.

6. Stephen B. Oates, "Children of Darkness," *American Heritage* 24, no. 6 (Oct. 1973).

7. Confessions of Nat Turner, Kindle Edition, loc 158.

8. Oates, "Children of Darkness."

9. Perhaps the best account of Nat's rebellion can be found in Stephen B. Oates, *The Fires of Jubilee: Nat Turner's Fierce Rebellion* (New York: Harper Perennial, 1990).

10. *Liberator*, Jan. 8, 1831.

11. *Liberator*, April 30, 1831.

12. *Liberator*, March 10, 1832. In this case it is probably redundant to define the hypothetical "citizen" as "white."

13. James H. Hammond, qtd. in Oates, "Children of Darkness." Again, the classics teach so much. Where would the "noble" *hoplites* have been without their *helot* slave class to carry their weapons, and toil for them, and to be hunted for sport in order to train future *hoplite* citizens?

14. Emerson, *Selected Journals 1841–1877*, 237.

15. George Bancroft. *The History of the United States from the discovery of the American Continent* Vol. 4 (Boston: Little, Brown, 1858): 150. See also Cheng, *The Plain and Noble Garb of Truth*, 176.

16. Emerson, *Selected Journals, 1820–1842*, 614–615.

17. Statement by John Jr. in Sanborn, *The Life and Letters of John Brown*, 91–93. Also captured in every other biography. The statement was reprinted in its entirety again in Ruchames, ed., *A John Brown Reader*, 174–175.

18. Qtd. in Oates, *To Purge This Land with Blood*, 23.

19. Salmon Brown, "My Father, John Brown," and Statement of James Foreman, Dec. 28, 1859, in Ruchames, ed., *A John Brown Reader,* 284, 171.

20. George Delamater, qtd. in Stephen B. Oates, *To Purge This Land with Blood: A Biography of John Brown,* 2nd ed. (Amherst: University of Massachusetts Press, 1984), 20.

21. Notes for a sermon in John Brown's handwriting. Boyd B. Stutler Collection, http://www.wvculture.org/history/wvmemory/jbdetail.aspx?Type=Text&Id=110

22. "Owen Brown's Autobiography," printed in Villard, *John Brown,* 14.

23. Redpath, *The Public Life of Capt. John Brown,* 25.

24. Richard Hofstadter, *Anti-Intellectualism in American Life* (New York: Vintage, 1966), 64–65, notes briefly Edwards's intellectual capacity before returning to the otherwise deplorable body of revivalism. In my estimation, the best characterization of the "Sinners" sermon—and whence the "Anger" came in that curious environment—was the charming title of a book review in *The Sewanee Review.* Richard W. Day, "Sinners in the Hands of an Angry Logic," *The Sewanee Review,* Vol. 49, no. 3 (July–Sept. 1941), 405–407.

25. *The Works of Jonathan Edwards: Volume 1: Freedom of the Will* (New Haven: Yale University Press, 2009), 137.

26. Ibid., 163.

27. John Locke, *An Essay Concerning Human Understanding,* Book II, ch. 21, sec. 17.

28. This was a theological position that John Brown employed at various times. Notably, during an episode in church in Franklin Mills, as well as at his trial. Emerson is also fond of using this phrase in his journals.

29. Russel B. Nye, *Great American Thinkers: George Bancroft* (New York: Washington Square Press, 1964), 119.

30. Bancroft's statement is quoted in numerous articles and books about Jonathan Edwards, including Vincent Tomas, "The Modernity of Jonathan Edwards," *The New England Quarterly* 25, no. 1 (March 1952): 60–84.

31. See Sam Harris, *Free Will* (New York: Free Press, 2012), for a rather simple treatment of this concept. In this case, Harris has made the entire concept comprehendible for the intellectually challenged by basing it largely upon research in neurology and clinical neuro-science. It might be refreshing, even groundbreaking, if it wasn't for the fact that the subject is illuminated more elegantly and convincingly by Edwards, Locke, Hume and Nietzsche. What Harris has accomplished in this essay is an act of linguistics, not of philosophy. This, however, is less an indictment of Harris than of his audience, though Harris neglects to mention Edwards even once, even in his chapter largely concerned with praise, blame and moral agency.

32. Hofstadter, *Anti-Intellectualism,* 96–97. By 1859, Methodism was the largest Protestant denomination.

33. Statement by James Foreman to James Redpath in Ruchames, ed., *A John Brown Reader,* 166. The questions could have been derived from the Westminster Catechism, the shorter of which is laid out in the form of 107 questions-and-answers. Intriguingly, the Westminster Catechism was presented to Parliament in 1648, the year of the Peace of Westphalia and the removal of historical causality from the "Heavenly City" to the absolutist state.

34. Notes for a sermon in John Brown's handwriting. Boyd B. Stutler Collection.

35. Recollections of James Foreman and George Delamater, in Ruchames, ed., *A John Brown Reader,* 163–173.

36. Notes for a sermon in John Brown's handwriting. Boyd B. Stutler Collection.

37. Letter, John Brown to his father, Aug. 11, 1832, in Ruchames, ed., *A John Brown Reader,* 41.

38. Duncan, "John Brown in Pennsylvania."

39. Letter, John Brown to Seth Thompson, Aug. 13, 1832. Photocopies in the KSHS John Brown Papers.

Chapter 5

1. Letter, John Brown to Seth Thompson, Aug. 13, 1832. Photocopies in the KSHS John Brown Papers. Foreman and Delamater in Ruchames, ed., *A John Brown Reader,* 164–173.

2. Villard, *John Brown,* 19.

3. Statement of James Foreman in Ruchames, ed., *A John Brown Reader.*

4. Villard, *John Brown,* 49.

5. Oates, *To Purge This Land with Blood,* 29–30.

6. Letter, John Brown to Frederick Brown (Dear Brother) Nov. 21, 1834, ibid., 42–43. Also Oates, *To Purge This Land with Blood,* 31–32.

7. Reminisces of Ruth Thompson, reprinted in Ruchames, ed., *A John Brown Reader,* 178.

8. Letter, John Brown to Frederick Brown (Dear Brother) Nov. 21, 1834, ibid., 42–43. This is the earliest document in Brown's handwriting regarding a plan to help liberate the slaves.

9. Ibid.

10. Oates, *To Purge This Land with Blood,* 31.

11. For an extended discussion of "benevolent supervision" and his arguments against colonizationists, see William Lloyd Garrison, *Thoughts on African Colonization* (Boston: Garrison and Knapp, 1832), e-book at, http://www.gutenberg.org/files/31178/31178-h/31178-h.htm, accessed March 2, 2012.

12. Letter, John Brown to Seth Thompson, March 1, 1834. Photocopies in the KSHS John Brown Papers.

13. Villard, *John Brown,* 23.

14. Oates, *To Purge This Land with Blood,* 40.

15. Ibid., 40.

16. Benjamin J. Klebaner, *American Commercial Banking: A History* (Washington, D.C.: Beard Books, 2005), 14.

17. Howe, *What Hath God Wrought,* 117.

18. DeWitt Clinton, qtd. ibid., 117.

19. Philip S. Foner, *History of the Labor Movement in the United States Vol. 1,* new ed. (New York: International Publishers, 1979), 55–56.

20. Business Agreement between John Brown and Seth Thompson, Jan. 13, 1836. Photocopies in the KSHS John Brown Papers.

21. See letter, John Brown to Dear Brother, Oct. 26, 1833, in Sanborn, *The Life and Letters of John Brown,* 26.

22. Oates, *To Purge This Land with Blood*, 35.
23. Letter, John Brown to Seth Thompson, Dec. 30, 1836. Photocopies in the KSHS John Brown Papers.
24. Emerson, *Selected Journals, 1820–1842*, 529.
25. Ibid., 525.
26. See Richard Hofstadter, *Anti-Intellectualism in American Life*, for a detailed description of the rise of deeply anti-intellectual spiritual self-help literature, antecedent to a comparable body of work today.
27. Emerson, *Selected Journals, 1820–1842*, 529.
28. Scott A. Sandage, *Born Losers: A History of Failure in America* (Boston: Harvard University Press, 2006), 6.
29. Lepler, "1837: Anatomy of a Panic," 140–143.
30. See Sandage, *Born Losers*.
31. For the origins of the word see Thomas K. McCraw, *Creating Modern Capitalism: How Entrepreneurs, Companies, and Countries Triumphed in Three Industrial Revolutions* (Cambridge: Harvard University Press, 1998), 3–8.
32. Harry E. Miller, "Earlier Theories of Crisis and Cycles in the United States," *The Quarterly Journal of Economics* 38, no. 2 (Feb. 1924): 294–329.
33. Ann Fabian, "Speculation on Distress: The Popular Discourse of the Panics of 1837 and 1857," *Yale Journal of Criticism* 3, no. 1 (Spring 1989): 127–42. Meteorological terms were in fact exceptionally popular, and remain so to the present day as a narrative device for "rationalizing" the irrational.
34. Fabian, "Speculation," 130.
35. Brown's most sympathetic biographers, notably Oates and Reynolds, have focused on the peculiarity of a man who believed in "signs and omens" and the intercession of Providence as mark of his folly, a folly multiplied by his own failure to heed the "signs" that were all about. Oates states that Brown "seems" to have been more reckless than the average speculator in a time marked by a wild lack of prudence and restraint. I fail to ascertain in any readings on the cultural/economic climate where he might "seem" to be so much more reckless, unless it is only in looking backwards from future incomprehensible events.
36. See Thomas Frank, *One Market Under God: Extreme Capitalism, Market Populism, and the End of Economic Democracy* (New York: Anchor, 2001) for an intriguing narrative about how this language and religious-like beliefs have filtered to the present in the form of modern-day market theodicies. Also, Hofstadter, *Anti-Intellectualism*, 253–298, for a description of the language of "religious self-help" and its fusion with market epistemology in the least intellectual quarters of religious capitalism.
37. Emerson, *Selected Journals, 1820–1842*, 527–528. Emerson did not describe the "Panic" of 1837 as a "panic." The term, as mentioned, was not available. Emerson's term was "crisis," a word that implies less moral judgment upon the individual actors within the system. Crisis rather implies judgment of the system itself.
38. Statement of John Jr. in Sanborn, *The Life and Letters of John Brown*, 88.
39. See Lepler, "1837: Anatomy of a Panic" for a description of how confidence and cultural beliefs ran the economy as much as—or more than—any theories that were actually formulated later to explain away what were essentially narrative beliefs covered in the language of science.
40. Emerson, *Selected Journals, 1820–1842*, 571.
41. Statement of John Jr. in Ruchames, ed., *A John Brown Reader*, 182.
42. Statement of John Jr., ibid., 182.
43. See Merton L Dillon, *Elijah P Lovejoy: Abolitionist* (Champaign: University of Illinois Press, 1961) for a detailed account.
44. Joseph C. Lovejoy and Owen Lovejoy, *Memoir of the Rev. Elijah P. Lovejoy: Who Was Murdered in the Defence of the Liberty of the Press, at Alton, Illinois*, reprint ed. (New York: John S. Taylor, 1838), 278–279.
45. Emerson, *Selected Journals, 1820–1842*, 529.
46. Henry Mayer, *All on Fire: William Lloyd Garrison and the Abolition of Slavery* (New York: St. Martin's Griffin, 2000), 237.
47. Emerson, *Selected Journals, 1820–1842*, 571.
48. See Oates, *To Purge This Land with Blood*, 42 for a discussion of this episode. The oath was first recalled in print in 1892 by the Reverend Edward Brown, a cousin of John Brown, in *The Northwestern Congregationalist*. The Reverend Brown's account is reprinted in Ruchames, ed., *A John Brown Reader*, 179–181.
49. Emerson, *Selected Journals, 1820–1842*, 568.
50. Letter, John Brown to Dear Wife and Children, Dec. 5, 1838. Boyd B. Stutler Collection.
51. Letter, John Brown to Dear Wife and Children, June 12, 1839, in Ruchames, ed., *A John Brown Reader*, 44–45.
52. W.E.B. DuBois, *John Brown* (Philadelphia: G.W. Jacob's, 1909), 50–51.
53. The sums and narrative have been documented in nearly every study of Brown since Villard's, and in some of the panegyrics. Observe the narrative weight of history, though: Many historians who sympathize with Brown won't use the word "stole." Others use it as welcome evidence of his perfidy. I use the word freely, but tag the additional description of "desperation" on for context. What then is truth? In this case I don't feel it matters; hungry people don't stay hungry for long, and Emerson has captured well enough the apocalyptic scale of the economic devastation for my satisfaction. The narrative weight goes beyond good and evil; it goes to freedom of the will. In this case, I believe that the system itself precluded any free will in this act all while basing itself on a lie of absolute free will.
54. Letter, John Brown to George Kellogg, Aug. 27, 1839, in Ruchames, ed., *A John Brown Reader*, 46.
55. Villard, *John Brown*, 37–41.
56. Oates, *To Purge This Land with Blood*, 46.
57. For further reading on early surveying, including the technology, tools, and schools, see Silvio A. Bedini, *Thinkers and Tinkers: Early American Men of Science* (New York: Scribner's, 1975).
58. See also Boyd B. Stutler, "John Brown and the Oberlin Lands," *West Virginia History* 12, no. 3 (April 1951): 183–99, available via the Boyd B. Stutler Collection.
59. See Villard, *John Brown*, 36–37 for a disposition of these suits.
60. Bankruptcy Inventory. John Brown, 1842 Sept. 28, U.S. District Court of Ohio; in the Boyd B. Stutler Collection.

61. Letter, John Brown to George Kellogg, Oct. 17, 1842. Qtd. in Ruchames, ed., *A John Brown Reader*, 49. Looking backwards with new theories, words and beliefs, one might decide that John Brown was a miserable businessman. His detractors have walked a fine line on this point, since to condemn Brown merely for the sin of being poor could be ethically compromising and therefore limit acceptance of the story, which in turn could be financially compromising in the realm of book sales. Robert Penn Warren was particularly unforgiving in narrating a transformation from business failure into murderous abolitionist; it is noteworthy that he wrote in an era which revered businessmen. It is the fall, not the poverty itself, which is thought to provide the insight into Brown's ethical and intellectual character. This, of course, is not without its irony. Warren—America's first poet laureate—published his volume in 1929, shortly before millions of Americans would have good reason to empathize with Brown, and material reasons not to buy the book. Sales were disappointing for Warren.

62. Foner, *The Story of American Freedom*, 50–51, 60.

63. Letter, John Brown to Dear Son John, July 24, 1843, in Sanborn, *The Life and Letters of John Brown*, 58–59.

64. Salmon Brown, *My Father, John Brown*. Reprinted in Ruchames, ed., *A John Brown Reader*, 184. Next quotation in a recollection penned by John Brown from the home of Gerrit Smith on Feb. 24, 1858, qtd. in Villard, *John Brown*, 322–3.

Chapter 6

1. Reminiscences of Ruth Brown Thompson, in Ruchames, ed., *A John Brown Reader*, 177–179.
2. Decaro, *Fire from the Midst of You*, 124.
3. Letter, Annie Brown to Garibaldi Ross, Dec. 15, 1887. Gilder Lehrman Collection.
4. Letter, John Brown to Dear Son John, Jan. 11, 1844, in Sanborn, *The Life and Letters of John Brown*, 59–60.
5. Letter, John Brown to John Jr., Jan. 11, 1844, in Ruchames, ed., *A John Brown Reader*, 52–53.
6. Account of Simon Perkins in Sanborn, *The Life and Letters of John Brown*, 57.
7. Letter, John Brown to Dear Afflicted Wife and Children, Nov. 8, 1846, in Ruchames, ed., *A John Brown Reader*, 56.
8. Letter, John Brown to Dear Mary, Nov. 29, 1846, ibid., 57.
9. Statement of John Jr. in Sanborn, *The Life and Letters of John Brown*, 88.
10. Decaro, *Fire from the Midst of You*, loc. 2449.
11. Ibid., loc 2465–2483.
12. Qtd. in Oates, *To Purge This Land with Blood*, 57.
13. The Erickson letter regarding John Brown's business first came to light in the Nevins account, which I regard with a great deal of scorn. "Childlike innocence" is a common deprecation applied to economic reformers who don't recognize the "natural law" of markets. It is also, ironically, the quality which a good capitalist is supposed to approach those markets with. Boyd Stutler believed that Erickson's assessment of Brown's business sense was agenda driven, since a class based pricing scheme, almost a progressive one, would have been detrimental to Erickson. See Boyd Stutler's correspondence with Stephen Oates at http://www.wvculture.org/history/wvmemory/images/jb/RP09–0110B.jpg.

14. Letter, John Brown to Dear Mary, March 7, 1847, in Ruchames, ed., *A John Brown Reader*, 59.
15. Letter, John Brown to John Jr. (Dear Son) ibid., 52–53.
16. Statement of George B. Delamater in Ruchames, ed., *A John Brown Reader*, 173.
17. Oates, *To Purge This Land with Blood*, 62.
18. Ibid., 63.
19. U.S. Department of the Interior, *Statistical View of the United States: Compendium of the Seventh Census*, open-file report, U.S. Geological Survey (Washington, DC, 1854).
20. See Ruchames, ed., *A John Brown Reader*, 66.

Brown wrote to Representative Joshua Giddings at this time in admiration, and to ask Giddings to sponsor this exhibit. It's unknown whether Giddings would have participated, as Brown's ability to pursue the plan was shortly pinched by previously described financial troubles.

21. Reprinted in Ruchames, ed., *A John Brown Reader*, 61–64.
22. Oates, *To Purge This Land with Blood*, 366.
23. Abby Kelley was an organizer for the American Anti-Slavery Society, and a prominent feminist activist, as many of Garrison's circle were.
24. Frederick Douglass, North Star, Feb. 11, 1848. Qtd. in Oates, *To Purge This Land with Blood*, 63.
25. Emerson, *Selected Journals 1841–1877*, 234.
26. Though it may get confusing, from this point the anti-slavery activities of Brown will often be referred to as "abolitionism." Brown did adopt the term occasionally, and there are few better ways to phrase it, repeating "eternal war with slavery" or "hatred of slavery" or the like would get tedious in short order.
27. Sanborn, *The Life and Letters of John Brown*, 96–97.
28. Foner, Labor 1, 57.
29. Oates, *To Purge This Land with Blood*, 67.

Chapter 7

1. Roger Boesche *Tocqueville's Road Map: Methodology, Liberalism, Revolution, and Despotism* (Lanham: Lexington Books, 2007) 85.
2. Fred Anderson, *Crucible of War: The Seven Years' War and the Fate of Empire in British North America, 1754–1766* (New York: Vintage, 2001), 7.
3. Emerson, *Selected Journals 1841–1877*, 197.
4. Fritz Stern, ed., *The Varieties of History: from Voltaire to the Present* (New York: Vintage, 1973), 57. The obeisance that early American historians paid to his seemingly unassailable position might be somewhat ironic, since as historian Peter Novick has noted, perhaps a better translation of his dictum is: "to show what *essentially* happened." See Peter Novick, *That Noble Dream: The "Objectivity" Question and the American Historical Profession* (Cambridge: Cambridge University Press, 1988), 21–31. Also Cheng, *The Plain and Noble Garb of Truth*, 162.

5. Hayden White, *Metahistory: The Historical Imagination in Nineteenth-Century Europe* (Baltimore: Johns Hopkins University Press, 1975) 149.
6. Qtd. ibid., 152.
7. Emerson, *Selected Journals 1841–1877*, 421.
8. White, *Metahistory*, 150–154.
9. Qtd. ibid., 158.
10. George Bancroft. *The History of the United States from the discovery of the American Continent* Volume 7 (Boston: Little, Brown, 1858): 295.
11. Carl L. Becker, *The Heavenly City of the Eighteenth Century Philosophers* (New Haven, CT: Yale University Press, 1951), 53–54.
12. See Eric Hobsbawm, *The Age of Revolution 1789–1848*, (New York: Vintage, 1996), 283–284.
13. Howe, *What Hath God Wrought*, 702–703.
14. Cheng, *The Plain and Noble Garb of Truth*, 18, 237.
15. Democratic Review 18 (June 1846), qtd. in Foner, *The Story of American Freedom*, 77.
16. David M. Potter, *The Impending Crisis, 1848–1861* (New York: Harper Perennial, 1977), 2.
17. Howe, *What Hath God Wrought*, 116, 792–795.
18. Timothy Mason Roberts, *Distant Revolutions: 1848 and the Challenge to American Exceptionalism* (Charlottesville: University of Virginia Press, 2009), 20.
19. Emerson, *Selected Journals 1841–1877*, 346.
20. Karl Marx, The Eighteenth Brumaire of Louis Napoleon.
21. Statement qtd. in Redpath, *The Public Life of Captain John Brown*, 56.
22. *Frederick Douglass Narrative of the Life of Frederick Douglass, an American Slave / My Bondage and My Freedom / Life and Times of Frederick Douglass: Autobiographies* (New York: Library of America, 1994).
23. Redpath, *The Public Life of Captain John Brown*, 56.
24. Statement, E.C. Leonard, in Sanborn, *The Life and Letters of John Brown*, 58.
25. Reminisces of Ruth Brown Thompson in Ruchames, ed., *A John Brown Reader*, 177.
26. Emerson, *Selected Journals 1841–1877*, 235.
27. Dana, "How We Met John Brown" *Atlantic Monthly*, 28 July 1871. Excerpted as well in Sanborn, *Life and Letters*, 102. It should be noted that Dana, who wrote the article *after* the Harper's Ferry raid, makes Brown's North Elba home a stop on the Underground Railroad and his two friends, fugitives. While this could have been most probable, it was also likely not possible, given that there were no "lines" through that location, and none of the local residents seemed to be fugitives. Brown was never of a character to join or invite organizations, and most historians do not believe that there was any "official" Underground Railroad activity there. Dana's 1849 journal does not mention any in his very brief account of the Brown house. See Robert F. Lucid, ed., *The Journal of Richard Henry Dana, Jr.*, Vol. 1 (Boston: Belknap Press of Harvard University, 1968), 364. Ruth Thompson (Brown) tells Franklin Sanborn in *Life and Letters* that the two who dined with them that night, Mr. Jefferson and Mrs. Wait, were not fugitives, but were neighbors. What really matters here is Brown's regard for them as human beings, not his work on Abolitionism. Dana would have been far more impressed in his journal at the time had this really been a "Railroad" stop, but he embellished the story later in order to both unite the Abolitionist cause in history and rationalize Brown's peculiar social habits.
28. Emerson, *Selected Journals 1841–1877*, 552.
29. Oates, *To Purge This Land with Blood*, 79.
30. Letter, Mary Brown to John Brown, Jr., Nov. 8, 1849. Boyd Stutler Collection.
31. "Words of Advice; Branch of the United States League of Gileadites, Adopted Jan. 15, 1851, as written and recommended by John Brown." Qtd. in Jonathan Earle, *John Brown's Raid on Harpers Ferry: A Brief History with Documents* (Boston: Bedford/St. Martin's, 2008), 43–47.
32. Letter, John Brown to John Jr., Feb. 21, 1853. John Brown, Jr., Papers, microfilm at KSHS, copies from Ohio State Historical Society via the Boyd B. Stutler Collection. Letter, John Brown to Ruth and Henry Thompson (Dear Children) May 10, 1853, in the Boyd B. Stutler Collection.
33. Letter, John Brown to John Jr. and Dear Children, Aug. 26, 1853, resumed on Sept. 13, 1853, in Ruchames, ed., *A John Brown Reader*, 81–83.
34. Letter, John Brown to Ruth and Henry Thompson (Dear Children) June 30, 1853, in Ruchames, ed., *A John Brown Reader*, 80–81.
35. Statement of John Brown, Jr., in Sanborn, *The Life and Letters of John Brown*, 88.
36. Emerson, *Selected Journals 1841–1877*, 326.
37. Lepler, "1837: Anatomy of a Panic," 27–28. For a look at the investment of the wider financial system in the markets of regional slave-trading, see: "An Abstract of the Lists of Debts Owed to the Bank of Virginia," referenced in a letter from Bacon Tait to R.C. Ballard, May 1, 1838, folder 24, Ballard Papers. Also, Harold D. Woodman, *King Cotton and His Retainers: Financing and Marketing the Cotton Crop of the South, 1800–1925 (Southern Classics Series)* (Columbia, SC: University of South Carolina Press, 1990).
38. Letter, John Brown to Frederick Douglass the Negro leader, Jan. 9, 1854, in *A John Brown Reader*, 84–5.
39. Redpath, *The Public Life of Capt. John Brown*, 58.
40. Letter, Anthony Burns to Richard Henry Dana, Jr., Aug. 23, 1855, at the Massachusetts Historical Society. http://www.masshist.org/longroad/01slavery/burns.htm#.
41. Susan Sutton Smith, ed., *Journals and Miscellaneous Notebooks of Ralph Waldo Emerson, Volume XIV: 1854–1861* (Boston: Belknap Press of Harvard University Press, 1978), 423.
42. Oates, *To Purge This Land with Blood*, 82.
43. Foner, *History of the Labor Movement in the United States Vol. 1*, 56.
44. James M. McPherson, *Battle Cry of Freedom: The Civil War Era* (New York: Oxford University Press, USA, 2003), 120. Not to disparage Lawrence's generosity, but by way of comparison, John Brown never sounded as crude in print or speech as that wealthy man.
45. Oates *To Purge This Land with Blood*, 83.
46. Emerson, *Selected Journals 1841–1877*, 625.
47. Letter, John Brown to Ruth and Henry Thompson (Dear Children) Sept. 30, 1854, in Ruchames, ed., *A John Brown Reader*, 86.

48. Letter, John Brown to John Jr. in Sanborn, *The Life and Letters of John Brown*, 191.
49. Letter, Salmon Brown to Mary Brown (Dear Mother, Brothers and Sisters) Aug. 16, 1855, in The Boyd B. Stutler Collection. http://www.wvculture.org/history/wvmemory/jbdetail.aspx?Type=Text&Id=712.

Chapter 8

1. Oates, *To Purge This Land with Blood*, 89–90.
2. Ibid., 90.
3. See Malin, *John Brown and the Legend of Fifty-Six*, chapters 3, 4, 6, 7, 8 and 9 for a fairly comprehensive review of the stories for which Kansas served as backdrop. At many levels, they were compelling and convincing fictions.
4. Dale E. Watts, "How Bloody Was Bleeding Kansas?" Kansas History: A Journal of the Central Plains 18, no. 2 (Summer 1995): 116–29.
5. W. Eugene Hollon, *Frontier Violence: Another Look* (New York: Oxford University Press, 1974), 75.
6. Watts, "How Bloody Was Bleeding Kansas?" 126. This is not to say that those men did not have names, but rather that whoever kept the records did not feel that their names were worth preserving.
7. Proceedings of the Convention of Radical Political Abolitionists, 1855. Boyd B. Stutler Collection.
8. Milton Meltzer. *Slavery: A World History* (New York: Da Capo Press, 1993), 225.
9. Proceedings, Boyd B. Stutler Collection.
10. Foner, *American Freedom*, 34.
11. Proceedings, Boyd B. Stutler Collection.
12. Proceedings. This observation is more or less in agreement with the population figures in the 6 and 7 United States Census.
13. Stephen B. Oates, *The Approaching Fury: Voices of the Storm, 1820–1861* (New York: Harper Perennial, 1998), 6.
14. Oates, *The Approaching Fury*, 7.
15. Proceedings; Boyd B. Stutler Collection Database.
16. Oates, *To Purge This Land with Blood*, 91.
17. Proceedings; Boyd B. Stutler Collection Database.
18. Ibid.
19. James Redpath, *The Public Life of Capt. John Brown: With an Auto-Biography of His Childhood and Youth* (Freeport, NY: Ayer, 1901), 26.
20. Proceedings; Boyd B. Stutler Collection Database.
21. John Brown. "Words of Advice: Branch of the United States League of Gileadites." Qtd. in Earle, *John Brown's Raid on Harpers Ferry*, 43.
22. Henry Mayer, *All on Fire: William Lloyd Garrison and the Abolition of Slavery* (New York: W. W. Norton, 2008), 308–310.
23. Proceedings; Boyd B. Stutler Collection Database.
24. Perhaps slightly more. It would appear that his benefactor, Gerrit Smith, personally contributed an additional $20 after the fact. See Oates, *To Purge This Land with Blood*, 90.

Chapter 9

1. Thomas Hobbes translation; deliberately both for his authorship of Leviathan, and for the absence of the word "revolution," such as appears in later translations. Hobbes chose other terms like sedition and insurrection, because he lived in a different age.
2. William Frank Zornow, *Kansas: A History of the Jayhawk State* (Norman: University of Oklahoma, 1971), 72.
3. Letter, John Jr. to John Brown, June 29, 1855. Qtd. in Oates *To Purge This Land with Blood*, 92.
4. C. S. Lewis, *Reflections on the Psalms* (Grand Rapids: Mariner Books, 1964), 77.
5. Psalms 18:7–15, 77:16–18, 97: 2–5.
6. Job 38–40.
7. Letter, John Jr. to John Brown, June 22, 1855. Kansas State Historical Society.
8. Ibid., and Letter, "John Brown to Dear Children," Feb. 13, 1855, in Sanborn *The Life and Letters of John Brown*, 192.
9. Henry Thompson's Statement to Franklin Sanborn in *Recollections I*, 128–129.
10. "An Act to Punish Offences Against Slave Property." Kansas State Historical Society, and Earle, *John Brown's Raid on Harpers Ferry*, 48.
11. T. H. Gladstone, *The Englishman in Kansas or Squatter Life and Border Warfare* (Lincoln: University of Nebraska Press, 1971), 14.
12. Letter, Wealthy and John Brown, Jr., to Mary Ann Brown, qtd. in Oates *To Purge This Land with Blood*, 102.
13. Ibid.
14. Letter, Wealthy Brown to Ruth Brown, June 12, 1855.
15. Salmon Brown, "My Father, John Brown." Qtd. in Ruchames, ed., *A John Brown Reader*, 186–187. This recollection also matches that given by Henry Thompson to Franklin Sanborn in *Recollections I*, 127–129.
16. Letter, John Brown to Father. Oct. 19, 1855. Brown-Gee Collection of John Brown Papers. Hudson Library and Historical Society.
17. John Brown, Letters to Wife and Children, Oct. 13, 1855, and Nov. 2, 1855. Kansas State Historical Society.
18. Letter, John Brown to Father, Oct. 19, 1855, in Ruchames, ed., *A John Brown Reader*, 88. Testimony of John Brown, Jr., to Franklin Sanborn in Sanborn, *The Life and Letters of John Brown*, 189–191.
19. John Brown papers, Kansas State Historical Society. The election is also briefly mentioned, along with commentary on the climate, in a letter, John Brown to his Father, Oct. 19, 1855.
20. Letter, John Brown to Dear Wife and Children, every one, Oct. 13, 1855. Kansas State Historical Society.
21. Ibid.
22. Letter, John Brown to his wife and children, Nov. 2, 1855, Kansas State Historical Society, Ellen's account is in Villard, *John Brown*, 112. Letter, John Brown to his Wife and Children, Nov. 20, 1855, Boyd Stutler Collection. Dispatch from Westport to E.C. McClarem, Nov. 27, 1855, in Sanborn, *The Life and Letters of John Brown*, 217.
23. See John Brown to the Akron *Summit Beacon*, Dec. 20, 1855, in Ruchames, ed., *A John Brown Reader*,

89–93. Also John Brown to the *Western Reserve Chronicle*, Dec. 22, 1855, in the Boyd Stutler Collection.

24. Ibid. Brown attributes the fact that they passed without molestation to the cowardly nature of bullies facing armed men capable of retaliating. He offers up a seemingly anecdotal story about that group later accosting an unarmed youth. While that story is feasible, it's uncertain how he could have known it was the exact same group. The distinction is of historical minutiae rather than of narrative integrity; to Brown it didn't matter—they were all largely the same.

25. Statement of G.W. Brown in Sanborn, *Recollections I*, 102.

26. Villard, *John Brown*, 121. Also the Lawrence *Herald of Freedom*, Oct. 29, 1859, in an article which tries to distance Kansas, and Lawrence, as far from John Brown as possible.

27. This was a later account by Henry Thompson, in Sanborn *Recollections I*, 129, and it may also be merging in memory with the Pottawatomie murders or even Harpers Ferry. It is entirely probable that such a brutal idea was conceived in the besieged city of Lawrence; in an environment of such urgency, under real and seemingly overwhelming siege, a mind as active as Brown's would have been questing for a way to break it. The *Herald of Freedom* relates a similar tale on Oct. 29, 1855.

28. William Addison Phillips, *The Conquest of Kansas by Missouri and Her Allies: A History of the Troubles in Kansas, from the Passage of the Organic Act Until the Close of July, 1856*, reprint (University of Toronto Libraries, 2011), 220–222.

29. Ibid.

30. Letter, John Brown to Orson Day, Dec. 14, 1855, Kansas State Historical Society. John Brown to the Akron *Summit Beacon*, Dec. 20, 1855, in Ruchames, ed., *A John Brown Reader*, 89–93.

31. John Brown letter to Wife and Children, Dec. 16, 1855. Kansas State Historical Society, Boyd Stutler Collection, Sanborn, *The Life and Letters of John Brown*, 217, and Earle, *John Brown's Raid on Harpers Ferry*, 51–55.

32. W. E. B. DuBois, *Black Reconstruction in America, 1860–1880* (New York: Free Press, 1998), 7.

33. Ibid., 8.

34. Ibid., 8.

35. Letter, Owen Brown to Samuel and Florella Adair, Aug. 8, 1855. Kansas State Historical Society.

Chapter 10

1. Letter, John Brown to Wife and Children, Dec. 16, 1855, Jan. 1, 1856, and Feb. 1, 1856.

2. Ibid. See also Sanborn, *The Life and Letters of John Brown*, 221–223.

3. Qtd. in Villard, *John Brown*, 127.

4. Letter, John Brown, Jr., to Friend Louisa, March 29, 1856. Boyd Stutler Collection.

5. Villard, *John Brown*, 130–131.

6. Letter, John Brown to Wife and Children, Feb. 1, 1856, in Ruchames, ed., *A John Brown Reader*, 93.

7. Kickapoo *Kansas Pioneer*, qtd. in Villard, *John Brown*, 129.

8. Oates, *To Purge This Land with Blood*, 114.

9. Letter, John Brown to Wife and Children, Feb. 1, 1856, in Ruchames, ed., *A John Brown Reader*, 93.

10. Letter, John Brown to Wife and Children, April 7, 1856. Kansas State Historical Society.

11. Oates, *To Purge This Land with Blood*, 118.

12. Alfred Vagts, *A History of Militarism* (Westport, CT: Greenwood Press Reprint, 1981), 136, 156–158. Though it sounds like "Social Darwinism," the term would be an anachronism since Darwin did not publish *On the Origin of Species* until 1859.

13. Alexis de Tocqueville, *The European Revolution and Correspondence with Gobineau* (New York: Doubleday, 1959), 227–229.

14. Alexis de Tocqueville, *Democracy in America* (New York: Library of America, 2004), 320.

15. Ibid., 349.

16. See Robert E. May, *Manifest Destiny's Underworld: Filibustering in Antebellum America* (Chapel Hill: University of North Carolina Press, 2004), The term itself came into the vernacular quite suddenly in the years 1848–1851, as Americans struggled to label the odd phenomenon. It was adopted from the French *flibutier* and the Spanish *filibustero*, both meaning "free-booter."

17. Jefferson Buford, letter in the Eufala *Spirit of the South*, Nov. 26, 1855.

18. Eli Thayer, *A History of the Kansas Crusade: Its Friends and Its Foes* (New York: Harper and Brothers, 1889) 175–177.

19. Foner, *History of the Labor Movement in the United States Vol. 1*, 259.

20. "Howard Report," *U.S. House Committee Reports*, 1855–1856, II. Affidavit of Mahala Doyle, June 7, 1856, and Villard, *John Brown*, 156.

21. Qtd. in Oates, *To Purge This Land with Blood*, 120–121. See also Villard, *John Brown*, 135–136, and Sanborn, *The Life and Letters of John Brown*, 228–230.

22. Malin, *John Brown and the Legend of Fifty-Six*, 559.

23. Sanborn, *The Life and Letters of John Brown*, 230.

24. Villard, *John Brown*, 142–143.

25. An appeal from the Lafayette (Missouri) Kansas Emigrant Society that appeared in *Debow's Review*, Volume 20, Issue 5, May 1856, 635–637, a journal for Southern plantation owners that covered agricultural and political matters.

26. In 1866 Hogback Ridge would be officially renamed "Mount Oread," a symbolically important geological feature to all University of Kansas students and alumni.

27. Walter L. Fleming, "The Buford Expedition to Kansas" *The American Historical Review*, Vol. 6, No. 1 (Oct. 1900) 38–48.

28. Oates, *To Purge This Land with Blood*, 125.

29. H.H. Williams, letter in the New York *Tribune*, Aug. 20, 1856. James Hanway, "Reminiscences," in Malin, *John Brown*, 329–330.

30. Ibid.

31. Statements of John Brown, Jr., and Salmon Brown in Villard, *John Brown*, 152. Letter, Salmon Brown to William E. Connelly, March 23, 1913, and May 28, 1913, Boyd Stutler Collection.

32. "Notes on the Pottawatomie Sword" by Herman M. Leonard concerning the swords used by John Brown's party in the Pottawatomie killings. In the

Boyd Stutler collection. Salmon describes the prepping of the weapons in a letter to William E. Connelly, May 28, 1913, Boyd Stutler Collection.

33. Sanborn *The Life and Letters of John Brown*, 264.

34. H.H. Williams, letter in the New York *Tribune*, Aug. 20, 1856. James Hanway, "Reminiscences," in Malin, *John Brown*, 329–330. Letter, Salmon Brown to William E. Connelly, March 23, 1913, and May 28, 1913, Boyd Stutler Collection.

35. This portion of the narrative has been the most contested of the entire story. The account given here, in the specifics if not in the motivations, is the sequence of events generally accepted. With certain disagreements, these specifics are seen in the affidavits of Mahala and John Doyle, James Harris and Louisa Jane Wilkinson in the "Howard Report," 1175–1182. Townsley's "confession" in the Lawrence *Daily Journal*, Dec. 10, 1879. Salmon Brown, "John Brown and Sons in Kansas Territory," *Indiana Magazine of History*. Vol. 31 (June 1935) 2:142–150. See also Mahala Doyle and Louisa Jane Wilkinson, "Accounts of the Pottawatomie Massacre," qtd. in Earle, *John Brown's Raid on Harpers Ferry*, 55–57.

36. Ibid., and Letter, Salmon Brown to William E. Connelly, May 28, 1913, Boyd Stutler Collection.

37. Reynolds has the body count at 28 free-state dead, 8 pro-slavery, 5 of whom perished by John Brown's hand. (April 20, 2005, interview on NPR.) It's uncertain where his figures are derived from. The best records of documented political killings in the territory, at the Kansas State Historical Society, indicate 25 free-state dead, 31 proslavery, 5 of those killed at Pottawatomie. See Dale E. Watts, "How Bloody Was Bleeding Kansas?" *Kansas History: A Journal of the Central Plains* 18, (Summer 1995) 2:116–29.

Chapter 11

1. Jason Brown's statement in Sanborn, *The Life and Letters of John Brown*, 273.

2. Letter, Jason Brown to F.G. Adams, April 2, 1884, Kansas State Historical Society. See also Villard, *John Brown*, 151–155.

3. Sanborn, *The Life and Letters of John Brown*, 273.

4. James Hanway, Journal entry June 1856, Hanway Papers, Kansas State Historical Society.

5. Statement of John Brown, Jr., in Sanborn, *The Life and Letters of John Brown*, 278–279.

6. *Autobiography of August Bondi (1833–1907)* (n.p.: Wagoner Printing, 1910), 113.

7. Ibid., 116.

8. Oates, *To Purge This Land with Blood*, 148.

9. Villard, *John Brown*, 142, 680.

10. August Bondi, "With John Brown in Kansas," *Kansas Historical Collection, 1903–1904* 8 (1904): 283–85.

11. Redpath, *Public Life of Capt. John Brown*, 112–114.

12. Walter L. Fleming, "The Buford Expedition to Kansas," 46.

13. Henry Thompson's statement in Sanborn, *Recollections I*, 130–132, Henry Pate's account in the New York *Tribune*, June 17, 1856. John Brown's rebuttal in the New York *Tribune*, July 11, 1856. And August Bondi's *Autobiography*. Also "Owen Brown's Account of the Fight at Black Jack" from the *Springfield Republican*, Jan. 14, 1889, Boyd Stutler Collection.

14. "Well, what do you think of this now?" Bondi called to him. "What should I think?" Weiner answered, amiably enough. "Man's life ends in death." August Bondi's account of the Battle of Black Jack, in the possession of the American Jewish Historical Society, qtd. in "Some Jewish Associates of John Brown," *The Magazine of History* 8 (July 1908): 1:210. The battle is better told by Aaron Kramer, *The Burning Bush: Poems and Other Writings (1940–1980)* (New York: Cornwall Books, 1983), "The Ballad of August Bondi," 205.

15. Henry Thompson's statement in Sanborn, *Recollections I*, 130–132, Henry Pate's account in the New York *Tribune*, June 17, 1856. John Brown's rebuttal in the New York *Tribune*, July 11, 1856. And August Bondi's *Autobiography*.

16. Ibid.

17. Report in Sanborn, *The Life and Letters of John Brown*, 301. The report is also with the Kansas State Historical Society. John Cook, who claimed to have been with the Old Man all the way from his middle creek camp until the breaking up of his band by Col. Sumner, was not on Brown's list. Brown appeared to have been very meticulous in recording those names. This, like many of Cook's movements, remains a mystery.

18. Prisoner exchange agreement drafted by John Brown, June 2, 1856, Kansas State Historical Society.

19. Letter, John Brown to Dear Wife and Children, June 1856, in Ruchames, ed., *A John Brown Reader*, 94–97.

20. Ibid.

21. Ibid.

22. The entire account of Phillips time with Brown is derived from W.A. Phillips, "Three Interviews with Old John Brown," originally published in the *Atlantic Monthly*, Dec. 1879, 738–744, qtd. in Ruchames, ed., *A John Brown Reader*, 208–218.

23. See Michael Lienesch, *New Order of the Ages: Time, the Constitution, and the Making of Modern American Political Thought* (Princeton, N.J.: Princeton University Press, 1988), for a detailed look at the horological and historical metaphors underpinning the Founders' political thought.

24. Hayden White, *Metahistory: The Historical Imagination in Nineteenth-Century Europe* (Baltimore: Johns Hopkins University Press, 1975), 40–48.

25. Galileo Galilei, *Discoveries and Opinions of Galileo*, trans. Stillman Drake (New York: Anchor, 1957). Excellent collection which includes both *The Starry Messenger* and *The Assayer*. This "revolution" incidentally gained its name-as-concept in the same manner as the Industrial one, though the word originated there.

26. Luther's enlisting of secular princes to his cause without any of the church's traditional safeguards between those monarchs and ecclesiastical power also helped to bring this occurrence about.

27. Becker, *The Heavenly City of the Eighteenth Century Philosophers*, 48–50.

28. Qtd. ibid., 56.

29. Ibid., 55–8.

30. Letter, John Jr. to Father, July 26, 1856. John Brown, Jr., Papers, Charles Frohman Collection.

31. Sanborn, *Recollections I*, 94.

32. Ibid., 95.
33. Letter, Aaron Stevens to Mrs. Spring in Hinton, *John Brown and His Men*, 499.
34. Sanborn, *Recollections I*, 96.
35. Letter, Lane to Robinson et al., Aug. 10, 1856, Letter, John Brown to Jason, Aug. 11, 1856, Kansas State Historical Society.
36. Sanborn, *The Life and Letters of John Brown*, 326–327.
37. Webb, *Life and Letters of Captain John Brown*, 423–426.

Chapter 12

1. John Brown's report, Sept. 7, 1856, in Sanborn, *The Life and Letters of John Brown*, 318–321. Samuel Adair, "Life of Frederick Brown," Kansas Collection, University of Kansas. "Kansas Experience of George Cutter," Jan. 1, 1857, Kansas State Historical Society. Villard, *John Brown*, 241–247.
2. Excerpt from a Missouri paper in Sanborn, *The Life and Letters of John Brown*, 321.
3. Villard, *John Brown*, 245–248.
4. Sarah Brown provides this added depth in Sanborn, *The Life and Letters of John Brown*, 322.
5. Sanborn, *The Life and Letters of John Brown*, 309, 321.
6. Villard, *John Brown*, 253–254.
7. Letter, John Brown to his family, Sept. 7, 1856, and "The Fight of Osawatomie in Sanborn," *The Life and Letters of John Brown*, 317–319.
8. Jason Brown's account in Sanborn, *The Life and Letters of John Brown*, 320.
9. Statement of John Brown, Jr., 1883, Boyd Stutler Collection.
10. Walter L. Fleming, "The Buford Expedition to Kansas," 46–48.
11. Letter, Charles Robinson to John Brown, Sept. 13, 1856, Kansas State Historical Society.
12. Allan Nevins, *Ordeal of the Union: A House Dividing 1852–1857* (New York: Scribner's, 1957), 482.
13. Ian Michael Spurgeon, *Man of Douglas, Man of Lincoln: The Political Odyssey of James Henry Lane* (Columbia: University of Missouri Press, 2008), 185–88.
14. Albert Castel, *Civil War Kansas: Reaping the Whirlwind*, Authorized ed. (Lawrence: University Press of Kansas, 1997), 43.
15. William E. Connelley, *A Standard History of Kansas and Kansans* (Chicago: Lewis Publishing, 1918), "Charles R. Jennison."
16. Reynolds, *John Brown*, 239–267.
17. Emerson, *Selected Journals 1841–1877*, 434.
18. Christian Wolmar, *Blood, Iron, and Gold: How the Railways Transformed the World*, Kindle Edition. (New York: PublicAffairs, 2010), loc. 1714. See also Larry A. Riney, *Hell Gate of the Mississippi, the Effie Afton Trial and Abraham Lincoln's Role in It*. Though it seems a minor thing, the bridging of the river was a powerfully symbolic act, networking the free-state northeast to the west while theoretically obstructing the slave-holding South's main line of commercial transportation. On May 6, 1856, 18 days before Pottawatomie, the steamboat *Effie Afton* ran into the bridge at full speed, and the ensuing fire and structural damage destroyed it, which did not stop the shipping company from suing the railroad for placing a bridge on the river. Here is where Abraham Lincoln enters the story, as an attorney for the railroad. The jury was tied in the end, which really meant that the railroad won; it had the capacity to rebuild the bridge and continue its westward integration, while the shipping company would not have survived long if it proposed to lose a ship for every act of protest. The Chicago and Rock Island line continued to steadily absorb and integrate branches, and reached Kansas City in 1879, linking with the Hannibal and St. Joseph lines. See Records held by legal counsel in Topeka, Kan., 1879–1933 (bulk 1880–1927), collection no 754, KSHS.
19. Emerson's journals X (ML), 184.
20. Allan Nevins, *Ordeal of the Union*, 156.
21. Sanborn describes Brown as "tall ... commanding," a point noteworthy in that EVERY account of Brown utilizes the adjective "tall" to describe him. He was, standing 5'9" or 5'10", but that didn't necessarily make of him a towering figure physically. The average adult male born in 1850 would grow to 5'7", and could expect to live to see 45. Certainly Brown's height was not enough to dominate memories by physical stature alone, though his age was somewhat exceptional for a life so hard. See Sanborn, *The Life and Letters of John Brown*, 341, 620–636, and *Recollections I*, 75, 83, 88. See Roderick Floud et al., *The Changing Body: Health, Nutrition, and Human Development in the Western World Since 1700* (Cambridge: Cambridge University Press, 2011).
22. Sanborn, *Recollections I*, 75–86.
23. Massachusetts Kansas Committee votes and minutes appropriating weapons, and receipts paid by Stearns, in the Boyd Stutler Collection. Stearns's testimony in the "Mason Report," 227–228.
24. Journal of Amos A. Lawrence, qtd. in Villard, *John Brown*, 273.
25. Mary Potter (Thacher) Higginson, *Thomas Wentworth Higginson: The Story of His Life* (1914; repr., Freeport, NY: Books for Libraries Press, 1972), 22–189.
26. Frank Preston Stearns, *The Life and Public Services of George Luther Stearns* (Philadelphia: J.B. Lippincott, 1907), 133–134.
27. Ibid., 134.
28. As is pointed out in William James Hoffer, *The Caning of Charles Sumner: Honor, Idealism, and the Origins of the Civil War* (Baltimore: Johns Hopkins University Press, 2010), 62.
29. Edward Baptist, "'Cuffy,' 'Fancy Maids,' and 'One-Eyed Men': Rape, Commodification, and the Domestic Slave Trade in the United States," *The American Historical Review*, vol. 106 (Dec. 2001) 5:1638–1640. Emphasis was in the original letter.
30. Crime Against Kansas.
31. Ibid.
32. David Herbert Donald, *Charles Sumner and the Coming of the Civil War* (Naperville, Ill.: Sourcebooks, 2009), 290–291.
33. Ibid., 293.
34. Emerson, speech at a meeting of the citizens in the town hall, Concord, May 26, 1856.
35. Reynolds, *John Brown, Abolitionist*, loc. 3316.
36. Hoffer, *The Caning of Charles Sumner*, 83.

37. Oates, *To Purge This Land with Blood*, 192.
38. Salmon Brown, "John Brown and Sons in Kansas Territory," in Ruchames, ed., *A John Brown Reader*, 192.
39. Letter, Annie Brown to Oswald Garrison Villard, March 25, 1908, Oswald Garrison Villard Papers.
40. Ralph Harlow, "Gerrit Smith and the John Brown Raid," *The American Historical Review* 38 (Oct. 1932) 1:32–34.
41. Reminiscences of Ruth Brown-Thompson, in Ruchames, ed., *A John Brown Reader*, 179.
42. Statements of Annie Brown in Sanborn, *The Life and Letters of John Brown*, 387, and Villard, *John Brown*, 277.

Chapter 13

1. Emerson, *Selected Journals 1841–1877*, 150–151.
2. See John Brown's "An Idea of Things in Kansas," in Earle, *John Brown's Raid on Harpers Ferry*, for Brown's notes for his more refined presentation regarding his travels in Kansas.
3. Sanborn, *The Life and Letters of John Brown*, 372–373. Brown's Feb. 18, 1857, speech to the Massachusetts legislative committee is in the Boyd Stutler Collection.
4. Charles W. Calomiris and Larry Schweikart, "The Panic of 1857: Origins, Transmission and Containment," *The Journal of Economic History* 51 (Dec. 1991) 1:Table 1, 812.
5. For instance, Amos Lawrence had given Brown a sum of $70 for his "personal use," and had stipulated that it actually not be used "for the cause in any other way than that." Letter, Amos Lawrence to John Brown, Feb. 19, 1857, Kansas State Historical Society.
6. Emerson, *Works* Vol. 11, 208, and Sanborn, *Recollections I*, 112.
7. Ibid., 198.
8. John Brown, March 4, 1857, in *The New York Tribune*, in Ruchames, ed., *A John Brown Reader*, 102.
9. Connecticut speech by John Brown, in Ruchames, ed., *A John Brown Reader*, 101.
10. Letter, John Brown to Wife and Children, March 12, 1857, Kansas State Historical Society, and John Brown to John Jr., April 15, 1857, Boyd Stutler Collection.
11. Statement of Hugh Forbes in the *New York Herald*, Oct. 27, 1859.
12. Villard, *John Brown*, 285.
13. Letter, John Brown to Mary Brown, March 31, 1857, Boyd Stutler Collection.
14. John Brown, "Old Browns Farewell," in Ruchames, ed., *A John Brown Reader*, 106.
15. Letter, John Brown to John Jr., April 15, 1857, Boyd Stutler Collection.
16. John Jr. to John Brown, April 23, 1857, in Villard, *John Brown*, 290–291.
17. Emerson, *Selected Journals, 1820–1842*, 434.
18. Ibid., 424.
19. Emerson, *Selected Journals 1841–1877*, 65–67.
20. Ibid., 121. Peter Norberg, ed., *Essays and Poems by Ralph Waldo Emerson* (New York: Fine Creative Media, 2004), "Experience," 234.
21. Emerson, *Journals*, 210, in an entry titled *The New John Baptist*.
22. Emerson, *Selected Journals 1841–1877*, 674 and "Speech on Affairs in Kansas."
23. Ibid., 100.
24. *Journals*. Emerson was in fact so fond of this statement, that he utilized it himself in the essay "Courage" later published in *Society and Solitude*: "Nature has made up her mind that what cannot defend itself shall not be defended. Complaining never so loud and with never so much reason is of no use. One heard much cant of peace-parties long ago in Kansas and elsewhere, that their strength lay in the greatness of their wrongs, and dissuading all resistance, as if to make this strength greater. But were their wrongs greater than the negro's? And what kind of strength did they ever give him? It was always invitation to the tyrant, and bred disgust in those who would protect the victim." What is most intriguing is that he was still using Brown's words *after* the war ... at least for a time.
25. These ideas were in Emerson's "Harvard Divinity School Address," given in 1838 as he was searching out the words and ideas that surfaced in his first series of famous Essays, which included "Self-Reliance."
26. Emerson, as recounted in his speech on Nov. 18, 1859, in Boston. *Works*, Vol. 11, 268.
27. Emerson, *Selected Journals 1841–1877*, 688.
28. These disagreements seem to appear in Forbes's recollections after the fact. While we are again getting into the basis of historical memory, at a purely subjective level Forbes does not strike one as the most forthright individual. Furthermore, he had motive to play up an angle of his "rational" plot versus Brown's doomed scheme. First, his name was all over it; after the failure of the Harpers Ferry raid, Forbes's manual was found in Brown's cabin. Not many were in the business of associating themselves with that raid immediately after the fact. Second, his name was all over a failed plot, hardly good marketing for a man who wished to sell his services as a sort of mental mercenary; he later popped up in Italy, once again peddling his services to Garibaldi. See Forbes in the *New York Herald*, Oct. 27, 1859, and the *New York Times*, Oct. 28, 1859.
29. Oates, *To Purge This Land with Blood*, 214.
30. Villard, *John Brown*, 293.
31. Testimony of H.B. Hurd in "The Mason Report," 245.
32. Calomiris and Schweikart, "The Panic of 1857," 817.
33. Ibid., Table 1.
34. Paul Finkelman, "Scott V. Sandford: The Court's Most Dreadful Case and How It Changed History," *Chicago-Kent Law Review* 3 (2007): 82.
35. John Missall and Mary Lou Missall, *The Seminole Wars: America's Longest Indian Conflict* (Gainesville: University Press of Florida, 2004), 21–27.
36. Ibid., 28–32.
37. Scott v. Emerson, 15 Mo. 576, 586 (Mo. 1852), retrieved Nov. 17, 2012.
38. Earl M. Maltz, *Dred Scott and the Politics of Slavery* (Lawrence: University Press of Kansas, 2007), 115.
39. Letter, Forbes to Howe, May 14, 1858, in *New York Herald*, Oct. 27, 1859.

40. Letter, John Brown to Samuel Adair, Nov. 17, 1857, in Villard, *John Brown*, 306.

Chapter 14

1. "Confession" of John E. Cook in Hinton, *John Brown and His Men*, 700–701.
2. See Hinton, *John Brown and His Men*, 453–504, Villard, *John Brown*, 679–691, and Letter, Annie Brown to Garibaldi Ross, Dec. 15, 1887, Gilder Lerhman Collection.
3. W. A. Phillips, "Three Interviews with Old John Brown," in Ruchames, ed., *A John Brown Reader*, 213–215, and "Confession" of John E. Cook in Hinton, *John Brown and His Men*, 700–701.
4. Owen recorded much of this encampment and the subsequent travels in his journal, to include instances where his irritable father vented at him for minor oversights. Dating from Aug. 25–Dec. 8, 1857, portions were published in the *New York Times*, Oct. 24, 1859. Letter, John Brown to Wife and Children, Dec. 30, 1857, Boyd Stutler Collection.
5. *The Life and Times of Frederick Douglass* (Mineola, NY: Dover Publications, 2003), 318–321.
6. Letter, John Brown to Mary Brown, Jan. 30, 1858, in Sanborn, *The Life and Letters of John Brown*, 440–441.
7. Letter, Franklin Sanborn to John Brown, Jan. 12, 1858, and Sanborn, *The Life and Letters of John Brown*, 427–428.
8. Letter, John Brown to John Jr., Feb. 9, 1858, in Sanborn, *The Life and Letters of John Brown*, 432–433.
9. Letter, Higginson to Brown, Feb. 7, 1858.
10. Letter, Brown to Higginson, Feb. 12, 1858.
11. Sanborn, *Recollections I*, 143, and *The Life and Letters of John Brown*, 436–438.
12. Sanborn, *Recollections I*, 145–148.
13. Sanborn, *Recollections 1*, 150–151. Emphasis added. Certainly Sanborn would not miss the intent of this very deliberate statement. He later referred to it as "prophetic," and cherished this letter always.
14. Ibid.
15. Joshua Giddings Papers, Ohio Historical Society.
16. Sanborn, *The Life and Letters of John Brown*, 451, and Hinton, *John Brown and His Men*, 169.
17. Letter, John Brown to John Jr., April 8, 1858, Boyd Stutler Collection.
18. The "Mason Report" contains a great deal on the Chatham Convention, including John Kagi's "Journal of the Chatham Convention," the testimony of Richard Realf, and the Provisional Constitution. Osborn Anderson gives a brief account in *A Voice from Harper's Ferry*, 9.
19. It would be presented at his trial by his own lawyer, Samuel Chilton, as evidence of his insanity. It was, in Chilton's words: "ridiculous nonsense—a wild, chimerical production" that "could only be produced by men of unsound minds." See Reynolds, *John Brown: Abolitionist*, 249.
20. The full text of Brown's Provisional Constitution is in Jonathan Earle, *John Brown's Raid On Harpers Ferry*, 65 Also http://law2.umkc.edu/faculty/projects/ftrials/johnbrown/brownconstitution.html.
21. James Cleland Hamilton. *John Brown in Canada: A Monograph* (Canadian Magazine, 1894), 15.
22. Sanborn, *The Life and Letters of John Brown*, 456.
23. William Seward's testimony in the "Mason Report."
24. Ironically, this wild accusation contains a subtle awareness of broader social and economic truths. Though Amos Lawrence did not help to fund the establishment of the city of Lawrence as a speculative venture—he did so out of outrage over the Anthony Burns affair—the ensuing speculation on the railroad made possible, indirectly, by the Kansas imbroglio certainly enriched many of the northeast capitalist class, which would of necessity include Amos Lawrence.
25. Letter, Senator Henry Wilson to Dr. Howe, May 9, 1858, in Villard, *John Brown*, 339.
26. Letter, Gerrit Smith to Franklin Sanborn, May 7, 1858.
27. Sanborn, *Recollections I*, 157–158, *The Life and Letters of John Brown*, 462–466, Higginson's memorandum on June 1, 1858, Higginson Papers.
28. Letter, Realf to "Dear Uncle" (John Brown), May 21, 1858, Kansas State Historical Society.

Chapter 15

1. According to Dale E. Watts, in "How Bloody Was Bleeding Kansas," the *political* body count at this time stood at 51.
2. Chas Blair, Letter to John Brown dated Aug. 27, 1857. Kansas State Historical Society.
3. Letter, John Brown to John Jr., in Villard, *John Brown*, 354–355.
4. Statement of Eli Snyder in Villard, *John Brown*, 357.
5. James Hanway to Richard Hinton, Dec. 5, 1859, Kansas State Historical Society.
6. Villard, *John Brown*, 358.
7. James Hanway to James Redpath, March 12, 1860, Kansas State Historical Society.
8. James Hanway, statement in December 1879, in Sanborn, *The Life and Letters of John Brown*, 280.
9. The entire conversation to follow is adapted from W. A. Phillips, "Three Interviews with Old John Brown," in Ruchames, ed., *A John Brown Reader*, 215–218. Originally printed in *The Atlantic*, a magazine that Ralph Waldo Emerson occasionally wrote for.
10. Gill, "Reminiscences," and Letter to F.G. Adams, Aug. 15, 1883, Kansas State Historical Society.
11. Ibid.
12. Villard, *John Brown*, 368.
13. Ibid., 369. Furthermore, while there are numerous stories of Brown taking property, there are zero accounts that he personally enriched himself doing so, and he was a man in dire need of enrichment. Additionally, he had never concerned himself with personal household effects, but rather with things that held more of a utilitarian value. If he had studied Napoleon as thoroughly as he claimed, this was likely to be expected. One of the great innovations of the emperor was to disperse and time coordinate his *Grand Armée*, allowing them to live off the land en route to the objective, rather than worry

about provisioning all of them for the entire march. "Live off the land" is really a rather clinical way to say plunder.
14. Villard, *John Brown*, 369.
15. Crawford to Eli Thayer, Aug. 4, 1879, Kansas State Historical Society.
16. John Brown, "Old Brown's Parallels," in Sanborn, *The Life and Letters of John Brown*, 481, and Earle, *John Brown's Raid on Harpers Ferry*, 62.
17. Testimony of Augustus Wattles in the "Mason Report."
18. Gill, "Reminiscences," and Letter to Richard Hinton, July 7, 1893, Kansas State Historical Society. Gill was awed by Brown's incredible endurance and willpower.
19. "The Battle of the Spurs and John Brown's Exit from Kansas," written by L.L. Kiene of Topeka, Kansas, for the Kansas State Historical Society. Originally printed in *Transactions of the Kansas State Historical Society*, Vol. 8, 1903–1904.
20. Ibid.
21. Ibid.
22. Ibid.
23. Letter, William F. Creitz to James Redpath, Dec. 17, 1859. Kansas State Historical Society.
24. Webb, *The Life and Letters of Captain John Brown*, 124.
25. Hinton, *John Brown and His Men*, 224.
26. Redpath, *The Public Life of Captain John Brown*, 224.
27. Letter, John Kagi to Friend Phillips, Feb. 7, 1859. Kansas State Historical Society.
28. Sanborn, *The Life and Letters of John Brown*, 491–492.
29. Gill, "Reminiscences," and Letter to Richard Hinton, July 7, 1893, Kansas State Historical Society.
30. W.E.B. DuBois, *John Brown* (Philadelphia: G.W. Jacob's, 1909), 114. Of course, Brown was not over six feet tall. Someone has again remembered him as a bit more than a man.
31. Sanborn, *The Life and Letters of John Brown*, 489. McPherson also remarks on Brown's fatalism regarding the gloomy outlook for the Harpers Ferry attack in *Battle Cry of Freedom*, pp. 205, referencing this letter. He seems to be passing along the conclusion reached by Oates. It is hard to argue with Oates, yet Sanborn viewed it in context as speech notes. Sanborn may have heard a version of the speech, but he doesn't say, and he wasn't present on this journey or in Chatham.
32. Ibid., 491.
33. Villard, *John Brown*, 684–686.
34. Letter, Higginson to John Brown, May 1, 1859.
35. Sanborn, *Recollections I*, 163–164.
36. Katherine Mayo interview with Mrs. Russell, qtd. in Ruchames, ed., *A John Brown Reader*, 237.
37. Inscription preserved in Ruchames, ed., *A John Brown Reader*, 103. Also (and probably originally for the record), in Thomas Wentworth Higginson, "A Visit to John Brown's Household in 1859."

Chapter 16

1. Letter, Jeremiah Anderson to his Brother, Sept. 1859, in Hinton, *John Brown and His Men*, 547.
2. Sanborn, *The Life and Letters of John Brown*, 551.
3. Merritt Roe Smith, *Harpers Ferry Armory and the New Technology: The Challenge of Change* (Ithaca, NY: Cornell University Press, 1980), 191.
4. Ibid., 206.
5. That was the assessment of Annie Brown, as she wrote to Garibaldi Ross on Dec. 15, 1887.
6. Statement of Annie Brown in "Kennedy Farm Notes," Oswald Garrison Villard John Brown Papers.
7. Villard, *John Brown*, 419–420.
8. Statement of Anne Brown in Sanborn, *Recollections I*, 173.
9. Sanborn, *Recollections I*, 177, and Letter, Annie Brown to Richard Hinton, May 23, 1893, Kansas State Historical Society.
10. Letter fragment, Annie Brown to Alexander Ross, Undated, Gilder Lehrman Collection #: GLC03007.49 and Statement of Annie Brown in Villard, *John Brown*, 417–420.
11. Statement of Annie Brown Adams, Chicago Historical Society.
12. Statement of Annie Brown in Sanborn, *Recollections I*, 173.
13. Statement of Annie Brown, in Sanborn, *Recollections I*, 152. Oddly, Harpers Ferry is *not* one of the cities he wrote down in the notebook he kept in Kansas.
14. Letter, Annie Brown to Richard Hinton, June 7, 1894, Kansas State Historical Society.
15. Sanborn, *Recollections I*, 183.
16. Letter, Owen "Smith" to Dear Sir, Aug. 18, 1859, in Villard, *John Brown*, 416.
17. Decaro, *Fire from the Midst of You*, 124.
18. Osborne Anderson, *A Voice from Harpers Ferry*, 23.
19. Frederick Douglass *Narrative of the Life of Frederick Douglass, an American Slave / My Bondage and My Freedom / Life and Times of Frederick Douglass: Autobiographies* (New York: Library of America, 1994), 158–160.
20. Ibid., 350–354. Annie Brown claimed in her letter to Garibaldi Ross that Douglass had paid Green to take his place. If so, it would be a most unfortunate stain on Douglass's legacy. Unless it was personal conjecture, the only place Annie would have learned this information would have been from Green, and Green never told anyone else. It may just be the Annie's residual bitterness at Douglass for not standing with her father when he was prepared to face death.
21. Letters, Harriett Newby to Dangerfield Newby, April 11, 22, and Aug. 16, 1859, *Calendar of Virginia State Papers*, 310–311.
22. Statement of Annie Brown, Chicago Historical Society.
23. Letter, John Brown to Wife and daughters, Oct. 1, 1859, in Sanborn, *The Life and Letters of John Brown*, 550.

Chapter 17

1. Oates, *To Purge This Land with Blood*, 280.
2. Thomas Paine, *Common Sense and Other Writings*, ed. Gordon S. Wood (New York: Modern Library, 2003).
3. Brown's Declaration. Emphasis added.

4. Letter, John Kagi to John Brown, Jr., Oct. 10, 1859, in Villard, *John Brown*.
5. Letter, Franklin Sanborn to Thomas Wentworth Higginson, Oct. 6, 1859.
6. Oates, *To Purge This Land with Blood*, 287.
7. Franklin B. Sanborn, *The Life and Letters of John Brown*, 546. Osborne Anderson, *A Voice from Harpers Ferry*, 32. I have often wondered if it was Frederick's cap he placed on his head.
8. Testimony of Daniel Whelan, "Mason Report," Boyd Stutler Collection.
9. Testimony of Lewis Washington, "Mason Report," Boyd Stutler Collection.
10. Statement of W.W. Throckmorton, *New York Herald*, Oct. 24, 1859.
11. Robert M. DeWitt, *The life, trial, and execution of Captain John Brown, known as "Old Brown of Ossawatomie": with a full account of the attempted insurrection at Harper's Ferry: compiled from official and authentic sources, including Cooke's confession, and all the incidents of the execution* (New York: R.M. DeWitt, Publisher, 1859), 69.
12. Mary Johnson, "An 'Ever Present Bone of Contention': The Heyward Shepherd Memorial," *West Virginia History* 56 (1997): 1–26., available at http://www.wvculture.org/history/journal_wvh/wvh56-1.html. This is a fantastic article about how southerners attempted to claim the memory of Heyward Shepherd not only to impugn Brown for having caused a black casualty, but also as an example of their bizarre myth of the docile and properly loyal slave.
13. A.J. Phelps to W.P. Smith, Oct. 17, 1859, *Correspondence Relating to the Insurrection at Harper's Ferry* (Annapolis: B.H. Richardson, 1860).
14. Alexander Boteler, "Recollections of the John Brown Raid by a Virginian Who Witnessed the Fight," *Century Magazine* 26 (July 1883): 405.
15. "Some personal recollections of 'John Brown's Raid' by an Eyewitness" Harpers Ferry National Historic Park.
16. Letter, Harriett Newby to Dangerfield Newby, Aug. 16, 1859. *Governor's Message and Reports of the Public Officers of the State, of the Boards of Directors, and of the Visitors, Superintendents, and Other Agents of Public Instruction or Interests of Virginia* (Richmond, 1859), 116–117. Special Collections, Library of Virginia, Richmond, Virginia.

Chapter 18

1. *New York Times*, Oct. 26, 1859.
2. Testimony of Joseph Brua, *New York Tribune*, Oct. 29, 1859.
3. *The* (Baltimore) *Sun*, Oct. 19, 1859.
4. Letter, Mary Mauzy to Daughter, Oct. 17, 1859, Harpers Ferry National Historic Park, and John Copeland to Addison Halbert, Dec. 10, 1859, "The John Brown Letters Found in the Virginia State Library in 1901," *Virginia Magazine of History and Biography* 10, (Oct. 1902) 2:170.
5. *New York Times*, Oct. 26, 1859.
6. *New York Tribune*, Oct. 29, 1859.
7. Statement of Edwin Coppoc, Nov. 22, 1859, in Hinton, *John Brown and His Men*, 488.
8. "Terms of Surrender," Col. Baylor to Gov. Wise, Oct. 22, 1859, *Governor's Message and Reports of the Public Officers of the State* (Richmond: William Ritchie, Aug. 1859.
9. Letter, Mary Mauzy to Daughter, Oct. 17, 1859, Harpers Ferry National Historic Park. *Richmond Daily Dispatch*, Oct. 20, 1859. Testimony of Terrence Byrne, "Mason Report." *Baltimore Clipper*, Oct. 20, 1859.
10. Boteler, "Recollections of the John Brown Raid," 407. *New York Herald*, Oct. 24, 1859. In July of 1857 As for Stuart's Kansas background, he was wounded in the U.S. Army's campaign of extermination against the Cheyenne. His commander, Edwin Sumner, went on to destroy the Cheyenne village.
11. Ibid., 407.
12. Israel Green, "The Capture of John Brown," *The North American Review* (Dec. 1885). Also Emory M. Thomas, "The Greatest Service I Rendered the State: J. E. B. Stuart's Account of the Capture of John Brown," *The Virginia Magazine of History and Biography* 94, no. 3 (July 1986): 345–57, and Lewis Washington's testimony in the "Mason Report."
13. Joseph Barry, *Strange Story of Harpers Ferry* (Shepherdstown, WV: Woman's Club of Harpers Ferry District, 1984), 80.
14. Letter, C.W. Tayleure to John Brown, Jr., June 15, 1879, Kansas State Historical Society.
15. *New York Herald*, Oct. 21, 1859.
16. *Baltimore American*, Oct. 21, 1859.
17. *Baltimore American*, Oct. 21, 1859. As far as his quote on gods and madness: *Quem deus vult perdere, dementat prius.* Imperfectly educated or not, this is an interesting choice of quotes. Misattributed to the Greek tragedian Euripides, it was quoted in the book *Daniel, a Model for Young Men* (1854) by William Anderson Scott, as a "heathen proverb." The book may have been among the materials at the Kennedy Farm that his own young men read from. The origin of the misattribution is unknown, though earlier variants exist. "Quem Iuppiter vult perdere, dementat prius" was a neo–Latin variant of obscure origin that may have been coined in Cambridge around 1640.
18. This proclamation is quoted in nearly every biography of John Brown, as the prophetic summation of his post-capture public questioning.

Chapter 19

1. Letter, Mary Mauzy to Daughter, Oct. 17, 1859. Harper's Ferry National Historic Park. Also *Richmond Daily Dispatch*, Oct. 20, 1859.
2. Letter, George Mauzy to Burtons, Dec. 3, 1859. Harper's Ferry National Historic Park. For brief biographies and the disposition of the bodies, see, Thomas Featherstonhaugh, "The Final Burial of the Followers of John Brown," Boyd Stutler Collection. Originally in *New England Magazine*, April 1901. W.P. Smith to J.W. Garrett, Oct. 18, 1859, *Correspondence Relating to the Insurrection at Harper's Ferry.*
3. *Baltimore American*, Oct. 21, 1859.
4. Testimony of Archibald Kitzmiller in the Mason Report, Boyd Stutler Collection.
5. Joseph G. Rosengarten, "John Brown's Raid: How I Got into It and How I Got Out of It," June 1865. See also Henry Wise, "Comments in Richmond, Virginia," Oct. 21, 1859, Boyd Stutler Collection.

6. Emerson, *Selected Journals 1841–1877*, 436.
7. *National Era*, Nov. 3, 1859.
8. Brian McGinty, *John Brown's Trial* (Cambridge, Mass.: Harvard University Press, 2009), 82.
9. Records of Jefferson Co. Circuit Court Clerk's Office, Boyd Stutler Collection.
10. John William Willis Bund, *A Selection of Cases from the State Trials Volume 1* (New York: RareBooks Club.com, 2012), 194.
11. Sir Matthew Hale, *The History of the Pleas of the Crown* (Philadelphia: Robert H. Small, 1847), 53.
12. Ibid.
13. http://supreme.justia.com/cases/federal/us/1/53/.
14. *The Baltimore Sun*, 22 Oct. 1859.
15. J.E. Norris, *History of the Lower Shenandoah Valley* (Chicago: A. Warner, 1890), 443–444.
16. George Caskie, "The Trial of John Brown," *Virginia State Bar Association Twenty-Second Report* (1909): 276.
17. *New York Herald*, Nov. 10, 1859.
18. John Brown's opening remarks to the Virginia Court, qtd. in Earle, *John Brown's Raid on Harpers Ferry*, 85–86.
19. Robert De Witt, *The Life, Trial and Execution of Captain John Brown*, 8. Also Earle, *John Brown's Raid on Harpers Ferry*, 86.
20. William Rasmussen and Robert Tilton, *The Portent: John Brown's Raid in American Memory* (Richmond: Virginia Historical Society, 2009), 39. *New York Times*, Nov. 3 and Nov. 21, 1859. *New York Tribune*, Oct. 19, 1859. *Liberator*, Oct. 21, 1859.
21. Henry David Thoreau, "A Plea for Captain John Brown."
22. *New York Herald*, Nov. 1, 1859. The full report of the trial, including speeches and testimony, can also be found at http://law2.umkc.edu/faculty/projects/ftrials/johnbrown/browntrial.html.
23. *New York Tribune*, Nov. 5, 1859.
24. *New York Herald*, Nov. 3, 1859.
25. *New York Tribune*, Nov. 5, 1859.
26. John Brown's last address to the Virginia Court, qtd. in Earle, *John Brown's Raid on Harpers Ferry*, 86–87.
27. Jefferson County Court Records, Boyd Stutler Collection and Oswald Garrison Villard John Brown Papers.
28. *New York Tribune*, Nov. 5, 1859.

Chapter 20

1. Henry David Thoreau, "The Last Days of John Brown."
2. Letter, John Brown to Mary Brown, Nov. 10, 1859, in Villard, *John Brown*, 540.
3. Letter, John Brown to Wife and Children, Nov. 8, 1859, in Sanborn, *The Life and Letters of John Brown*, 586.
4. Letter, John Brown to Jeremiah Root, Nov. 12, 1859, in Ruchames, ed., *A John Brown Reader*, 142.
5. Letter, John Brown to Dear Friend E.B., Nov. 1, 1859, in Earl, *John Brown's Raid on Harpers Ferry*, 90.
6. Letter, John Brown to Rev. H.L. Vaill, Nov. 15, 1859, ibid., 93.
7. Letter, John Brown to Rev. Luther Humphrey, Nov. 19, 1859, ibid., 95.
8. Letter, John Brown to Hon. D.R. Tilden, Nov. 28, 1859, ibid., 99–100.
9. Telegraph, George Sennott to Thomas Wentworth Higginson, Nov. 5, 1859. Letter, George Hoyt to Mary Brown, Nov. 11, 1859. Boyd Stutler Collection.
10. Letter, John Brown to Higginson, Nov. 4, 1859, in Earle, *John Brown's Raid on Harpers Ferry*, 91, and John Brown to Family, Nov. 8, 1859.
11. Letter, John Brown to Devoted Wife, Nov. 10, 1859, Oswald Garrison Villard John Brown Papers.
12. Letter, Gov. Henry Wise to Lydia Maria Child, Oct. 29, 1859.
13. Letter, Lydia Maria Child to Gov. Henry Wise, Undated, 1859.
14. Governor Henry Wise, "Message to the Virginia Legislature," December 5, 1859, in *John Brown's Raid on Harpers Ferry: A Brief History with Documents*, by Jonathan Earle (Boston: Bedford/St. Martin's, 2008), 122–129.
15. Letter, John Brown to the Rev. McFarland, Nov. 23, 1859, in Earle, *John Brown's Raid on Harpers Ferry*, 97.
16. Statement of Milton Lusk in Sanborn, *The Life and Letters of John Brown*, 34.
17. *Baltimore American*, Nov. 26, 1859.
18. Letter, Mary Brown to John Brown, Nov. 13, 1859. Oswald Garrison Villard John Brown Papers.
19. Letter, John Brown to Mary Brown, Nov. 26, 1859, in Ruchames, ed., *A John Brown Reader*, 159–160.
20. *New York Herald*, Nov. 19, 1859.
21. *Baltimore American*, Dec. 3, 1859.
22. *New York Tribune*, Dec. 6, 1859.
23. John Brown's Will, Dec. 1, 1859.
24. Andrew Hunter, "John Brown's Raid," *Publications of the Southern History Association, Vol. 1* (July 1897) 3: 178.
25. Letter, John Brown to My Dearly beloved Wife, Sons: & Daughters, *every one*, in Earle, *John Brown's Raid on Harpers Ferry*, 101–102.
26. Letter, John Brown to Aaron Stevens, Dec. 2, 1859. Gilder Lehrman Collection.
27. *New York Herald*, Dec. 3, 1859.
28. *New York Tribune*, Dec. 3, 1859.
29. Elizabeth Preston Allan, *The Life and Letters of Margaret Junkin Prestion*. (Boston: Houghton, 1903), 114.
30. *Evening Star*, Dec. 3, 1859.
31. *New York Herald*, Dec. 3, 1859.
32. *Right or Wrong, God Judge Me: The Writings of John Wilkes Booth*, ed. John Rhodehamel and Louise Taper (Urbana: University of Illinois Press, 2000), 125.
33. John Brown, "Final Written Message," December 2, 1859, in *John Brown's Raid on Harpers Ferry*, 102. This final message was barely reported at the time, just one last curiosity. The first dedicated attention paid appears to be an article by Franklin Sanborn entitled "The Virginia Campaign of John Brown," *Atlantic Monthly*, Dec. 1875.

Chapter 21

1. This formulation draws heavily on Jung's essays on archetypes and the collective unconscious, and his discussions of the "martyr," and the "wise old man," as well as the traditions of the prophet in the three

Abrahamic faiths and of the prophet as interpreter in Greek myth; hermeneutics, the art of text interpretation, is derived from Hermes, whose role as prophet and psychopomp required him to become mediator and interpreter between the mortal and divine. The Sage is far more prominent in Eastern traditions, but also appears in some of the more mystical branches of Judaism and Christianity.

2. Johann Wolfgang von Goethe, *Wilhelm Meisters Lehrejahre*.

3. Emerson, *Letters V*, 178.

4. Judah Goldin, *The Living Talmud: The Wisdom of the Fathers and Its Classical Commentaries*. This is not a quote of Emersonian origin.

5. Thoreau, "A Plea for Captain John Brown," in Earle, *John Brown's Raid on Harpers Ferry*, 112.

6. Emerson, *Journals IX*, 81–83.

7. Emerson, *Selected Journals 1841–1877*, 843. In Emerson's journals, he said, "Zoroaster has a line saying..." Zarathustra was another name for Zoroaster, the one that Nietzsche utilized for the central figure of *Also Sprach Zarathustra*.

8. Emerson, *Selected Journals 1841–1877*, 726.

9. Emerson to Sarah Swain Forbes, Oct. 26, 1859. *Letters V*, 179–180.

10. *Journals, IX*, 248.

11. *New York Daily Tribune*, Nov. 8, 1859, in Ralph L. Rusk, *The Life of Ralph Waldo Emerson* (New York, 1949), 402. The comment was also carried in Garrison's *Liberator* on Nov. 11. Emerson appears to have heard it said by suffragist/feminist activist Mattie Griffith in conversation, and liked it well enough to utilize the line himself. See, Ralph Waldo Emerson, *Selected Journals 1841–1877*, 726.

12. Moncure Daniel Conway, *Emerson, At Home and Abroad* (Boston: J.R. Osgood), 1882, 310–311.

13. Ralph Waldo Emerson, "Harvard Divinity School Address," 1838.

14. Sanborn, *Recollections I*, 196.

15. Sanborn, *The Life and Letters of John Brown*, 623.

16. *Letters V*, 182.

17. *Baltimore American*, Dec. 6, 1859. Letter, Louisa Williamson to Jedidiah Williamson, Dec. 8, 1859, and "Notes on John Brown's Body in New York," Boyd Stutler Collection.

18. *New York Weekly Tribune*, Dec. 17, 1859.

19. Warren, *John Brown*, 29.

20. Letter, Annie Brown to Garibaldi Ross, Dec. 15, 1887. Gilder Lehrman Collection.

21. Letter, Annie Brown to Alexander Ross, Dec. 28, 1887. Gilder Lehrman Collection.

22. http://www.kshs.org/kansapedia/abraham-lincoln-in-kansas/12132.

23. http://www.kshs.org/kansapedia/abraham-lincoln-in-kansas/12132.

24. Mayer, *All on Fire*, 515.

25. http://www.digitalhistory.uh.edu/learning_history/brown/public_davis.cfm.

26. William Lloyd Garrison. *The "New Reign of Terror" in the Slaveholding States for 1859–1860*. (New York: American Anti-Slavery Society, 1860), 5–12.

27. "The Harpers Ferry Conspiracy," *Petersburg Express*, Oct. 25, 1859, in Earle, *John Brown's Raid on Harpers Ferry*, 107–108.

28. "The Cloud in the Distance No Bigger then [sic] a Man's Hand—The First Battle of the 'Irrepressible Conflict,'" *Cincinnati Enquirer*, Oct. 19, 1859.

29. "What Shall the South Do?" *Wilmington, North Carolina, Daily Herald*, December 5, 1859.

30. Bruce Catton, *The Coming Fury* (Garden City, New York: Doubleday, 1961), 37–40.

31. This is the assessment of James McPherson in *Battle Cry of Freedom*.

32. Foner, *History of the Labor Movement in the United States Vol. 1*, 289.

33. www.archives.gov, uselectionatlas.org.

34. Qtd. in Foner, *History of the Labor Movement in the United States Vol. 1*, 294.

35. Qtd. ibid., 292.

36. Emerson used this wry device in his Journals in a cutting remark about Andrew Jackson.

Chapter 22

1. Charles Robinson, Letter dated December 21, 1879, in *The Life and Letters of John Brown, Liberator of Kansas and Martyr of Virginia*. By Franklin B. Sanborn (Boston: Roberts Brothers, 1891), 269.

2. Emerson, *Selected Journals 1841–1877*, 825.

3. See Charles H Wesley, *The Collapse of the Confederacy* (New York: Russell & Russell, 1968).

4. Armstead L. Robinson, "In The Shadow of Old John Brown: Insurrection Anxiety and Confederate Mobilization, 1861–1863," *The Journal of Negro History*, Vol. 65 (Autumn 1980) 4:279–297.

5. Ibid., 286.

6. Ibid.

7. Ibid., 288.

8. Ibid., 292.

9. Emerson, *Selected Journals 1841–1877*, 806.

10. Lerone Bennett, Jr., *Forced Into Glory: Abraham Lincoln's White Dream* (Chicago: Johnson Publishing, 2000), 513–516.

11. Robinson, "In The Shadow of Old John Brown," 293.

12. Ibid., 293.

13. Richard Hofstadter, *The American Political Tradition: And the Men Who Made It* (Norwich: Vintage, 1989), 132.

14. Emerson, *Selected Journals 1841–1877*, 806.

15. Ibid., 785.

16. Doris Kearns Goodwin, *Team of Rivals: The Political Genius of Abraham Lincoln* (New York: Simon & Schuster, 2006), 390–400.

17. Emerson, *Selected Journals 1841–1877*, 835.

18. Ibid., 840–841.

19. Seymour Drescher "Servile Insurrection and John Brown's Body in Europe," *The Journal of American History* (Sept. 1993): 501.

20. *Daily Alta California*, Sept. 18, 1885. And Graham Robb. *Victor Hugo, A Biography*. (New York: W.W. Norton, 1999), 390.

21. Ibid., 509.

22. Ibid., 511.

23. Becker, *The Heavenly City of the Eighteenth Century Philosophers*, 16–17.

24. Ilya Prigogine, *Order Out of Chaos* (New York: Bantam, 1984), 62–64.

25. Ibid., 63–65. The italicized word is selected to highlight the language of *animism*, the most primitive

of human belief structures. Traces of genuine animistic worldviews can be found in Newton's writings, and in the language and thoughts of many Westerners today. How many modern readers have ever had the privilege of seeing an "inspired" performance? Such a quaint, animistic, medieval term.
   26. Frank Edward Manuel, *Isaac Newton, Historian* (Cambridge, MA: Belknap Press of Harvard University Press, 1963), 139–65.
   27. Herbert Butterfield, *The Whig Interpretation of History* (New York: W. W. Norton, 1965), 42.
   28. White, *Metahistory*, 205.
   29. Ibid., 194.
   30. Ibid., 196–197.
   31. Ibid., 199.
   32. Qtd. ibid., 202. Emphasis added.
   33. Ralph Waldo Emerson, "The American Scholar."
   34. White, *Metahistory*, 203–204.
   35. Emerson, *Selected Journals 1841–1877*, 119–120.
   36. Walt Whitman, "Year of Meteors," *Leaves of Grass*.

Chapter 23

   1. Emerson, *Selected Journals 1841–1877*, 727.
   2. Emerson, Works, XI, 277–279 for the Salem speech, 334 for the Lincoln speech.
   3. Emerson, Works, XI, 603.
   4. Emerson, Works XI, 279–280.
   5. Sanborn, *Recollections I*, 109–110.
   6. Emerson, "Speech at a Meeting to Aid John Brown's Family."
   7. Ibid.
   8. Ralph Waldo Emerson, "Fate."
   9. Emerson, *Selected Journals 1841–1877*, 851.
   10. Ralph Waldo Emerson, "Courage."
   11. Asia Booth Clarke, *John Wilkes Booth: A Sister's Memoir*, ed. Terry Alford (Mississippi: University Press of Mississippi, 1999), 88.
   12. Ralph Waldo Emerson, "Progress of Culture." The address was given 3 years before "Courage" was published, but roughly contemporaneously with the writing of most of the essays in Society and Solitude.
   13. Ibid.
   14. Emerson, *Selected Journals, 1820–1842*, 174. This particular observation about the military class was made when Emerson was reflecting on the War of 1812.
   15. "Progress of Culture."
   16. "Progress of Culture."
   17. Emerson, *Selected Journals 1841–1877*, 750.
   18. *New York Times*, Oct. 24, 1868, qtd. in Hofstadter, *Anti-Intellectualism*, 173. This is not to say that Butler did not make admirable contributions to the freedom of blacks during the war; he was one of the first to specifically liberate them during the course of his military campaigns. But he was decidedly not of the intellectual class that had reared Dana and Emerson, and not one of the "gentlemen" of Massachusetts. He gloated often that his success grew from the disdain shown towards him by those men, and by Harvard College. He was a wealthy industrialist who may have engaged in corrupt profiteering in the South with his enemies at the same time he was taking their slaves.
   19. Ibid., 417.
   20. Emerson, *Selected Journals 1841–1877*, 437 (1848), 858 (1866). This, however, is a complicated sentiment. I often wonder whether Emerson meant that it was better to.
   21. Ralph Waldo Emerson, "Illusions."
   22. Emerson, *Selected Journals, 1820–1842*, 77.
   23. David Hume, *An Enquiry Concerning Human Understanding*, 42.
   24. Thomas Carlyle, *Oliver Cromwell's Letters and Speeches: With Elucidations* (New York: Wiley & Putnam, 1845), 162. Carlyle's writings on Hero-Worship and Heroism in history were also a strong influence on Emerson.
   25. Ralph Waldo Emerson, "Courage." Thoreau recounts this statement with equal fondness in his "Plea."
   26. Ralph Waldo Emerson, "Illusions."
   27. Ralph Waldo Emerson, "Power."
   28. Ralph Waldo Emerson, *The Correspondence of Emerson and Carlyle*, ed. by Joseph Slater (New York, 1964), 575. Or *The Correspondence of Thomas Carlyle and Ralph Waldo Emerson*, Vol. 2, 372–373.
   29. DuBois, *John Brown*, 225–230.
   30. William James, American psychologist and philosopher, summarized wisdom as such. Among his many intellectual influences was his godfather, Ralph Waldo Emerson.
   31. Warren, *John Brown*, 446.
   32. Malin, *John Brown*, 437. Malin also seems to have willfully ignored the family correspondence and artifacts in the Boyd B. Stutler collection, as well as the Boston Library Abolition files (available now at archive.org), the Atlanta University John Brown Letters (available through the Kansas State Historical Society at present), the Ohio Historical Society, among many others. Malin indirectly thanked Stutler in his preface, but Stutler wrote to Oates that he never provided Malin with any direct help. What assistance was rendered was on behalf of one of Malin's graduate students for work on her own dissertation. That student, however, apparently earned a passing grade only by writing a biography which Malin was amenable to. After all, it's science. See Oates, "John Brown and his Judges," 13.
   33. Harold Bloom, *Where Shall Wisdom Be Found?* (New York: Riverhead Hardcover, 2004), 191.
   34. Letter, Mary Brown to Owen Brown, Jan. 31, 1864.
   35. Diary of John Brown, Jr., Ohio Historical Society. John Brown, Jr., to Franklin Sanborn, Nov. 11, 1887, Boyd Stutler Collection. Simeon M. Fox, *The Story of the Seventh Kansas* (Topeka: Kansas State Historical Society, 1902), 14.
   36. John Brown, Jr., to Ohio *Chagrin Falls Exponent*, Dec. 12, 1883, and *Akron Beacon*, Jan. 1881. Boyd Stutler Collection.
   37. Sarah Brown interview in Villard, *John Brown*, 406–407.
   38. John Brown, Jr., to Ohio *Chagrin Falls Exponent*, Dec. 12, 1883, and *Akron Beacon*, Jan. 1881. Boyd Stutler Collection.
   39. Katherine Mayo interview with Salmon Brown, Oct. 11–13, 1908, and with Sarah Brown, Sept. 16–20, 1908, Oswald Garrison Villard Collection. Also Salmon Brown, "My Father, John Brown," in Ruchames, ed., *A John Brown Reader*, 182–189.

40. Letter, Jason Brown to Franklin Sanborn, July 13, 1892. Boyd Stutler Collection.

41. Letter, John Brown to Rebecca Spring, Nov. 24, 1859, in Sanborn *The Life and Letters of John Brown*, 600.

42. Katherine Mayo interview with Jason Brown, Dec. 13–14, 1908, Oswald Garrison Villard Collection.

43. Statement of Annie Brown in Sanborn, *Recollections I*, 180.

44. Katherine Mayo unpublished notes, "The Trip to Annie Brown-Adams," Boyd Stutler Collection.

45. Letter, Annie Brown to Franklin Sanborn, Sept. 25, 1892. Boyd Stutler Collection.

46. Letter, John Brown, Jr., to Mary Stearns, May 1, 1860. Boyd Stutler Collection.

47. Letter, Annie Brown to the editor of the *Boston Transcript*, Nov. 11, 1892. Letter, Annie Brown to Alexander Ross, Feb. 19, 1892. Gilder Lehrman Collection. This is one of the most fascinating sources to quote regarding myth and reality concerning John Brown. The letter, and Annie's sentiments, are certainly her own. Alexander Ross, however, published a book entitled *Recollections of an Abolitionist* that owed at least a portion of its material to his correspondence with Annie, and with her brother John Jr. Ross claims a rather glorious role for himself, including a friendship with Brown, but it is almost entirely a fabrication.

48. Annie Brown, interviewed by Katherine Mayo, Oct. 2, 1908, Oswald Garrison Villard Papers. Letter, Annie Brown to Franklin Sanborn, Dec. 23, 1894, Boyd Stutler Collection, and Narrative of Annie Brown in Sanborn, *Recollections I*, 177.

Bibliography

Amar, Akhil Reed. *America's Constitution: A Biography*. New York: Random House Trade Paperbacks, 2006.

Anderson, Benedict. *Imagined Communities: Reflections on the Origin and Spread of Nationalism*. Revised and extended ed. London: Verso, 1991.

Anderson, Fred. *Crucible of War: The Seven Years' War and the Fate of Empire in British North America, 1754–1766*. New York: Vintage, 2001.

Baptist, Edward. "'Cuffy,' 'Fancy Maids,' and 'One-Eyed Men,': Rape, Commodification, and the Domestic Slave Trade in the United States." *The American Historical Review* 106, no. 5 (December 2001): 1619–50.

Barry, Joseph. *Strange Story of Harpers Ferry*. Shepherdstown, WV: The Woman's Club of Harpers Ferry District, 1984.

Beard, Charles A. *An Economic Interpretation of the Constitution of the United States*. 1913. Reprint. Mineola, NY: Dover Publications, 2004.

Becker, Carl L. *The Heavenly City of the Eighteenth Century Philosophers*. New Haven, CT: Yale University Press, 1951.

Bedini, Silvio A. *Thinkers and Tinkers: Early American Men of Science*. New York: Scribner's, 1975.

Bennett, Lerone, Jr. *Forced Into Glory: Abraham Lincoln's White Dream*. Chicago: Johnson Publishing, 2000.

Bloom, Harold. *Where Shall Wisdom Be Found?* New York: Riverhead Hardcover, 2004.

Boesche, Roger. *Tocqueville's Road Map: Methodology, Liberalism, Revolution, and Despotism*. Lanham, MD: Lexington Books, 2007.

Bondi, August. *Autobiography of August Bondi (1833–1907)*. N.p.: Wagoner Printing, 1910.

———. "With John Brown in Kansas." *Kansas Historical Collection, 1903–1904* 8 (1904): 283–85.

Booth, John Wilkes. *Right or Wrong, God Judge Me: The Writings of John Wilkes Booth*, eds. John Rhodehamel and Louise Taper. Urbana: University of Illinois Press, 2000.

Boteler, Alexander. "Recollections of the John Brown Raid by a Virginian Who Witnessed the Fight." *Century Magazine* 26 (July 1883): 399–411.

"The Boyd Stutler Collection: West Virginia Division of Culture and History." West Virginia Memory Project—John Brown/Boyd B. Stutler Collection Database. http://www.wvculture.org/history/wvmemory/jb The Stutler Collection should probably be listed first in any John Brown bibliography in the internet age. Boyd Stutler acquired over his life the most extensive single John Brown document and artifact collection in the country, almost all of which is available for viewing online through the efforts of the West Virginia Division of Culture and History.

Breisach, Ernst. *Historiography: Ancient, Medieval, and Modern*. 3rd ed. University Of Chicago Press, 2007.

Brown, Salmon. "John Brown and Sons in Kansas Territory." *Indiana Magazine of History* 39, no. 2 (June 1935): 142–50.

Bund, John William Willis. *A Selection of Cases from the State Trials Volume 1*. New York: Rare BooksClub.com, 2012.

Calomiris, Charles W., and Larry Schweikart. "The Panic of 1857: Origins, Transmission, and Containment." *The Journal of Economic History* 51, no. 4 (December 1991): 807–33.

Carlyle, Thomas. *Oliver Cromwell's Letters and Speeches: With Elucidations*. New York: Wiley & Putnam, 1845.

Carr, James. "The Battle of New Orleans and the Treaty of Ghent." *Diplomatic History* 3, no. 3 (July 1979): 273–82.

Case, Lora. *Hudson of Long Ago: Progress of Hudson During the Past Century, Personal Reminiscences of an Aged Pioneer: Reminiscences, Written in 1897*. Hudson, OH: Hudson Library and Historical Society, 1963.

Caskie, George. "The Trial of John Brown." *Virginia State Bar Association Twenty-Second Report* (1909).

Castel, Albert. *Civil War Kansas: Reaping the Whirlwind*. Authorized ed. Lawrence: University Press of Kansas, 1997.

Cavell, Stanley. *Emerson's Transcendental Etudes*. Stanford University Press, 2003.

Cheng, Eileen Ka-May. *The Plain and Noble Garb of Truth: Nationalism and Impartiality in American Historical Writing, 1784–1860*. Athens: University of Georgia Press, 2008.

Clarke, Asia Booth. *John Wilkes Booth: A Sister's Memoir*. ed. Terry Alford. University Press of Mississippi, 1999.

Connelley, William E. *A Standard History of*

Kansas and Kansans. Chicago: Lewis Publishing, 1918.
Correspondence Relating to the Insurrection at Harper's Ferry. Annapolis, MD: B.H. Richardson, 1860.
Davis, David Brion. *The Problem of Slavery in the Age of Revolution, 1770–1823*. New York: Oxford University Press, 1999.
Decaro, Louis A., Jr. *Fire from the Midst of You: A Religious Life of John Brown*. New York University Press, 2005.
DeWitt, Robert M. *The life, trial, and execution of Captain John Brown, known as "Old Brown of Ossawatomie": with a full account of the attempted insurrection at Harper's Ferry: compiled from official and authentic sources, including Cooke's confession, and all the incidents of the execution*. New York: R.M. DeWitt, 1859.
Dillon, Merton L. *Elijah P. Lovejoy: Abolitionist Editor*. Champaign: University of Illinois Press, 1961.
Donald, David Herbert. *Charles Sumner and the Coming of the Civil War*. Naperville, IL: Sourcebooks, 2009.
Douglass, Frederick. *Frederick Douglass Narrative of the Life of Frederick Douglass, an American Slave / My Bondage and My Freedom / Life and Times of Frederick Douglass: Autobiographies*. New York: Library of America, 1994.
_____. *The Life and Times of Frederick Douglass*. Mineola, NY: Dover Publications, 2003.
Drescher, Seymour. "Servile Insurrection and John Brown's Body in Europe." *The Journal of American History* (Sept. 1993): 499–524.
DuBois, W. E. B. *Black Reconstruction in America, 1860–1880*. New York: Free Press, 1998.
DuBois, W.E.B. *John Brown*. New York: Modern Library, 2001.
Duncan, Rev. John S. "John Brown in Pennsylvania." *Western Pennsylvania Historical Magazine* 11 (January 1928).
Earle, Jonathan. *John Brown's Raid on Harpers Ferry: A Brief History with Documents*. Boston: Bedford/St. Martin's, 2008.
Edwards, Jonathan. *The Works of Jonathan Edwards*. New York: Nabu Press, 2010.
Egerton, Douglas R. *Gabriel's Rebellion: The Virginia Slave Conspiracies of 1800 and 1802*. Chapel Hill: University of North Carolina Press, 1993.
Emerson, Edward Waldo, and Waldo Forbes, eds. *Journals of Ralph Waldo Emerson; With Annotations—Vol. 4 1836–1838*. Boston: Houghton Mifflin, 1910.
Emerson, Ralph Waldo. *The Conduct of Life: A Philosophical Reading*, ed. H. G. Callaway. Lanham, Md.: University Press Of America, 2006.
_____. *Emerson's Complete Works*. Kindle, from archive.org. Vol. 11. Boston: Houghton Mifflin, 1883.
_____. *Journals and Miscellaneous Notebooks of Ralph Waldo Emerson, Volume II: 1822–1826*. Boston: Belknap Press of Harvard University Press, 1961.
_____. *Selected Journals 1841–1877*, ed. Lawrence Rosenwald. New York: Library of America, 2010.
_____. *Selected Journals, 1820–1842*, ed. Lawrence Rosenwald. New York: Library of America, 2010.
_____. *Self Reliance*. New York: Empire Books, 2011.
Emerson, Ralph Waldo, and Edward W Emerson. *Emerson's Complete Works*. Vol. 4. Boston: Houghton Mifflin, 1883.
Fabian, Ann. "Speculation on Distress: The Popular Discourse of the Panics of 1837 and 1857." *Yale Journal of Criticism* 3, no. 1 (Spring 1989): 127–42.
Feyerabend, Paul. *Tyranny of Science*. Cambridge, UK: Polity, 2011.
Finkelman, Paul. "Scott V. Sandford: The Court's Most Dreadful Case and How It Changed History." *Chicago-Kent Law Review* 3 (2007): Vol. 82.
Floud, Roderick, Robert W. Fogel, Bernard Harris, and Sok Chul Hong. *The Changing Body: Health, Nutrition, and Human Development in the Western World Since 1700*. Cambridge University Press, 2011.
Fogel, Robert William, and Stanley L. Engerman. *Time On the Cross: The Economics of American Slavery*. New York: W. W. Norton, 1995.
Foner, Eric. *The Story of American Freedom*. New York: W. W. Norton, 1999.
Foner, Philip S. *History of Black Americans: From the Emergence of the Cotton Kingdom to the Eve of the Compromise of 1850 (Contributions in American History)*. Westport, CT: Greenwood Press, 1983.
_____. *History of the Labor Movement in the United States Vol. 1*. New York: International Publishers, 1979.
Fox, Simeon M. *The Story of the Seventh Kansas*. Topeka: Kansas State Historical Society, 1902
Frank, Thomas. *One Market Under God: Extreme Capitalism, Market Populism, and the End of Economic Democracy*. New York: Anchor, 2001.
Galilei, Galileo. *Discoveries and Opinions of Galileo*. trans. Stillman Drake. New York: Anchor, 1957.
Garrison, William Lloyd. *Thoughts on African Colonization*. Boston: Garrison and Knapp, 1832. http://www.gutenberg.org/files/31178/31178-h/31178-h.htm (accessed March 2, 2012).
"Gilder Lehrman Collections" at the Gilder Lehrman Institute of American History. http://www.gilderlehrman.org/collections Searchable database containing numerous letters written by Annie Brown, among other subjects.
Gladstone, T. H. *The Englishman in Kansas or Squatter Life and Border Warfare*. Lincoln: University of Nebraska Press, 1971.
Goodwin, Doris Kearns. *Team of Rivals: The Political Genius of Abraham Lincoln*. New York: Simon & Schuster, 2006.
Green, Anna. *Houses of History*. Manchester, UK: Manchester University Press, 1999.
Green, Israel. "The Capture of John Brown." *The North American Review* (December 1885).
Hale, Sir Matthew. *The History of the Pleas of the Crown*. Philadelphia: Robert H. Small, 1847.

Hamilton, Alexander, James Madison, and John Jay. *The Federalist Papers (Penguin Classics)*. New York: Penguin Classics, 1987.

Hamilton, James Cleland. *John Brown in Canada; A Monograph*. (Canadian Magazine, 1894)

Harlow, Ralph. "Gerrit Smith and the John Brown Raid." *The American Historical Review* 38, no. 1 (October 1932): 32–60.

Hickey, Donald R. "New England's Defense Problem and the Genesis of the Hartford Convention." *The New England Quarterly* 50, no. 4 (December 1977): 587–604.

Higginson, Mary Potter (Thacher). *Thomas Wentworth Higginson: The Story of His Life*. 1914. Reprint, Freeport, NY: Books for Libraries Press, 1972.

Hobsbawm, Eric J. *The Age of Revolution 1789–1848*. New York: Vintage, 1996.

———. *Nations and Nationalism Since 1780: Programme, Myth, Reality*. 2nd ed. Cambridge: Cambridge University Press, 1992.

Hobsbawm, Eric, and Terence Ranger, eds. *The Invention of Tradition (Canto)*. Cambridge: Cambridge University Press, 1992.

Hoffer, William James. *The Caning of Charles Sumner: Honor, Idealism, and the Origins of the Civil War*. Baltimore: Johns Hopkins University Press, 2010.

Hofstadter, Richard. *The American Political Tradition: And the Men Who Made It*. Norwich: Vintage, 1989.

———. *Anti-Intellectualism in American Life*. New York: Vintage, 1966.

Hollon, W. Eugene. *Frontier Violence: Another Look*. New York: Oxford University Press, 1974.

Howe, Daniel Walker. *What Hath God Wrought: The Transformation of America, 1815–1848 (Oxford History of the United States)*. New York: Oxford University Press, USA, 2009.

Iggers, Georg G. *Historiography in the Twentieth Century: From Scientific Objectivity to the Postmodern Challenge, with a New Epilogue by the Author*. Middletown, CT: Wesleyan, 2005.

Jaffe, Irma B. "Religious Content in the Painting of John Stuart Curry." *Winterthur Portfolio* 22, no. 1 (Spring 1987): 23–45.

"The John Brown Letters Found in the Virginia State Library in 1901." *Virginia Magazine of History and Biography* 10, no. 2 (October 1902): 161–76.

"John Brown Papers" at The Kansas State Historical Society. An overview of the collection can be viewed at http://www.kshs.org/p/john-brown-papers-1826–1948/13993. Contains microfilm and photocopy reproductions of letters and manuscripts, to include those contained in the Boyd B. Stutler Collection, Atlanta University's "John Brown Letters," and holdings of the Ohio State Historical Society. Many are available via interlibrary loan, and all can be viewed by researchers visiting the research room at 6425 SW 6th Avenue, Topeka, KS 66615. The museum in Osawatomie has several artifacts on display. 10th & Main Streets, Box 37 John Brown Memorial Park, Osawatomie KS 66064. The Kansas Historical Society also hosts easily searchable records at http://www.territorialkansasonline.org

Johnson, Mary. "An 'Ever Present Bone of Contention': The Heyward Shepherd Memorial." *West Virginia History* 56 (1997): 1–26.

Keating, Jerome Francis. "Personal Identity in Jonathan Edwards, Ralph Waldo Emerson, and Alfred North Whitehead." PhD diss., Syracuse University, 1972.

Ketcham, Ralph. *James Madison: A Biography*. Charlottesville: University of Virginia Press, 1990.

Kilbourne, Richard Holcombe, Jr. *Slave Agriculture and Financial Markets in Antebellum America: The Bank of the United States in Mississippi 1831–1852 (Financial History)*. London: Pickering & Chatto Ltd., 2006.

Klebaner, Benjamin J. *American Commercial Banking: A History*. Washington, D.C.: Beard Books, 2005.

Kramer, Aaron. *The Burning Bush: Poems and Other Writings (1940–1980)*. New York: Cornwall Books, 1983.

LaCroix, Alison L. "A Singular and Awkward War: The Transatlantic Context of the Hartford Convention." *American Nineteenth Century History* 6, no. 1 (March 2005): 3–32.

Lepler, Jessica. "1837: Anatomy of a Panic." PhD diss., Brandeis University, 2007.

Lewis, C. S. *Reflections on the Psalms*. Grand Rapids, MI: Mariner Books, 1964.

Lienesch, Michael. *New Order of the Ages: Time, the Constitution, and the Making of Modern American Political Thought*. Princeton, NJ: Princeton University Press, 1988.

Long, R. Seymour. "Andrew Jackson and the National Bank." *The English Historical Review* 12, no. 45 (January 1897): 85–99.

Lovejoy, Joseph C., and Owen Lovejoy. *Memoir of the Rev. Elijah P. Lovejoy: Who Was Murdered in the Defence of the Liberty of the Press, at Alton, Illinois....* Reprint ed. New York: John S. Taylor, 1838.

Lucid, Robert F., ed. *The Journal of Richard Henry Dana, Jr*. Boston: Belknap Press of Harvard University, 1968.

Maier, Pauline. *American Scripture: Making the Declaration of Independence*. New York: Vintage, 1998.

Malin, James C. *The Contriving Brain and the Skillful Hand in the United States: Something About History and Philosophy of History*. Lawrence, KS: James C. Malin, 1955.

———. *Essays On Historiography*. Lawrence, KS: James C. Malin, 1948.

———. *John Brown and the Legend of Fifty-Six*. Philadelphia: Haskell House, 1971.

———. *On the Nature of History*. Ann Arbor, MI: Edwards, 1954.

Maltz, Earl M. *Dred Scott and the Politics of Slavery*. Lawrence: University Press of Kansas, 2007.

Marx, Karl. *Capital: A Critique of Political Econ-*

omy. 1867. Reprint, New York: Penguin Classics, 1992.
Mattheson, Tim. "Jefferson and Haiti." *Journal of Southern History* 61, no. 1 (May 1995): 209–48.
May, Robert E. *Manifest Destiny's Underworld: Filibustering in Antebellum America.* Chapel Hill: University of North Carolina Press, 2004.
Mayer, Henry. *All On Fire: William Lloyd Garrison and the Abolition of Slavery.* New York: St. Martin's Griffin, 2000.
____. *All On Fire: William Lloyd Garrison and the Abolition of Slavery.* New York: W. W. Norton, 2008.
McCraw, Thomas K. *Creating Modern Capitalism: How Entrepreneurs, Companies, and Countries Triumphed in Three Industrial Revolutions.* Cambridge, Mass.: Harvard University Press, 1998.
McGinty, Brian. *John Brown's Trial.* Harvard University Press, 2009.
McNeill, William H. "History and the Scientific Worldview." *History and Theory* 37, no. 1 (February 1998): 1–13.
McPherson, James M. *Battle Cry of Freedom: The Civil War Era.* New York: Oxford University Press, USA, 2003.
Meltzer, Milton. *Slavery: A World History.* New York: Da Capo Press, 1993.
Miller, Harry E. "Earlier Theories of Crisis and Cycles in the United States." *The Quarterly Journal of Economics* 38, no. 2 (February 1924): 294–329.
Miller, Perry, ed. *The Works of Jonathan Edwards: Volume 1: Freedom of the Will.* Yale University Press, 2009.
Missall, John, and Mary Lou Missall. *The Seminole Wars: America's Longest Indian Conflict.* Gainesville: University Press of Florida, 2004.
Morison, Samuel Eliot. "Our Most Unpopular War." *Proceedings of the Massachusetts Historical Society* 80 (third series, 1968): 38–54.
Nelson, Truman John. *The Truman Nelson Reader.* ed. William J. Schafer. Amherst: University of Massachusetts Press, 1989.
Nevins, Allan. *The Emergence of Lincoln—Volume II—Prologue to Civil War 1859–1861.* New York: Scribner's, 1950.
____. *Ordeal of the Union: A House Dividing 1852–1857.* New York: Scribner's, 1957.
Nietzsche, Friedrich. *Basic Writings of Nietzsche*, ed., transl. Walter Kaufmann, Modern library ed. New York: Modern Library, 1992.
____. *The Portable Nietzsche*, ed. Walter Kaufmann. New York: Penguin Books, 1977.
Norberg, Peter, ed. *Essays and Poems by Ralph Waldo Emerson.* New York: Fine Creative Media, 2004.
Norris, J.E. *History of the Lower Shenandoah Valley.* Chicago: A. Warner, 1890.
Nye, Russel B. *Great American Thinkers: George Bancroft.* New York: Washington Square Press, 1964.
Oates, Stephen B. *The Approaching Fury: Voices of the Storm, 1820–1861.* New York: Harper Perennial, 1998.
____. "Children of Darkness." *American Heritage* 24, no. 6 (October 1973): 42–47, 89–91
____. *The Fires of Jubilee: Nat Turner's Fierce Rebellion.* New York: Harper Perennial, 1990.
____. *Our Fiery Trial: Abraham Lincoln, John Brown and the Civil War Era.* Amherst: University of Massachusetts Press, 1983.
____. *To Purge This Land with Blood: A Biography of John Brown.* 2nd ed. Amherst: University of Massachusetts Press, 1984.
"Oswald Garrison Villard (John Brown) Papers," Columbia University Rare Books and Manuscript Library.
Paine, Thomas. *Common Sense and Other Writings.* ed. Gordon S. Wood. New York: Modern Library, 2003.
Perkins, Bradford. *The Cambridge History of American Foreign Relations Vol. 1: The Creation of a Republican Empire, 1776–1865.* New York: Cambridge University Press, 1993.
Peterson, Merrill D. *John Brown: The Legend Revisited.* Charlottesville: University of Virginia Press, 2004.
Phillips, William Addison. *The Conquest of Kansas by Missouri and Her Allies: A History of the Troubles in Kansas, from the Passage of the Organic Act Until the Close of July, 1856.* 1856. Reprint, University of Toronto Libraries, 2011.
Pomeranz, Kenneth. *The Great Divergence: China, Europe, and the Making of the Modern World Economy.* Revised ed. Princeton, N.J.: Princeton University Press, 2001.
Potter, David M. *The Impending Crisis, 1848–1861.* New York: Harper Perennial, 1977.
Rasmussen, William M.S., and Robert S. Tilton. *The Portent: John Brown's Raid in American Memory.* Richmond: Virginia Historical Society, 2009.
Ratner-Rosenhagen, Jennifer. *American Nietzsche: A History of an Icon and His Ideas.* Chicago: University of Chicago Press, 2012.
Redpath, James. *The Public Life of Capt. John Brown: With an Auto-Biography of His Childhood and Youth.* Freeport, NY: Ayer, 1901.
Renan, Ernest. *Qu'est-Ce Qu'une Nation?: Conférence Faite en Sorbonne, Le 11 Mars 1882.* Paris: Calmann Lévy, 1882. http://books.google.com/books?id=IngGAAAAQAAJ&printsec=frontcover&source=gbs_ge_summary_r&cad=0#v=onepage&q&f=false (accessed March 6, 2012).
Reynolds, David S. *John Brown, Abolitionist: The Man Who Killed Slavery, Sparked the Civil War, and Seeded Civil Rights.* New York: Vintage, 2006.
Riney, Larry A. *Hell Gate of the Mississippi: The Effie Afton Trial and Abraham Lincoln's Role in It.* Santa Barbara, CA: Talisman Press, 2007.
Robb, Graham. *Victor Hugo: A Biography.* New York: W.W. Norton, 1999.
Roberts, Timothy Mason. *Distant Revolutions: 1848 and the Challenge to American Exceptionalism.* Charlottesville: University of Virginia Press, 2009.

Robinson, Armistead L. "In the Shadow of Old John Brown: Insurrection Anxiety and Confederate Mobilization, 1861–1863." *The Journal of Negro History* 65, no. 4 (Autumn 1980): 279–97.

Rosen, Gary. *American Compact: James Madison and the Problem of Founding*. Lawrence: University Press of Kansas, 1999.

Ruchames, Louis. *A John Brown Reader: The Story of John Brown in His Own Words, in the Words of Those Who Knew Him, and in the Poetry and Prose of the Literary Heritage / Edited with Introduction and Commentary by Louis Ruchames*. London: Abelard-Schuman, 1959.

———. *John Brown, The Making of a Revolutionary*. New York: The Universal Library / Grosset & Dunlap, New York, 1969.

Russell, Bertrand. "On the Notion of Cause, with Applications to the Free-Will Problem." In *On the Notion of Cause, with Applications to the Free-Will*, eds. Herbert Feigl and May Broderick, 387–407. New York: Appleton-Century-Crofts, Inc, 1913.

Sanborn, Franklin B. *The Life and Letters of John Brown, Liberator of Kansas and Martyr of Virginia*. Boston: Roberts Brothers, 1891.

———. *Recollections of Seventy Years V1*. 1909. Reprint, Whitefish, MT: Kessinger Publishing, 2009.

Sandage, Scott A. *Born Losers: A History of Failure in America*. Harvard University Press, 2006.

Smith, Merritt Roe. *Harpers Ferry Armory and the New Technology: The Challenge of Change*. Ithaca, NY: Cornell University Press, 1980.

Smith, Susan Sutton, ed. *Journals and Miscellaneous Notebooks of Ralph Waldo Emerson, Volume Xiv: 1854–1861*. Belknap Press of Harvard University Press, 1978.

"Some Jewish Associates of John Brown." *The Magazine of History* 8, no. 1 (July 1908).

Spurgeon, Ian Michael. *Man of Douglas, Man of Lincoln: The Political Odyssey of James Henry Lane*. Columbia: University of Missouri Press, 2008.

Stack, George J. *Nietzsche and Emerson: An Elective Affinity*. Athens: Ohio University Press, 1993.

Stearns, Frank Preston. *The Life and Public Services of George Luther Stearns*. Philadelphia: J.B. Lippincott, 1907.

Stephenson, Wendell Holmes. *Isaac Franklin: Slave Trader and Planter of the Old South; With Plantation Records*. Baton Rouge, LA: Louisiana State University Press, 1938.

Stutler, Boyd B. "John Brown and the Oberlin Lands." *West Virginia History* 12, no. 3 (April 1951): 183–99. http://www.wvculture.org/history/journal_wvh/wvh12-3.html (accessed March 7, 2012).

Thayer, Eli. *A History of the Kansas Crusade, Its Friends and Its Foes, by Eli Thayer*. 1889. Reprint, New York: Harper, 2010.

Thomas, Emory M. "'The Greatest Service I Rendered the State': J. E. B. Stuart's Account of the Capture of John Brown." *The Virginia Magazine of History and Biography* 94, no. 3 (July 1986): 345–57.

Tocqueville, Alexis de. *Democracy in America*. New York: Library of America, 2004.

———. *The European Revolution and Correspondence with Gobineau*. New York: Doubleday, 1959.

Tomas, Vincent. "The Modernity of Jonathan Edwards." *The New England Quarterly* 25, no. 1 (March 1952): 60–84.

U.S. Department of the Interior. *Statistical View of the United States: Compendium of the Seventh Census*. Open-file report, U.S. Geological Survey. Washington, DC, 1854.

Vagts, Alfred. *A History of Militarism*. Westport, CT: Greenwood Press Reprint, 1981.

Villard, Oswald Garrison. *John Brown 1800–1859: A Biography Fifty Years After*. 1859. Reprint. New York: Kessinger Publishing, LLC, 2010.

Warren, Robert Penn. *John Brown: The Making of a Martyr*. Lanham, MD: J.S. Sanders Books, 1993.

Watts, Dale E. "How Bloody Was Bleeding Kansas?" *Kansas History: A Journal of the Central Plains* 18, no. 2 (Summer 1995): 116–29.

Watts, Steven. *The Republic Reborn: War and the Making of Liberal America, 1790–1820 (New Studies in American Intellectual and Cultural History)*. Baltimore: Johns Hopkins University Press, 1989.

Webb, Richard D. *The Life and Letters of Captain John Brown, Who Was Executed at Charlestown, Virginia, Dec. 2, 1859, For an Armed Attack Upon American Slavery; with Notices of Some of His Confederates*, ed. Richard D. Webb. London: Smith, Elder, 1861.

Wesley, Charles H. *The Collapse of the Confederacy*. New York: Russell & Russell, 1968.

White, Hayden. *Metahistory: The Historical Imagination in Nineteenth-Century Europe*. Baltimore: Johns Hopkins University Press, 1975.

Wilson, Hill Peebles. *John Brown Soldier of Fortune: A Critique*. New York: Nabu Press, 2011.

Wilson, John F. "Jonathan Edwards as Historian." *Church History* 46, no. 1 (March 1977): 5–18.

Wilson, Major L. *Space, Time, and Freedom: The Quest for Nationality and the Irrepressible Conflict, 1815–1861*. Westport, CT: Greenwood Press, 1974.

Wolmar, Christian. *Blood, Iron, and Gold: How the Railways Transformed the World*. Kindle Edition. New York: PublicAffairs, 2010.

Woodman, Harold D. *King Cotton and His Retainers: Financing and Marketing the Cotton Crop of the South, 1800–1925 (Southern Classics Series)*. University of South Carolina Press, 1990.

Zornow, William Frank. *Kansas: A History of the Jayhawk State*. Norman: University of Oklahoma, 1971.

Index

Abolitionists, racists 26
Age of Revolution 55
Alcott, Bronson 146
American Dream 19
Amistad mutiny 72; influence on Brown's League of Gileadites 73
Anderson, James 169
Anderson, Jeremiah: death 171; joined John Brown 150
Arminian argument 31
astronomy 101

Ballard, Rice 113
Bancroft, George: career 56–57; historical treatment of slavery 29; *History of the United States* 11; on Jonathan Edwards, 31–32
banks, doubling during 1832–1837 37
Baring Brothers 23
Battle Hymn of the Republic 221
"Battle of the Spurs" 143–144
battles 202
Beecher, Henry Ward 75
Benét, Stephen Vincent 230; and *John Brown's Body* 230
Biddle, Nathan 22
Bismarck, Otto von 60
Black Americans 221
Black Jack, battle 98
Bladensburg Races 15
Bleeding Kansas: casualties 68; reinforcements 84
Bondi, August 96
Booth, John Wilkes, on John Brown 219
Breckenridge, John C. 200
Brooks, Preston 114
Brown, Amelia 49
Brown, Anne: after Harpers Ferry 229; birth 47; grief 195–196; joined father in Harpers Ferry 152; left Harpers Ferry for home 156; maintained Harpers Ferry raiders' cover 152–153; on Potawatomie killings 115; relationship with father 48–49; version of the story 229
Brown, Austin: 45, 46
Brown, Charles 42, 46
Brown, Dianthe (Lusk) 18, 33

Brown, Ellen (b. 1854) 64, 147
Brown, Ellen (b./d. 1848) 53, 54
Brown, Frederick (brother) 35
Brown, Frederick (1st son) 19, 24
Brown, Frederick (2nd son): birth 33; developmental problems 42, 61; found James Redpath 97; killed 105; traveled to Kansas 64
Brown, Jason 42; after Harpers Ferry 228; captured 95; refused to go to Harpers Ferry 147; thoughts on Black Jack and Osawatomie 108; traveled to Kansas 65; version of the story 228
Brown, John: on abilities of daughters 153; addressed crowd at Harpers Ferry 170; adult personality 7; allowed train to leave and revealed plan 163; appointed Captain 80; arrived in Harpers Ferry 150; asked Mary not to prison letters 180–181; assisted Underground Railroad 51; attachment to church 184; belief in capabilities of black people 154; biographies 225–227; birth 4; brief respite at home 115; built homes for family in Kansas 79; buried 194; business ineptitude 50, 61; canal laborer 37; on capital 62; captured 168–169; childhood personality 5; church bells commemorate hour of death 194; civilization's monster 224; common physical description 7; comparison with other violent partisans 109; contracts for 1,000 pikes 118, 147; death 187–188; decided to kill 90; Declaration of Liberty, structure of 157–159; defended Westlands, arrested 44; deteriorating health 138; disguised number of raiders 163; disillusionment with military 7; dispute with Franklin Mills church 41; dispute with Freemasons 18; doctrine of Atonement 29; drafted Provisional Constitution 131; early education 17; embezzled money 43; end of political participation 16; European travels 60; evacuated family from Kansas 108; execution, European views of 209; family move to North Elba 61; family move to Randolph 18; final bequests to children 185; final message 189; final payment to George Kellogg 185; first financial decline 20; first tannery 17; foundational childhood story/cattle drive 6–7; at Frederick Douglass home 131; fundraising tour 116–118; granted Oberlin lands 44; herded cattle to CT 42; hiding from U.S. Marshall 119; infiltrated Buford camp as surveyor 88; journey and condition of body 194; journey from Kansas with liberated slaves 142–146; last letter to family 186; last meeting with father 82; lawsuits and bankruptcy 45; learned to shoot 18–19; lived in Kansas wilderness 99; location of crimes 175; lost four children at once 46; married Dianthe 18; and Methodist preacher 32; moved to Ohio 36; myths about during Kansas fighting 107; new business partnership with Simon Perkins 49; "Old Brown's Farewell" 119; organized housing protests 19; parenting 47; and Perkins partnership ends 63; planned to build school 35; positive northern opinion of 184; predicted war 139–140; proposed instigating insurrection in the South 97; proposed to Mary Ann Day 34–35; Randolph tannery 19; read *Liberator* for the first time 35; refused to kill Martin White 138; rejected southern ministers 184; relationship with Annie 48–49; requested Mary to visit 185; returned to Kansas 136; revealed Harpers Ferry plan to

255

men 130; and Sabbath observation 30; searches for black leadership 154; sermon on reason 33; sheltered runaway slave 18; on significance of Kansas 139; sons learned of killings 94; sons left Kansas for Iowa 103; spoke at Convention for Radical Abolitionists 72; stole cattle with Kansas Regulars 104; summation of Black Jack battle 99; supra-historical overman 223; in Tabor, Iowa 124; traveled to Boston 109; traveled to Kansas 76–78; trial 176–179; on trial in Virginia 173; turned the Free State Assembly 85; viewed as archetype 147; views on own execution 180; visited in prison 181; on Wakarusa War 81; walked with prisoners 144; worked as shepherd 49; worked as surveyor 44; with wounded to Nebraska 103; wrote autobiographical origin story 120; wrote "Old Brown's Parallels" 142

Brown, John, Jr.: after Harpers Ferry 227–228; agnosticism 47; attended Grand River Institute 45; biblical language in writing 75–76; birth 18; captured 95; left behind by father 134; scars from imprisonment 108; traveled to Kansas 65; won election 83; wrote to father about Kansas 67

Brown, Martha: death 195; joined Oliver and John Brown in Harpers Ferry 152; left Harpers Ferry for home 156

Brown, Mary: after Harpers Ferry 227; arrived in Charles Town 185; death 227; as historical character 195; listened to Lucy Stone 62; married John Brown 34–35; refused to go to Harpers Ferry 152; and Salmon 48

Brown, Oliver: birth 43; death 167; traveled to Kansas 76

Brown, Owen (son): after Harpers Ferry 228–229; birth 18; crippled 42; travels to Kansas 64

Brown, Owen (father): childhood poverty 4; moved to Hudson 5; Oberlin college 35; wife died and remarried 6

Brown, Peter 44, 46

Brown, Ruth 19, 42, 47

Brown, Ruth (Mills; mother) 6

Brown, Salmon (brother) 6, 7, 37

Brown, Salmon (son): 48; after Harpers Ferry 228; birth 37; suicide 228; traveled to Kansas 64; refuses to go to Harpers Ferry 147

Brown, Sarah (1st): birth 35; death 46

Brown, Sarah (2nd) 49

Brown, Watson: birth 37; death 169; joined father in Harpers Ferry 152; shot 165–166

Brown family 227

Brownson, Orestes A.: *The Laboring Classes* 45

Buchanan, James 117

Buford, Jefferson 86; raised army 87; fled Kansas 108; main army arrived in Kansas 88

Bull Run, battle 205

Burns, Anthony 63–64

California: and the Compromise of 1850 70; occupation of 57

Campbell, William (executioner of John Brown) 187

canals, connection with coal and steel 37

capitalism 39

Carlyle, Thomas 222–223

Caskie, George F., on Virginia court 175

Cato Court 85

Charles Town armed camp 184

Chatham Convention 134–135

Chenay, Paul 208

Child, Lydia Maria 182–183

Cinques, Joseph 72–73

Civil War, U.S.: disappointing results 221; European views 208; first shots 201; as illusion 203

Clay, Henry 26

Cleanthes 102

Cochrane, Sir Vice Adm. Alexander 15

colonization societies 25

comets 211–212

Communist Manifesto 55

Compromise of 1850 70

Confederacy: expectations of quick victory 204–205; garrison deploying and difficulties 204; as manufactured rebellion 202–203

Confederate army 205–207

Consolidated Association of Planters of Louisiana (C.A.P.L.) (Planter's Bank) 23

Constitution, U.S.: 14, 120

Continental system 14

Convention for Radical Abolitionists 69–75

Cook, John 96; dispatched to Harpers Ferry 136; Harpers Ferry activities 150–151; on trial 173

Copeland, John Anthony: arrives Harpers Ferry 159; captured 166; joined John Brown 146

Copernicus, Nicolaus: *On the Revolutions of the Celestial Spheres* 101

Coppoc, Barclay 134

Coppoc, Edwin: joined John Brown 134; on trial 173

corporal punishment 29–30

cotton 21

Cowper, William, on slavery in England 71

Crandall, Prudence 36

Cromwell, Oliver 222–223

Dana, Richard Henry 61, 64

Daniels, Jim 141

Darwin, Charles 224

Davis, Jefferson 197–198

Day, Mary Ann: hired as Brown housekeeper 34; married John Brown 34–35

Declaration of Liberty 157–159

Declaration of Sentiments 55

declarations/revolutions and historical discontinuity 157

The Democratic Review (magazine) 58

Douglas, Stephen A. 196, 200

Douglass, Frederick 26; abused in *Liberator* 73; life in England 60; met John Brown 51–52; tried to dissuade John Brown from raid 155

Doyle, James 87, 91–93

Doyle, Mahala 87, 91–93

Doyle, William and Drury 87, 91–93

Drake, Edwin 154

DuBois, W.E.B. 224–226

Dutch Henry's Crossing 85

economic growth 21

Edwards, Jonathan 29; "Freedom of the Will" 31–32; "Sinners in the Hands of an Angry God" 30–31

1812 War 11; American entry 14

Election of 1860 196–200

Emancipation Proclamation 206; effects of release 207; John Brown party 209

Emerson, Ralph Waldo: aloofness ended by John Brown 123; alternative history of U.S. Civil War 203; on Bancroft 16; began mythologizing John Brown 191; Brown biography unfinished 216; Brown compared to Cromwell 222–223; on capitalism 63; career a mirror for the age 121; condemnation of the age 223;

Conduct of Life 219; courage 192; death of son 122; Emancipation Proclamation as military strategy 206; Harvard Divinity School address 192–193; on history 11; initial reaction to John Brown's execution 190–191; John Brown as hero 219; John Brown historiographic Christ comparison 192–193; and John Brown legend 122; met John Brown 117; on John Brown's speech 123; on Mexican-American War 59; on Michelet 58; perspective on John Brown 216; philosophical detachment 121; *Progress of Culture* 219–224; rationalism and religion 218; reasons for entering ministry 9; as sage 190; *Self Reliance* 122; studies 10; on Sumner assault 114
Erie Canal 37
execution as ceremonial spectacle 186

factory system 55
fancy maids 113
Fayette visits John Brown 43
fear and panic in Harpers Ferry region 171
feminism and abolitionism 153
filibustering societies 86
Fillmore, Millard 86
fire-eater agenda 198–199
Forbes, Hugh: caused trouble for John Brown 131–132, 135; met John Brown 118; vanished 128
Foreman, James 20, 32
France, Second Republic and Second Empire 60
Franklin, Isaac (slave-trader) 22–23, 113
Franklin Land Company 38
Franklin Mills 37
Free-State: men increased attacks 99; party criminalized by President Pierce 83–84
free will and destiny 58
freedom 224–225
French Revolution (other) 59

Garrison, William Lloyd 25; "Another Dream" 28; blamed for Nat Turner's uprising 27; met John Brown 110
Geary, John W.: appointed KS territorial governor 104; fair governance in Kansas, resigns 117
German Socialists: impact on 1860 primary 199
Gettysburg Address 188
Glorious Revolution 55

Gobineau, Comte de: *Inequality of Races* 86
God as engineer 102
Goethe, influence on Emerson 190
Great Awakenings 30
Green, Israel 169
Green, Shields 131, 155

Haiti 13
Hall, John H. 151
Halley, Edmund 211
Hallock, Moses 17
Hamlet: relationship to John Brown story 190–191
Hanway, James: opinion on Pottawatomie killings 95; on Potawatomie killings and Free-State cause 138
Harpers Ferry: alarm sounded 162–163; armory 151–152; captured 160; combatants negotiated 165; description 150; ended 168–169; fell 168–169; mayor killed 167; militia reinforcements arrived 164; near mutiny against Brown 153–154; news spread 163; raid began 159; raiders began organizing 131; railroad bridge captured 160; train stopped 162; under siege 165
Hawkins, Nate (alias) 131
Hazlett, James 173
Hegel, Georg Wilhelm Friedrich 57
Higginson, Thomas Wentworth: and Burns trial 63; met John Brown 111
historical process 212
Hobbes, Thomas 58
Holst, Herman von, biography of John Brown 226
Hotchkiss, Wealthy (wife of John Brown, Jr.) 61
Houston, Sam 197
Howe, Julia Ward 111, 221
Howe, Dr. Samuel Gridley 111
Hudson, David 5
Hudson, OH 5
Hugo, Victor 208
Hull, Gen. William 6
Hume, David: *Dialogues Concerning Natural Religion* 102; *Enquiry Concerning Human Understanding* 222

identity and history 121
illusions, as control 202
individualism as new idea 20
irrepressible conflict 198

Jackson, Andrew: Battle of New Orleans 15; fight with U.S. Bank 23; similarities to John Brown 24

Jacksonian Democracy 16
Jefferson, Thomas: on the future of slavery 71; and Sally Hemmings 43
Jennison, Charles 109, 141, 201, 227
John Brown's Body (song) 206
Jones, Sherriff 88

Kagi, John 129–130, 139; drafted General Order 1 159; joined John Brown 129; met John Brown 103; ordered retreat and was killed 166
Kaine, Gov. Tim 226
Kaiser, Charles 96
Kansas: Act to Punish Offenses Against Slave Property 76–77; admitted to Union 200; black people disenfranchised 200; first casualties connected with slavery fight 69; Free State Opposition formation and meeting 77; land speculation 110, 127; landscape and psychology 76; narrative meaning of 160–161; peace and Brown's funds 124; speculation bubble collapse 125; Territorial Legislature and voting fraud 75; threatened funds for John Brown 133; winter 83
Kansas-Nebraska Act 64
Kellogg, George 43–45, 185
Kennedy house 172
Kent, Zemas 36

Lane, James 103
law in a modern nation-state 172–173
Lawrence, Amos 64; conspiracy alleged by Hugh Forbes 135; met John Brown 111
Lawrence, Kansas: attack on 98; attacked by pro-slavery army 88–89; founding of 64
League of Gileadites 62
Leary, Lewis Sheridan: arrived in Harpers Ferry 159; joined John Brown 146; killed 166
Lee, Robert E. 168
Leeman, William 166
Liberator (magazine) 25, 35
Liberia 26
Lincoln, Abraham: beliefs about slavery 198; colonizationist 26; commented on John Brown and preservation of Union and slavery 197; deportation agenda 206; emerged as candidate 196–197; "Fiery Trial" speech 206; pro-labor statements 200
literacy laws 28
Locke, John: on despotism 58; "Essay Concerning Human

Understanding" 31; on slavery as warfare 158
locomotive as metaphor 109
Lost Cause trope 203–204
Louisiana Purchase 12
Lovejoy, Elijah 41
Lusk, Milton 52; feud with Hudson Church 184

Madison, James 16
Malin, James 226
Malthus, Thomas 58
Manifest Destiny 58
Marais des Cygnes massacre 142
Martin, Luther 29
martyrdom, letters worried about 183–184
Marx, Karl 55, 59, 178
Mason, Sen. James 169–170
mass production 151
Massachusetts Emigrant Aid Society 64; sends reinforcements to fight Buford's army 87
Mayo, Katherine 227
Melville, Herman: "The Portent" 209–210, 213
Merrian, Francis 159
Methodism 32
Mexican-American War 57; role of race/racism 59
Michelet, Jules: contrast with Tocqueville 212–213; romantic worldview 57
Les Misérables 208
money and monetization 21
Morgan, Shubel (alias) 137
Morgan, William 18
Morse, Samuel 55

Napoleon Bonaparte 11–12
Napoleon III (Louis-Napoleon Bonaparte) 60
nationalism 26, 59
natural law 213–214
nemesis 225
New Orleans slave rebellion 27
Newby, Dangerfield: joined John Brown 155; killed 164
Norfolk, Lord 174
North Elba 53

Oates, Stephen 226
Oedipus, sphinx riddle 225
Ohio Life, failure 125
"One Drop" laws 226
Osawatomie, KS 104–106
Overman 193
Oversoul 10
Oviatt, Heman 40

Panic of 1837 38–39
Parker, Judge Richards 173–175
Parker, Theodore 110
Le Pendu Ecce 208–209
Phillipe I, Louis 60

Phillips, William: met John Brown 100; met John Brown for second time 129; met John Brown for third time 139
Pierce, Franklin 83–84
Pinckney Resolutions 37
Planter's Bank 22
politics, U.S., slaveholder control of 13
Polk, James K. 56
"The Portent" (Melville) 209–210, 213
positivism 57
Potawatomie: election 79; killings 91–93; rifles 85–87; and Sumner assault 114
Principia 211
property, as political discriminator 20
Prospect Bluff (Negro/slave fort) 126
Prosser, Gabriel: "pardoned" 226; slave rebellion 13
Provisional Constitution: drafted 131; revealed at Chatham Convention 134–135
public opinion of John Brown after raid 176
Puritans 29

Quakers 134, 145

Rachel v. Walker 126
rail networks 109–110
Ram's Horn 52
Ranke, Leopold von 57, 212–213
rationalism and occult 210–211
reconstruction 221
Redpath, James: biography of Brown, John 225; finds John Brown camp 97, 159
Reeder, Andrew (Kansas territorial governor) 77
religious self-help 38
Republican Party, new 199
Respublica v. Chapman 174
La Révolution 55, 193
Revolution, origin of term 101
Reynolds, David S. 226
ritual death, purpose 213–214
Robespierre, Maximillien 193
Root, Sally, marries Owen Brown 6

"Sambo's Mistakes" 52
Sanborn, Franklin: biography of John Brown 225; meets John Brown 110
scientific history 57
scientific revolution 101
Scott, Dred 125–127
Scott v. Sanford 127
secession 200
Second Bank of U.S. 21
Secret Six 132, 193

Seminole War 125–126
Seneca Falls Convention 55
Seven Years War 56, 212
Seward, William H.: beliefs about slavery 198; irrepressible conflict 196
Shannon, Wilson (Kansas territorial governor) 77
Sharps rifles 75
Shepherd, Hayward 162, 166
Sherbody, Ellen (wife of Jason Brown) 61
Sheridan, Daniel 142
Sherman, Henry (Dutch) 85
Sherman, William 85
Shore, Samuel 98
slavery: economy and debt 63; as a form of warfare 158; labor output 22; new meanings 225
Smith, Gerrit 53
Smith, Isaac (alias) 150
Southern states 198, 204
speculation bubble of 1824 22
Stearns, George Luther 111
Stearns, Henry 112
Stevens, Aaron D. (Captain Whipple) 96; captured bounty hunters 143; hanged 194; killed a man 141–142; last meeting with John Brown 186; met John Brown 103, 129, 131–134; shot 165–166; on trial 173
Stowe, Harriet Beecher 52
Stuart, Jeb 168
Subterranean Pass Way 51
Sumner, Charles: assaulted by Preston Brooks 113; "Crime against Kansas" speech 112–113
Sumner, Edwin 99
swords, artillery 90

Taney, Roger B. (Supreme Court justice) 127
tannery work 17
Tappan, Lewis: and Convention for Radical Abolitionists 73
Taylor, Stewart 167
telegraph: and 1848 revolutions 163; invention of 55
The Terror 209
Thompson, Dauphin: death 169; joined John Brown in Harpers Ferry 152
Thompson, Henry: refused to go to Harpers Ferry 147, traveled to Kansas 76
Thompson, Seth 20
Thompson, William: captured 165; executed by mob 167; joined John Brown in Harpers Ferry 152
Thoreau, Henry David: met John Brown 116; rallied support for John Brown 176–177

Titusville, PA 154
Tocqueville, Alexis: on American Revolution 55; historical perspective 212–213; on slavery and race 86
Toussaint L'Ouverture: imprisonment and death 12–13; influence on Nat Turner 27
treason 174
Treaty of Ghent 15, 126
Treaty of Paris 212
trial of John Brown: insanity defense 176; reasons for being in Virginia 173–175; validity of charges 174
Turner, Nat 27
"Twenty Nigger Law" 206–207

Uncle Tom's Cabin 51–52
Underground Railroad, impact on slavery 51
U.S. Army 207–208
U.S. Bank 22
U.S. Capitol 15
University of Kansas 226

Villard, Oswald Garrison: biography of Brown, John 226

Virginia court, conduct of 175
Virginia Military Institute 28
voting rights, of blacks 81–82
Wadsworth and Wells 42–43
Wakarusa War 80–81
Walker, Robert: appointed KS territorial Governor 118; brought peace to Kansas 124; resigned as governor 137
Warren, Robert Penn: biography of John Brown 226; on Ralph Waldo Emerson 227
Washington, George: crossing Delaware, painting 161
Washington, Lewis 161
Webb, Richard D., biography of Brown, John 226
Weber, Max 178
Well-Matured Plan 124
Wellington, Duke, inspiration for Well-Matured Plan 124
Wesley, John 32
Western Reserve black laws 36
Westlands (Brown family land) 38; repossession 40
Whitefield, George 32
Whitman, Walt 213–214
will to power 223

Wilson, Hill Peebles: biography of Brown, John 226
Wisconsin system of education 32
Wise, Gov. Henry: attacked Harpers Ferry armory 201; filibustering society 183; met John Brown 169; roused Union opposition 172; treasonous statements 183
wool growers cooperative: Brown and Perkins 50

Year One 193
Yeoman farmer 19

www.ingramcontent.com/pod-product-compliance
Ingram Content Group UK Ltd.
Pitfield, Milton Keynes, MK11 3LW, UK
UKHW050537150426
5217IPUK00026B/1972